ENDING AGEISM, OR HOW NOT TO SHOOT OLD PEOPLE

☾

GLOBAL PERSPECTIVES ON AGING

Sarah Lamb, Series Editor

This series publishes books that will deepen and expand our understanding of age, aging, ageism, and late life in the United States and beyond. The series focuses on anthropology while being open to ethnographically vivid and theoretically rich scholarship in related fields, including sociology, religion, cultural studies, social medicine, medical humanities, gender and sexuality studies, human development, critical and cultural gerontology, and age studies. Books will be aimed at students, scholars, and the general public.

Jason Danely, *Aging and Loss: Mourning and Maturity in Contemporary Japan*

Parin Dossa and Cati Coe, eds., *Transnational Aging and Reconfigurations of Kin-Work*

Sarah Lamb, ed., *Successful Aging?: Global Perspectives on a Contemporary Obsession*

Margaret Morganroth Gullette, *Ending Ageism, or How Not to Shoot Old People*

ENDING AGEISM, OR HOW NOT TO SHOOT OLD PEOPLE

MARGARET MORGANROTH GULLETTE

RUTGERS UNIVERSITY PRESS

NEW BRUNSWICK, CAMDEN, AND NEWARK, NEW JERSEY, AND LONDON

Library of Congress Cataloging-in-Publication Data
Names: Gullette, Margaret Morganroth, author.
Title: Ending ageism : or, how not to shoot old people / Margaret Morganroth Gullette.
Description: New Brunswick : Rutgers University Press, [2017] | Series: Global
    perspectives on aging | Includes bibliographical references and index.
Identifiers: LCCN 2016046282| ISBN 9780813589299 (hardcover : alk. paper) |
    ISBN 9780813589282 (pbk. : alk. paper) | ISBN 9780813589305 (epub) |
    ISBN 9780813589312 (web pdf) | ISBN 9780813590875 (mobi)
Subjects: LCSH: Ageism. | Aging—Social aspects. | Aging—Psychological aspects. |
    Older people—Social conditions.
Classification: LCC HQ1061 .G86334 2017 | DDC 155.67—dc23
LC record available at https://lccn.loc.gov/2016046282

A British Cataloging-in-Publication record for this book is available from the British
Library.

∞ The paper used in this publication meets the requirements of the American National
Standard for Information Sciences—Permanence of Paper for Printed Library Materials,
ANSI Z39.48–1992.

www.rutgersuniversitypress.org

Manufactured in the United States of America

Senexa

The goddess of age studies, whose motto is "End Ageism," would look a lot like Michelangelo's Libyan Sibyl—strong shoulders, muscular arms holding an open book. Imagine her with more lines in her face and with silver-gray hair. Senexa is interrupting her instruction of the children behind her, who reverently discuss her anti-ageist lore, to cast a deprecating glance at the macro perpetrators of ageism, invisible beneath her feet.

Call the crone-goddess Senexa. This book is dedicated to the survivors of ageism, scholars, teachers, agitators, and well-wishers of all ages who are doing her good work.

Photo courtesy Wikimedia Commons.

"The awakening of consciousness is not like the crossing of a frontier—one
    step and you are in another country."
                    —Adrienne Rich, *On Lies, Secrets, and Silence*

I knew a man, a common farmer, the father of five sons,
And in them the fathers of sons, and in them the fathers of sons.

This man was of wonderful vigor, calmness, beauty of person,
The shape of his head, the pale yellow and white of his hair and beard, the
    immeasurable meaning of his black eyes, the richness and breadth of his
    manners,
These I used to go and visit him to see, he was wise also,
He was six feet tall, he was over eighty years old,
    his sons were massive, clean, bearded, tan-faced, handsome.
They and his daughters loved him, all who saw him loved him,
They did not love him by allowance, they loved him with personal love. . . .
You would wish long and long to be with him. You would wish to sit
    by him in the boat that you and he might touch each other.
                    —Walt Whitman, "I Sing the Body Electric"

In a village in a remote area of the world, an old man is lying on a pallet talking
to his son.
    "Maybe the time has come," he says, "for you to get the cart and take me up
the mountain and dump me there. I'm only a burden to you and your children."
    The son gets the wheelbarrow, bundles his father into it.
    "One more thing," the father says, "when you leave, be sure to take the wheel-
barrow with you. Your son will need it."
                    —Fable told to me by a psychoanalyst

"There's not much that feels better than a firm, urgent No to someone else's big,
restrictive Yes. If that someone has power over us. . . ."
                    —Stephen Dunn, *The Poet's Notebook*

CONTENTS

Preface
Fight Ageism, Not Aging: The Discovery of Trauma   xi

1 #Still Human
Into the Glare of the Public Square   1

Five Special Sessions   21

2 How (Not) to Shoot Old People
Breaking Ageist Paradigms through Portrait Photography   22

3 The Elder-Hostile
Giving College Students a Better Start at Life   54

4 Vert-de-Gris
Rescuing the Land Lovers   85

5 The Alzheimer's Defense
"Faking Bad" in International Atrocity Trials   112

6 Our Frightened World
Fantasies of Euthanasia and Preemptive Suicide   136

7 Induction into the Hall of Shame and the Way Out   163

8 Redress
Healing the Self, Relationships, Society   192

A Declaration of Grievances   205

Acknowledgments   207
Notes   211
Bibliography   227
Index   253

PREFACE

FIGHT AGEISM, NOT AGING:
THE DISCOVERY OF TRAUMA

The history of liberation movements reserves a special place of honor for the documents that reveal inflicted suffering. Enlightenment struggles—for American independence from Great Britain, the abolition of slavery in Britain and the United States, women's rights everywhere—needed such evidence to reframe public opinion. Reform depends on having the wrongs described, feelingly.[1] In the cultural study of ageism, credit for crucial concepts often goes back to Simone de Beauvoir's exposé of bias, *Old Age* (*La Vieillesse*, 1970). But the first important age critic, over a century before, may be Ralph Waldo Emerson, a radical nineteenth-century abolitionist and a vastly popular orator and essayist. In flashes of insight, the Sage of Concord revealed the hidden injuries of age.

Centuries, indeed millennia, of advice about aging had treated it as a primarily biological process closely linked to death. Biology, not culture or individual will, ruled. But by the age of fifty-nine, Emerson had become astutely conscious of the social impositions that impacted his age peers far short of death or illness. In his essay "Old Age" (1862), he explained.

> That which does not decay is so central and controlling in us, that, as long as one is alone by himself he is not sensible of the inroads of time, which always begin at the surface edges. If, on a winter day, you should stand within a bell-glass, the face and color of the afternoon clouds would not indicate whether it were June or January; and if we did not find the reflection of ourselves in the eyes of the young people, we could not know that the century-clock had struck seventy instead of twenty.[2]

A power exercised by younger strangers, Emerson saw, unleashed destructive interior forces in those exposed to it. That power was epitomized for him by the *age gaze* of the young. Making a mountain of differentiation out of minute bodily differences, that judgmental gaze minimizes our durable qualities, imposing decrepitude by magnifying tiny defects and linking them to "the century-clock."

Everything that "does not decay" in us *feels* "central and controlling." Emerson's sentence makes sense. It refers to a strong feeling of continuing selfhood. It explains (more appealingly than "denial" or ageist self-hatred) why many people say "I don't feel old" or "Inside, I am only thirty." Our inside affect can seem to override the weather outside. But Emerson responsibly added that enormous caveat, "as long as one is alone by himself." Only the subjective life can be lived as if under a glass dome, a protective translucent bell jar. But no one lives for very long alone, or completely, in that solipsistic, potentially airless way. So, looking down from somewhere beyond weather, Emerson strikingly describes the effect of the withering January gaze.

And, as he rightly says, our vulnerable point is our "surface edges," the place where our skin, that membrane that holds self together, offers our appearance to the watching world. (A writer who can get such metaphors right, compactly effusive, to express a big new idea, deserves our attention.) And then, in a tone that grows bitingly sardonic, Emerson expands on how dangerous that outside world can be for older adults.

> Youth is everywhere in place. Age, like woman, requires fit surroundings. Age is comely in coaches, in churches, in chairs of state and ceremony, in council-chambers, in courts of justice, and historical societies. . . . Age is becoming in the country. But in the rush and uproar of Broadway, if you look into the faces of the passengers, there is dejection or indignation in the seniors, a certain concealed sense of injury, and the lip made up with a heroic determination not to mind it. Few envy the consideration enjoyed by the oldest inhabitant. We do not count a man's years, until he has nothing else to count. . . . In short, the creed of the street is, *Old Age is not disgraceful, but immensely disadvantageous*. Life is well enough, but we shall all be glad to get out of it, and they will all be glad to have us [do so].
> This is odious on the face of it.[3]

Where Emerson says "Old Age" (because his era lacked a term for the bias), many now know to call that "creed of the street" *ageism*. Ageism, the infliction of suffering by mere fact of birthdate. Illustrating one situation, Emerson edges toward some fundamental principles of contemporary age theory. This preface lays them out for those people who are not familiar with them.

Chapter 1 then introduces the latest contemporary sources of sorrow. The set of prejudices we face has become a worse evil than in Emerson's time, when he considered it only "immensely disadvantageous." Pressures and interests he could not have imagined make of later life a great Demotion, not only in the USA but globally.

The rest of the book goes deep into some of these particular stories.

The first two principles of age theory are that people are aged by culture and that *decline* is the narrative about aging-past-youth systematically taught to us from on high. "Unremarkable actors in everyday interactions"—on the trolley, in the kitchen, at the office, in church, or in the rush and uproar of Broadway—are immediately responsible for decline's unyielding grip over so many hearts and minds.[4] Looking at his dejected age peers, Emerson felt their depression, their "sense of injury," "the lip made up with a heroic determination not to mind it." "The emotions of those who are in a position of oppression should be accorded special privilege epistemologically," writes Alison Jaggar, a feminist ethicist.[5] Through empathy or self-recognition, Emerson gave importance to the particular oppression and depression of ageism. Above all, social complicity and widespread suffering make ageism an ethical issue, not acceptable but "odious."

But, 150 years later, the struggle against ageism still has no manifesto like the Seneca Falls "Declaration of Sentiments," no stirring canonical speech like Martin Luther King Jr.'s "I Have a Dream." Many observers agree: compared to sexism, racism, or transphobia, ageism is the least censured, the most acceptable and unnoticed of the cruel prejudices. *Ending Ageism* collects materials for such a document of struggle.

No one who shies away from noticing the unnecessary griefs of ageism understands aging, however much they know about medicine or love their grandma. *Ending Ageism* says little about "geroscience": that needle-narrow focus on disease is an overwhelming reduction of the meaning of "aging," as if there could be human events without sentient subjects. Instead, in this book I stress the malign discharges of social systems and their sobering subjective impacts.

Aging, ageism—the two slippery concepts are often confused. The difference between them needs to become rudimentary. Let us devise a new consensual definition of "aging" that fixes it more squarely in culture. Whatever else it may be, *aging is the process that serves as the trigger for ageism.*[6]

Can we sharpen the distinction between a trigger and the pain caused by discharging the gun? To make that meaningful, we need a fleshier concept of age-related trauma.

A GREATER WE

In each era, many people wake up to immoral suffering inflicted by a system. For Emerson, that awakening was slavery. For me, it was Vietnam. Your awakening may have been McCarthyism, *Brown v. Board of Education*, Stonewall, sexism, the Contra War, Abu Ghraib, global warming, Occupy's revelations about the 1 percent, NSA spying, threats to deport Mexicans and Muslims. . . .

Many say the timing of that "first" divides us by generation. Untrue. The generations of those who dare to confront history often march together.

In this book, another "we" embraces those who identify deeply as members of a family. Mine is multigenerational (the oldest is ninety-five; the youngest, four months). For us, history is intimate, anecdotal, fabulous. It's in our genealogy, more powerful than genes. We don't care to be addressed as if each age cohort shared values primarily with those who chance to be the same age. Like the man in a Harry Bliss cartoon, people in families like ours look up from their human-centered life to ask, "Honey, I forget—are we Millennials, Gen-Xers, or Baby Boomers?"[7]

Family history is precious: stuff of memory, source of endless gossip, pride, amazement, jokes, conjecture—stories polished and handed down like silver. As kids, we cousins listened rapt. We learned the tales by heart. Grandpa Herman arrived on Ellis Island in the nineteenth century! The year McKinley was assassinated! He married four times, the last at eighty-six! Eww, did the other Grandma really cut her daughter-in-law's eyes out of the photos in her album?! My parents returned to Brooklyn after the Florida nursery business failed; I was seven. My father taught my brother and me to walk on stilts, choke up on a hammer, and weed crabgrass. Family legend-building went on and on. Our parents marched against the Vietnam War. My father contracted ALS and my mother cared for him at home until he died. She married his oldest brother. Years later, divorced, she had a love affair in her late seventies. At the D.C. March for Women's Lives in 1992, twenty-one members of the family turned up together.

"Love is loyalty," Marilynne Robinson, the author of *Gilead*, writes, in a semi-hopeful essay on family. "The real issue is, will [family members] shelter and nourish and humanize one another? This is creative work, requiring discipline and imagination." "The antidote to fear, distrust, self-interest is always loyalty," Robinson says of this microcosm.[8] Because this creative kinship matters so much, in my family we worry about whether all of us, from the youngest to the oldest, are going to be able to move successfully through our entire life courses. Our younger relatives, brought up with our traditions, tragedies, and peculiarities, are able to live inside our skins, even now when some of these show wrinkles. People operating as members of families—like Jessie, the student we will meet in chapter 3 who describes her unemployed uncle—are the likeliest to be aghast at discovering contemporary forms of ageism, and to reject them indignantly.

I use a third "we," which includes myself, to express the potential utopian solidarity of those who are here and now aging-beyond-youth. Some of my peers sagely observe the inflictions of ageism. Others start out not noticing, or even denying, our risks. Slowly it dawns on them, the protagonists of their own lives, that they are becoming minor defective characters in someone else's story.

The collective "we" I often use here joins these vast overlapping groups in a natural union of those willing to face the inconvenient truths of their era responsibly, and ready to treat the politics of age with defiance. But what is our inconvenient truth, exactly?

THE GRAYING-NATION "PROBLEM"

The template of writing about old age was set in 44 B.C. by Cicero, Emerson's model, in *De Senectute* (*On Old Age*). That tradition is based on a false premise: that there is an essential truth about being old, independent of history and cultures.

Demanding deep obeisance to the woes of physical decay, this "truth" is leavened by a dollop of maturational accumulations. Like Cicero, Emerson plumped up the list of the "capital advantages" of growing older. "The Indian Red Jacket, when the young braves were boasting their deeds, said, 'But the sixties have all the twenties and forties in them,'"[9] Emerson wrote, somehow imagining that "the young braves" believed this wisdom, although he saw clearly that younger white men did not. His own list of aging's advantages, balm to successful men as they age, has enrolled the American Montaigne among the legions of positive-aging gurus. His more profoundly original and disturbing discoveries about ageism have been overlooked.

The paradigm of harping on physical decline or compensations rather than on imposed social losses has been fortified in the twentieth and twenty-first centuries. Writers persist in the age-old old-age tradition, still trying to close in on that will-o'-the-wisp, the Truth of Aging. The tradition sheers off in two directions. A large faction of "Happy Gerontologists" explains *Why Almost Everything Gets Better after Fifty*. If your expectations are bad, as researchers say they typically are, you may indeed eventually agree that *Life Gets Better*.[10] An opposing faction insists that it only gets worse: "extreme old age can be nasty, brutish, and long."[11] Scientific humbuggery about "agelessness" also swirls through the public air, displacing ways to keep dignified and comfortable the longevity that many enjoy.

Age theorists say, *"Enough!" How does this dichotomy map onto people who Skype versus "Pluggers" with no computers and poor life chances? The "ill-derly" versus the "well-derly"?*[12] *What about the other intersections?* Even the most thoughtful book cannot predict my own old age. I am my own specific time capsule, and am still pretty busy filling it up. It can be opened only in retrospect. The meta-argument against the Ciceronian convention is this: neither empirically nor philosophically can there be a universal truth of elderhood, any more than a single truth about "adolescents" or "women." Getting "inside" aging is thus an idle boast. In the era of the new longevity, anyone interested in true weights and measures must, like a barometrist, know this: nothing is unaffected by society's weather.

Study ageism. At this historical conjuncture, that's the detour around the impasse. Truths about the *harms* to old(er) people don't line up neatly with either positive aging or biodecline—although the assaults certainly do make life nastier and, sometimes, shorter. Some of the worst downgradings are ignored or misrepresented to the public, and invisible even to the very people most affected. Whenever these can be identified, it makes sense to subsume them together under the umbrella term *ageism*.[13]

Obnoxious Untruths and Disregarded Facts

Emerson also sussed out the geography of ageism (it was worse in cities than villages), located one of its sources (young men), and, like Plato's Cephalus in *The Republic*, noticed an attribute afflicting many targets: they occupied a lower social class. If you travel by trolley, you don't get the respect attached to those who wear gowns and sashes and roll along in private carriages; you are more blighted by the creed of the street. Emerson thus edged toward a basic truth of all cultural studies: that, in given historical circumstances, superior powers create systems of inequality and inferiority that bleed into individual lives. The "woman problem" turned out to be sexism, not the supposed nature of women. The "Jewish problem" was and is anti-Semitism, not Jews. The "Negro problem" is still squarely racism. Now the whole world is said to be facing the "Graying Nations problem": too many old people, sickly, unproductive, costly, selfish. . . .

The system behind the ugly "Graying Nations" charges is *decline* ideology, stating pointblank that people normally aging are ruining nations. Age critics finger the underanalyzed truth: ageism. This should be obvious, not a revelation. If it is still shocking, it's partly because so many trust the powers that malign the minority group of older people. They don't hear the thousand journalists on the age beat who supplement the scholars,[14] all trying to broadcast counter-information into the air like a sheaf of arrows: "The old are *so* productive." "Healthier longer, *less expensive* than you think." "They *do* like sex." "They are not only white-and-rich; they are increasingly ethnic/racial." "They *don't* vote as a bloc against the young." "They earned their Social Security." Do social science data and humanistic interpretations pierce through the fog and filthy air? No doubt they solace some good hearts. As we'll see, facts seem to have little effect on the armored decline machines, using the media (slothful or complicit) to shoot glossy, loud propaganda into the minds of the majority. Absent a political force, what can truths matter when power rules?

Although there is no single truth about aging-past-youth, there are many despicable falsehoods. Consider physiological weaknesses, supposedly "naturally" accumulating or the fault of ill-chosen lifestyles. In fact, power foists biological declines on many. From the prenatal period on, the body's fate is grounded on what money buys: access to nourishing food, healthy surroundings, higher education, medical attention, avoidance of dangerous work. Being married correlates with later, and less, disability. If these are lacking, a life accrues disadvantages that may lead to premature illness and death. In life expectancy, the United States actually ranks only fiftieth in the world. Dying at fifty rather than eighty is a sign of grim inequalities in wealth. This disparity ought to be "the next frontier of the inequality discussion."[15] It is a feat to reach the ages at which disparagement begins.

Even more cleverly obscured are decline's other impositions, this book's focus: bias in all its forms, whirling middle and later life askew from normal human development. Visual, discursive, medical, economic, political, bureaucratic, legal. . . . In fact, we should learn to speak of *ageisms*, in the plural.

Do older people enjoy equitable conditions and social inclusion? A question to be asked. The insidious demotions that many experience are produced by the inveterate, well-funded activity of elites, often transnational in their power, who decide for us "what is allowed or expected in every specific domain," as political scientist Victor Wallis notes.[16] Neoliberal capitalists control discourse and much of the global economy either directly, through supranational agencies, or through the votes they influence and the mass media they literally own. In their panic for reliable profit they are racing to the bottom in earthly and human resources. They cut wages and the option of work, even for prime-age workers. Good midlife jobs are outsourced to low-wage nations. Small-government, low-tax conservatives are indefatigable in trying to slit the safety nets of the welfare states.

In the United States, the middle years (not long ago, a peak age) are riven by inequality, wage stagnation, and poverty. Adverse Supreme Court decisions—*Murgia, Gregory, Kimel*—weakened Congress's intent in the Age Discrimination in Employment Act to protect people over forty against unfair job loss.[17] When anyone older is unemployed long-term, especially when unemployment benefits end, we can be treated as unemployable. *Middle-ageism* (a term I invented so such failures cannot be ignored)[18] now strips, in every generation as it ages, many people's prized accumulations of respect, salary, family well-being, health, and equal protection of the laws. By shredding wages and benefits that rose with age and thus supported seniority in the broad sense, the "prime drivers of exclusion" render the midlife increasingly precarious and stressful, even for the middle class.[19]

In the slacker fable of neoliberal rhetoric, Social Security recipients are "idle, they are well off, and they live off the hard work of others."[20] The poorest of those alleged to be undermining national well-being—many of them single women, lesbians, and women of color—survive on their hard-earned monthly benefit alone. In 2014 the average benefit for all retired American workers amounted to $1,294 a month.[21] Can people with no other income eat? Although the most successful antipoverty program in US history, Social Security, is intended to maintain seniors in personhood and dignity, Republican legislators chisel away our "parasitical" benefits.[22] President Barack Obama briefly agreed. The Cost of Living Adjustment (COLA) was cut to zero in the very same year, 2015, that the economy had allegedly improved enough for the Federal Reserve to raise interest rates.

Ageism is built into the commerce of aging as well. Pharmaceutical companies benefit from promoting how bad aging-past-youth must be. All the dysfunction and uglification industries champion remedies against getting sexually, esthetically, physically, and cognitively "old," having already taught the coming inferiority to the not-yet-old. The pseudoscience of rejuvenation exacerbates the modern fixation on the "body" (ideally youthful, fit, tall, male, white, and topped by an educated brain). The numbers of those in the United States alone who sell unapproved "anti-aging medicine" indicate almost three times more snake-oil salespersons than specialized trained doctors. The cash motive drives the medical researchers who assert, "Old age is a collection of diseases."[23]

We know that the "ideal citizen is one who remains youthful as long as possible."[24] That judgment—*"Is she youthful enough?"*—is, however, out of our control. Outside of Emerson's protective glass dome as well as within, the no-longer-so-young typically fall toward a sense that our status is declining after having been maturing and valued for so very long. I become suspect to myself, asking, in a kind of limbo: do I have the wrong body, the wrong mind? In this way, by being sprung on us late, ageism differs from racism and sexism, the born-into-them biases.

We cannot choose not to be old. And once we are considered "old" in important settings, no amount of theoretical deconstruction or individual behavior or good attitude makes it reversible for any of us. The continuing subtractions from selfhood hurt even when the body carries on just fine. If the body is suffering organically, the attacks on selfhood worsen all ills. In her novel *Gilead*, Marilynne Robinson's narrator, John Ames, a well-liked preacher in his early seventies who deals well with his angina, discovers there are other injuries that hurt his heart.

> I really feel as though I'm failing, and not primarily in the medical sense. And I feel as if I am being left out, as though I'm some straggler and people can't quite remember to stay back for me. . . . It could be true that my interest in abstractions, which would have been forgiven first on the grounds of youth and then on grounds of eccentricity, is now being forgiven on grounds of senility, which would mean people have stopped trying to see

the sense in the things I say the way they once did. That would be by far the worst form of forgiveness.[25]

It's worth lingering over the complaints Ames is supplied with, noticing social misery. Novelists rarely convey that it's how we are treated rather than our physiology that hurts. Gerontologists studying "successful" aging rarely ask how we are treated. And the resultant leathern silences of those who might listen muzzle those who suffer from racism and sexism, often worsened by age.

As birthdays arrive, we get only *more* oldness, not wisdom, attributed to us. I contend that, in our historical conjuncture, age (which theorists usually consider a moving target) becomes, in legal language, "an immutable trait." Nina A. Kohn writes, "The characteristic of immutabilty—the inability to control an immutable trait . . . is generally used [by the Supreme Court] to justify greater scrutiny."[26] The Court treats sex and race, but not age, so protectively. That needs to change. Decline need not be a social fate.

As the wars against the midlife and age escalate, they are noxious to younger people too. Praise of their beautysexandbrains provides them no certainty of higher education, jobs, or decent wages. Treat people poorly at lower ages—pay them less, treat them rudely, minimize their attributes—and no matter how young they are, they will look inferior to others, and worth less. How, then, can growing-past-youth look good to the young, when they see so many ahead of them becoming second-class citizens? Fearful of that fall, some Silicon Valley employees are getting cosmetic face-work when barely over thirty.[27] (Indeed, Silicon Valley may be the most ageist place on earth.) Why don't the young fight ageism instead of "aging"?

In a slack labor market, with more people looking for jobs than there are jobs created, age-linked competitiveness adds to the well-known rivalries created by sexism, racism, and ableism. About the economy, younger people are intentionally misled, told that people called "the Boomers" are "deadwood." But also that older adults are super powerful and wealthy, and represent giddy marketing opportunities. Intergenerational rivalry, a factor in ageism in many countries, encourages the young to blame midlife workers for greedily holding onto their jobs. Blame is a cudgel that employers use to shame midlife workers out of claiming higher wages and seniority benefits. The cult of youth is one reason incomes have been stagnating without more protest. Those who harp on the nation's dangerous demographics, older workers' deficiencies, a misleading dependency ratio, supposedly scarce public resources, and high youth unemployment interpose intergenerational warfare where there should be solidarity and common sense. Cultural snipers forget that the 1 percent includes thirty-year-olds. Instead, they teach that *age* is what divides a society.

The older age classes will always remain a minority. In 2060 in the United States, people over sixty-five will be only 22 percent of the population.[28] And, despite alarming statistics about the "graying globe," this minority status is true internationally. The fact, as I see it, is that heterogeneous as old people are, privileged as some may be, we endure many attributes of other numerical minorities: invisibility and hypervisibility, intolerance of our appearance, lack of audiences for our subjectivities and our grievances, underestimation of our trials, dislike of our alleged characteristics or disgust at our apparent weaknesses, and unwillingness to look us in the eye or spend time in our company. Sometimes these are mixed with the chilling sentimental look that Jean-Paul Sartre, referring to anti-Semites, termed "brotherly love."[29] ("How cute she is," "How sweet they are.") Anyone may be capable of doing harm through a freezing age gaze, verbal condescension (*elderspeak* is only one form), dismissive personnel decisions, careless voting. "Minority" is used by other cultural critics to refer to ethnic/racial people over sixty-five, not to all of us in later life. However, the generic term is applicable to all and illuminating in many contexts.

Innumerable motives explain the reluctance to hear the hard news about ageism, including, of course, ageism itself. If some people think only the most marginalized are liable to suffer from avoidance, disdain, and other risks of being old, they are wrong. Do those who follow the commercial rules for delaying "aging" actually trust that they will find themselves exempt? Do those who enjoy healthy later life and leisure feel serene? Many people are eager to see agency, or potential agency, in themselves or in the age class—feminists, gerontologists, me. But it doesn't help to ignore the elements of our minority powerlessness.

Even those who swear they are neither socially afflicted nor internally infected may see there are evil consequences that it behooves us to mind. A shift in thinking might rescue people from internalizing ageism to their sorrow. At some level, we do all intuit that the imposed demotions—not old people in themselves—are what, for everyone, make the life course ahead fearful. People tend to distance themselves from individuals or groups that frighten them. Fear can be taught, heightened, or redirected: after World War II, against communists; after 9/11, Muslims; today, immigrants. Social-identity and terror-management theories, informed by age theory, explain how fear can be manipulated against old people. A handy new group to target.

Ending Ageism, or How Not to Shoot Old People, is arranged to present increasingly grave instances from the array of ageisms. In each chapter, something fails the test of fairness, equality, or basic humane dealing.[30] It might be a glaring neglect in private or public life, grossly hostile speech, abusive images, cruel practices, threats, incitements to self-harm, or violence. In each chapter, suffering is allowed to speak. The question is often not what, but whether, remedies are possible. Justice may be as simple as distinguishing the targets, listening to the survivors, and naming the malefactors; or as fundamental as asserting our right to live as long as each of us can and wants to.

ENDING AGEISM, OR HOW NOT TO SHOOT OLD PEOPLE

☾

CHAPTER 1

❨

#STILL HUMAN

INTO THE GLARE OF THE PUBLIC SQUARE

PART ONE. THE GREAT DEMOTIONS, UPDATED

Like racism and sexism, ageism has a history. Much that has lately occurred with regard to old age and aging relations is historically quite peculiar. The production of age is like the cunning of bankers: the evils never stop mutating. Our best cultural analysts scramble to keep up, which means that discoveries about later-life demotions are slow to emerge in the public square. The state of the ageisms (as it is sometimes useful to call them) begs for constant updates.

Although the term "ageism" was invented in 1969, a year after "sexism," "sexism" found early hard-won success: taught in classrooms, a boon to consciousness-raising, the source of damning epithets like "sexist pig." Unlike all the bigotries now recognized as evils (among them sexism, racism, homophobia), "ageism" has yet to become an everyday pejorative. But this is not because the reality has ended.[1] It is rarely named and little examined, even in gerontology. (Institutionally, the field started to highlight the lack of study of ageism in 2015).[2]

People may mistakenly think ageism is behind us because of federal, state, and local agencies serving older people—the agencies that remain after Congressional budget-slashing and means-testing since 1983.[3] These are "service-oriented" responses[4]—Social Security, Medicare, Older Americans Act, Meals on Wheels, the programs of AARP, OWL (formerly the Older Women's League); plus the statutory attempts to end various discriminations (in the USA, the Age Discrimination in Employment Act, ADEA; the Equal Employment Opportunity Commission, EEOC; and the private NGO, Justice in Aging). Activists anywhere may turn for inspiration to the Madrid International Plan of Action on Ageing; HelpAge International; the UN's International Day of Older Persons, which focused on ageism in 2016; and the European Union's Charter of Fundamental Rights and its Employment Equality Directive. Welcome as these documents and programs are, in many places they do little to temper a frosty climate. And the statutory plethora supports an illusion that struggling against the powers-that-be is no longer urgent.

In the United States, Obamacare is a rare, particular, midlife boon, even though rates rise higher for midlifers. Before the Affordable Care Act, the high death rate suffered by people over fifty-five who were uninsured and too young for Medicare's rescue was a scandal. Annually, 10.7 percent of them were dying.[5] *Breaking Bad*, a dramatic series that proved obsessively watchable, ended the night before Obamacare went into effect on October 1, 2013. This was no coincidence. The show began in 2008, at the very beginning of the unending Recession, when unemployment became terrifying. A timid high-school chemistry teacher, Walter White, works two jobs, each demeaning. He learns he has lung cancer the day after his fiftieth birthday. Treatment is possible but White's insurance is inadequate and he's broke. He resorts to manufacturing meth. White's transformation from a midlife loser to a drug-dealing killer kept the plot churning. His widely shared conditions—his age, malignancy, lack of job prospects or insurance, maybe even Bryan Cranston's whiteness—made the show plausible and affecting. By offering subsidized health insurance to people like White, Obamacare forced the series to end and alleviated the anxiety or grief of millions.[6] By the spring of 2014, the number of people fifty-five to sixty-four signing up was greater than insurers had expected but not more than age critics had anticipated.[7] A coalition of progressive groups led President Obama to turn around and argue for expanding Social Security's Cost of Living Adjustment (COLA). But the material side of helping a poorer, sicker population is used as an argument against indispensable government programs.

Much as I might wish to salute progress in a book like this, *Ending Ageism, or How Not to Shoot Old People* is not a progress story. It strives to answer the questions, *How do we recognize ageism now? How bad is it? How might we best try to end it?*

The safety nets end, insofar as they do, only what might be called the "first-generation" issues, like health care and medications, that had clear policy solutions. My historicizing language is taken from Justice Ruth Bader Ginsburg, discussing worsening racialization when the Supreme Court majority gutted the Voting Rights Act. #BlackLivesMatter tells us Ginsburg was right to dissent.[8] Old people should also be included among those losing fundamental voting rights: in many states the new ID requirements will disenfranchise those (often people of color and immigrants) who do not have access to their birth certificates. The second-generation issues of ageism that this book deals with tend to be immune to legal and institutional efforts, less visible than the first, and increasingly devastating and intractable. Many also have lethal consequences, but they do not come with hashtags.

Here are a few updates on exclusions and demotions for which it is hard to prove discriminatory "intent" but easy to recognize discriminatory outcomes.

Midlife men used to be considered *prime-age* workers at the peak of their experience and ability. The stories and data on midlife job discrimination are appalling. Related to unemployment outcomes (beyond divorce, home and farm foreclosure, children dropping out of college) is midlife suicide. The unending recession saw a sharp rise in suicides of unemployed men. The steepest rise was for men age fifty to fifty-four—almost 50 percent more. A Baltimore man lost his job at the steel mill at Sparrows Point, where he had worked for thirty years. At age fifty-nine, Bob Jennings couldn't get into a retraining program. He felt he was a failure with no future. " 'No no,' his wife said, 'The system is the failure,' but she couldn't convince him," and he shot himself.[9]

Although recognizing that "ageism is not experienced over the entire life course, as racism typically is," a professor of public health, J. O. Allen, nevertheless finds that the mechanisms of body-mind distress work similarly. Studying this kind of ageism is in its "infancy," Allen says, but she sees evidence that "repeated exposure to chronic stressors associated with age stereotypes and discrimination may increase the risk of chronic disease, mortality, and other adverse health outcomes."[10] And once you are ill, many specialists treat you differentially, denying not-so-very-old people with lung, colorectal, and breast carcinomas, and lymphoma the life-saving treatments they would offer younger people, though the former could benefit as much. The odds of *not* receiving chemotherapy if you are a woman over sixty-five with breast cancer are seven times greater than for a woman under fifty.[11] Undertreatment of older patients may be a primary reason for their having poorer outcomes than younger patients.

For doctors, aversion to the old as patients starts young. Although compassion can be taught, almost every exhausted impatient medical resident is warned about GOMERs—Get'em Out of My Emergency Room: older people with complex problems. (Nurses don't seem to get that tainted message.)

GOMERS are said to "block" hospital beds. Older people who come in sick may leave disabled, if medical staff fail to feed them properly or control their pain.[12] The health of people on Medicare is represented in the mainstream media as being protected, even cosseted, but malpractice with an ageist/sexist edge should sharpen our second-generation focus on doctors, hospitals, and medical training.

Now Alzheimer's has been inextricably shackled onto old age. Neuroageism prophesies that any of us might dodder toward death, as Alexander Pope said of Jonathan Swift, as a dribbler and a show, only now more expensively than was ever before possible. In the Age of Alzheimer's, as medical/pharmaceutical entrepreneurship bumps up against the heightened terror of memory loss, we may be called "demented" while still having wit to deny it. Normative ideals deem all of us, eventually, unsuccessfully aging. An Internet hate site wishes that "these miserable old once-were-people not survive as long as possible to burden the rest of us."[13] In chapter 3, on teaching age in college classrooms, I refuse to dismiss troll slobber, because many sober pundits also complicitly foretell how awful it will be to live on into old-old age. In Congress, partisan deficit-mongers want the "gray tsunami" to renounce Medicare as soon as our cancers need treatment. Supposedly we owe it to ourselves and our offspring, not to mention the budget, to "not survive as long as possible." The supposed demographic "catastrophe" of longer life—a stressor our grandparents didn't have—has taught many to dread a future of "becoming a burden" or taking one on. We are meant to let ourselves ebb by nature, accepting our "duty to die" as a patriotic imperative.

Dehumanization is the inevitable outcome of having a culture that relentlessly questions the value of the later-life age classes. Like other critical gerontologists, two highly regarded British theorists, Chris Gilleard and Paul Higgs, also see the trend worsening. "While the putative abjection of those with an appearance of agedness can be and is being challenged," they noted in 2011, "other linked processes have been at work bringing about an intensification of agedness."[14] They refer to "real old age," but a person can be targeted while still ensconced in what I call "the long midlife." Younger people can't tell the difference between us. In our current frigid eugenic imaginary—a twenty-first-century repeat of Anthony Trollope's *Fixed Period* (1882), in which *sixty-eight* was the literal deadline—it's as if "the appearance of agedness" is becoming forbidden.

In this atmosphere, wife-killing is rising among male care-givers over fifty-five. A sixty-eight-year-old Ohio man, John Wise, brought a gun to the hospital and shot his wife after she had had triple cerebral aneurysms. He knew she was already close to death.[15] As chapter 6 reveals, wife-killers who plead "euthanasia" rarely do time. Sometimes they are not even indicted. The legal regime shows that government can accept a "right to kill" old people. Not all old people, of course. These old women appear to have a lessened claim to the protections of the state. In the following chapters—called, in a judicial metaphor, "sessions"—I explore further the kinds of suffering that are unprecedented and unseen, engendered by ageism's growing global power.

"Old age" can be represented as becoming deficient in the ways an unequal economy demands and a decline rhetoric confers. "The old," visual spectacles of decrepitude, are either *feeble*, *unproductive*, or *demented*, appropriate objects of revulsion, or *politically powerful* Boomer voters whose job security is so unassailable that they do not need a COLA or the heightened scrutiny of constitutional law. The age group can be held responsible for an increasing portion of the national crises (fiscal deficits, high youth unemployment), serving as a scapegoat, a bogeyman, a mass of hysterical projections.

Movements that have made progress—feminism, antiracism, gay rights—also reckon with disastrous failures while trying to counter the ascendancy of market ideology, the relentless undermining of welfare states, political slyness, popular ignorance, and ethical laxity. But they are nevertheless mainstream movements. Lacking its own passionate movement, ageism remains the most stubbornly, perplexingly naturalized of the isms. Although bias is sometimes driven by malice, aiming to wound the Other, often blows are aimed at a non-human target (like deficit-reduction or casual profiteering). This enables the perpetrators to ignore the human victims whom they are creating. Damaging those of us who are aging past midlife almost never damages the professional or political careers of perpetrators or puts thugs behind bars.

Everyone should be concerned about ending ageism. Many people care and are open to enlightenment. Some may be frustrated at not finding an anti-ageist political interest group to join. But the distracting power of decline discourse distances the well-disposed from seeing how great the need is for truth and justice. And beside the benign reason already cited for this detachment—believing democratic governments already provide well for "them"—there is another cause of not knowing what to do next. "We do not have a well-developed language for arguing . . . against things that we never imagined people would seriously propose."[16]

Blindsided

People feel confused about what assails us. Many forces hostile to the no-longer-young (including decisions already mentioned, by the Burger, Rehnquist, and Roberts courts and the 114th Congress) are not clearly identified as ageist. I speak here both as one of "us" and as an age critic who has had to work to clear my own way through the confusions.

And many are held under by the affects that ageism foists on them, understandably reluctant to identify with our defamed age class. They feel shame, dread, depression—the psychosocial sorrows that Ralph Waldo Emerson movingly noticed so long ago. Once they have suffered an attack they see as "aging"-related, further painful experiences may loom as inevitable. They blame their "aging," and, oblivious of ideology, perceive no escape. They transmute the cultural attacks into what Audre Lorde called "the piece of the oppressor planted within" us.[17] Having been shoved out houseless into January's frigid weather, they act as if they deserve to shiver. The most worrying, we'll see later, are those in whom self-dislike leads to despair or for whom desperate exclusions lead to suicide.[18]

This unhappy range of feelings ought to be identified as outcomes of ageism. Cognitively, people are pressured to accept this social construction, where old age is vilified, as if it were natural. They don't feel sure what the word means. Popularly, it's trivialized, as someone offering you a seat on the bus, rather than specified as letting midlife jobs be outsourced to Asia, not being offered a hopeful treatment, being shunned for some impairment. Some think it is unconnected to them. A woman who asked me the title of this book then joked, about her ninety-one-year-old father, "I'd like to shoot *him*."

We can't repudiate an evil we don't recognize. The abstract terms in use—attitudinal bias, job and credit and judicial discriminations, disparate treatment on the basis of irrelevant traits—increasingly important as they are, do not grip us until we grasp their effects. Ideology distorts human interactions and then muddles our perceptions of what we call "experience."

As remedy, in this book I pay attention to a relatively neglected arena, "the affective dimensions" of ageist ideology.[19] A thorough investigation must integrate causes and affects. As Jan Baars and his colleagues say, integration means tying "microsocial or narrative analysis" to "the macro level forces that are beyond the control and often beyond the sphere of knowledge" of those living our bewildering everyday life.[20]

It is difficult to show how the too-secret troubles of personal life reel back to mighty structures. To start, I align myself with the bold discoverers of suppressed traumas. Trauma studies has evolved. Scholars have expanded the categories of events considered traumatizing to include experiences of oppression that do not meet the original criteria for post-traumatic stress disorder. The "punctual" conception of trauma—war, rape—occludes another kind, "the insidious, cumulative, and daily experiences of poverty, persecution, enslavement, and abuse," in Marianne Hirsch's useful distinction.[21] I expand the term further, bearing witness to the continual assaults on this minority population— old people—who often do not find ways to articulate their griefs and turn them into grievances.

When this book discerns self-absorbed, neglectful, mean individuals, it does so to disclose their relations to indifferent or hostile systems. The systems are on record. The neoliberalizing of old age through budgets and statutes, capitalist wage stagnation and inequality, the commerce in aging, worm into human life from childhood on. But because the system hides certain kinds of suffering or justifies them, much harm to old people is undocumented or is deemed insignificant. Certain looks, behaviors, allegations, hate speech, images, fantasies, laws, and practices are weapons of oppression. Let's disparage them. My method starts with exposure, listening to the oppressed, telling submerged stories, calling perpetrators out by name. A lasering light is necessary to prove to the incredulous that aging serves as the trigger for ageism, the way skin color serves as the trigger for racism or secondary-sex characteristics as the trigger for sexism. And, precisely because merely aging-into-old-age is the trigger for bias, we ourselves growing older *are not the cause of ageism*.

The basic goal is encapsulated in the metaphor of "not shooting" old people. Grim circumstances demand appropriate metaphors. To whatever reduces our dignity and personhood, let us retort, en masse, *We are still human.*

Under the Glass Dome

Beneficent influences also flow around us, the warming winds of the cultural approach to age and the operations of age-friendly organizations to solve obvious grievances. Discovering resources to withstand the macro powers, whether we can now marshal these resources or not, is part of age studies' liberating mission.

On my seventieth birthday, for the first time in decades I wanted a party. I got one. The house was filled with friends, tables were lit with candles, laden with wines, nuts, seasonal strawberries, custard-fruit tarts, mocha cake. Using an Internet program, my husband adroitly produced a gift I wanted: a photograph album of our favorite pictures of me. They started with one taken at a few months old, with my father—face alight with shy happiness—holding me tight to his chest ("afraid the insurance company would take her away" my mother wrote next to that one). The latest was a snapshot my husband had taken in Tangier, with our granddaughter's hands on my shoulders.

The guests too came from all epochs of my life. Many brought short texts to read aloud, respecting a request I sent that the topics have nothing to do with old age. I didn't want poetry about dying or jokes that would make me grit my teeth behind a formal smile. (A 2001 survey by gerontologist Erdman Palmore revealed that the most frequent type of prejudice, reported by 58 percent of respondents, was a micro-aggression, being told a joke that pokes fun at older people.[22]) I could anticipate my day being smudged with tee shirts inscribed "Aging—It's Not for Sissies!" Wouldn't I have been protected by the kind of friends amassed over my lifetime? I didn't want to risk even one chance in fifty.

Friends crowded into the living-room to read their party pieces. Freed from clichés, they read poetry that was satirical, grave, charming, wise; creative non-fiction about animals, love, liberation. The idiosyncratic choices cohered into one atmosphere of heightened language. People gathered, gossiped and argued, flirted. Some came up to say touching things. The spirit was cordial, something taken for the heart.

My younger brother had died young, and been buried on my quarter-century mark. Grief takes long to subside, and as it does so (over a lifetime, as I know) it takes unexpected forms. I had never mourned Lewis particularly around my birthday; it was on his own that we specially remembered him. Nevertheless, I didn't have parties for forty-five years. Instead, my husband and I ate a good meal. One year I counter-picketed to support a Boston abortion clinic that had been bombed. Parties seemed childish and unnecessary.

So why choose to hold one on my seventieth? One can never know one's motives to the bottom, but a brief age autobiography is in order. My mother— the person who had so warmly rejoiced at our being, the object in her mid-nineties of much of my profound anxiety and loving care—had died a year before. I became simultaneously an orphan and a matriarch. I had been an age critic for decades. My heartfelt anti-ageism must have slowly stirred and felt a call, at the insistent thought of others suffering from being thought "old" (the *bad* old, the knell) on that canonical but arbitrary day, three-score and ten. My health was good. This is no boast. Most people say the same in old age, even those living with significant illness or hardship. We are resilient.[23]

When people turning thirty-five hang black balloons, a festive party at seventy can seem unexpectedly subversive, delicious. We not only said nay to decline ideology but gaily cocked a snoot, outfacing both the age-deniers and the age-catastrophists. A truth practiced by a single person and experienced by others may have a delicately spreading influence. Personally, the event left me feeling launched onto the path of expectable work, soaring into the decade with aplomb. I was still lodged in the midlife, in the Daughters' Club. In a book I published that year, a main section concerned menopause, cosmetic surgery, and sexuality. Two chapters on being old referred to my mother, not me.

Seventy is far from eighty or ninety, but it risks looking "old" to people more than ten years younger. I knew I was sliding toward the category, as everyone who survives in our culture does. In limbo, have I been a victim? I am unsure. Am I unconsciously storing up bad expectations for the time I am struck? Am I reluctant to admit the hits, as if I were ashamed? Shaming is a neglected aspect of age theory, as age is a neglected aspect of shame theory. (I try to rectify these disregards in chapter 7.) In some circles I had a reputation as the chair of the Department of Silver Linings. Undeserved, given that for decades my method involved exposing midlife decline's lowering storms. Still, my long defense of the progress narrative, and my concern for those who are prevented from telling it, began in 1989 with *Safe at Last in the Middle Years*. Defense and concern, they both culminate here. It was inevitable that what thwarts the extension of the progress narrative into later life—ageism, for short—should come dead center into my scope in this book and fill my lens entirely.

Loving families may protect against ageism even better than friends or community. Yet no one aging can feel permanently safe. Far short of violence, fraud, medical neglect, or murder, family members can neglect their partners' or parents' needs, belittle or exclude them socially, threaten institutionalization, or demand money. None of these is criminalized. One story here suggests how slight decline cues can be and yet still burden family life, crushing a stout spirit.

In Tove Jansson's subtle novel *The Summer Book* (1972), the astringent, perceptive grandmother is caring for her son's daughter, Sophia, whose mother has died. Jansson, a Finnish-Swedish writer and artist, is considered "one of the 20th century's most brilliant, enigmatic prose writers."[24] "Grandmother" leads

Sophia where the child needs to go emotionally. Her ways are gnomic lessons in parenting. Sophia claims there is a hell. No. "We get comfort when we die, that's the whole idea," the Grandmother says, knowing to rebut strongly.[25] Though handicapped by dizziness, she crawls under a thicket to carve outlandish entertaining animals. When another child comes to visit, Sophia runs for advice to her finer companion.

Toward the end of the novel, however, this woman whom we find admirable is odiously ignored by her son. Going off-island to visit friends, he leaves her behind with a note—"Love and kisses to those too old and too young to come to the party"—obtusely revealing that excluding her was deliberate. "Tactless," she mutters. Worse, he fails to tell his mother that she and Sophia will be moved to another island when he departs for a week. Sophia tells her. To her son she has become a mere dumb object, his mother thinks. "It was a nuisance. Even potted plants needed to be cared for, like everything else you took care of that couldn't make decisions for itself."[26]

The son's treatment calls her into being as an "old" person in a way that her cane, her false teeth, and chronology had not. It shows readers that "old," whatever else it means, means negligible. The novel's evidence of her violated personhood is doubled by the wounds her only friend receives from his family. They mean well. " 'But you're only 75,' the Grandmother said in astonishment. 'Surely you can do what you like.' " Verner says they don't let him, "And when you get right down to it, you are mostly just in the way."[27] Ill-judged interference and cold-heartedness are not the worst intimate abuses. Worse is recounted in later chapters. But without fulfillable desires—without autonomy—life turns insipid.

Some victims of ageism struggle. Their life force and their allies stiffen their resolve. But the end of being recognized as an equal is for this woman a starved state. The dramas of exclusion have been played out with her own granddaughter as witness. Helpless in the face of such identity-stripping, she wizens, turns quiet. She loses interest in eating: "for Grandmother, no matter what happened, it was only time on top of time, since everything is vanity and a chasing after wind." Other summers come. "As with all the most traumatic injuries, the pain followed later," Aminatta Forna writes in her novel, *The Memory of Love*.[28] In Jansson's last chapter, without having become frail, the woman silently says goodbye to the island in a way that appears to be final. Families may deal the unhealable wounds.

This story is fiction. But having adult children who at a certain time of our lives begin to inflict subtle violence on our personhood—this is the way many people, even those luckily graced with means, courage, and independence, who are insulated by an affectionate pro-aging community, discover ageism. "How sharper than a serpent's tooth it is / To have a thankless child" (*King Lear* I, 4). Several mothers I know, and one father, heretofore feeling safe from filial disregard or paternalism, risk telling me they are starting to experience it—but not for attribution. They don't know what to do. The recent plethora of *King Lear* productions (five in New York City alone in 2013–2014) is a sign of intergenerational anxiety, going both ways, about resentment and caregiving. And some productions of *Lear* find previously undreamt-of ways to take the side of the wicked daughters against the overbearing dad.[29]

How do offspring decide to wield their latent power? Perhaps parents exude a benign signal, saying, "I no longer wish to exert any of my hierarchical power. We can be equally adults together." Some adult offspring take advantage of our egalitarian renunciation. They may have absorbed from the system careless jokiness, impatience, rudeness, or feigned interest. They inhale the fear of potential frailty, disease, misery. Dr. Stephen Post, director of the Center for Medical Humanities, Compassionate Care, and Bioethics at Stony Brook, noting that "Honor thy father and mother" comes first among the social precepts in the Decalogue, summarizes a chilling trend: "The demographic transition to an aging society *has put more pressure on this Commandment than any other.*"[30]

Emerson's "glass dome" is really no stout wall but a porous membrane. Against the ageist rearrangements of society, the mind trembles like the screen of a porch in a fierce storm. Agewise influences from within us do flow outward. The screen does admit warm wind. But the smoke and dirt wuthering around the streets blows remorselessly into the house of our life. Some of the strangers outside have hearts furred with dust.

Who Strikes the Century Clock?

A good friend of mine was minding her own business one day when she was unexpectedly attacked by one of those young men of today, all-too-quick to bong the century clock. The friend was Alix Kates Shulman, a highly praised memoirist and novelist, a renowned second-wave feminist, and a hardy walker who wears a pedometer. On that day she was striding outdoors "in the rush and uproar of Broadway."

I was walking on a crowded Manhattan sidewalk on my way to see the new Woody Allen movie when a guy on a bike plowed his way among the

pedestrians. I shouted out that he shouldn't be riding on the sidewalk but
in the street. "Seriously?" he said, peering down at me, then he examined
my face and spat out, "Old hag!" This was a first for me, so it took a moment
before I realized my opportunity and shouted back "Ageist!" I doubt that
the young man cycling away knew the word, if he even heard me, but for a
moment I felt that old activist rush of triumph all the same.[31]

"Old hag" has nothing to do with my pretty, athletic friend, or me, or you,
gentle reader. No Goya witch, no Rodin grotesque. The young man attacks
a phantasm, not a particular human being. One explanation is that in panic
at receiving a reproof from an older woman, he attacked his hyper-powerful
internalized mother with an atavistic five-year-old's rage. Even a psychoanalyst can be blindsided by an older patient and try to diminish her stature. A
sixty-five-year-old woman, a potential client, made a forceful impression on
the analyst in question, on the phone. He found himself carefully giving her
instructions about finding his office, as though "she were a helpless old lady
who had to be told everything twice."[32]

Just as "Jews" are imaginary in fascist speech, "old people" are increasingly
imaginary in ageist ideology.[33] The hostile age gaze landing on a female face
determines the epithet, "hag." The anachronistic epithet is still current. The
witchy image of the evil hag from the film *Snow White* has been seen around the
world, because Disney is a vast infotainment conglomerate, by eight-year-olds.
(A panic syndrome known as "sleep paralysis" is also popularly imagined as an
old woman crouching on one's chest.) In belligerence, legions find this particle
of misogynistic ageist hate speech at the tip of their tongues. As Judith Butler
remarks about those who yell "Queer!" "it is always an imaginary chorus that
taunts." "The interpellation echoes past interpellations, and binds the speakers,
as if they spoke in unison across time."[34] Feeling powerfully united with his
age-peers, in two words a single ageist may produce a shaken or shamed—or
resistant—female subject.

"Old woman" becomes a choral taunt when the crone is feared and rejected.
Actual old women, trivialized, ignored, laughed at, holding little social value,
can be regarded as "burdens," writes Ruth Ray Karpen, a feminist gerontologist. Her crone is a female sage like Senexa: the oldest of the three-headed goddesses who represent a female life course. Psychoanalyst Jean Shinoda Bolen
says, "When the crone archetype is activated, the old woman is valued, her
image is widely circulated and actual women of crone age become more visible

and influential."[35] There are now many women of crone age, including the influential political women of the second wave (Hillary Clinton, Nancy Pelosi, Elizabeth Warren), but this trend does not render the biker incident—far from the most threatening—impossible. Long before the 2016 election, Clinton was being called an "old hag."

Public micro-aggressions need to be singled out because, often resistant to challenge, they can lead to worse. A brand new ageism is where you have to step out of the way when a younger person is about to walk through you. One tall woman friend, only seventy-three but slender enough to appear weak, says, "They are playing chicken with you. They want the sidewalk. '*Make that old lady move out of the way.*'" Conscious that this is a chronic urban danger, she avoids main streets. Female professors as young as fifty, find (mostly male) students bumping into them on campus sidewalks or in hallways.[36]

Men are not exempt from violence. My friend "Daniel" is white, Harvard-educated, a high-level public servant and head of a vast NGO, retired: at eighty, a big six-foot-two, over 200 pounds, well-dressed. From the back, though, an observer might see white hair, careful walking—insignia of age. What does that sight trigger? Kindness, often enough. But a reckless man hurtling down the stairs of the subway kneed Daniel from behind. He wasn't seen, he didn't stop. Daniel fell. He endured a painful knee operation, hallucinatory opioids, weeks of rehab; then a cascade of ongoing problems. His condition is now being called "aging" rather than depraved-heart battery. It was a new classic hit and run.

The epithet in the street, the bumps on the walks, the shove down the steps, "the forgiveness" that John Ames thought "the worst," in turn exist because of the macro-aggressions arraigned earlier. In the holy era of the new longevity, decline's emphasis falls like a bludgeon on what excludes old people from the human majority: weakness, closeness to mortality. Our being monstrous in number, a data point endlessly yammered about by friends as well as foes, stirs fear and encourages fantasies and oppressions.

Women, by living some years longer than men, are by this screwy reckoning *more* abject, at younger ages. *What is the gender of death?* the philosopher John Lindemann Nelson astutely asked.[37] The question is startling, implying not genes or cells but cultural history. The traditional "medieval night-rider in a hoodie," as Roger Angell calls him, used to be an emaciated old *man*.[38] Now the charge of dying expensively is feminized. Insofar as there is a duty-to-die cheaply, it is therefore an obligation implicitly laid on women. In point of fact, men get sicker younger than women, and their healthcare costs more beyond age sixty-five.[39] It doesn't matter how healthy the hag is, or how little dying is on her mind as she hurries to buy a baby present or catch the bus. Within the new ageisms, bias makes the faces of my kind—we charming old women—deaths'-heads. Noting the symbolic link between loss of autonomy, decline, old age, dying, and women, Diana T. Meyers, a feminist philosopher, concludes "There's no reason why women's aging faces should bear the whole burden of anxiety about death."[40] When old men also bear that projected burden, it is still unfair.

"Epidermalization," was the name Frantz Fanon conferred on the focus of the master gaze. The radical psychiatrist, analyzing racism in *Black Skin, White Masks*, invented a term that emphasizes how inferiors look to privileged others at first glimpse. His term also explains the operation of encounter-ageism (as contrasted to those many situations where no recognizably "old" person is present, but phantasms of old people dance in the air, as on the street, in classrooms, and in Congress). "Epidermalization" works better than the term "embodiment," which seems oddly bodiless. It is our surface edges alone that rile up the ill-disposed. They are not looking closely, looking to see. The age glimpse is quick, summary, dismissive. It sees defenselessness first, far ahead of whiteness, class privilege, even maleness. Then it rushes on. It doesn't look back.

Ageism can no longer be ignored when it threatens people with palpable violence. It means that in any setting you, growing older, might serve as a target. It becomes strikingly like part of everyday racism: an unpleasant, scary possibility, mostly good to keep out of mind. The *sidewalk encounter* is a metaphor for the entire decline system. As a vile atmosphere, an expectable hazard of aging, ageism can be an insidious continuous stressor. The body wants safety. Violent ageism undermines the need to feel safe. The classic psychoanalytic example of chronic stress is having been beaten as a child and expecting physical assaults as an adult. A classic racist example is living in a society where you expect to have to step aside when a white person is walking toward you on the sidewalk. "Walking while old"—we need that new meme.

Ageism like racism leads to an arm unconsciously ever half-rising to ward off a possible blow. The frailer the world sees you as, the more tremulous the tension in that arm. The writer with her pedometer and the big man groaning at the bottom of the subway stairs deserve to lead normal lives every day, not to be flung into irritation or pain. Will people who suffer from similar experiences ever get back to a previous level of serenity in public settings? We all deserve to have our immense powers of resilience kept quietly in reserve for the ordinary sorrows of life.

Trauma can be most appalling when it arises from despair. As long as untrained people must provide billions of hours of unpaid care for family members, the absence of affordable long-term care insurance is a source of preventable anguish. President Barack Obama wanted to include such a modest premium-driven program in the Affordable Care Act. A fair nationwide program would provide families with social empathy and paid respite. It would also reduce the "burden" that no one notices: the allegation, laid meanly on people with cognitive impairments, cancer, or chronic illness, of being ruinously expensive. The project was cancelled on the grounds of expense.[41] Individuals are left confronting the private long-term care insurance market, where there is still no protection against one "preexisting condition": The suspicion of Alzheimer's disqualifies an applicant.

The Air We Breathe

One can find the character of an era in its unnoticed issues and suppressed voices. What I hope to have indicated so far is that ageism is not a psychological aberration on the part of a few, but a systemic vice. Not a random daub of dirt on a fair day, but a climate change engulfing a society diffusely, like toxic gas. Look for it as a possible factor anywhere—in every self-understanding ("under the dome"); in every encounter (in the family, the workforce, and on "Broadway"), in every projection (of negative emotions onto older people), in life-and-death health decisions; and, as we'll see, in visual culture, opinion pieces, TV, films; in care-provision, legal decisions, and public policy.

We need to focus on the harms ageism inflicts until we comprehend its vast spectrum. Not all are quantifiable. Not every heinous speech or callous omission leads to dire effects. But innocently aging provokes crippling and immoral oppressions. From the careless filial rudeness that Jansson illustrates to the reductive age gaze that Emerson poignantly described, to grave bodily harm. From neglect and inadvertence to symbolic violence to battering, rape, porn, fraud, and other material harms. From violation of personhood to publicly wishing us dead to senicide.

We haven't heard yet from the vulnerable all the emotions they feel, when they are allowed to feel them. But they lead up and up to the almost inexpressible shock, sorrow, grief, bitterness, anger, and outrage that others would rather have our place and space instead of prizing our one and only life. Those who look closely, like Margaret Cruikshank, can see instances of dehumanization so painful that the word *ageism* cannot convey it.[42]

PART TWO. THE REPUDIATION OF AGEISM

Whence cometh our help? "The big cultural shifts," activist Jim Hightower says, involve "the dawning on society that a way of thinking has been wrong."⁴³ After thousands of years in which "aging" has been treated without question as ruled by nature, age critics are writing back to right the wrongs. Influenced by feminism, black, gay, and disability rights, and labor activism—movements that do not always take into consideration the ages of the vulnerable—a host of writers, artists, and scholars are profoundly deepening our comprehension of the experiential and mediated aspects of aging-past-youth. Like-minded people share our judgment, that the maltreatment of our minority is unjust.

Age studies is visionary, a field for those with both eyes open to the underpinnings of the phenomena. I invented the term in 1993 out of enthusiasm for collecting neglected life-course intersections in a range of academic disciplines and the arts.⁴⁴ The approach, ever-broadening and ever-deepening, has been embraced by creative people of various birthdates and nationalities. These scholars, critics, artists, and writers see age as the next humane, imaginative, intellectual, political focus of our time. We are well aware that for much of the world, age as a theme to dwell on is considered at best dull. But boredom is itself a deep-seated phenomenon: it can be a symptom of fear and ignorance. In this climate, the field of age studies has a way to go to make age nonboring, nonfearful, nonstupid.

Investigating ageism is for now, as I see it, that way. To those fascinated by contemporary culture, this cultural turn can be saddening, but it is not only that. I sometimes feel an amazed stupor at the excesses I was compelled to exhibit in this book. But the turn to ageism is primarily vivifying. (Not because "the Boomers are aging" and can reverse decline ideology. They can't, or they would have.) This is work done with conviction. The people pushing back against ageism view explaining *how* we are aged by culture now, and who is most vulnerable, and determining what to do next, as difficult and urgent projects. A cause.

How can hegemonic power—the Wars Against the "Old," the great Demotion—be overturned? Arguing for individuality is a typical response. "When you've seen one old person," wise geriatricians say, "you've seen one old person." I disaggregate the terrifyingly homogeneous age class another way. The damagers rapidly sketched in the Preface, the damages aggregated so far, serve like a dark painted diorama in an ethnographic museum. They are the necessary background for the flesh-and-blood protagonists, hailing from the global South as well as the North, who appear next. I focus on eclectic assemblages of people and the diverse collective concerns that each inspires.

Among them are those few lucky older persons whose photographers shoot them in imaginative ways that break the common visual paradigm of ugliness, decrepitude, isolation, superfluousness, and self-neglect. Students in college, with the help of teachers and, at times, people they call *Sages*, confront Internet bullies who treat old people as zombies, better off dead. Actors in some films make oldsex look delightful. Women refusing to be shamed by "aging" fight back. Lawyers try to undo bad court decisions. Caregivers extend personalized care to people who are very old, frail, ill, and sometimes speechless.

Other stories beg to be dragged into a space of glare and critique. People with cognitive impairments are written into newspaper articles, films, and plays as *wanting* to no longer live. Aging dictators, who definitely want to live, try to escape being tried for war crimes at international tribunals by claiming they have full-fledged Alzheimer's. Hard-scrabble farmers, hard pressed, commit suicide when they lose their land. My unassigned topics run across the arts and humanities, the social and political sciences: law and cognition; food and water on a planet of slums; ageist persuasions on the Internet, in films and theater; the difficulty of making accurate cognitive diagnoses when prison time depends on it; and nude and headless photography. Tracking ageism into its lairs—so many with transnational implications—makes this the most adventurous of my books as an age critic. It may seem like a wide purview, but in age studies' terms it is a mere sampler.

The gamut of subjects I cover is emblematic. They are introduced here to be pondered—loathed and arraigned, envied or pitied, admired, rescued, emulated. Their absorbing, unspoken stories derive from specific contexts: classrooms; nursing homes; a courthouse in Cambodia where aging (alleged) perps tell lies in front of survivors, equally old, who are panting for justice; the nearly dry hand-dug well surrounded by the gaunt faces of the global food crisis. In diverse settings, real characters and fictional ones go about their business, seek their pleasures, endure their troubles, put on their best face, succumb or rebel against the forces that hound and surround them.

This book's updated catalog unearths stories that merge the micro and the macro.

Juxtaposed and cumulative, the following Five Special Sessions also bring news from worlds seldom considered together. If old people are everywhere, as we're so often told, the distresses and threats dealt by ageism might be any-where. I found these without, in point of fact, exactly looking. Whatever I read or heard, I was merely asking, as a cultural critic tends to do, an innocent objec-tive question that anyone practicing intersectionality can learn to ask. "What (if anything) does *age* have to do with this?" Asking proved as revelatory as equivalent questions have been about, say, ableness, gender, or race.

Uncovering trauma in fact often came as an unexpected byproduct of my answering, "Nothing. Not much." Almost all the characters I focus on are "old," whatever that means to those who decide. It could be fifty, or ninety. Yet being old is often *not* primary among their identities and projects. When people fake Alzheimer's, age is only a convenient pretext. For the innocent, the look of age exacerbates their other troubles. In portrait photography, it can be a trigger for nastiness or genius. In global farming, geography, poverty, government neglect, and unrelenting physical work outdoors, not chronological age, are crucial; but older people are overlooked because the focus is on the young pouring into the cities. The real question turns out to be, "What does *ageism* have to do with it?" The keyword that bothers some and is unknown to others is indispensable.

The news is also heartening. Learning the hardships of the groups I re-searched, I came to respect their human gifts. There are stories of amazing patience under tribulations and perplexities that would fell others. There is the moral beauty of justified anger. Most of my subjects deserve allies and champions. Even the criminals and willfully obtuse deserve a chance for repen-tance, a chance to help their victims heal. Craigie Horsfield said of the home-less people he photographed what I say of most of my subjects: They "seem to have about them a kind of heroism, not the heroism of great gestures, though that may be there, but of resistance, of actions; small actions in the world."[45] Incommensurate though they may be, they state, in effect, "We too are human." Old and nonold alike, we might come to feel toward some inhabitants of these worlds emotions like kinship, admiration, envy, desire, or love. These are paradigm-shattering, heart-changing attractions. It does indeed matter that these groups are all chronologically, undeniably, "old." New emotions toward them can make anti-ageism a *feeling* as well as a conviction.

Battles for change aim to expunge the psychosocial agents of affliction. Emerson's insight into how older men were humiliated suggests that he himself had endured the devastating age gaze of youth, distinguished though he was by fifty-nine. Twenty years before, bedazzled by the endless possibilities of thinking, he had derided old people as excluded from the rising spiral of mental development. "Nature abhors the old, and old age seems the one disease; all others run into this one."[46] Such is the mindset of our time that this shocking summation is disinterred, quoted. Emerson rejected it once his perception of trauma had converted him into an age critic.

"Induction into the Hall of Shame," chapter 7, which starts with a woman writer saying she is "ashamed" of turning sixty-five, shows how emotional intelligence can reject the charges of inferiority accepted by the Oppressor Within. Moral imagination can replace the blinkered creed of the street, item by item. For almost every situation of trauma, *Ending Ageism, or How Not To Shoot Old People*, offers milestones. "Milestone" is another term from Frantz Fanon, who, good therapist that he was, honored the smallest steps out of subordination. The key is masses of radical anti-ageists who dismantle the collusive habits of thinking of "aging" as a disease or a solely *natural* process or a fault. Every new step of liberation is a pleasure and a triumph.

"Redress" is the theme of the final chapter. Jansson's Grandmother returns there, with her son, as does the crude biker; others from intervening chapters; people contemplating revenge. Much redress depends on individuals practicing how to think and speak—even how to *look* at others—more responsibly. If they think we are so different, it is their thinking so that makes us so. They can imagine new institutional and collective responses. Art and information, theory and story-telling can create pleasanter alternate countries of later life. It takes millions of changes across a range of platforms by various actors to produce sizable epistemic change. My focus on ageism's dehumanizations, beyond appealing for empathy, gives reasons for solidarity. When injustice is the leitmotif, isolating its hidden manifestations gives us better-defined goals for rectifying them.

We might then have hope worthy of belief. Grace Paley wrote, "The only recognizable feature of hope is action." Given that so many other appalling imbalances of power and wealth are now piercingly described, indicted, and passionately contested, ageism in its myriad overlapping forms may be the great underestimated evil of our time. *Blame ageism, not aging.*[47] That is a slogan marchers might wear proudly into the street. It asserts that our troubles and traumas matter and that their causes can be addressed. Blaming power means that anti-ageism joins feminism, antiracism, gay and trans rights, disability rights, progressive labor, as a critical reform project that needs a movement for fulfillment. *Fight* ageism. More exactly and riskily, fight ageists. In purifying the air we all share, blaming is only a start.

This nexus of trauma and suffering, exposure and new definitions, enlightenment and judgment, prevention, fresh representations, grievances and resistance, can set a movement's agenda.

☾

FIVE SPECIAL SESSIONS

As in the South African Truth and Reconciliation Commission, justice begins with listening to the unheard stories. In such tribunals, victims or their survivors tell theirs.

Age is comely in courts of justice. Let age sit at the bar, let it listen, let it judge. Let a bailiff now pound the staff three times, as in the Théâtre Français before the action begins.

This Court of Age Appeals sits in special session until, in some brighter future, it becomes a daily ordinary, a standard mental and moral fixture everywhere. The victims and the witnesses will come forward to testify.

The perpetrators shift uneasily in their chairs. They listen as survivors recount their harsh experiences.

Ladies and gentlemen of the jury, summoned here by curiosity, stay. Take your seats. Attend. You may find you are corroborators. There are five hearings and an analysis of the shame-throwing that underlies the way we live now. On the way to *Redress*, we need to envision a kinder, more just world. A world that is good for old people is a world that is good for everyone. Along the way, I estimate the chances of its possible emergence in various domains.

Let the sessions begin.

☾

CHAPTER 2

HOW (NOT) TO
SHOOT OLD PEOPLE

BREAKING AGEIST PARADIGMS THROUGH
PORTRAIT PHOTOGRAPHY

What another person looks like to you is your responsibility.
—Michael Lessac

VISUAL PATHOLOGY

Why does the young man on the bike "see" Alix as a hag? Why does the bully on the subway *not* see my six-foot-two friend Daniel ahead of him, descending the stair? How is it possible that, these days, students walking across campus bump into professors? Older women say they feel "invisible." Do we think this is literal, a demon cloak draped over our shoulders? Invisibility or hypervisibility—both are recklessly endangering. What is the cause in culture for these hard hearts?

The hardhearted see "agedness" and read it as disposable, beneath attention. "Old age," the great divide before terms like "greedy," "expensive," "ugly," "asexual" (as a pejorative, not a choice) can be forcibly applied, has no fixed threshold.[1] (Is it eighty, the "new sixty"? Are we officially old at sixty-five, or whenever Social Security kicks in? Is the threshold when employment begins to dwindle, around fifty?) The differences matter to those from various age groups; but to the perpetrators, we all look the same. Verbal or physical abuse by strangers is based on the visual homogeneity they instantly perceive.

In any given culture, people are trained whom to look at and how to regard them, and sometimes whom not to see at all. "Visual culture" is the name given to the universe of depicted forms that we humans live among. Charles

Baudelaire in *The Painter of Modern Life* said that beauty, the perception of the beautiful, had a huge historical component, dependent on fashion, passion, morals. The volatile contingencies of any era are even more striking when it comes to the perception of ugliness. Nazi and racist cartoonists educated viewers to believe that the dehumanizing traits of physiognomy and the character flaws they drew to elicit disgust really belonged to Jews or Negroes. Visual prejudice has terrible consequences.[2]

Like cartoons, "instead of representing emotions, photography might also provoke and stimulate them."[3] Emphasizing the politics of visual representation is an enlightening approach to art, highly appreciated in antiracist, anti-sexist, anti-ableist circles. This decades-old theory has been upping the ante on photography by demonstrating that seeing is a cultural practice—thus, a practice whose failures can be avoided. In the past, photographic discourse rarely took the side of the objectified human object. Now many photographers grapple with their own bias. "One eye open, one eye closed" was once their literal description of the way people shot (with film, before digital cameras).[4] That (metaphorically) closed eye is the danger.

I don't need to argue here that photography is not a "record" of the real, that it can never be "objective" or "a mirror." Early in the nineteenth-century history of the realism debate, even scientific photographers understood that they were altering the so-called automatic image by changing lighting or retouching with color.[5] Subaltern groups increasingly rebel and look for esthetic allies to make them visually equal. In this session, it is an age group that stares back, objecting. We see you and we raise you. "One eye closed" can now be read as a sly critique of bias, and thus as a call for artists to undo the "isms" that betray us.

In our ageist culture, I feel that my friends and I, past a certain age, are at risk in front of a lens. Ageism is not solely a visual pathology, far from it, but our social optic does several kinds of dirty work in hypervisual, body-focused societies. Although pundits complain far too often about the demographic "tsunami" of old people, we remain eerily scarce in public. In an era of spectacular reproduction, there are billions of images of the young in the "still-and-mute division" of the optical universe[6]—magazines, fashion ads, huge movie posters. There, cathexis on the young is reinforced all day every day. There, young adults (and an increasing few in the long healthy midlife, the occasional actor of seventy-three or model past fifty) disport. About advertisers who ignore older people although many have disposable income, Ashton Applewhite comments, "Ageism trumps even the profit motive."[7]

The prevalent age gaze is youthful, meaning, as Kathleen Woodward says of viewers, that "in general we cast ourselves as younger in relation to the old person we see on the screen or in a photograph (*as spectators we inhabit the position of an uncritical 'younger than'*) unless, importantly, we are invited otherwise by the nonnormative nature of the cultural text, or if we have educated ourselves to see past conventional and reductive ageist responses." Everyone, including future photographers, editors, curators, and art critics, grows up within the youth ghetto of our visual culture, and most reproduce what Woodward calls "the youthful structure of the look."[8] Older people embedded in this culture often don't notice how absent we are, as uncritical as if we too "see young." Unconsciously we may conclude that we and our age peers are terminally unphotogenic.

This oblivion damages younger people too. We need to see more old people, in life and commerce and art, shot well enough to be interesting, fascinating, and appealing. I know I do. With the deaths of most of the elders in my family, I have lost the old living flesh, faces and bodies, that I looked upon with love. The framed photos of my mother in my home include images from her eighties. From looking achingly and admiringly every day into her benign oldest face, I learn to believe that my own future looks may be appreciated by some—by my family, friends who survive me, curious strangers. Margaret Cruikshank suggests that obituaries "reinforce age shame" by often running photos taken forty or fifty years earlier.[9] The cult of youth and youthfulness in public locations, the absence of people looking older than I am—looking at me comprehendingly and protectively—makes me feel more deeply orphaned and unmentored. The beloved old people living now will disappear. Nothing is more certain. Optical oblivion banishes us in advance as not worth seeing while alive.

The Boomers' mass disappearance is seen as bringing relief from an unbearable national economic burden. Whether people over sixty-five are going to be as much as a third of the social family in a few decades or, more likely, not, we want the public to welcome our minority *right now*. The idea that, in an age of increasing longevity, visual culture cuts off the entire end of the life course is painful, paradoxical, disastrous, unacceptable.

And Then They Found Us

But what happens when the age gaze, swiveling around, finally finds us? When putting certain human subjects in the viewfinder, even good photographers may distort them. No one's selfhood is transparent from outside, where photography awaits its moment. From behind our epidermis, we are as it were hiding, shyly or boldly playing peekaboo through facial expressions and body language.

Moreover, the curious photographer is not always seeking our evasive personhood, as she or he would do with a "superior." A German age critic, Christopher Ribbat, asserts, "The 'not-yet-old' become merciless observers of the old. . . . the gaze of the young is potentially violent."[10] Bill Bytheway described a UK ad of a woman, dressed unfashionably and with stockings wrinkled; the caption reads, "This Christmas, shoot Granny and put her in a box." This brutal humor appeared in an ad for cameras.[11] Those who laughed at it then, in 1993, are now old enough to try to avoid being photographed.

Younger persons' depictions of older people may be frightened or distancing. Once fear of old people has been created and heightened, they may be considered an alien outgroup with whom the young wish to disidentify. Images that are mocking, hooting, or ribald appear on websites. Google the seventy-nine pages of http://weirdoldpeople-blog.tumblr.com, or "ridiculous old people" or "old people having fun" or "weird old women" to see photography aping cartoonishness. Nursing home attendants take "explicit" photos of their clients; some post these on Snapchat. "They just blew everything out of proportion," whined one attendant, who spent three days in jail. "It was just a picture of her butt."[12] Viewers may find ridiculous images a chuckle, and pathetic ones disgusting, because they are unable to criticize either kind as projections of a foolish, biased, dangerous cast of eye.

The "weird old" woman in the above-mentioned Tumblr blog (http://weird oldpeople-blog.tumblr.com), seated in a kind of highchair, wearing a bib, all expression on her ill-lit face erased, her neck and downturned mouth highlighted, was taken inside the woman's private space. Entry onto private property usually requires permission; one doubts she gave it. In some jurisdictions, filming subjects in a healthcare facility without consent is a crime. This image has the effect of much street photography, where the subject is anonymous and unaware. The age gaze here is obtuse and harsh. This woman, resting with her cuppa, meditating or dozing, is made to look stony-faced, withdrawn, planetary—the way many of us look when taken unawares. Just as "Jews" are imaginary in fascist imagery, "old people" can be imaginary in ageist imagery:[13] *"Yeah, sure, that's what old people look like."*

Even people who reject the concept of realism in theory may fall back on it when looking at images that represent to them that strange, *other*ed group, the no longer young. I called this instant perception the age *glimpse*. A fast shutter abets its carelessness. Unnerved sitters might cringe were they ever to stumble upon such a result, and blame themselves for having aged beyond the pale of human body norms. Such shots demand a large red Guerrilla Age-Warriors' digital stamp and sticker to cover the photographer's trespass and protect the sitters' privacy. Such a stamp would read, in a dignified and indignant voice, "I Too Am a Person."

Faced with such photos, I want to do what the artist Carrie Mae Weems did to archival photos of black American slaves in her memorable show, *From Here I Saw What Happened and I Cried*. The photographers were whites looking at people they considered inferiors. A repudiator and paradigm-smashing vision-ary, Weems sandblasted her own pained, scandalized, scornful texts over these images, addressing the photographers indirectly by speaking to the persons travestied. Emulating her, I could write, with passion, keeping in mind also the people who post and the viewers who deride, "You became in their eyes a vision of decrepitude . . . the horrible image of old age. . . . You were made to descend from your throne. . . . Some said you were the spitting image of looniness . . . of ugliness. . . . of greed. . . . A death's head."

At a minimum, a portrait should suggest, in Elsa Dorfman's dry phrasing, "Character, perhaps more than personality. There is a sense that someone is home."[14] Typically, anonymous old people portrayed in art exhibits, websites, and journalism convey decline ideology. There are exceptions, but the age gaze fetishizes perfect skin and mortifyingly magnifies innocuous departures from the ideal body and face, the blighted surface edges it anticipates: a bent neck, sags, harmless hair loss, epidermal changes. There is a role for ethnographic images of wrinkled and perplexed helplessness (as in raising money for famine relief, or illustrating the poverty of women who live on Social Security alone). But many images that don't challenge the status quo suggest that old people are uniformly of low status, obese or emaciated, grotesque, strange, sick, lonely, or simply passé.

The risk for serious photographers is that almost any person who looks "old" may look to them like a dejected body without agency–as if the bodily compo-nent becomes heavier as we age past the middle years. Early in an important book about consciousness, aging, and photography, the author writes of artists using "the paradoxical dynamic of attraction and repulsion that we *inevitably* associate with bodies marked by time or disease" (my emphasis).[15] A careless adverb. Would anyone but adolescents dare say out loud that teenagers marked by youthful acne are repugnant? Or that people with purple bruises from Coumadin disgust them? To state that any aversion (or for that matter, any attraction) is "inevitable," free of construction, is disheartening for those who do not want now or eventually to be considered repulsive.

The public, doting on even ugly babies in photos, is indifferent to representations of later life. Despite reliable reports warning that they too will age, not yet old eyes may fail to recognize an old subject as akin to them. As people grow older, however, all that they have absorbed in their alienated unconscious younger years comes back to kick them in the teeth. It's a dangerously slow learning curve.

THE POLITICS OF VISUAL REPRESENTATION

Epidermalization overrides our interior play with identities, our gratitude for having a useful body, our pleasures in inhabiting it at any age and in many conditions of impairment, and even what is visible to any responsible eye: our obvious physical and expressive charms. The repetition of ageist visual stereotypes bores and worries me. I want to bring the gasp of disappointment, the stiff lip of resignation, the glare of outrage, the chastening knowledge that some artists already do better, into our conversations about photographing old people. "Posing while black" (unless done for other African Americans) used to pose a danger to people of color. "Posing while old" (even if done for family members) may likewise prove dangerous to our well-being and cultural health, without anyone, on either side of the camera, quite recognizing the harms.

In the politics of the body seen as old, as in all body politics, visual difference is squeezed out under tremendous pressure from socioeconomic regimes of productivity and psychosexual realms of desirability. So clumping together all "aging" individuals is not mere mental laziness or cognitive "efficiency," as sociologists sometimes explain group-think. It's an outcome. It influences how we are seen when seen. As long as recipients of Medicare and Social Security are said to be decrepit and in need of anti-aging makeovers, can we be made to look good in black and white or color?

Creating an anti-ageist gaze—recuperating the label "old" through portrait photography—however urgent, will not be easy. "Art shakes the dust off ordinary life," Picasso declared with more certainty than many observers can muster.[16] Yet drastic changes in visual culture are sometimes unexpectedly possible. This may be a propitious time in portraiture of the old. There is certainly a desire for relief and appreciation, on the part of older viewers. Other progressive impulses are roiling the arts. Alertness to ageist representations may be a matter of how much experience a person has with cultural critique.

Photography, our era's new pet art and market success, has great power. "Photography has long primped and preened its subjects, warming their flesh tones to an agreeable glow, more recently brightening colours to an unnatural intensity," writes Julian Stallabrass, a British art historian.[17] There are, as I said, exceptions to decline imagery: these include portraits of politicians, celebrities, the very rich, well-known artists, friends of the photographer. Some ad campaigns use the charismatic old. In 2015, looking as if she were shrinking from the camera, eighty-year-old Joan Didion lent herself to a brief campaign for accessories. It made a stir, but is unlikely to have the same impact as the long-lived Blackgama series for mink coats, headlined from 1968 on by older stars under the pro-aging caption, "What Becomes a Legend Most?" A current legend, Caitlyn Jenner, at age sixty-five answered that question for our time by letting herself be corseted, made up, and posed to look like a Playboy Bunny for her transwoman coming-out image on the cover of *Vanity Fair*. The photographer who shot the image, Annie Leibovitz, was also sixty-five. Leibovitz, Jenner, and the magazine connived on the impeccably ageist decision.[18] The "Nay" of culture allows a few contradictions: only a few. Of any commercial shoot, let's learn to ask: How old are the current deciders? Does internalized ageism affect their taste?

Some editors actively seek photos for illustrating "successful aging," photos such as those used in AARP publications or in ads for products that older rich people prefer. These show people who are never *very* old or poor or even ordinary-looking. CEOs, society hostesses, models on cruises or in tennis togs inhabit a category so different from ours that even if there were thousands more images of *them*, the effect could not be to prove that "Old is Beautiful" or admirable. Some photographers sincerely want to change the tide, if we judge from thematic volumes like Ed Kashi's *Aging in America*, Imogen Cunningham's *After Ninety*, or, online, Vicki Topaz's *Silver: A State of Mind*.[19] A fifty-three-year-old trans woman, a cartoonist, told me that Ari Seth Cohen's dressy Upper West Side women, in his affectionate book, *Advanced Style*, made her look forward to getting old. Some viewers are thirsty for anything positive, however anodyne; some critics applaud the brimming teaspoons. I praise the intention, but a work of agitprop (to me a noble goal, rarely accomplished) has to be judged on its singular impact, not on its intention. Only if an image strikes the eye first as a work of art and a shock of insight can it carry a radical idea. So being asked to

Figure 2.1. Piotr Trybalski, "Leda Antonia Machado" from
the mural series by JR and José Parlá, *Wrinkles of the City*,
2012. Piotr Trybalski / Trybalski.com. Courtesy of the artist.

page through a series weakens each solo image.[20] Bill Bytheway thinks that setting out to "represent later life" lumps old people together, often to show only
privileged people.[21] I turn such pages languidly, looking for distinctiveness.

One series worth close attention, however, is a group of public art pieces
by perhaps the best known of group portraitists, the French *photograffeur* JR,
working with his Cuban American partner, the painter José Parlá. In 2012 the
two plastered the bare walls of Havana with murals called *Surcos de la Ciudad*
("Wrinkles of the City"). Their much larger than life images were of ordinary
people they discovered in the streets of Havana, all old enough to have been
witnesses of the revolution, all charmed to be interviewed and courted for their
images. The people were elegantly shot and then framed by Parlá's sweeping
calligraphic drawing in umber, violet, grass green.

One image in the series figures first in my collection, here, of singletons:
Parlá's photograph of their outdoor mural of Leda Antonia Machado, taken a
few years later when most of the mural's wall had been obliterated (fig. 2.1). Parlá
had an eye to see that "what is ceremonious and curious and commonplace will

be legendary." The mural had been reduced to a narrow red-gold column, with Machado's fine, cool, sad, elegant countenance disdainfully rising above the ruins. Something that might be a regal train, as it were, pools at her ankles like a plinth. Machado's tall pillar of form has the look of a statue in a temple that has been assaulted by vandals, like Bamiyan.[22] (The cover of this book uses another, even later, image of Machado, by a Polish photographer, Piotr Trybalski, who was also captivated by the grandeur of the image in the squalor of its setting.)

Scale matters. The other ephemeral Havana images survive primarily as small prints in Parlá's book or as thumbnails, Internet-impermanent. The world would be better with billions of similar images colossally swarming in public space alongside those of the temporarily young.

In discussing these images, the question I am raising is *how* to bring more age justice. It would be well if this became an explicit and even heated debate. It's not as if there are rules, or ever could be, even in a more agewise society. Instead of rutted paths, we ask for inventions, discoveries. So how does startling, widespread change in visual culture come about? Not through ghettoizing older people as a group. Not through "tolerance," another distancing response. Mere pleasantness does not open an eye shut tight.

The Shock of Seeing Appropriate Long-Lived Embodiment

Stuart Hall, the peerless and charismatic British cultural critic, identified two far stronger emotions that can jolt our imaginations into a new culture of feeling. Getting "release" from stereotyping can come about, he says in a video interview, only through "an epistemic shift" in the visual imaginary of the body in question. If an episteme is a tectonic plate of ideology, it needs a shock that shivers the perceptions and concepts of those crawling on its surface. Hall argues that this can come about by artists creating the powerful emotions of "identification and desire."[23] He felt that Robert Mapplethorpe had done this for naked black male bodies. Mapplethorpe had made it possible for viewers to undo their racism and/or homophobia enough to identify with and/or desire black men—or to admire the statuesque beauty of bodies sometimes considered ugly or even vicious. Hall liked to look, and he guessed that many others, straight and gay, did too. A civil rights movement provided the energy and cognitive confirmation for anyone sharing this frank new vision of bodies of color or repudiating the old contempt.

Likewise, Deborah Bright's *Dream Girls* series (1990) works, in the ways Hall described, for lesbians. By inserting herself as a butch into the Hollywood dreamscape, Bright habituated or shocked viewers into identifying with, being charmed by, or desiring her madcap figure. Queer theory, AIDS, lesbian activism, and gay rights provided her movement context. Feminists, fat-acceptance activists, disability-rights workers, cancer activists, and others fight every day to remake the visual culture in which the bodies they care about are violently sexualized, or desexualized, or ridiculed, dismissed, or pathologized. In tandem with positive visionaries, a liberation movement needs the major repudiators, like Jean Kilbourne in her *Killing Us Softly* series, http://www.jeankilbourne.com/videos. Syreeta McFadden, a Feministing blogger who complains that African Americans like her come out sometimes purple, sometimes black, and often ugly, argues that photography has a technological bias against dark epidermis and that "the camera" needs to learn "to see [her] skin."[24] To successfully disrupt everyday prejudice, critics show how it gets reproduced ideologically and technically, and mock it out of the street. Age critics, questioning misrepresentations of older people, need to frame more audacious critiques.

Hall's video interview gave me the thrill of recognizing there might be a way out of visual ageism, the new frontier to be crossed by the imaginative power of photography. This is no more impossible than the Black Is Beautiful movement seemed—and no more liable to the tedious charge of being politically correct. Think instead: politically sensitive. To produce the edgy, memorable images that do this, photographers need consciousness raising in the anti-ageist imaginary, because, as Hall says about skin color, "It's a question of seeing the body . . . the insignia written on the body," differently.

Photographers have the tools to do it. Primping may flatter celebrities of a certain age, but *food* is often photographed more carefully than old people are. (The magazine *Saveur* describes how their staff does it: "In the photo of pork with apples and cider cream sauce, backlight creates a dramatic effect, bathing the food in a play of light and shadow."[25]) If artists truly want older people to look—I won't say *appetizing*, but not like leftovers, the soon-to-be dead, clowns, or society's marginalia—they can't ignore the emotions that arise in response to their use of the tools of image construction: size, composition, light and shadow, camera angles, textures, posing, framing and cropping, distance from the camera, selection of the moment, lighting, facial expression, body conformation, context. And they need to focus on the major tool that drives technology and style: their own attitude.

My project in this session is to show photographic ways to create affects that may seem inconceivable to some: identification with or desire for, old people. "Desire" requires a subject who fascinates visually, perhaps by suggesting vital energies (sexual, sensuous, spiritual, intellectual, moral) or attainable serenity, or both. Walt Whitman conveys such overlapping and driving emotions in "I Sing the Body Electric," narrating his attraction to a farmer, a man of "wonderful vigor, calmness, beauty of person—he was wise also," noting only in passing that he was eighty years old.

I have spent years perusing still images, looking for that shock. I found it. Some photographers are hypersensitized to avoid illustrating age stereotypes, the way they would avoid enacting racism, sexism, ableism.[26] They live in a world of the larger embrace. My finds convinced me that viewers can learn to see better, from photographers who defuse our ageist resistance to being charmed or impressed or touched because they themselves have been bowled over. We lean forward to look through their delighted eyes. "Identification" enables us to see models who embody, as Kathleen Woodward puts it, "alternative futures for ourselves as we live into lives longer than we had imagined."[27] Young viewers may then hold in memory images that evoke sympathetic companionship, beneficent power, or the simple brag of selfhood.

There is also a third way: to create admiration, broadly defined. It was Diane Arbus who envisaged the third way, when, in her Guggenheim application about finding subjects, she wrote (as quoted earlier here), "I want simply to save them, for what is ceremonious and curious and commonplace will be legendary."[28] Arbus's way to save was to bring out the uniqueness of her subjects. Admiration carries many meanings, from the Latin sense of wonder, through respect and appreciation, even if slightly appalled. *I may not want or be able to become that person, but value comes from their existence.*

Older people in an ageist culture crave images of charm or power—as emanations of our ordinary selfhood—ensconced in bodies that look like ours. We need them for our current fantasy life and for self-love. And some younger people have reasons to crave such images. A *New York Times* writer, noticing a teaspoon of "pedigree oldster" in the media, observed that "a mother Botoxed to have fewer wrinkles than her college-aged daughter might very well create an elder-shaped hole in her daughter's heart."[29] If parents' ageist self-dislike inhibits their normal coming-to-agedness, this may well create longing in younger hearts to fill the "elder-shaped holes" with connections to the selfhood ensconced in older bodies. I believe this longing to be widespread and underestimated. Ageism is so antihuman that it makes us thirsty for a life course we can plausibly look forward to. The life course is meant to bring *more*—more of whatever we crave—or at least not to strip us of what we are able to amass of selfhood.

Desire, identification, admiration, companionship. These few precious keywords are the basis of my analyses in this session. Hoping to bring a utopian future a step closer through this fine art, I have curated a small set of still portraits (by professionals and one experienced amateur, all appearing since 1953) that illustrate some successes. Thematic shows like this that put social contexts in high relief are becoming welcome in expositions, according to the curator of photography at MoMA in New York, Quentin Bajac.[30] Like other art lovers, collectors, and critics choosing favorites, I found this disparate collection by intuition at first. Close comparative looking and research developed the theories by which I have justified the items in my own petit Armory show. I tried to match the expectations for an exhibition to be considered "rigorously curated." Susan Bright, a former curator at the National Portrait Gallery in London, specifies: "It has to be a reflection on societal values; show a recognition of art history or culture; come from a personal perspective; reflect upon the media it presents . . . and operate in a multi-platform way in order to extend beyond the gallery walls and reach as wide an audience as possible."[31] I have shown the images several times, each time to an audience that included photographers. To me an important outcome of this session would be having gallerists decide to curate their own similar shows, deploying and extending the principles enunciated here.

From the first glance, my images, however stylistically diverse, had something in common that stopped me in my peregrinations. They each deal well with the "insignia" of age. By giving the illusion of capturing selfhood, they create emotions that make anti-ageism a feeling as well as a conviction. They directly oppose the dominant group's cruel assumptions that physically we do not belong. They fit our submerged longings; they may rush our society toward the visual future.

The following sections are titled: Not Naked. Not Headless. Not Clichéd. Not Abjectly Lonely. Each Not will have a Yes attached, more complex to explain. Yes to Context. Yes to Plenitude. Yes to Surprise.

Not Naked

Selfhood being a complex body-mind phenomenon, being photographed naked at any age past infancy does almost no one's subjectivity any favors.

Figure 2.2. Jeff Wall, *The Giant*, 1992. Transparency in lightbox, 39.0 × 48.0 cm. Jeff Wall. Courtesy of the artist.

Babies cannot be harmed by being treated as viewable objects, until the age at which they start to pose. Teenagers, however, probably can't afford to lose any hard-won selfhood to an objectifying eye.

All right, sometimes naked, if old enough and shot right. Figure 2.2, Jeff Wall's *The Giant*, takes as given that "representation should be understood through the metaphors of enactment, dramatization, performance, and masquerade." The statement is from Griselda Pollock, the art historian and cultural theorist.[32] If we think photos ought to appear to hide the "performance," we can nevertheless be seduced by drama.

Goddesses can be shown without clothes, dressed as they are in their charisma. So in *The Giant*, almost before we register the age of the woman, we are confronted by her immense size and nakedness.[33] Wall, a Canadian photographer, appropriated environmental portraiture by giving his figure a context that is plausible for a thirty-foot high sculpture (the library, the mezzanine, the puny students). She is a stander, not a sitter. As a symbol of dignified grandeur in a place of learning, this real woman of many years lifts our spirits by her in-your-face visibility, the visual pleasures of the mise-en-scène, and Wall's iconographic allusiveness.

We rarely see images of naked old bodies, Julia Twigg, a British age critic, has observed. Classic and Renaissance respect for the naked body in the round only when that body is young is doubled down by contemporary avoidance, or, as the nursing-home shutterbugs indicated, nasty laughter. The nonporn images one recalls are often not arranged to appear attractive. Twigg reminds us that "we have little sense culturally of aesthetic pleasure in old flesh, or of what a beautiful old body might look like." I wrote in *Agewise* about an exceptional photo by Miriam Goodman. She took pleasure in the flesh of a hefty unclothed friend and titled her image, beside that of a painting of the slender Egyptian goddess, Nüt, *The Two Nüts*.[34]

Many of Wall's devices—the scale of the setting, the upright unscandalized posture, the undaunted bright lighting (Wall's work is presented as backlit transparencies)—make this image a surprise. *The Giant* is a fictional tableau. Practically speaking, it involved negotiation with the subject, who had to take off her clothes to make it possible. In answer to my questions, Wall told me in an email,

> I made that picture 20 years ago, so some things are hazy. The model was
> 64 at the time, I think. I found her through a talent agent in Los Angeles,
> where she lived, and presumably, still lives. She'd been a dancer profession-
> ally so that probably had a lot to do with her being in good form. I told her
> pretty much exactly what I wanted to do and how I was going to do it, so far
> as I knew in advance. She was a professional performer so it wasn't difficult
> for her; we had a nice time doing the shoot, which took maybe a week. I
> don't know that I had any motive except to make this particular image,
> which came to me from I don't know where. But I was glad to be doing an
> older female nude, it seemed different and fresh.[35]

Wall has read his Baudelaire. He spoke in 2001 of his work in general in relation to actual social conditions: "The painting of modern life would be experimental, a clash between the very ancient standards of art and the immediate experiences that people were having in the modern world. . . . So, I think that *The Giant*, which is an imaginary scene, is a painting of modern life."[36]

Like Parlá's "Leda Antonia Machado," *The Giant* succeeds by imposing symbolic grandeur on later life, or, more precisely, old womanhood. Seeing this piece can be a mind-changing experience. Although the image is actually small, and the detail of the figure holding a note card mildly humorous, Hall rightly calls it "an imagery monument."[37] Art appreciators see, not a paid model, but a sculpted Roman-style goddess. Or, from her lifted arm, an echo of the Statue of Liberty: this female Colossus thwarts the sexist ageism of our disrespectful world.

> Not like the brazen giant of Greek fame,
> With conquering limbs astride from land to land;
> Here at our sea-washed, sunset gates shall stand
> A mighty woman with a torch, whose flame
> Is the imprisoned lightning, and her name
> Mother of Exiles.
>
> —Emma Lazarus, "The New Colossus"

Asked "What do you see?" at an exhibit of *The Giant*, one anonymous person wrote cryptically, "Surrounded by a miniature of youth. The obedience of youth is small, whereas the defiance of the old is bold and above standard."[38]

Starting with an image of nakedness allows me to make another point about later-life nudity and gendered sexuality. *The Giant* is not posed in a curvaceous, provocative way. Well and good. Many people are irritated by the proliferation and escalating sensationalism of sexualized images, approaching porn in the public sphere. Wall's esthetic choices block out possible comparisons with, say, porn or selfies or images of anorexic adolescent girl models. The fresh truth of later life is that desire, identification, or admiration is possible without youth-inflected eroticism.

In particular, *The Giant* may help grown women get over the anachronism of continuing to marvel like adolescents at our bodies as if they were still only newly sexualized. Early auto-eroticism enforced by culture, harmful to the young, becomes increasingly harmful as we age past the admiration conferred on youth. Plain unashamed nudity, such as a focus on Hall's sixty-four-year-old model torn from her richly imagined context, might still seem sexy to some. Go for it. But the image's symbolic function is to construct matriarchs undaunted by society's worship of younger bodies. Goddess-matriarchs link age to other kinds of power: mature sex; serenity; assurance; the seeking of wisdom.

Not Headless

Having a face was a surprising late addition to my growing list of suggestions for portraying selfhood. More often than you might guess, old people are photographed headless. John Coplans's distinctive self-portraits are beheaded (fig. 2.3).

One critic said, "The absence of the most unique part of his body—by which he would be recognized as a specific individual—makes the images less about a distinct person and more about a sort of icon or symbol."[39] Coplans's back, photographed when he was sixty-four, appears to be a giant rectangular slab of meat, like a standing boneless roast, whose scary antennae high above turn out to be puny fists. Coplans habitually turns his *corps morcelé* into oddly shaped inhuman objects while emphasizing the male object's human hairiness, burliness, or other attributes.

Coplans says that his project is political in rejecting standard ideals of youthful beauty. An assistant takes photos of the poses Coplans selects. On video, however, he says, "And I pretend that my body is young. . . . Yeah, I want to look as young as I can, because I want to be like Everyman. . . . I want my body to be representative."[40] To me, what Coplans's unforgettable photo discloses instead (with some disgust despite the wit) is unretouched maleness, the fleshy excess of it. He finds masculine ugliness formally and texturally interesting, but a younger man who was porky and bristly could produce the same effects. Coplans's treatment of his older body, in my opinion, summons its contemporary opposite, the anorexic hairless teen males of ads. Painting older, stockier, muscular, masculine backs or chests in art was a joy that Michelangelo and Rubens taught later painters. Those images have faces.

My friend Roswell Angier, in his illuminating book *Train Your Gaze*, uses Eugene Richards's photo of a headless *Nursing Home Resident, Dorchester, Massachusetts, 1976*. Richards caught this woman defending or comforting herself. Her arms are crossed across her breasts, as if shielding them from the photographer's gaze; her hand is lying protectively on her chest. Angier indicates how an image creates, or implies, the artist's evaluation of his represented object. "The photographer's own gesture, his act of framing, literally marginalizes his subject, implying thereby an opinion, certainly a feeling, if not a judgment, about the nature and quality of life as represented in this moment."[41] In 1976, Richards, a great social documentarian, may have thought he was protecting his

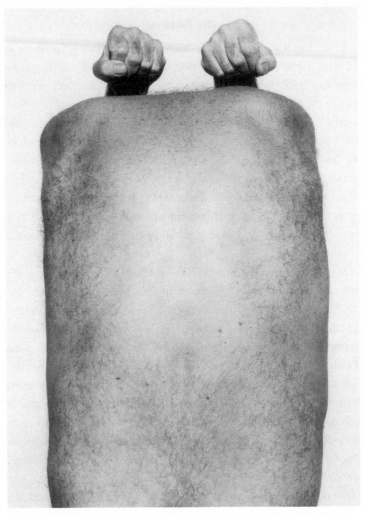

Figure 2.3. John Coplans, *Back with Arms Above*, 1984. Gelatin silver print, 42 × 32 in. © 1984 The John Coplans Trust. Courtesy of Coplans Trust.

model's privacy by cropping her head. But forty years of social theory later, we see that if this woman wanted to look back at him, perhaps with aggression—as in the phrases "the subaltern speaks" or "The Empire Strikes Back"—Richards wanted to avoid that.

But, let me argue against myself: a naked headless person can sometimes be a study of shapely form. Gorgeous formalism, as in the luscious high-contrast lighting of the 1930s and 1940s for modeling youthful bodies like marble sculpture, can be applied to bodies that are old, heavy, fleshy. The outcast body can be redeemed in many styles. But I prefer the illusion of selfhood. I want portraits with faces.

Not Clichéd

Photographs of groups of old people (with faces), usually women, who look alike: they may look sweet or they may look witchy, but the attribute the photographer sought and then found is often the expected boring or repulsive sameness of age. Given the consequences, group photos should be taken and looked at with caution.

Not Abjectly Lonely

Few portraits attend to how a person relates to someone else, although it is rare that people live in the utter solitude a formal portrait implies. Old people in particular are often shown isolated—on a park bench, along an empty stretch of beach, in an institutional setting, as in Eugene Richards's photo—in a way that implies their having been abandoned by friends, family, lovers. This is somewhat the way Samuel Beckett uses old men in his novels, as an allegory of all wounds, within a world of bafflement, frailty, regretted sexual dysfunction, and loss of affect. Yet compared to a teenager who has no children, the older we are, the likelier we are to have younger family: children, grandchildren, nieces and nephews, or godchildren. As in Whitman's tribute to the farmer as father, grandfather, and great-grandfather, some elders seem the very fount of life with their families arrayed around them.

Figure 2.4, taken in a rural house in Nicaragua, exhibits none of the typicality of so-called ethnic photography of old age, where expressionless people, often looking confused or vacant, do nothing but show off extreme wrinkles or native dress. Although Petrona Martinez is not placed in the exact center of the photo, she is a figure of self-possessed stature in her domestic universe. The children's faces are still, rather than animated, as in many typical American family albums

Figure 2.4. David Gullette, *Petrona Martinez, San Jeronimo*, 2013. © David Gullette 2013. Courtesy of the artist.

where it is the children who are featured. And this image reverts to the age hierarchy of an earlier century in another way: it is Martinez's broader and taller form that quietly dominates the family scene (replacing the traditional patriarch). The photographer did not tell her where to stand or tell the youngsters to cluster around her like *putti* around a saint. A fifteenth-century Renaissance painter would love the touches that ennoble her: the backcloth that frames her figure as the central one even though it is off-center; the Madonna blue of her dress that picks up other blues on the wall; the winged canopy over her head (in a painting, *putti* would have been holding up the folds), the soft light from below showing the even lines of her forehead and the set of her mouth.

Unlike us, who chronically expect to be surveilled in public—at the ATM, the market, in a club—Doña Petrona Martinez doesn't have expressions ready-made for the camera. She doesn't feel the need to smile, and although she may never have stood in front of a camera in her entire life, she looks calmly forward at the photographer. One feels she would move purposefully. She has what I would call a firm soft face. Her arms or hands reassuringly touch each of her grandchildren. Her girth is protective. The religious symbolism supports her selfhood, aging toward old age within the generations of a family.

Doña Martinez represents the polar opposite of Ari Seth Cohen's over-dressed New Yorkers of the same age or older. Martinez isn't cutting a fig-ure. No elaborate make-up, outré costume, oversized jewelry, or eye-catching stance. Her Virgin-blue smock is faintly stained. The photo neither denies her economic context nor fetishizes poverty. The cloth covers a window into a dark room; the canopy is a hammock tied up; the walls of her house are old wood from trees of giant circumference; the wires show the house boasts electric-ity. The framed photo behind her is of a family member graduating from high school, one of the rare times that a farm family like this would lay out money for a photographer.

Realism does not have to be a synonym for abjectness. Indeed, this is a leg-acy photo for a family that has no albums. Photographers of old people can be considered saviors of the living, providing the persistence of vision that makes the memories of the eventual orphans brighter.

Unrelated viewers receive another legacy, which lifts this particular image out of the family context. Jennifer Coplon, a sociologist who photographs formerly homeless older Bostonians while doing life reviews with them, says: "Those who are visibly in extreme poverty in our society, often compounded by physical disabilities, are less likely to be recognized for their strengths and merits. They can appear defeated. Even their self-respect can be in jeopardy. . . . I believe that there is much dignity and wisdom from years of living—with resilience and determination and plain old grit—in the faces of elders. Photo-graphs of old people *in the context of their environments* have a lot to teach us."[42]

We now have many photographers who believe this, and some take non-ageist photographs. The photograph here of Doña Petrona is by my husband, David Gullette, an experienced amateur who was working with members of her community, building bio-sand filters to purify their contaminated water. Amateurs can sometimes portray people who are old better than profession-als because, not having to sell their work, they escape commercial (which can mean youthist) pressures. Given the spread of social media, a noncommercial image potentially has many viral viewers.

There must be billions of snapshots that show pleasant old people shar-ing a space with family members. But they are not paradigm-breaking unless they capture relationship, the network in which meaning arises, as this photo captures the children's reliance as well as the woman's iconic power. Can I envisage a darkly brilliant photo of a controlling matriarch, with her family warily detached, faces averted, that is not a cartoon? Yes, certainly. Yet this image gives me the opportunity to hope that more images may operate as this grand-madonna does, in symbolic and esthetic registers that make generous statements about trust, dignity, persistence, and the importance of age hierarchy. Her value, deriving from the integration of the entire image (her posture and expression, and the esthetic/religious/domestic context) is something we can identify with and, perhaps yearningly, desire to possess.

Old as Old, with Attitude

Scholars in aging studies, according to Christoff Ribbat, believe that "displaying the old *as old* usually serves purposes of exclusion and marginalization." Age critics have good reason to be suspicious. So far, I have shown how a photo artfully pushes age into the second tier of a viewer's consciousness. But sometimes a photo that shows the old as old can be, as Ribbat says, "less constricting, more flexible and liberating."[43] Here is one, distinguished by its utter disregard of or casual contempt for our prejudices. (The photographer refused permission for use of her image in this book. Although creative nonfiction can do much, it cannot produce the instantaneous effect of so remarkable a portrait. To appreciate the commentary, please go online.[44])

This is a small image, sixteen inches high by twenty inches wide—a landscape orientation rather than the typical portrait vertical—of an old woman in profile and her open right hand. Atypically, she is *not* facing front; her eyes seem nearly closed. She does not bother to look at us.

The striking image was taken in high resolution with raking light from the side—the better to display the woman's strong profile, bone structure, and wrinkles across half the picture plane. The woman, then in her mid-eighties, could well have been shot to look less lined. But the shot intentionally stresses old age. Then the landscape shape permits the interesting hand to take up the other half of the space, saying, as the sitter, a sculptor, once said, "I am not what I am, I am what I do with my hands." My gloss: *Stop! My gestures too require attention to be paid.* The exceptional choice of profile, which may remind us of ancient cameos, or the chiseled sweep of a Native American chieftain, emphasizes the impressive age effect, and so do the nearly closed eyes, as if saying, *I don't care who looks.* Together, the averted profile and eyes declare,

By not looking at you, by simply sitting still, I permit you to look at me. You may look as long as you like, it won't affect me. Get used to the unappreciated strangeness of wrinkles, the complexity of their design, my unabashed acceptance of what writers describe so grotesquely. The entire image says, You may work through your fears. I am already unafraid, of myself or the photographer standing in for you. You may try to say that this is "beauty" or "wisdom" or "temporality," the result of time; you may say any fancy thing the culture has taught you. You may trot out all your clichés of positive aging. The discourse you propose is neither here nor there. Look, while I go about my business.

The decline view of this image could not be more different. A UK student writes, "The blank expression of [Louise] Bourgeois with perhaps closed eyes and her pose which seems as though she has died in her sleep, lying on her side with her hand up by her head scream death."[45] Watch out, ladies, not to close your eyes in public, so you don't *scream death.*

This is a celebrity, posed, coiffed, poised, with inner power to defy, but also an old woman, to whom the photographer, Annie Leibovitz, has chosen to apply her grandly mannered style. Perhaps with Bourgeois, an innovative feminist, Leibovitz realized that other portraitists had not yet been daring enough to exploit the full panoply of design elements stored like treasure in the vitrine of an old face. In 1997, she also decided that this sitter's hand—her imperious hand—would be almost as prominent as her face.

This image, as well as another landscape-oriented portrait by a French photographer, Raymond Collet, of an Egyptian man, convey something important: an attitude, as caught by the artist's alert eye (fig. 2.5).

You don't know the charming Cairo ambulatory street vendor—smiling, Collet told me, because he saw he was being photographed—but, like Bourgeois, he has poise and a distinguished profile. He may never have been photographed before, but he believes it is a pleasant thing to have happen. "The light loves him," as photographers say, who woo light. The beiges favor his skin tones. No object distracts from the deep lines carved in his face. In fact, the empty, softly blurred backdrop concentrates the eye on those lines, placed in almost the exact center of the image. The clean white folds of the turban pick out the curling Rembrandt-like wires of his neat beard; these and the dark shadow on the nose further frame those highly lit wrinkles. An artist with a certain eye wants *that.* The whole image reads: *People can be proud of their old faces, can*

Figure 2.5. Raymond Collet, *Street Vendor, Cairo, Moezz Street near Khan and Khalili*, 2010. © photo 2010. Raymond Collet / www.1001images.com. Courtesy of the artist.

display their lines with as much ease as their profiles. Shame on you if you imagine you must be ashamed when you are old.

There has long been an honorific portrait tradition, retrieved from painting by photography, in which sitters, if they could afford to, paid to be portrayed as respected elders. In attenuated form, this tradition of admiration complicated by paid flattery still exists. And some become legendary, like the venerated artists in Eugene Richards's *Time* magazine spread of September 12, 2013. But only one of my own choices is a recognizable person. Old need not be pretty, famous, rich, or beautiful, if desire, identification, or admiration can be created in other ways. In this imaginary exhibit, I have avoided not only the stereotypes of decline but also the opposite homogenization: positive aging.

Our Parents, Not Ourselves

Roswell Angier, an important teacher, warns about "the difficulty of undertaking a portrait project with your own parents as subjects, in which the exercise of critical awareness and compassion alike, become part of a collaborative enterprise."[46] Sometimes a parent looks at an adult child who is taking their photo with a look that says, *Don't do me any harm*. And that frightened non-collaborative relationship to the offspring is what you see first. The fact that photographers shoot their own families does not guarantee any meaningful result about being old or in relationships.

Portraits of people living with dying, if taken without full consent, betray the person and the concept of respect for vulnerable selfhood, by showing the body permanently thrown out of the control of the will. Richard Avedon's father was already ill with cancer when Richard shot him; the father died in 1973. "In 1970, I showed my father for the first time one of the portraits that I had made of him in the years just before. He was wounded. My sense of what is beautiful was very different from his."[47] Avedon's famous result claims esthetic "beauty," while empathetic viewers see only the artist's obsession with "interesting" suffering. His father's expressions are sometimes so peculiar that they might be illustrations for Arthur Danto's complaint that camera speed catches not what people are significantly feeling, as painters had to do, but only "the transitions between expressions." Danto, a philosopher and art theorist, pointed out that an image might possess some "optical truth" while failing to capture "visual truth."[48]

Larry Sultan's father, who was not ill, also doesn't like the photos his son takes of him. Larry Sultan honestly quotes his father saying "All I know is that when you photograph me I feel everything leave me . . . my thoughts disappear." The elder Sultan thinks he ought to have more control: "It's your picture but my image." He becomes wary, perhaps angry. "You're not procrastinating are you, waiting for me to die so that your book has a dramatic ending? . . . And listen, I hope you're not going to end your book with one of those pictures of despair."[49] In contrast, I think appreciatively of Marcel Proust's Marcel, recalling that in his youth he hadn't understood why his beloved grandmother was hiding her face from a photographer. Marcel had called it vanity, because he couldn't accept how sick she was. Later he feels intense regret. A midlife man, he knows that people want to control the image their survivors have of them.

The next portrait (fig. 2.6), however, was also taken by an adult child. It's a still used to advertise Stephen Dwoskin's documentary, *Age Is. . . .* Dwoskin chose it. He writes, "The same society which tries to make you live as long as possible does everything in order to stop helping you after a certain age. . . . What strikes me when seeing these people [in his film] is the value, the invaluable which those eyes have seen, those hands have felt, much more than certain younger faces which look rather 'photoshopped.' "[50]

Figure 2.6. Valerie Massadian, *Mamoushka—Age Is . . .* © valerie massadian 2013. Courtesy of the artist.

The still is by Valerie Massadian, a filmmaker, of her mother. It is beautiful, provocative, and surprising enough almost to be funny. Against the dark swirling background, the woman's white hair shines and her naked skin is warmed like a Gauguin. The photographer must have loved the blue lines of her pencil against the apricot colors of her flesh. Christiane Massadian is attractive, with gorgeous strong shoulders. (Many older women have them.) What is arresting, I think, is that Christiane is *doing* something, one desideratum in portraits of a group stereotyped as useless.

The pleasurable shock comes from a mirror scene in which a woman is *not trying to make herself look younger.* On the contrary. For whatever mysterious reason, she is highlighting her wrinkles. And one can warm to another surprising countercultural message: she is looking in a mirror *without self-criticism* of the imposed female kind. No shame, no discontent. Simply a craftswoman's concentration on getting the desired effect right. The artist's bold image keeps us riveted on this gesture and attitude. Susan Sontag says, "In some way a still image is and always will be more memorable" than a few minutes of film.[51]

Certainly we can look longer. Captivated by the triple fascination of the person, the action, and the image, we look long and long enough.

None of my subversive images shows a subject passing for younger. None was chosen for beauty; I did not go looking for beauty in subjects. The Nots are not pet peeves. My choices are based on what I consider anti-ageist, ethical, and esthetic sensibilities, technically conveyed by the images.

YES TO CONTEXT

Selfhood is enriched by context, as we saw in Wall's *Giant* or in Petrona Martinez's family photo. "On location" or environmental portraits are usually of people in a situation that they live in (or work, rest, or play in) or a place that they choose, such as a beach or museum.

One image manages a final subtle and indirect effect not yet mentioned, which is to aggrandize a particular older person—in this remarkable case, a man who is not even "present" except in an image. Gordon Parks, an African American photographer who worked for *Life* in its heyday, took a painterly close-up of a bureau or table in an old-fashioned room (fig. 2.7).

The top has been made into a shrine, presumably to the man in the ornate frame. The light is a burnishing gold, which warms the metals but not the photograph, whose blueish-gray light seems to belong to another, colder realm of being. The man wears an old-fashioned moustache, an artist's or partisan's smock and a workman's cap. This is not a formal portrait, but a high-resolution snapshot of him taken in a somber moment. Someone—a lover, a widow, an adult child—keeps his pipe, his wire-framed round eyeglasses, one cufflink, as precious relics. "A good life summed up by the possessions on a desk," Philip B. Kunhardt Jr., then an editor at *Life*, writes in his introduction to Parks's collection of images and poems.[52] Presence is artfully signified.

"In many black homes, photographs, particularly snapshots, were also central to the creation of 'altars,'" bell hooks explains. "These commemorative places paid homage to absent loved ones."[53] hooks, too, uses the word "shrine." Here, Parks's pictorialist style finds intimate charm in the possessions the absent man used. A viewer may feel imbued with the atmosphere the imagined widow has created. Usually we need narratives to accomplish so much, because they can portray love or lust and describe appearances without depicting a body the youthful age gaze can condemn. Here, we see the physical man, loved by the

Figure 2.7. Gordon Parks, *Untitled* [*Portrait in a Frame*], n.d. Courtesy of and copyright The Gordon Parks Foundation.

maker of the shrine, thought worthy of a treasured photograph, with the whole ambiance captured by a reverent lens.

YES TO PLENITUDE AND PLEASURE

My last image, a photo without text—by Kosti Ruohomaa, a Finnish American artist who also worked for *Life*—shows a couple in a swing, he standing on the seat behind her, pumping; she seated, with an expression of unalloyed delight (fig. 2.8). There is nobody else around. It is as if the two came upon the swing while passing by, she in her hat and good shoes, and decided on the spur of the moment to test it out.

Hard to imagine such an image being taken nowadays. It wouldn't work as an AARP ad for leisured retirement living, replacing middle-class golf players. It comes from a show and book that were long dismissed as sentimental, *The Family of Man*. The caption used there—specifying their ages, the event, his job—unnecessarily narrowed this photo's imaginative possibilities.[54]

I see this image, gratefully, as being about the longevity of the physical pleasure we take in motion, as possible at eighty-nine as at age three. I see his strong pull on the chain, her arm carelessly wrapped around the links; the landscape deep beneath as if they pushed themselves up quite high. Because of

Figure 2.8. Kosti Ruohomaa, *Untitled* [*Couple on Swing*]. Gelatin silver print. Courtesy of The Black Star Collection, 1947. Ryerson Image Centre, BS.2005.279117/174–741.

the dynamic diagonal, because of their joy, here again we don't see "age" first, but rather mingled in the action. These people are having bodily fun and the surprise of enjoying physical closeness and motion-in-relationship in an unexpected setting. Old-fashioned as his garters and her hat are, this fresh image makes a novel statement about long-term marital pleasures. It kindles our desire for a plausible future like this. The joys of later life are true joys.

Why does my curated show not fall victim to the charge of merely "representing old age"? I didn't take any of them myself. They are heterogeneous. Each on its own is esthetically distinctive enough to make the idea of breaking the paradigm plausible. Each image projects its subject's significance by deploying, in Julian Stallabrass's words again, "extreme individuality of style and [or] composition . . . congruent with the supposed uniqueness of the subject."[55] Not all the images suggest agency: there are other ways of being unique. Collet and Leibovitz convey the subjects' importance by throwing the undisguised insignia of age in our faces, making the attitudes of the admired subjects more striking than their wrinkles. All manage to foreground feelings that have no age-negative buried in them: grandeur, resistance, amusement, family cohesion, elegiac loss, physical delight. Together, they succeed by linking, in an indissoluble way, an imposing state of being, to being old.

That play with connotations is what I must have been looking for, turning over hundreds of images. Possibly the finest anti-ageist art does not arise, so far, from an intention to make it so, but as a side effect or serendipitous outcome of an attitude the artist has deeply internalized, called forth by the human subject(s). I call the effects "subversive," handling that overused word cautiously, because the works prepare our not-yet-quite-ready eyes for a new episteme.

The photographers' individual visions are their gift. As a strategy for looking responsibly, it strikes me as just and useful. It is useful, because it distracts the ageist inheritance of the gaze long enough for an image of unavoidable "oldness" to engender other responses, as it did for me. It is just, because people past youth need not feel obliged to identify willy-nilly with age as their primary identity. Some will call this "denial." Some call it pragmatic. Why should we give this lately acquired or peremptorily imposed identity first place, given the hostile world we inhabit?

And there's a theoretical consideration, linking my finding in visual culture to psychology and society. We all need a wide cultural turn toward age pride, like those evinced in race, gender, queer, and crip pride. But no identity, however proudly borne, ought to be made to feel primary at the behest of others—neither "woman," "person of color," "gay," nor "old." No need to blame identity politics for this primacy, since bias imposes exaggerations and limits rebuttals. The slogan-identities are good on parade and for de-internalization, but less useful in daily life, where we want whole selves in relation to others in equally diverse worlds.

Whatever we say and do in public forums, let us decide for ourselves, as we mature, which identity surges up to true pride of place from time to time, and then what images best represent that identity. If agewise self-reflection decides that "being old" is not primary in front of the lens, this need not be confused with self-hating ageism. The best portraits satisfy sitters (whose primary identity is not always epidermal) that some aspects of their opaque selfhood have been seen.

For us the unphotographed, the unpinned, the un-Instagrammed, if such images were to become widespread, aging-into-old-age could be more easily accepted as prideful, with complex meanings that each person determines. There's freedom to be found that doesn't exist now. Yet.

Responsible Looking

In this vast politico-conceptual space—changing age politics by esthetic means—this is a small body of examples. As decline ideology keeps on shooting different bolts at those it renders vulnerable, I seem unable to stop throwing up my tiny shields. What can be the cumulative effect of looking at these photos, or even ten times their number? Some of the young may not see anything but extreme otherness or near-death. But for others the effect may not be small. It may inspire efforts to seek exceptional photographs. Merely recognizing that they exist enlivens a seeker's vision. Seeking, whether done deliberately or desperately, constitutes a political act that any of us should feel free to make.

The saying I use as the epigraph, "What another person looks like to *you* is *your* responsibility," may seem gnomic as theory, or impossible to put into practice. But being led to look properly at the Other can be a life-changing experience. Anca Cristofovici in her book on aging and photography says that what we want from deeply imaginative representations is not "immediate identification as [much as] their potential to increase our emotional knowledge."[56] Expanding our ability to empathize corrects misconceptions. We feel different and more whole precisely because the Other comes to look more human. The epigraph comes from a theater and film director/ producer, Michael Lessac, long dismayed by the idea that race hatred in South Africa was based on Afrikaners *seeing* blacks as violent, murderous, unreasonably hostile to whites. The word "seeing" is not metaphorical. After South Africa's Truth and Reconciliation hearings, Lessac, an anti-apartheid activist, thought that the people who attended it would see around them more human visages and expressions. Through knowing *why* we see the formerly neglected or despised differently, we take more responsibility for how others look to us.[57]

Absorbing Lessac's *sententia*, people may find themselves affected more deeply by faces whose first apparent identity is *being old*. This warmer affect can come as an illuminating flash of comprehension, an epiphany, or it can feel like the result of an arduous process, both cognitive and emotional, in which our will to see more benignly forces us to look again and differently. My own anti-ageist trajectory in looking is far from complete.

Being moved by exceptional images begins a process of understanding an economy that uses old people hostilely as proxies for vulnerability. Susan Sontag wrote at the end of *On Photography*, "A capitalist society requires a culture based on images . . . to stimulate buying and anesthetize the injuries of class, race, and sex."[58] *That* explains why there are billions of images of younger people, now more frequently multiracial—who, whatever the product, at the same time sell "anti-aging" as a concept and desire—while there are few public images of older people who aren't politicians, popes, or patrons of sports teams. What anesthetizes the injuries of ageism and ableism?

Maintaining the cult of youth, visual culture serves as a perennial enforcement mechanism. By suggesting that the unphotogenic nonyoung are undeserving—why else would they be invisible?—generational rivalry blunts the facts of stagnant wages and the loss of seniority for people over fifty. Everything festers together: belief in our ascribed characteristics, behavioral avoidance and impatience, hate speech. Scapegoats now include Muslims, young black men, and trans women; but with longevity's expense account and the Alzheimer's boom heightening fears of the old, this additional outgroup can be sent, as it were, into the wilderness. Are these necessities that capitalism, democracy, and neoliberalism cannot do without? Only struggle can decide.

This Is the End of the First Session

Still imagery cannot satisfy all the craving that later life be shown as worth living. In the next four chapters, I discuss other means, for other zones of human activity. The turn toward visual anti-ageism needs critics to explicate and repudiate, artists to create and disrupt, and a movement to keep the pressure on. When enough of us complain, *and threateningly, look elsewhere,* or curate tendentious shows of what we like, who knows what further transgressive imaginations we may inspire? The revolutionary anti-ageist energy we provide may seep into the milieus of artists.

New work, Stuart Hall said in the same provocative video, "if it has any authenticity, and power, and depth," will reflect how countercultural forces have impacted artists. Who wants to ask, "Might my work *sadden* old people within the human family? Might it abet the attempts to make those seen as decrepit lose heart and want to die early?" As artists respond to ageism from their own divergent impulses, many more will shove us toward the longed-for paradigm shift we deserve. The movement needs millions of counter-images—of people who look like me and (please, please), people older than me.

Only a movement can make sure that revolutionary art gets not only made but also purveyed in public arenas, critiqued and admired for the right reasons. I have a vision: that with luck and hard work we may look back in twenty years on this era's visual guarantees of disgust, condescension, or avoidance, and find them incomprehensible.

CHAPTER 3

（

THE ELDER-HOSTILE

GIVING COLLEGE STUDENTS
A BETTER START AT LIFE

IN BARS, LOCKER ROOMS, SOCIAL MEDIA

The Internet is notorious for commenters who feel grossly entitled to dismiss vulnerable others. Ageist hate speech is not hard to find there.

"God forbid these miserable once-were-people not [*sic*] survive as long as possible to burden the rest of us." This fantasy wish—that a large and easily identifiable group, "miserable once-were-people" should die prematurely for the convenience of youngers—was found on *Hatebook.com* by Alison Stripling and two psychology colleagues. Their discoveries, presented at the Gerontological Society of America conference in 2011, were my first exposure to verbal ageism on social-networking sites. The researchers call ageism there "ubiquitous."[1] I was unprepared, taken aback. There was more to come.

Anyone "over the age of 69 should immediately face a firing squad." This imperious declaration appeared on Facebook. Of the Facebook groups that focused on older individuals, with a combined twenty-five thousand members, one study found that 74 percent "vilified" older people, and 37 percent would like to ban them from public activities like driving or shopping. More than one wanted somebody to get a gun and kill them en masse. This data was collected by Becca Levy, a psychologist at the Yale School of Public Health, and her team. Levy studies prejudice (as well as pro-aging attitudes) in innovative ways. "These are the groups older people are likely to come across," Levy commented.[2]

These Facebook groups were created by adults, whose mean age category was between twenty and twenty-nine. Ten of the groups were "offensive" in terms of Facebook's own Community Standards list. Since Facebook is used by a billion people a day, how its reviewers moderate its content matters. But Facebook did not list "age" among its protected categories and ignored the Levy group's complaints: eight of these groups remained in operation nearly a year later. On Facebook, extreme youth rules. The average age of the company's employees is twenty-eight. A gay writer and painter, David Conner, writes, from "the other side of 35," "I've been told by young gay men online that I should have killed myself after 30—young, white, worked out gay men who see me and say or think 'Eww, die.'" "Criticism from other gay men . . . is meaner than the meanest scene from *Mean Girls*."[3]

On unmoderated sites, anonymity encourages frightening de-individuation, a herd mind. In "Trolls just want to have fun," Erin E. Buckels and colleagues state from self-report that men, already known to be higher than women in general Internet usage and in antisocial behavior online, spend more time putting up hostile remarks. The plural of LOL, "lulz," means a nasty laugh at someone else's expense. Some trolls admit they feel "glee at [imagining] the distress of others," if that distress is caused by their words.[4] Their sadistic pleasure is a fantasy about possessing power over the vulnerable.

Rampant fear-mongering about our graying nation and the implied horrors of Alzheimer's may drive up some young people's fears of old people, in line with theories that mortality salience can be manipulated against an out-group, and that some young people have more death anxiety than others. Numerous attacks on lulz culture have pointed out its arrogant sexism and white-supremacist racism, but so far few critics have attacked its barbaric ageism and ableism. Readers who were dismayed by the visual ageism highlighted in the previous chapter may be alarmed at such verbal contempt and terrorist threats, a troubling peephole into the widespread ageism of (some) young First World adults. Mary Beard, a British feminist, was the target of ugly mysogynistic ageism. Although she finally received an apology from one reformed attacker, Beard, quoted in the *New Yorker*, believes that "comment sections expose attitudes that have long remained concealed in places like locker rooms and bars."[5]

Not so concealed. Much that is public against an older age class is unashamedly signed. The men's magazine *GQ* interviewed a dismissive twenty-three-year-old rapper, Young Thug. "If you're 30, 40 years old, you're not getting listened to by minors," Thug asserted. ("Minors" would be the preferred demographic.) "Like, Jay Z has some of the sickest lyrics ever, but I would never buy his CD, just because of my age and because of his age. By the time I turn that old, I ain't gonna be doing what he's doing." Jay Z, whose net worth lies in the $500 million zone, was then forty-five.[6]

Other lords of cool—the IT industry as a whole, a cynosure for a tech-obsessed society—are offhandedly ageist. Billionaire CEO Mark Zuckerberg, then twenty-two, told an audience at Stanford why he stressed hiring young techies: "Young people are just smarter." The slur reverberates still as if it were true. Industry employment ads ask for "recent grads."[7] Although the median age of Americans is close to forty, "The average age at founding [a tech company] in our dataset was just over 31, and the median was 30." Middle-ageism smashes even those in privileged job categories. A wrongful termination lawsuit brought against Google by a former employee, age fifty-two, quoted numerous age-based derogatory remarks from coworkers. Almost half the respondents to an IT job board survey felt it was impossible to get ahead after the age of forty.[8] And forty is too old elsewhere, as the show *Younger* on TV Land hammers home, with its heroine pretending to be twenty-six to get a newbie job in publishing.

These victims are, obviously, not members of the vilified oldest age classes— retired people or the small percentage who live in nursing homes—but simply people edging in that direction a few years sooner than those with power to judge. For decades I have been warning that middle-ageism is backing down the life course, to younger and younger ages. Now that the trend of job discrimination may be irreversible, it is finally being noticed. A few celebrities critique youth-preference. When comic Andy Samberg reported sexist age discrimination at the 2015 Emmys, millions had already seen Helen Mirren, Madonna, and younger stars complaining.

Hate speech on the lawless playground of the Internet is fully protected in the United States unless it threatens violence against a particular individual (and not always then, as feminists and victims of police violence know). Hate speech against older people, unlike midlife job discrimination, has barely been noticed. Danielle Citron, in *Hate Crimes in Cyberspace*, makes the general case that online harassment is a serious civil rights issue. "Civil interferences" mean the intentional infliction of emotional distress. In the case of people considered old, hate speech may well not be "intentional," if that means *meaning to hurt*. Hate-speakers have no sense that human beings are involved, capable of being hurt.

Are there any fresh insights into how this wanton insensibility comes about?

THE GENESIS OF YOUNG JUDGE

A twentyish young man—writing Internet hate mail, judging a slightly older entertainer condescendingly, unwilling to relate to older employees—is setting himself up with an assertive subidentity I want to call Young Judge. Cocky by virtue of the alleged superiority of testosterone and youth, like Zuckerberg, Young Judge rejects those he's stuffed into the category "old." Perhaps insecure about work or love, he enjoys moments of grandiosity, flings himself into self-important anger on the comment sites. Mocking old people is a mob distraction that solidifies the in-group identity. (Being sure they have such a cohesive and exclusive thing is a category mistake, like thinking all old people are alike. It is an outcome of the havoc ageism wreaks on common sense.[9]) The basis is an unstable illusion that "being young" means "I'll stay in this age class forever." In youth, one's age can seem just as fixed as one's sex and race appear to be. The oldest age one has ever been is bound to be "privileged" in a way that "privilege" is not usually understood. I want to call this subjective attitude *age essentialism*, treating age here not as a sliding signifier (as most theorists do), but as a fixed fantasy.

A female Young Judge also feels prideful. The female, however, embedded in perfectionist sexist culture (perhaps she is a reader of fashion magazines), already condemns her own skin and figure, and scolds or scorns older women for (in her eyes) not keeping their looks. With the male YJ telling her she is "Not a 10" about her looks or sexual readiness, she may incorporate him as "the male in the head" for her later life.[10] A *Vogue* writer notices how young women are, when "branding themselves, usually *slamming* themselves, as 'old.' I see it all the time on Facebook—'Help, I'm officially old' on a woman's 25th birthday."[11]

Youth supremacists, dreading the aging narrative as provided by our life-course imaginary, are vastly more numerous than the trolls. Their bias is imposed before being self-fashioned. Children may first absorb ageism from about six to eight years of age.[12] Not all do. My granddaughter, entranced from the age of eight by the grandmother-admiring *American Girl* series of books and movies, may skip some age-avoidance. Ageism may worsen for adolescents, perhaps from overhearing the sotto voce complaints or jokey-fearful allusions of their parents to "aging" or the cost of elder care, or from repeating comedic put-downs.

Silicon Valley, TV, films, magazines, and the Internet are some of the ageist unsourced sources that influence the discourses of the young as they go

"forming attitudes independent from knowledge."[13] In a survey of eighteen-
to thirty-four-year-olds by the American Press Institute, 88 percent percent
say they get their crypto-news (which includes attitudes) from Facebook; 83
percent use YouTube; others, Reddit. None involves fact-checking.[14] Americans under age thirty-five are more likely to think that "older workers" are less
effective, and that "old people" are lonely, miserable, suffering from defective
memory, and "pretty much alike," according to AARP.[15] Taking the well-known
Implicit Association Test devised by Harvard professor Mazharin Banaji, people of all ages tend to be slower to associate positive adjectives with old faces
than with young faces. Whatever the problem with the IAT photographs, in a
world saturated with bias it makes sense that anyone (including me), seeing a
stranger with an older face, is slower to think "sharp," "brilliant," "admirable,"
"Hire her," "Invite him out to lunch."

But people don't need an implicit-bias test to reveal prejudice. Those responding to explicit statements are surprisingly shameless. They agree with
facile generalizations (e.g., "Most old people are not interested in making new
friends, preferring instead the circle of friends they have had for years") that
they would dismiss out of hand about their own age class (e.g., "Most young
people are not interested in their old friends, preferring instead to make new
ones online"). The clannish-olders statement comes from the Fraboni Stereotype subscale, widely used since 1990. Ignorance about old people has behavioral concomitants, which can be measured by Fraboni's Separation subscale.
This comprises eight items: for example, "I sometimes avoid eye contact with
old people when I see them." The Behavioral subscale might well now include
"I have bumped into a professor walking on campus"; Leni Marshall, an English
professor at University of Wisconsin–Stout, a tall woman with an infectious
smile, describes faculty members as fuming at this. She added, in an email,
"Often, I'll just stop walking (so they can't say I walked into them) but not
move out of the way."[16] The offenders are mostly male. The Affective Attitude
subscale includes, "I personally would not want to spend much time with an
old person."[17] Obviously, people who respond so unguardedly fail to question
their feelings or censor their stereotypes. Common carelessness and avoidance
make ours an interesting period to record, as well as an urgent one to change.

I was not exempt from bias even though I became a young adult in a different era. I want to tell another fragment of age autobiography, like the story
about my seventieth birthday in chapter 1. Age autobiography typically notes
an important psychological change over time, which leads to a discovery about

your selfhood in relation to "aging." Discovery comes from reflecting on how your life history connects to your culture's constructions of reality.[18] Simply put, this is a confession about a revelation, submitted to informed introspection.

When I first started visiting my mother in Florida, where she had retired from elementary-school teaching when she was sixty, I often failed to behave nicely, arrogant and snobbish thirty-five-year-old that I was. I was a textbook Fraboni freak. What improved my humanity was getting to know my mother's women friends over the years—chatting on the beach, lunching, hanging out together naked in the steam room, smiling, making eye contact. I treated them with respectful friendliness. We became "equally adults together," a value I have theorized elsewhere.[19] I wasn't yet an age critic (obviously). I was simply lucky to have some of my social life there arranged for me. But my encounter therapy should have come earlier—or not been necessary.

In helping younger people undo what is sometimes treated as *innate* mortality-fear, probably nothing beats social interaction with older strangers, under the right conditions. (Gerontologists know this: students have grandparents who are real to them in some sense that doesn't preclude stereotyping and avoiding nonfamilial old people.) Without such opportunities to meet, actually crossing the great divide in a timely fashion—that is, undoing a juvenile belief that the Great Demotions are deserved—may be a matter of dumb luck.

Ideally, thanks to merely aging-past-youth, the Young Judge subidentity would wither by itself as its endorser, the cult of youth, subsides. But Young Judges are alarmed to feel their essential age identity trembling. Prior to aging-denial (the self-dislike that gets so much attention) is the harmful tendency of younger people to cling to their trained aversions.

Young people often eliminate other prejudices. "Students would rather have the dry heaves than make outward utterances of racial stereotypes (although some may inwardly hold such sentiments), because they have been learning about the problems associated with racism all of their lives." The researcher who sent me this note, Don Umphrey, taught for decades at Southern Methodist University in Texas. "However," he continued, "ageism is not so high on our nation's agenda."[20] By now, prejudiced remarks are likely to be contested in many classrooms; and not only by the affected targets (African Americans, feminists, LGBTQ students) but by other students, sometimes passionately. But ageism and its twin, ableism, are excluded from most agendas.

That a self develops unevenly is not a difficult concept. People do relinquish certain identity-maintaining boundaries—but not all, and not all at once. They can lose their homophobia and hold onto their aversion to the disabled. What is stranger is that development may involve *replacing* other biases by drawing on the available fund of ageism. Lisa S. Parker and Valerie B. Satkoske give some examples: "An older African-American man who, because of his age, no longer seems threatening . . . no longer prompts a young white woman to cross to the other side of the street. [She] avoids her racist fear only in virtue of [subjecting him] to ageist disregard. In viewing an older African-American woman as a matriarchal figure, one may indeed venerate her for her wisdom and life experience, but without specific knowledge of her, such regard is mere ageist, sexist, and racial stereotyping that marks her as beyond her sexual prime and valued primarily in terms of her family or community role."[21]

Although a straight man may be satisfied that his inner self has unlearned sexism and homophobia, and a gay African American male feel pretty cool in the tolerance sweepstakes, the Young Judges inside them may still think that an *older* gay man is creepy, an *older* black man pathetic, and *any* older woman ugly. Many of our stereotypes are "compound."[22] They pool at the intersections of two or more gross misrepresentations.

These examples show that people suffer from uneven developments in emotional intelligence and that, without the benefit of age critique, ageism adds a new twist of prejudice to their mental stock. Aside from other definitions, ageism is what may be called a *replacement bias*.

The insight can be taken farther by thinking about the anachronism of this psychic situation. In some life-course theorizing, later selfhood "contains" our previous selves. One such identity might be Young Judge, an immature ageist, never overcome, carried along like a zombie. If it survives, the self in the body will feel shamed by aging-past-youth. In chapter 7, I show how shaming can play out in later life. Tracking this unhappy early age-identity through its potential life-course outcomes suggests that immersion in a culture like ours causes long-term damage.

YOUNG JUDGE GOES TO COLLEGE

Researchers used to disagree about whether undergraduates were ageist. Our best and brightest? Yes. Leni Marshall, also a gerontologist, observes, "Most students arrive at college with a set of stereotypes about ageing firmly but unconsciously embedded."[23] Marshall is one of many emerging educators who have learned how crucial age education is to our society and who cross over into interdisciplinary age studies.

Her conclusion is no longer controversial. Toni Calasanti, who teaches courses on the sociology of aging, asks students "how we know when someone is old." You might think they would be circumspect, given the professor's reputation as the co-author of *Gender, Social Inequalities, and Aging*. "They begin to answer with such benign descriptions as 'gray hair,' or 'wrinkles,'" Calasanti writes. "But then someone mentions slow drivers, unfashionable clothes, or that 'they smell funny.' Others laugh; students grow bolder, more pejorative, and come up with more humorous [sic] indicators."[24] Michael North, a psychologist who now studies ageism, was once offered a paying job to talk to "old people" about wisdom. "I nodded and said OK, but as a 22-year-old kid I wasn't really excited about sitting in a basement interviewing old people, as I saw them. I thought they would be really boring. I thought they would smell."[25] ("Smelly" is an atavistic and dangerous attribute. As a child in the 1950s, I read a book that explained *why* "Negroes" smelled funny. Now older people get their turn at olfactory deviance. It's not funny. Ageism, once again like racism or sexism, means one has to work twice as hard to get over particular stereotypes.) Laughter at unimaginable otherness, like driving *slowly* or wearing previous fashions, is often a twisted demand for behavior. Patricia Williams, a critical race theorist, believes that at times "the demand isn't just to laugh but to humiliate, to degrade, and to expel the offending object from the body politic." The demand asks us to "give up speaking in support of the oppressed, or the derided."[26]

If, as the Fraboni statements show, there is avoidance of anything to do with older people, "anything" might include studying them. Erin Gentry Lamb, who had seven years of experience teaching a remarkable course in medical humanities when I attended her class, has described basic conceptual obstacles to teaching age. Most students "do not recognize age as an identity category similar to race or sex, have never heard of ageism, and find it difficult to picture themselves growing old. Thus a significant deficiency exists not only in students' critical awareness of the subject but also in self-motivated interest to learn more." Four years of teaching psychological gerontology taught Brittany Siegal and Sarah H. Kagan that "any discussion of sexuality, dementia, and death" needed special care.[27]

At Boston College, I have several times been invited to lead a class in a semester-long business course that explicitly promotes age as an "identity category" and accurately assumes its students are highly motivated to deal well with gender, age, and racial diversity in the workforce. The students in Terry Byrne's course, all working, some already employers, ranged in age from twenty to forty-five. I have been invited not to provide pro-aging content ("Look how healthy and intelligent old people are") but to introduce self-examination, data, ethics, and theory, and to applaud signs of ageism consciousness. I treat these students as adults operating on a larger professional stage. As soon as they begin to wonder if their behaviors conflict with egalitarian organizational/societal values, they can figure out how to change. So, with the first obstacles that Erin Lamb listed removed, what others remain?

On the whiteboard, one year, I started by writing keywords: "Social Security's congressional critics," and, on a list headed "decline ideology," the terms "neoliberalism," "Big PhRMA," "'burden' discourse." The students had read articles (some by me) on job-related middle-ageism, so I put up "EEOC. CDC on unemployment and suicide." I add to the lists as the students come up with more; taking dictation from the conversations indicates my respect. After I wrote "Hate speech," I read a few vituperative Internet examples aloud from a handout they had received beforehand. Troll-speak might feel enough beyond the norm to overcome indifference and provoke surprise or outrage.

"How would *you* respond to one of these remarks," I asked, "if someone said it in front of you?"

"I'd laugh," one white man in his early twenties, whom I'll call Fred, responded first.

"And if you were old enough so that this is aimed at *you*?" I asked. Showing students the precariousness of privilege invites them to share a bit of vulnerability vicariously. Gloria Pierce teaches future counselors by this method. Like her, I was challenging Fred to "problematize how [his own] identifiers such as age, appearance, socioeconomic status, and ableness might change over time."[28] This can prove salutary, or frightening.

"I'd still laugh."

Laughter might be a plausible strategy for an old person confronting a micro-aggression like a disparaging joke, but quotes like the Internet ones I had just read, when they call for death for black people or gays, come only from the Klan or the Westboro Baptist Church. From Fred, with midlife peers (including his father) present, a laugh seemed a startling brush-off, not to mention a lack of basic politeness.

My friend Frances A. Maher, the co-author of *The Feminist Classroom*, a landmark book on pedagogy, tells me that as soon as teachers explicitly introduce an identity category, whether it be gender, race, or sexuality, the theory of positionality warns that many in the classroom will quickly become sedimented into their most relevant group—in this case, the age class, *youth*. A group that holds workshops for adults from hostile groups, CEDAR, notices that the encounter with the Other may "require the policing of my own boundaries, lest that which is essential to me be lost."[29] "Policing" is a metaphor of rigid self-protection. What seemed "essential" to Fred is being youthfully exempt from ageism. Ignorance of the fluidity of age can last a long time.

When students are confronted with any biased text, it is not unusual to be met with a denial by someone in the class that injury exists—or isn't serious enough to contemplate further. ("But that's just *funny*." "Being offended is a choice" is found on many comment sites describing bias.) One study concluded, "a male dominant worldview constitutes an important element in the support for inequity between groups. . . . Such a belief system may include a tough-minded approach to civil rights issues—that is, hate crime laws are an 'excuse abuse' and it is up to the individual to 'get over it' on their own."[30] The "toughen up" response "automatically places the student in a position of determined disengagement from critical analysis," Jennifer Proctor and her colleagues write, "And if this argument is directed to a female faculty member, it further positions the instructor as having special interests, being out of touch, or lacking a sense of humor."[31]

The brief Boston College interaction I have just described could be a starter case in a future volume of *Case Methods for Teaching Anti-Ageism*. Part A would end here, with a student stonewalling. Then the faculty group's discussion begins with open-ended questions, *What should this teacher say? Do?* For those who don't teach, let me tell you, if discussing "Fred" seems like a tiny fragment of wasted time, frank admission of problems around teaching age turns out to be dense, scary, fruitful preparation for engaging anyone who comes on with ageist speech or behavior.

In the classroom with Fred, I had to persist. The others had just been exposed to the mouthy assurance of Young Judge. Poor options sweep through your head. Should I turn on him? *When do we get to stop smiling? Does change ever come, when we're forced to swallow every insult and provocation?* Fortunately, I know Todd Nelson's kindly formulation: beneath many a nasty projection and vilification of others, ageism is "prejudice against our feared future self."[32] Fred was one of those many people who cannot see their own hand uplifted against themselves in later life. I had trained with the great Harvard teacher of teachers, Chris Christensen, and edited a book on *The Art and Craft of Teaching*.[33] I bit my tongue and opened the conversation to all.

Slowing down, I repeated in a neutral tone, as a way of protecting Fred, " 'Firing squad.' 'Not survive.' Not allowed out in public. This counts as offensive and even murderous speech. Would you mind if someone said, about a group you identified with, 'Let's gas them'?" A pause. "Is there anyone in the room who belongs to a group at whom hate speech is aimed? Jews, Native Americans, Muslim men, women gamers? Is ageism comparable to other hate speech? How would you respond? How should we?"

Given a second chance, I might have asked, "Is laughter a good strategy?" to see if anyone agreed with Fred. Paolo Freire assures us that "the role of critical pedagogy is not to extinguish tensions." "Finding the 'sweet spot' where there is some discomfort but not too much, is key to learning," the authors of *Living with Difference* learned.[34] But I avoided building tension in my only class with these people, before we had built any group cohesion.

Fred stayed silent. Others spoke. One boon of discussion is being able to count on a spectrum of opinions. It can be broader than you anticipate. Go in wary and welcoming, both. A man from the subcontinent, and two African American women, all older than Fred, launched the discussion fruitfully. The Indian used the word "respect." This made the atmosphere comfortable again. We moved one or two baby steps farther into seeing how ageism could intensify sexism and racism and homophobia and reduce social status.

If Part B of a teaching case ended with the students not offering much, however, faculty discussion could begin by tackling "Why was the class silent?" Indeed, the challenge may be to prise out any debate at all, if a group has uniform, entrenched ideas about older people. One clever UK study gave mental health nursing students a vignette about "Jane," asking them to write down how they would deal with her deep confusion about sexual issues with her bullying male partner. One group got a Jane who was sixteen years old in a two-year relationship with a boyfriend; another, a Jane of seventy who was long married. Each group believed there was only one age to consider. That assumption proved a test for implicit bias.

The group that discussed young Jane at sixteen emerged with interesting debate about what to do for her "complex personal and professional dilemmas," whereas about Jane at seventy in the same circumstances there was "no sense of such dilemmas." Toward this Jane the group tended to interpret the word "confusion" as dementia, despite the clear reference to sexuality. They exhibited little sense that a woman's sexual life might be lively, or be changing, or even exist, at seventy.[35] When the class reunited, their age biases stood out as sharply as fresh graffiti on a wall.

Every teacher who uses examples of ageism, has to decide on vocabulary—whether to call it "ageism." Resistance to strong challenging expressions (like "racism") might prove unpleasant. In describing what the IAT measures, Banaji's team was "careful to use phrases such as 'implicit attitude,' 'implicit preference,' and 'automatic preference,' while avoiding the unqualified word 'prejudice.'"[36] There are occasions, however (some provided by putatively civilized pens), when if you don't use the general term "ageism" and the specific term "hate speech," words have no meaning.

Hiding behind laughter, as Fred did in the Boston College classroom, or behind reticence, as others do, may have many causes. Some students resist information that disrupts what they already "know." Feelings factor in. Because ageism, unlike racism, is not considered a cause of suffering, I often expose students to the idea that it is crude and hurtful. Some then realize or suspect that they have been guilty. The editors of a journal issue treating "social suffering" write, "The circulation of narratives of trauma and suffering in public domains produces troubled and troubling emotions: shame, guilt and, perhaps, aversion in those who give witness."[37]

In open conversations, students may, however, introduce difficult feelings by themselves. That day in the Boston College class, one man—Fred's father—gave examples of discrimination against midlife workers. He mentioned that "No unemployed need apply" is an intolerable Catch-22 for people who have run out of ninety weeks of unemployment benefits. One fortyish man, a department manager, chose that moment to criticize older bosses for "hanging on to jobs." I raised an eyebrow, pointed to the words "Middle-Ageism" on the board, and waited for the dialogue to ensue. It did. Often, student input enabled me to summarize a basic theoretical point. "A named group like 'aging Boomers' is no more homogeneous than 'gays' or 'Asians.'" I wrote "heterogeneity" on the board. Some people took shots of the board with their phones as they left.

Any teacher would need more class time. Jennifer Proctor and her educational group wisely suggest that "a strategy of in-class response cannot be our primary strategy of intervention. We must consider pedagogical interventions that permeate course design."[38] (Later in this chapter, a writing teacher named Sofi shows how that might work.)

YOUNG JUDGE HIDES OUT IN THE ADMINISTRATION BUILDING

In most classrooms, one group is left out, both as fellow learners and as subject matter: older people (and their concerns, and the systems that produce those concerns). Students spend most of their time with age peers. Their social groupings may be diverse in gender or race, but not at all diverse in age. About half of college students are now "nontraditional age," but that means only over twenty-two.[39] A single older authority figure, who may be as young as twenty-five, doesn't change attitudes simply by being there. Unless she is an age critic, she may never even hear the ageisms soiling the air around her.

The age-hostile and/or age-indifferent milieu that surrounds the classroom also subtly seeps down from above. An emerita English professor at a distinguished state research university, whom I will call Linda Serenata, wrote me, hesitantly, about her own "painful encounters with age discrimination," "not wanting to relive" them.

> Oh yes, I was lucky and had tenure from a young age, but at the very end of my career, my department became very biased against the senior professors in various ways; it became difficult to get a graduate seminar to teach because they were all given to the new junior hires; there was an assumption that the older faculty were hopelessly out of touch, even though many of them were conspicuously in the vanguard of developments in their various specialties. The dean kept our birthdays on his desk blotter, hoping he could encourage us into early retirement so he could use our salaries to hire junior people for less. I feel a lot younger since I retired.[40]

Department chairs like Serenata's, provosts, presidents—the kind of administrators who once used "excellence" to keep people of color out of academe—now use it against older scholars to urge them out. Invitations come to emeriti to teach again, but at lower wages, often as adjuncts. This is one of the more obvious demotions. "The median age of the professorate now surpasses [that of] all other occupational groups," TIAA-CREF laments. Cost accounting, dominating other values, may make resistance to these trends seem futile. Managers are ageist also out of unexamined convictions. Barbara DeMille earned her Ph.D. at forty-seven. Chairs who gladly invited the recent Ph.D. to interview noticeably lost enthusiasm when they saw she was a woman with some gray hair. DeMille describes age discrimination as so insidious "it is like trying to draw the outline of a cobweb."[41] Younger colleagues talk to DeMille in tones of voice they wouldn't use to those perceived as equals. (Such situations may sound familiar to members of racial/ethnic minorities.) Younger women's anxiety about the loss of career ladders can fuel hostility toward the tenured women, some of them second-wave feminists who fought for opening departments to women. Despite a façade of bonhomie, intergenerational resentment in academia is fostered by the pile-on of ageist contexts.

What situation can you imagine that might be worse for the future of aging, or the future of higher education, than a privileged space of learning, in which students getting prepared for life are permitted to be carelessly ageist in class discussions, some academic employers actively discriminate against their midlife faculty or needle them to retire; some departments seethe with scapegoating, and there are few students of the age class to protest on their own behalf?

The preventative, to protect ourselves personally and socially from the epidemic of ageism, is to educate people young. The process of nipping Young Judges in the bud should start in childhood. But in individual families, age education is haphazard and, when successful, isolated. Middle and high schools would certainly be next best, if there weren't obstacles to adding any intervention, especially subject matter that might be (wrongly) considered inappropriate for the age group.

For now, the college years may be the best time. Emerging adults not yet in the workforce have not been repetitiously exposed to the "make room for the young" arguments about work or the malevolent "duty-to-die" discourses. Entering students expect much of the college experience, the so-*not*-high-school experience. Forming their first adult selves, they trustingly believe their professors are the best guides they have yet encountered for development. Many want to become competent decoders of reality, masters of systemic ideologies like sexism and racism, upholders of ethical standards. Many arrive with impressive records of civic engagement. They may hold onto the once widespread image of the university as a "subversive institution, designed to overturn entrenched attitudes of inhumanity, arrogance and intolerance."[42]

And whatever the problems of higher education, interventions to raise age consciousness can still be procured more widely and effectively on campuses than off. Some faculty members and some colleges aim to provide more egalitarian incubators for interpersonal and civic engagement. Where young people learn about cultural otherness from a broad spectrum of peers and can take courses interested in diversity, is where space can be made for teaching age.

Teaching has always been, for some, a calling. I persisted in getting a Ph.D. because I thought the vocation would be mine. Before I started writing full-time, I was able to do enough teaching and teacher training to experience the night-before anxiety of teaching, its self-doubt and fear, and the moments of excitement when students seem rapt and collaborative learning is obviously taking place. Teaching is often a high, but we rarely know its outcomes—called, in educational testing, the "value [we] added." Perhaps because of all that, I love movies honoring teachers. Denzel Washington as Melvin B. Tolson, a professor at an African American college in Depression-era Texas, forms the school's first debate team. In *The Great Debaters* (2007), his team suffers debilitating racism but goes on to challenge Harvard in the national championship. In real life, good teachers change hearts only thirty people at a time. In reel time, bootstrap movies—*Music of the Heart* (1999), *Stand and Deliver* (1988)—obscure systems of poverty and bias too lousy for individual teachers alone to redeem. But as narratives about the exhilarations of the profession, these stories of pure challenge and triumph touch millions. We need a movie about *agewise* teachers and their effects.

Vast areas of culture-mediated age have been as opaque as were the dragon-filled seas of medieval maps. Agewise teachers can help develop sensitivity and practice in critical thinking in young people who have been deprived of these. If a Young Judge lurks inside, students may learn to disclaim it. Those who are given opportunities to recognize their ageism and become more attuned to older adults, express surprise, pleasure, and gratitude.

SOFI TEACHES AGE STUDIES

So far there's been little converse between age studies and writing studies. But one excellent site for transformation can be the first-year composition course. Teaching such a course, Sofi Gregorian goes to the whiteboard to spend the first five minutes asking students to contribute to this week's "Old Age/Ageism Barometer."[43] In 2016 the students have already offered Seth Meyers's spiel about why Bernie Sanders was polling so well (he was in "The Betty White Zone" of coolness). By now, her students often provide so many examples that the whole class could be spent on pop culture: #OscarsSoWhite, the allegations of racism, followed by new Academy rules making some members "emeritus" so they lose voting rights (Sofi asked, rolling her eyes, "Aren't 'nonworking members' likely to be people of color, too? Older, too?") Lili Tomlin's *Grandma*, a movie about a woman counting on her grandmother for money to get an abortion. Senator Elizabeth Warren, trying to redress the 0 percent Cost of Living Adjustment in Social Security with a one-time $581 pay-out.

Students are eager to opine. They don't realize their clever competitive analyses are raising one another's consciousness about both media and ageism. For their Facebook fanpage, Sofi finds that giving the students responsibility for finding kicky input—still images, videos, ads, links to other media—creates a habit of observation of where age enters common discourse, and what puts it out there.[44] This virtual discussion board lets them go personal and get corrected by peers if they expose ageism. Herd conformity can work for good, too.

Sofi is imaginary; the multimodal class and most of the students' remarks in the following scene are not; I have heard or read them or had them reported to me. In the short screenplay that follows, Sofi's knack of talking in complete paragraphs, like Oscar Wilde, with no "uh uh," included, is heuristic. This screenplay, no more a transcript than Plato's Socratic dialogues, shows a bit of what I have gleaned of best practices. All readers (I hope) can use these examples to think about misperceptions, lies, insults. If you teach, this section might suggest creative assignments.

In the backstory I invented, which Sofi has shared with her students, she is thirty-nine, a feminist Ph.D. in history, divorced, with a twelve-year-old son. An adjunct in a state university, for four years she has been teaching first-year writing as multicultural studies with a pronounced age component. Today, five weeks into the semester, she is finishing a short PowerPoint presentation by wrapping up Becca Levy's material on hate-sites with an excerpt from the *New York Times*. She has yellow-highlighted a verb and a noun. She asks a student to read aloud "with expression."

MANUEL

(*reads*)

"One reason for America's fiscal problems is that the population is aging, meaning that there are relatively many old people to care for and relatively

few young workers to *support* them. (Immigrants are helping *with this burden*, though.)"[45]

SOFI

That verb "support." What does that metaphor have in common with
"burden"?

Sofi waits. Her students have had some practice analyzing tone, word
choice, rhetorical strategies, and genre. Sofi spends little time on counter-
facts but here she reminds them.

SOFI

And how are they characterizing *you*, young people?

MALIK

We're too weak to support the bundle . . . the burden? The heavy old people?

MELISSA
(cuts in)

It's like saying "young workers" are *feeble*. "Relatively few"—that's to make
us feel weak. They're telling us how to feel.

SOFI

Excellent, Melissa. That powerful direct address, at *you*. "The public has little literacy about the political evocation of deep feeling," Patricia Williams
writes.[46] *You* are getting literate! Even more since the crash of 2008, the
media displace anger about unemployment and inequality by categorizing
old people as *your* "burden"—too great for you to bear. This message comes
at you from all sides: crude Internet sources, economists in the paper of
record, leaders in the tech world. Under the guise of protecting *you*. You
are bystanders now, but you will vote.

Discovering this cultural script, with themselves cast as bludgeons of retir-
ees, can shock the students' sense that they are autonomous and agentic, or, for
that matter, harmless.

Sofi had started with gender and race, modeling her structure on a British
social work course that impressed her. She personalizes concepts like agency

and intersectionality. She once quoted, from a novel by Ruth Ozeki, a passage that begins, "Adjunct teachers are the professorial equivalent of the migrant Mexican farm laborers hired during harvest."[47] In the British course, studying ageism was what helped the class reflect on the macro forces linking discriminations. There, age turned out to be "one of the least threatening oppressions for students to talk about and more importantly 'own.'" There was no "intra-group confrontation or conflict since there was no obvious 'oppressed' group [present], and all the students accepted how they could be and were ageist." As a student wrote in her evaluation of that unit, "Penny did drop on structural oppression."[48]

In every unit, Sofi cultivates questions of age and class. At this point in the rhythm of the semester's learning, most of her students are wary of sounding stupidly ageist and some eagerly discuss formerly estranging material. Now Sofi reads two sentences, the second yellow-highlighted, from her next slide.

"In the coming years there will be generational conflicts over Social Security and Medicare. *Young people may get tired of paying for baby boomers who refuse to die.*"[49]

SOFI

This is from a column in the *Boston Globe*. Ed Meek, the author, wants to show there is a "Millennial-Boomer Alliance" between him and his son, based on more than both loving rock-and-roll. Tell us, "Millennials," what Meek is aiming for in just two sentences. Michael?

MICHAEL

There's the *burden*. Us against them, again. But what does that mean "*refuse to die*"? How do people refuse to die? That's weird.

MALIK

(*gets it*)

Would Meek say that about a *young* guy with cancer who wants treatment? He's not supposed to want it?

SOFI

Bingo.

Students are ready at this point to do some paradigm-breaking, intersectional thinking. Medical humanist Erin Lamb explains how her students, having accepted that a wheelchair with a young person in it can be okay, might "squirm while trying to defend how a wheelchair . . . with an old person in it would be negative."[50] Let them squirm who justify offering cancer treatment to a forty-year-old but not to a sixty-five-year-old. Sofi writes "under-treatment" on the board.

SOFI

Now see for yourselves; for the assignment, go online, see if you can find a few more hate quotes, not from trolls but from "thought leaders." In the *Atlantic* here's Dr. Ezekiel Emanuel, a major health official. Having just described his own father since his heart bypass at seventy-seven as "sluggish," he lays down the law about how "we want to be remembered": Watch those "we"s. A "we" implies a "them." Keisha, would you read?

KEISHA

"We wish our children to remember us in our prime. Active, vigorous, engaged, animated, astute, enthusiastic, funny, warm, loving. Not stooped and sluggish, forgetful and repetitive, constantly asking 'What did she say?' We want to be remembered as independent, not experienced as burdens."

SOFI
(*grins*)
"*Our* prime"? Well, I'm supposed to be flattered—you know how astute, enthusiastic, funny, warm, and loving *I* am. But this bad son is insulting elderly disabled people. Do hate-speakers assume these people aren't listening? Emanuel's father, a retired doctor, might subscribe to the *Atlantic*. The Gerontological Society of America made Ezekiel the keynote speaker at their last national meeting. Amazing. Would you invite Donald Trump to speak to the National Association for Chicana and Chicano Studies?

And Emanuel's adult children may also be reading *this*. As a mother, I am amazed that any father would expose his own children to his malice toward old age. Remember the wheelbarrow! (Sofi had read them the fable that appears on the epigraph page of this book.)

STUDENTS
(*a slow double-take, some laughter*)

"Additional education decreases negative stereotypes about aging," writes Leni Marshall, reviewing thirty years of research on incorporating age into humanities curricula.[51] With a full semester course, Sofi asks students to read short fiction, media, and popular and scholarly work in age studies, with the aim of developing distinctive styles and integrating their readings. She has gotten this group of students past the initial age-hardened positions that Frances Maher warns about. Erin Lamb does the same. In an important essay with marquee stereotypes in its title ("Polyester Pants and Obstetrical Shoes"), about teaching age studies to undergraduates of all years and disciplines, Lamb concludes, "Because their critique is self-generated, I find that my students react with buy-in rather than resistance."

Kate de Medeiros teaches an undergraduate course, Global Aging, which fulfils university requirements for diversity in two ways. She says, "Ageism is something completely new to them. It's always exciting to see their attitudes change."[52] The culture wars have not infiltrated age and toxified the discourse around it, as they have race, gender, and sexuality. Students do not call defending elders "politically correct" as if that were a bad thing. One friend of mine who directed a freshman writing/cultural studies program for fifteen years told me, "There had to be, at a minimum, a convincing appearance of asking an open question." But that question cannot be "Is ageism warranted? Justify."

Sofi wants to broach feelings that some struggle with, while avoiding the pity-aversion dyad. To get to the tremulous topic of "dying," for example, she started not with old people, often thought of as close to death, but with young people who *wish* the old would die. *Which group is more to be feared?* Some materials that students read—about loss of rights, depraved-heart negligence, porn—may be vicariously traumatizing. Agewise teaching needs to be gently supportive as well as challenging. Today Sofi will give assignments that, like the discussion, keep the focus on verbal agents of harm.

SOFI'S ASSIGNMENTS

SOFI

You can find out for yourself what unashamed hate speech is about. Listen to your dorm-mates in casual conversation. See what "ageism" means on Reddit, which has been called a cesspool of hate. What keywords, aside from "burden," might you use online?

(Hands are raised. Some students shout out.)

VARIOUS VOICES

"Old and disgusting."

That's a joke Valentine!

Huh?

It's a Valentine. It *is*. "Grow old and disgusting with me!" Shows two kids holding hands.

How about "old hag"?

"Geezer."

SOFI

(dryly)

You're such good researchers already. Be sure to cite the URLs in your bibliography.

By being asked to do some original research online, Sofi's students generate both content and analysis. They are nicely positioned as self-educators in incipient control of edgy material that other students can't handle analytically.[53]

SOFI

This seems like a good time to start asking, "What *is* ageism?"

VARIOUS VOICES

I couldn't drive until I was sixteen.

Nobody can drink—buy liquor—until you're twenty-one in this state.

Sofi is prepared for this. At this question, many students revert to their own age-class interests and need to be reminded about life-course vulnerabilities. She writes "age grading" on the whiteboard.

SOFI

Let's call the drinking and driving limits "age grading" rather than "ageism," because such regulation is geared to provide more liberty and empowerment as you get older. "Too young" is a temporary condition. You will gain by getting older, which is not a bad life-course system. But what if you don't gain benefits as you go on getting older? If they seem to stop? You become "too old." And that will never reverse. You lose respect and identity as an individual. You hit some Great Demotions. Do you know instances of bias or injury based on *getting* older, not *being* younger?

JESSIE

I dunno if this is ageism, 'cause my uncle isn't so old. My dad told how he was laid off at their work. He's older than my dad, making him maybe sixty. The excuse and the term the company used when laying him off was "job elimination." My dad began to discuss with me on how this is an excuse that companies use due to age discrimination. Later my dad's theory was solidified when he learned that his brother's former title was just renamed and given to another much younger employee.[54]

SOFI

(*looks at her carefully, suspecting she is talking about her father*)
Jessie, how does your father feel about this?

JESSIE

(*looks down*)
This man may never get work again, my mother says. In the office, it's about how old people are "deadwood," they say people like her are taking jobs away from the young. That's like what they used to say about women "taking men's jobs"! Whuh the . . ? Why aren't there enough jobs?

SOFI

(*writes "outsourcing" and "deindustrialization" on the board*)
Right. "Middle ageism," firing and not rehiring people over a certain age—as Jessie said, it goes with language that justifies the bosses' decisions through more bias.

Let's turn to the assignments. We'll go on defining ageism from your papers and videos.[55]

With the class already having done some writing on sexism and racism, Sofi will now require a written or video assignment on age, due in three weeks.

SOFI

You get four choices of topic and approach. I'll be learning alongside you. I'm not trained as a gerontologist. As you know, I study modern American history. But I'm going to write up our experiment for the comp teachers' retreat in the spring. Not too many students get such assignments. Upper-class students in sociology or anthropology of aging, maybe. Some comp teachers I know won't like what we're up to. We'll brave that, okay? (*She smiles.*) If it produces good writing, we'll all triumph.

(*smiles on a few faces*)

Okay, now for the four options. The first choice could be called "Feed the Troll." Respond to the Internet hate speech. Your audience is the troll, himself. The question for you as writers is, "Can you use your skills to respond to the mindset that considers old people no longer human?" Don't think you can't. One man apologized to an older feminist profusely for making fun of her dead father online. In option 1, use any evidence or rhetoric you think likeliest to sway him. If he changes his mind, have him say why. Would you do this in a serious, Bill Moyers voice? Or like Sarah Silverman? Always with some data. This could be a video piece.

Strategies for challenging oppressive practices sometimes come at the end of a course. Sofi starts her students with the *problem* of strategizing a response.

SOFI

(*people are taking notes*)

Okay, option 2. I'm looking for the best responses written in the first-person, in the persona of an old person who accidentally comes across an article like Meek's or Emanuel's. You might interview someone, any unrelated older adult. Not a relative. Try for someone who is over sixty-nine. Or you can do this from imagination, as an imaginary interview with, say, Emanuel's father. I am going to give extra credit for option 2.

CLARK

Uhh, why for this one?

SOFI

(*writes "intersectionality" and "empathy" on the board*)

Because it takes more imagination to pretend to be an older person or to get a good interview, than to impersonate Jon Stewart or Bill Moyers. The goal is to get this person, or your character, to rebut the allegation that she and her age class are "once-were-people." It is a philosophical challenge to any of us to prove that we still count ourselves among the human, if our entire category is excluded a priori by dominant groups.

Future Hollywood screenwriters, take note of this choice. They're pas-
turing older screenwriters these days, even though there is a huge audience
for films with older stars; as we saw with Harrison Ford, people are loyal to
the stars of their youth.

Write creatively. Give your imagined character the characteristics a fiction writer might: an age, a gender, a state of health, a sexual history, a job
history—a bunch of "intersections" or social locations: old and trans, say,
with a race, a health history, adult offspring. A vocabulary! And, of course,
feelings. Was this person amused? Injured? Irritated? Stay in character.
(*Afterthought*): Don't have the character be ageist. Don't let her excuse the
attackers, or let herself be belittled.

Sofi answers some questions about Option 2, then goes on:

SOFI

Option 3. Become the president of the United States. Barack Obama wants
to make a major address to the nation about ageism. The POTUS feels ageism has crossed civil bounds, that it threatens our unity and human dignity: These are values that any society should try to develop. Think of this
as your bully-pulpit speech.

This is good for poli-sci majors; you can practice for your later jobs as
speech writers, campaign managers, politicians. It is also good for philosophy majors and ethicists. Give yourself a presidential style. Read Roose-
velt's Second Inaugural Address for inspiration.

Pick grievances worthy of a president. Read the Age-Friendly University
Initiative, started by the Irish in 2012.[56] Or read the *Chicago Declaration
on the Rights of Older Persons*; the URL is in the assignment sheet. If the
issue is threats to receiving good health care, you might start with President
Obama saying that giving his grandmother a new hip was not "sustainable."
That was in 2009, before Occupy and the move to expand Social Security,
which he has now joined. Ageism is not static: it has a political history,
sponsors, financial interests.

Sofi wants her students to get excited as writers about these creative choices,
from interviewing to channeling styles, from rebutting extreme instances to
moving into proactive mental positions. The writing involves imaginative work

and moral reasoning. Such assignments can disrupt the essentialism that comes from being wedged deep into one's current age.

SOFI

Some of your essays might be suitable for YouTube or would make great opinion pieces in local newspapers. A philosopher who publishes often in the letters column of the *New York Times* tells me that anti-ageist letters are the easiest to publish.

And finally. The lit choice, option 4. You'd be reading Anton Chekhov, the Russian playwright and short story writer. This story involves a woman who is dying. Chekhov was a doctor who said his medical work with poor people and outcasts seriously affected his literary work. The dying woman is the wife of a poor coffin-maker, Yakov, in a village. Yakov also plays the violin. This is Anton Chekhov's "Rothschild's Fiddle" (1894).

Sofi clicks on a link to the story, chooses a student to read excerpts out loud.

CARLOS

"It was a tiny town, worse than a village, inhabited chiefly by old people who so seldom died that it was really vexatious." (*He skips to:*) "It somehow seemed to Yakov that he had never once spoken a tender word to [his wife, Marfa] or pitied her; that he had never thought of buying her a kerchief or of bringing her back some sweets from a wedding. On the contrary, he had shouted at her and abused her for his losses, and had shaken his fist at her."

SOFI
(*in a low voice*)
He borrows a horse to take her to the doctor.

CARLOS
(*reads*)
"She sat on a stool, a wasted, bent figure with a sharp nose and open mouth, looking like a bird that wants to drink.

"In her presence, the doctor's assistant says, 'Influenza and possibly fever. There's typhus in the town now . . . How old is she?'

"'She'll be seventy in another year, Maxim Nikolaitch,' says the old man humbly.

"'Well, the old woman has lived her life, it's time to say goodbye.'
He turns briskly to the next patient."[57]

SOFI

Yakov doesn't leave after having been coldly told that his wife Marfa will
die. In fact, he insists she be given attention—what we would call palliative
care. When this is impatiently denied, despite his usual servility Yakov flies
into a rage. Describe what is going on in this story. Whose mind do we
inhabit? Why is it called "Rothschild's Fiddle"? Is it only about old age in
a tiny town, "worse than a village"? How is gender made important? How
does it exress grief? Other themes? Chekhov is a writer capable of keeping
many threads going.

Overall, 40 percent of Americans eighteen to twenty-four were enrolled in
postsecondary education in fall 2013. One quarter of the total undergraduate
enrollment amounts to four million people.[58] If anti-ageist education begins
in the first year of college, as it should, one inevitable space is in composition and creative writing courses. Every college requires comp courses (some
require writing across the curriculum). There are about six hundred creative
writing programs in the United States. Writing courses, with their careful
attention to modes of discourse and structures of argumentation, give students powerful tools for growth. Directors of such programs could devise
with their faculty a range of exercises that require an imaginative response to
ageism. Train the trainers. It would be good to promote an intervention that
might affect millions of students, year after year, as they start on their education for life.

WRITING AGE ACROSS THE CURRICULUM

But it would not be enough. The Florida psychologists who discovered Web-
based hate speech did a fine-grained study that shows the need to teach anti-
ageism to college students beyond the first year. The researchers—Ashley
Stripling, J. M. Calton, and Martin Heesacker—enlisted thirty-one psychology
students at the University of Florida in a writing project to respond to the hate
speech. (I borrowed Sofi's option 1 from this project.)

These researchers' results are hopeful as well as appalling. A heartening 84
percent of the students disagreed with the statements and devised some ways

to rebut them. Most were aged eighteen to twenty-one; 74 percent were women. Psychology students are trained to note stereotypes; and younger women, aware of gender bias, possibly know they will be the majority among the old and so may notice and resent age bias. The researchers concluded, "For the most part collegians . . . can probably be counted on to counter-argue virulently against ageist rhetoric if motivated." *If motivated.* Their own evidence undermines their optimism. Sixteen percent of students in fact agreed with the Web slurs, and provided more preposterous generalizations: for example, "The problem with the elderly is that their [*sic*] are very hypocritical." Even when defending old people, some of the other 84 percent added slights. Students who want to reject ageist hate speech are too misinformed, too unsteady about their own beliefs, to know how to do it.

Two professors of advertising, Don Umphrey and Tom Robinson, devised a survey to learn whether four years of education in a communications major improved ageist attitudes. In marketing, success depends on avoiding stereotypes in order to not offend target audiences, but to allure them. Did the communications major in fact change the students' attitudes? Was stereotyping older targets more common among entering first-year students than among seniors from thirteen universities who had majored in the field? A third of all three-hundred-plus respondents, asked to analyze four ads, used stereotypes ("crone," "incontinence") when offering reasons why seventy-year-olds would be influenced by an ad for Depends. No surprise. When Umphrey and Robinson asked, "What ideas/experience/ information, etc., did you draw upon to estimate the influence of the advertising?" they found that the majors did not utilize any of their training: for example, analyzing ad content, quality, art, or the likely consumer.[59] Students didn't wonder whether any seventy-year-olds they knew would buy paper panties. Why this failure?

By and large we are in the *Before Anti-Ageism* era of higher education. Far from being sensitized, students rarely hear ageist remarks rebutted in classrooms. (At Boston College, one slight rebuttal stimulated more.) They aren't given the tools that would make them eager to wise up. Most graduates then drag the burden of their acquired and unleavened ageism into work settings. In hierarchies where respect for midlife workers is strangled and the stakes of failure get higher, intergenerational rivalry grows, unheeded. Indeed, some young adults become members of the cybermobs that wish older people might be flushed off the face of the earth.

BUILDING SOLIDARITY ACROSS THE LIFE COURSE

How do we get younger people to buy into solidarity, now that the endeavor must be made in the teeth of growing apartheid between "younger" and "older"? Not by reiterating the stupefying truism that we all age. If theorists forget how keenly Young Judge cuddles his essentialism, or what youth supremacy accomplishes for ideology, we will never outwit either. Telling students that being age-positive may help them live 7.5 years longer (a frequent recent ploy, based on Becca Levy's correlations[60]) won't make them care, if those "encore years" seem to them disgusting.

The sine qua non is learning enough about what to expect, at a young enough age, to reduce prospective dread of aging. Critical age studies, as I describe one of its strategies here, prepares students to dread *ageism* instead. Seeing the worst bias toward others and then anticipating it will be aimed at them, makes them stakeholders. Sofi started by drilling down onto hate speech, teaching analysis of stereotypes, and requiring imaginative advocacy for change.[61] Other disciplines might start with despicable visuals (as in chapter 2); economists and environmentalists might begin with other harms (like those in the following chapter).

If young people long to fill "elder-shaped holes" in their hearts, some courses give them the chance to do so. National programs like Elly Katz's Sages and Seekers model one future. Sarah Lamb (no relation to Erin Lamb), the author of *White Saris and Sweet Mangoes*, runs this curriculum at Brandeis University as a credit-bearing add-on to her anthropology courses. Students (the "Seekers") must volunteer. The assignment is to meet with someone from the Brandeis Osher Lifelong Learning Institute for nine sessions.[62] Warm encounters with interesting elders are offered as the Fieldwork Practicum across Generations. Lamb rounds out the course with readings and class discussions.

The undergraduates start off very conscious of the age gap, perhaps afraid that "old people" will be too different, or shy about their own conversational abilities. Yet they wind up thrilled and delighted with the experience. All of them. One young man has taken the curriculum twice. At the end the Seekers read aloud essays about their Sages that turn out to be hymns of pleasure and praise, called the "Tribute." Here are four excerpts.

"Ben also encouraged me to step out of my comfort zone and meet more mature people in order to learn from them, and this works." A sophomore who had been worried about choosing a major read Plato on the Sage's recommendation. "It may be cheesy to say, but I see part of myself in his personality. . . . [I] retracted my original apprehensions about being in college." "I now know Barbara and I are much more similar than different, which for lack of a better word, is just so cool." "I have started to feel more comfortable asking my parents questions about their life, experiences, and relationships."

So this is what "experience" means! QED: the longer the life course has been, the richer the flow of material—considerably more life lessons than can be conveyed in nine interviews. Probably all the students become, as one said, "fascinated that one person could know so many facts about art, nature." The Seekers are grateful to be listened to by grown-ups, chuffed by the elders' politeness and curiosity about themselves.

Admiration, so hard to achieve via visual culture, seems to emerge readily from open-ended talk that already assumes value in the encounters. As I learned with my mother's friends in Florida, such relationships offer the sweet taste of hugging otherness, in lieu of the sourness of estrangement. On the website for Katz's programs, a Seeker named Emily says, "For me to be able now to walk down the street and look at someone seventy-plus years old, and know I could connect with them on any level, is just the greatest feeling in the world."[63]

The grail, in my opinion, is to help one another overcome our learned inability to imagine being much older than whatever age we presently are. Simon Biggs, the author of *The Mature Imagination*, conceives of "generational intelligence" as "a relative ability to put one's self in the position of other generations. . . . accept the aging process, contain ambivalence, while acting in a way that enhances harmonious relations between generations."[64] The Seekers, I hypothesize, acquire something grandly metaphysical: Although newly conscious of their relative inexperience, they are comforted. The Sages have somehow conveyed that seniority will be theirs too, in time. "Seniority," the sense that age brings some betterment—I call it "life-course progress"—is profoundly necessary. Ashton Applewhite, in her manifesto *This Chair Rocks*, calls the result of having a healthy culture the widespread ability to "live agefully."

Theorizing ageism and teaching about age is rare outside of gerontology programs, but life-changing courses are being taught by current leaders in the humanities, including English (where ageism can be found in classic novels, vampire fiction, the romance, and contemporary poetry); in economics, sociology, anthropology, and social and developmental psychology; in medical humanities; in women's studies and sexualities. Sarah Lamb, Erin Gentry Lamb, Leni Marshall, Kate de Medeiros, Terry Byrne, and many others can be proud of being in the vanguard. The teachers in NANAS—the North American Network of Age/Aging Studies, with 150 members as I write—are giving their students rich gifts.

My 1990s dream, that age studies would spread through the disciplines, is thus being realized by many. Imbued with the concept of the politics of culture, we agree that it is existentially and ethically necessary to understand age (more or less, since much about "age" is contested) as a mediated category, in historical flux, under the sway of macro forces, imposed on bodily self-concepts, and unconsciously internalized by a developing self, living in a specific place, over time. Age studies, vibrant and revolutionary, ought to be part of any educational experience. One day this approach will be expected as firmly as women's, gender, and sexuality studies. It's an "embarrassing backwardness," as Steven Katz says, that it is not.[65]

We—not age scholars alone, but presidents, deans, social thinkers, and all faculties—have a responsibility to help students obtain a more life-affirming education. Universities that place more emphasis on experiential learning and civic engagement might institute a Sages' program. Anyone who teaches subjects touching on culture, including neurology, history of science, medicine, or nursing, should consider integrating the critical analysis of age into their curriculums. As "Sofi" shows, knowing some gerontological information is desirable, but most faculty who teach age have no formal training, anymore than feminists had before women's studies was institutionalized. Ample materials, scholarly and theoretical, exist in all fields.

Graduates of age studies may not call out ageism at every chance, but they will have some equipment to do so. Students may forget their calculus, debating strategies, or the violin. But if revelatory ideas change their erroneous expectations of the life course, that wisdom will give them a better start at every aspect of life.

THE END OF THE SESSION

It's never too late to change your spots. Even those thugs who want elders to fall off the face of the earth, epitomized so far by Internet trolls, might benefit from the right encounter. So could the yelling cyclist and the mocking photographers of "Weird Old People." So too the ill-mannered son in *The Summer Book*, the legislators imposing scarcity on everyone but the global 1 percent, the tech CEOs, and those heading outsourcing corporations. Over the course of this book's sessions, we'll notice pundits, agricultural experts, clinicians and bioethicists, judges, filmmakers and writers, who could make good use of the new curriculums of age studies.

Mastering an actual course does not necessarily make students optimistic that ageism will disappear. One student, after taking a critical media course about age, wasn't hopeful. She wrote, "Some could argue that there is no way we could discriminate against a group that big but our society has done it with African Americans."[66] In advance of a movement, formal education to create energized stakeholders is an important piece of any campaign. Widespread salutary change, coming from such stakeholders, may well arise from relatively small, timely, preemptive interventions that teachers across the nation hold within their own creative power.

Be the change we want. It is inside colleges and universities (these equivocal, privileged, contested, overheated, and chilly spaces of learning) that educators who care must make their stand. As time passes, more and more parents and teachers will refuse to let children grow up ageist. Future American presidents will lean in. One of them, using her executive bully pulpit for the cause, may remember how she felt and what she learned in her agewise classroom decades before.

CHAPTER 4

((

VERT-DE-GRIS

RESCUING THE LAND LOVERS

"When eating fruit, remember who planted the tree."

—Vietnamese saying

FIELD OF AWE

I was prepared from childhood to look up to the wisdom of gardeners and, by extension, farmers.[1] This pattern was set by my father. We had a tiny backyard behind the little row house in Brooklyn, where my father with grimed nails rooted geranium cuttings, planted a yew hedge, and tried to get mutinous me to weed the grass. I was not a promising beginner in home-made Edens.

Yet years later when my new husband and I rented a sharecropper-style house in North Carolina, I discovered I had developed instincts. Somehow I knew to twist a sprawling weed's wiry tendrils tight in my fist, pull straight up and yank it out whole. I could translate book-learning into practice. I must have watched my father closely, unconsciously mirroring him. He had owned a nursery in Florida for a year, and would have profited in his too brief retirement from having more than a backyard to tend. Land—arable land, with sufficient water and accommodating weather—is the first need and the last.

Our North Carolina landlord was a real farmer in overalls, and a successful, careless planter. Seeing J. D. on his tractor tossing seed over red clay and not looking back gave us the courage to plant tomato seedlings. Their rank growth in that rust-colored soil led me to believe that growing food had to be easy. This delusion lasted only so long, to be replaced by appropriate awe at those with know-how.

Because of my father and that competent farmer, I was luckier than most urban-raised youngsters, whose lives are so estranged from dirt and photosynthesis. In the 1970s, my son's class only once put seeds in soil: the humble lima in a plastic cup. Now in the twenty-first century, my granddaughter's Manhattan school has an entire green roof. California aims to have a garden in every school.[2] In some countries, schools are jackhammering concrete playgrounds and bringing in rich fill. In Australia a few years ago, twenty-four thousand children in 193 primary schools were being taught plantsmanship. Later they would prepare and eat the fresh vegetables that they would grow.[3] Healthy eating—attacking childhood obesity, embarrassment that children don't know peas come in pods, irritation at "pickiness"—motivates some of these educational changes. As cities sprawl, nostalgia for outdoor, rural life and the color green kicks in.

Farming is always subliminally about age, because it's another teaching profession. (There should be feature films about old farmers as teachers, too.) You don't have to grow up in a farm family to experience, as a novelist says, "a connection between generations that represents a pipeline of information, knowledge, and experience that . . . dwarfs anything delivered via high-speed modem or Cisco router."[4] In a disadvantaged southern California town, Manuel Jimenez, a midlife man who is a small-farm advisor with the university, has attracted and trained high-school volunteers, partly to save them from joining gangs. They have transformed fourteen waste acres into orchards and vegetable and rose gardens.[5] The Intergenerational School in Cleveland, run by the wife of Dr. Peter Whitehouse (the co-author, with Daniel George, of *The Myth of Alzheimer's*), brings kindergarten through eighth-grade kids together with elders who have cognitive impairments to create "food-forest" permaculture.[6] Tuskegee agriculture professors bring students to the Federation of Southern Cooperatives' Training and Research Center in Alabama to witness a farmer dig his or her hand into the soil, crumbling it to judge the tilth and what is needed to improve it.[7] A South Korean farmer activist named Lee Kyung Hae, now legendary among antiglobalization activists, started a nationwide Young Farmers organization.

Farming is a powerful domain of knowledge, not so different from what is admired as technology. Older food producers inspire younger ones by their activity (in spite of possible physical issues) and the effectiveness of the techniques they teach. They learn, too. In thousands of moving projects around the globe, estrangement between younger and older people breaks down. The habit of respecting seniority in gratitude for expertise must have begun wherever hunter-gatherers made way for settlers. Now science comes in to correct harmful horticultural traditions or restore forgotten lore, but not much beats oral traditions and watching practices with one's own eyes.

Young back-to-the-landers are emerging from college courses on the environment and from the most popular internship among American students, World Wide Opportunities on Organic Farms (WWOOF).[8] In the right conditions—with enough capital—farming is losing its stigma as a profession incompatible with education, culture, and moneymaking. Yet most of the young, although touted as the rescue team rather than dismissed like the 1960s counterculture and its back-to-the-land practitioners, will not become long-term farmers. One-fifth of new American farmers left farming, between 2007 and 2012.[9] The programs such as WWOOF, young people's eagerness, the novels about raising goats or growing bivalves and falling for a hunk, do not signal the changes needed to address the crises of food production across developed and developing nations alike. They are likelier to distract us from an under-acknowledged human and food crisis, the aging of farmers.

Most studies or accounts—from the plethora of cooking shows to the serious books on climate weirdness, "ghetto pastorals," food sovereignty, or migration, and the bulk of farm fiction—lack a focus on old people. The gerontological contexts often miss the growers of food.[10] Although farming is recognized widely as a rural enterprise, indexes of edited books on rural old people typically do not include farmers. Poverty and social exclusion are overlapping categories. They "have not been engaged with, in a meaningful way, for older people in rural places."[11] People concerned with "age-friendly" cities do not estimate how age-hostile rural areas can be.[12] Oral historians, who need older informants, tend to ask farmers about their distant pasts rather than what it's like being old growers now. In the public square, the humanity of old farmers and the conditions of their labor are largely ignored.

The complex reasons why this is so took me awhile to figure out. Food has become "the bearer of unwieldy questions about the survival of a planet whose destiny we can't foresee and the fate of people whose problems aren't the same as ours."[13] The others whose problems we don't see include the half billion hardpressed small-scale producers (rural and urban) who actually provide 70 to 80 percent of the world's food, according to Frances Moore Lappé. Lappé, the author of Diet for a Small Planet, adds that the world could produce far more than enough calories for humans—2,900, or three or four pounds per person, per day—if not for biofuels, hamburgers, and waste. Distribution is also an issue. Much of the food for humans comes from these low-input family farmers. Seventy percent of them, according to the Food and Agricultural Organization (FAO) of the United Nations, are women. So "old small-holders" should summon up an image of old women. Bill McKibben, like Lappé using FAO data, notes that "small farms in fact produce more calories per acre": "if you want to feed the world, clever peasant farming will be effective."[14] Small-holders are both the source of most of the food consumed in the global South and the majority of people who are food insecure. How else would the cash-poor eat, if they didn't feed themselves?

The salient fact is that many of the indispensable people who feed the world and whom we do not see are old. Without them, you and I would not starve, but others would. Around the world, the farming population is old. In Japan, the average age is sixty-seven; 40 percent of farmers will quit farming before 2022. In the UK, the average age is fifty-nine. In the United States, it is fifty-eight. Principal American farm operators over sixty-five, the hands-on farmers, now outnumber those under thirty-five by more than seven to one.[15] Not a typo, but a frightening statistic that is not generally known. Older labor-force participation in the global South is also high. In Jamaica, the average age of farmers is over fifty-five. In Mozambique, more than two-thirds of the members of the Small Farmers Union are over fifty.[16]

Even when these facts about the age of global food producers are announced as news, which happens occasionally, the human beings involved are obscured. Ageism and agriculture politics play mendacious roles. If we hear too much about "global graying," we may be led to assume that the people shut up in that category are unproductive mouths, safely nourished from their pension income. False. Not all countries offer pensions, and, in some, farmers don't receive them. That old farmers' food production will dwindle is assumed and dismissed, not denied or explained and grieved. They are seen as problems, not as active, engaged solutions. And because Big Farma, the monopolistic industrial-agrifood complex, reigning supreme, is assumed to be the great anonymous provider, the small-holder must be passé.

The interests of wealth hide the troubles of immiseration. Little news about the problems of low-income farmers comes to urbanites. In the five years after the Great Recession of 2007–2008, did Americans learn about foreclosures of farms, let alone what havoc was wreaked on older farmers? Yet the number of farms declined, and average farm size increased, the USDA reported. Did editorials lament the suicides of older farmers?[17] In India, yes. Meanwhile, triumphal media articles appeared in my country, the United States, about inflation-beating rises in land values, or about hedge fund managers and conservationists buying up acreage dirt cheap—a process that, along with another euphemism, "development," is known in antipoverty circles as "land grabbing."

Once I had uncovered disturbing signs that old women and men were the missing images of current transnational troubles, I started with these people—sun-stained faces found in the remote (to us) places where everyone works outdoors and heads inside at dusk—men working "from sun to sun," women whose work is "never done." While writing the farm novel *Wish You Well*, David Baldacci pored over family photos. "I would trace their curled and leathered hands, their lean but mountain-strong torsos and then finally reach their faces." He found inspiration in those portraits, as I do in those of my mother in her later years. Behind rural faces—not ageist "objects of the tourist gaze" on picturesque postcards, but framed in reality by withering landscapes[18]—I perceive the looming crises that fill this session.

Age proved to be a generative concept and category. But when seeking the silenced voices and the important issues of small-holding elders, one finds mainly tatters of information and ethnography. In general, the conditions of these elders differ tremendously—how much land they own or rent, whether they participate in commodity markets, how oppressive their age-gender system is for women, what (if any) governmental provision is made to assist farming, how much the adult children can or do help, what the terrain, pollution, and weather constrain or encourage, and how these people feel about their situations. But some hard-to-find common strands emerge in this session—in Nebraska, Spain, the UK, India, Nicaragua, Korea.

By asking, "What part of this 'aging' story is ageism?" I was led far from the local, suburban, and pastoral regions where I began. Although "aging farmers" is a known category, ageism makes it a hollow and underestimated one. And ageism probably has obscured a hard truth: that the tiny family farms that feed so many have become a place of exile for old people. Often these people cannot or will not leave. All the crises—loss of land and workers, climate destabilization, food insecurity—affect them. Older producers go on, sowing and cultivating and harvesting, to prevent, as far as they can, hunger and famine. Worldwide, that makes them indispensable. Thank heaven for the old woman, the old man, with the hoe. Their situation is a cause for both gratitude and alarm. It is urgent that they receive attention and support. It is their shared skills and achievements, hardships and traumas that beg for emphasis. No crises can be solved without better information and appropriate respect for the human resources we eaters depend on. I don't romanticize them, but everything starts, as it must, from admiration of the indomitable workers who provide this crucial labor and its indispensable output. Never passé, eating.

LASTING LORE

Some pleasures continue from childhood on, and messing around with dirt is one. If it becomes a lifelong activity, intimate knowledge of the practices never leaves you. Børge lives in a nursing home in Copenhagen, active but quite speechless. Eva Algreen-Petersen, a Danish gerontologist I met in the Netherlands at an age studies conference, told me his story. She met Børge when she was helping design a working garden. "Consider it your future Paradise," she said to the clients, families, nursing staff, administrators; "What do you most want?" An artist drew their desires on a mural. Through this ideal collaborative process they got everything: a pool with fish; tables and umbrellas for sheltered kibbitzing; waist-high planters for growing herbs and vegetables; hard-surfaced paths for wheels; shrubs and herbs as a haven for butterflies; flowers for color and aroma and bees; evergreens for shelter and esthetics; a greensward; food sources.

That fall, when they were planting seven fruit trees, Børge came outside. He knew how to hold the sapling, wordlessly showed the digger the right depth, packed the soil, watered the roots in properly. Gardening may start as child's play or child labor, but those muscle memories last a lifetime.

So do long-cultivated skills and knowledge. In Minnesota, good gardeners come from the older Hmong, with their long horticultural heritage. In a garden developed in New Orleans after Hurricane Katrina, although many older African Americans were still in the diaspora, Leola and Eola, both in their eighties, were known as good growers of greens.[19] Gertrude Jekyll, the British designer of ravishingly vivid gardens, never lost her sense of color in old age, even as she was losing sight.[20] In San Juan del Sur, Nicaragua, where my husband, David, and I go annually, David met an old farmer, named José Adan Baltodano, who made up a list for him of native trees. When they stopped at a count of about ninety-five, an old woman who was listening said, "You missed some" and added eight more. Our farmers are our professors of practice.

Henry David Thoreau sat at the feet of one small-scale farmer, an older man named George Minott. "Minott adorns whatever part of nature he touches," Thoreau wrote, like a Seeker about his Sage; "whichever way he walks he transfigures the earth for me." The "poetry" of his mentor's existence still defines agrarianism: Minott's independence ("in all his life, he never went to market") and his willingness to share his lore and sharp observations. The "yeoman" in the early years of the Republic, an owner working his own land, was considered a creative, innovative professional, foundational to the nation.[21] As agriculture became more industrialized in the nineteenth century, the banks took the land, then as now. For a person to stay the course lifelong, given the pressures even then to scale up or sell out, was an achievement. The man Walt Whitman revered, "of wonderful vigor, calmness, beauty of person, . . . six feet tall, . . . over eighty years old"—the one "You would wish long and long to be with"— was "a common farmer."

LADDER OF YEARS

Over the decades, this special identity—gardener or farmer—remains in touch, in spirit if not tactilely, with soil, seeds, humus, leaves, worms, insects, sunshine, buds, flowers, seeds, the cycle of seasons. Maintaining a sensuous continuity over the life course assures land lovers of some stability amid flux and losses. Certain flowers or produce become identified with us, by our children or grandchildren, forever.[22] Robert Frost, making dirt sublime, wrote, "But I was one of the children told / Some of the dust was really gold . . ."

Over the life course the workload changes. In a subsistence family, a girl may start by weeding and graduate to collecting firewood. Women's work is often overlooked. In Africa women do 60 percent of the marketing of excess crops, 70 percent of hoeing and weeding, 90 percent of carrying water.[23] In almost all contexts, women, even without owning the land, play a central role in ensuring household food security, a job that in turn affects crop choices and other agricultural decisions.[24] The main providers tend to be older women. Their uncounted labor includes not only cropping but other skilled occupations. Preserving, cooking, making beer, or raising livestock do not stop in middle life.

In a middle-class family, a life course in the garden comes with luxurious choices. The supervisor of the outdoor space may start by trucking sand for children. Later the child-centered space becomes a vegetable garden, a peony border, a quincunx of fruit trees. And gardeners try to go on working through pain and disability. They organize raised beds to avoid bending. To ease the chores, as well as for sound ecology, the space may be turned over to inter-planted permacrops like asparagus, rhubarb, Jerusalem artichokes, ground nuts, apricot or pear trees. These are some of the edibles my husband (now seventy-five) grows in our suburban garden. Maintaining even a small "potager" (for the *potage* or soup) requires, year in and year out, an urgent commitment to planning and manual labor. For forty years we have been eating out of our small plot in southern New England from mid-May until after frost.

As time passes, orchards and evergreens require more care. In our thirties, enchanted by great ornamental gardens (those conjured up by the word *jardin* and glossy illustrated books), and in particular by Vita Sackville-West's Sissing-hurst garden rooms in England, we planted a hedge of capitata yews that makes a sheltering microclimate for our small vegetable garden. Now I climb a ladder every August to keep that green wall, which wants to soar fifty feet in the air, cutting off southern exposure, at twelve feet. I mount that ladder with some pride and some fear, in recent years, now twice the age I was when we sketched the plan. Perched at the top, balancing, weighing deep in with belly against branches, I sometimes wonder how much longer I dare. Wielding the shears while encumbered by too much learning, I recall, alas, the medieval ladder of years with its tumble down the far side. I persist. Like old farmers, I want to go on doing what I do as long as I can.

Green Longevity

Rudyard Kipling advised, "Live as if you are going to die tomorrow, garden as if you are going to live forever." Some serious gardeners do. Gertrude Jekyll died at eighty-nine. The poet Stanley Kunitz kept hoeing, deadheading, and carrying water, into his late nineties. Writers who garden—I'm thinking of Eudora Welty and William Maxwell, who wrote to each other about gardening and who, also, died in their nineties—have longer (and more interesting) lives. A study in *JAMA* found that Iowa farmers under sixty-five, given to vigorous exercise and little smoking, had a 10 percent lower coronary heart disease risk than their same-age neighbors in town.[25]

Noticing that farmers in Africa and Asia do not live so long, however, geriatricians could well attribute the longevity of middle-class gardeners and farmers to their having eaten nutritious food starting in childhood, and having received medical care all their lives. Doctors could point to the farmers' continuous cardio exercise—like walking a dog or doing yoga, but with a product. In the field of psycho-neuro-immuno-endocrinology, gardening is highly recommended.[26] Gardening was found good for Katrina survivors with PTSD.

There are more holistic explanations of why people in contact with nature sometimes live longer, not to say better. The giant Antaeus needed to touch his mother, Earth, to regain strength. Nature is no abstraction: it is dirt, shovels, weather. Eva Algreen-Petersen was walking through the Copenhagen nursing home one day when she heard a man, Egon, in a wheelchair repeating, persistently, "Get me out of here."

She stopped; she asked, "Can I help?" She knew Egon as one of those who rarely spoke.

"Out," he said, "I want to get out."

"It's raining," she said. "Pouring, really."

"Doesn't matter," he said.

Wonderfully, kindly, she got her raingear, and his. She wheeled him just outside the door. He put his head up to feel the rain, and kept it there, face to sky, skin to water. After a while he said, "That's enough. That is what I wanted."

A Moroccan proverb says, "A downpour in April [in the dry season] is worth all the money in Madrid."[27] Rain is a profound poetic metaphor in a dry century. And for a person cooped up indoors in a wheelchair, it is a tang, a bracing chill, a reminder of the hardships of youth or the gladness of drinking water dropping from heaven; a break in the monotony of blue-sky days; a timely promise of a good harvest.

Farmers tend to stay put on their piece of earth. In our crazily mobile globe, they have a fixed foot. Our North Carolina landlord told us, "I ain't never been out of the county but once, to go to Morehead on the weekend to take Loretta ta see the ocean. Had to get my nephew to mind the cows." If farmers don't have alternatives for making a livelihood—and the older they are, the fewer the choices—departure won't occur to them, despite isolation from town life or family.[28] Lack of nearby doctors, pharmacies, and vehicles forces them into buses and self-care. But aging in place where everyone knows you and you know everyone has social and health benefits. Doña Petrona, in her village in San Juan del Sur, has grandchildren (as seen in the photo in chapter 2) right nearby. Neighbors gossip, lend or borrow an ox or an ax. They tell their stories to the young. A favorite is how they or their ancestors acquired the land.

Farmers, loving their land, want to hold onto it. They tend to be possessive, and thus possess long views about inheritance. With enough capital, they sometimes plant valuable trees—apple, mango, black walnut, teak. In her memoir, *The Orchard*, Adele Crockett Robertson tells how she and her father planted "the smooth-barked whips" of peaches on a Massachusetts farm after World War I. " 'They will take care of me in my retirement,' my father said with satisfaction, looking down at the neat rows of frail little sticks from which so much was hoped and promised."[29] Grandchildren might inherit a living capital. We terrestrials are all pro tem. But handing on small farms is one of the less narrowly individualistic forms of progress narrative. Native Americans thought to assure the welfare of the seventh generation.

"Intergenerational responsibility," of which Pope Francis spoke in the encyclical *Laudato Si'* (2015), usually means a commitment toward those younger and to be born. It doesn't require acting responsibly toward those who are old now. To be just, however, "green longevity" must refer not only to the long lives some farmers enjoy but also to the living elders in trouble. They embody the long thread of continuity and obstinacy that has kept land and lore intact to be inheritable over the centuries and millennia, despite all challenges.

EAST OF EDEN

Farming can also be sheer misery. Food, the most basic of human needs, is pleasure—tastes and textures, the smoothness, the succulence, the juice, colors, smells of ripeness, feel of heat or cool, the good chew, the smacking swallow, the belly's satisfaction. But food is work—hard, anxious, open to the ills of chance, simultaneously independent and insecure. Work—punishing work, and risk— has been linked to gardens since Eden.

Except for gardeners who hire field hands and never put a dibble into the ground, even gardening is no shallow ditch, no primrose path. Trained horticulturist or on-the-job learner, a grower must break ground, improve soil fertility, provide shelter from wind, drain soil. Composting requires storing peelings, adding carbon, cozying up to aerobic decomposition. One may have to water often, maintain machinery. From this point of view, that of hands-on labor, the hard and fast borders between gardeners and poor people living off the land break down a bit. Gardeners are well placed to respect people truly dependent on what they grow. Despite their hardships, some advantages accrue to the latter, who may be illiterate but know traditional secrets for improving soil, deciding when to sow, and a million other variables. When farmers begin to lose inherited lore, that's serious for everyone.

If a garden feels as exigent as a baby, on a farm you can't miss a chore. Self-sufficiency is harsh natural law. The pastoral view of green recumbent fields or Breughel-like harvest festivals doesn't take up much space. For older peasants and small farmers, growing food or raising animals is neither an avocation nor a choice. It is a way of living: not romantic; fraught, inescapable. Family farm production is focused not on avoiding obesity but on staple grains and subsistence. Many try to feed themselves on land they sharecrop, or on land made smaller by past inheritance or cut up for crop rotation. If some who grow food enjoy the cycles of nature and appreciate soil and rain, hills and mist, the most valued outcome is the produce.

Even in the developed world, many people go hungry. The "green revolution" did not solve the problem of hunger, even in the United States. Growing your own food is becoming a necessity in middle-class families, and food pantries in affluent suburbs are common. Like low-income children, people over sixty are often malnourished despite targeted programs. They may not know about the programs (in the United States: the Commodity Supplemental Food Program, the Senior Farmers' Market Nutrition Program), and the barriers to register can be high. Globally, poor older women may get less access to food than older men in the same families or than younger family members.

Earth may roll forever, with or without us, but human life depends on the food supply. Worldwide droughts and apocalyptic floods remind us that human agency worsens the natural case. Topsoil and seeds that don't wash away may blow away. Plants wither. Fruit rots. Pests thrive. Rivers disappear, wells run dry. If the sun doesn't shine enough, or rainfall goes wrong, a harvest is lost. Disappointing for the avocational gardener, this is traumatic or fatal for sharecroppers or small-holders sowing subsistence crops, such as quinoa, maize, platanos. Given global climate weirdness and population growth, food provision is done amid increasingly hostile conditions.

LACKLAND

Owning farm property is the symbol of agricultural identity, and that identity is prized. Farming on family land was once a legacy career. For generations, even in countries where people retained only small plots, as they grew older, growers proudly passed on land to their offspring. But for many old providers, it can no longer be handed on. Some feel this is their own personal failure. But "failure" is a keyword in a complex history: According to whose subjective view? Who or what failed whom?

Many rural young adults have left their parents and the land. For the first time in history, more people live in cities than not.[30] In Africa, Asia, Latin America, younger people have been decamping for shanty megacities, ragged bidonvilles, and overcrowded favelas. Urbanization has meant the transformation of the green Earth into what Mike Davis has called our *Planet of Slums*. The global youth exodus is the cause of the thirty-year trend in which farmers' average ages appear to be rising. A focus on the problems of youth crowding the megalopalises obscures the push-pull of economic history and the painful losses of the older farmers in the parents' generation.

Globally, city life, promising urban incomes and education, calls to the young. Women, whose rural work is considered less essential, leave to seek manufacturing or service jobs or husbands who have more secure income. Some young people farm part-time, but have trained for and found other jobs; Jane Guyer, tracing thirty-odd years of Nigerian labor conditions, calls them "sideliners."[31] Simultaneously, farming became expensive even in the global South. Starting a new farm of one's own with mechanical equipment and fertilizer, along with fancy seeds, became cash-intensive. "Parents started failing in their [traditional] responsibilities," one view has it. Perhaps they were able to provide a patch of land from the family lot, but no other start-up costs.[32] Over the last forty years, as this overwhelming out-migration has occurred, many families have been torn apart. The absolute numbers of peasant and small-holder farmers in the South have remained stable.[33] But in many places, that means fewer people left to do the risky, labor-intensive, knowledge-rich work that agrarian philosophers admire.

The abandonment of rural life began in the developed countries two centuries ago. In 1930s America, about half of the employed (30 million) were still primary producers of food, and farmers' unions were the backbone of Progressive politics, alongside urban labor. The number has dwindled to two million, with fewer than 2 percent of the now much larger workforce farming.[34] A teacher in Maine, Garrett Keizer, writes about the few adolescents in his high school who wear the Future Farmers of America jacket:

> Back in the old days a kid who wore that dark-blue gold-lettered jacket was as often as not a kid who came to school smelling like a barn, sometimes

with manure in the tread of his boots. It takes me a while to realize that of the half-dozen or so FFA members I have in my classes, only one lives on a farm; that is to say, the parents of the others have become lifetime members of Past Farmers of America.[35]

A woman I interviewed, born in Nebraska, a geriatric nursing educator now in her sixties, tells me about her three brothers who have farmed there all their lives.

Corn, soybeans, wheat, a few cattle. None of their children or grandchildren wants to take over the farm, nor could they. Some have found professional careers; others don't have the practical knowledge and skills for farm management. Some of their adult children help my brothers with things like irrigation, driving trucks or moving equipment to various fields during planting and at harvest time, filling and cleaning out grain bins that store dry grain, mowing and cleaning up around the farm. The same circumstances afflict some of their neighbors who are aging toward retirement. My brothers used to help older farmers in the past by renting and farming their fields. But now they themselves are aging beyond midlife and experiencing health problems.

Parents may decide that benefits balance their personal losses. A northern Greek farmer who now cultivates fewer crops explains: "I am not so young now and my sons are not living in the village. I urged them to go to the university. They both live and work in Thessalonika; the older one is a lawyer and the younger is a doctor. It was my life dream! Sometimes they come and help me."[36] In San Juan del Sur, where the high school I cofounded in 2002 had graduated 1001 people by 2016, at least half the rural parents now have the same "life dream" the Greek father has. The superintendent of schools tells me they *want* their children to attend and not be farmers.[37] Migrant farmers everywhere work land they don't own; their better-educated children probably will not. Some owners who leave find legal ways to keep land in the family, even if it is not farmed by kin.[38] Mostly, when parents die, the heirs sell it. It's a developer's bonanza.

"Lackland" may have arisen as a name for any unlucky family that lost its property. In many places, the important story of noncultivation is not about the young leaving, but about people who farmed all their lives being deprived of the necessities that make for continuity, including ancestral land itself. The land grab is a global phenomenon that has driven millions off their land, after dire circumstances have forced small and mid-sized farmers, often less well-educated or illiterate, to sell.[39] They could be credit-starved, they could have had too many years of poor harvests. The macro causes might include competition from larger mechanized farms, costs of new seed, distance from markets, and state abandonment of small farmers. Some sell to developers. Nicaraguans I knew sold precious cooperative lands conferred during the postrevolutionary agrarian reform, saving only small private plots. The prices per acre were risible to the buyers, but it was more cash than the sellers had ever imagined. Countries like China or corporations like Harvard buy up land. Most transfers are legal, but in some countries goons enforce takeovers. Farmers can't afford to sue or defend themselves if big companies sue them.

Experienced and successful farmers can lose land, without any fault of their own, through racism, classism, or the caste system; through bad foreclosure deals; or from fraud. Japanese farmers in America, many American-born, lost their land to government-sponsored internment during World War II. In the United States, it took the largest class-action civil rights settlement in the history of the country (known as *Pigford* and *Pigford II*) to prove Department of Agriculture (USDA) discrimination against people of color, and women of all colors, who had farmed between 1981 and 1996. The court found that county agents of the Farmers Home Administration denied requests for loans without just cause, and failed to service these farmers' loans in a timely manner or offer other USDA programs that might have saved their operations, land, and homes. The African Americans who testified had grown up under Jim Crow: they were old. Many had to overcome ingrained fear of retaliation to tell their stories.

The vindicated wanted their land back, but many received inadequate financial restitution instead.[40] The settlement also silenced their stories. "My parents weren't the only ones to die waiting for their settlement," says Gary Grant, of the Black Farmers and Agriculturalists Association. "Many of the farmers in Pigford died before the case was closed. It was a 20-year battle, and the average age of the Black farmer is about 63. . . . We went from one million strong in 1920 to not much more than 15,000 today."[41] Many also left for better-paying urban jobs, during the Great Migration north that went on from 1920 through World War II and beyond. Some who may want to return mistrust the USDA and lack the capital without it.

Within the fierce macro-history of land losses, physical aging seems a lesser factor. Many researchers count sixty as "old" in censuses of farm work. It might be truer to conditions on the ground to put "old" at fifty-five or even fifty, depending on rural life expectancy in a given country. Ill health in later life represents the accumulated effects of life-long deprivations: farming, despite its cardiovascular benefits, is hard on the body. The risk of injuries and death is higher than in other professions.[42] Exhausting labor and repetitive motions take their toll on the musculoskeletal system. The exposure to sun ravages the skin and damages the eyes; exposure to pesticides can cause organ failure. A 2014 report by the FAO and HelpAge International found that 76.8 percent of the elderly small-holders they surveyed suffered from chronic ailments, including hypertension, backache, vision problems, diabetes, and HIV/AIDS.[43] Women live longer than men in many developing countries, too. Those who married young and had many children too young are likely to suffer more than men from ill health as they age. One Chinese woman of seventy-three offered a definition: "When one feels too weak to work, one becomes an old person."[44]

As people lose strength, the need to tend either a garden or a farm can be "acutely depressing and enforce feelings of powerlessness as others may need to be employed to carry out tasks once carried out by oneself with ease." Frustrations undermine "the long-felt ontological security of 'home,' and give rise to the feeling of 'not being at home.'"[45] Past prime working age, some leave. They move closer to their urbanized families to be looked after or to get better access to social and health services and transportation than exist in their isolated and dispersed communities. Others defiantly choose to age in place in overlarge troublesome houses precisely because they can't face a dismal urban future. They plant seeds in a south-facing window.

Moving away from whatever land they possessed, displaced land lovers find themselves in places where almost everything at ground level is hard-scaping: brick, mortar, concrete, iron. They sit in parks with flowers they can't touch, grass they are forbidden to walk on, shrubs they could prune better, not a vegetable in sight. Some may like surcease from toil, but to my mind the neatly tended public park fails the public. In cities suffering from disinvestment, residents walk past expensive or substandard grocery stores, toxic dumps, and vacant lots that attract trash, drug dealers, junked cars, and kids with no other place to play. Where are their healing gardens, their fresh vegetables, their aerobic exercise, their chances for chat and longevity?

The losses are not only personal. Former farmlands get turned into water-guzzling golf courses, cattle land (more profitable for owners but useless as a source of calories for most eaters), or industrial farming, all generating environmental problems.

The epithet "lackland" could be applied to all involuntary land-leavers. Many are elders, who have no way to turn their griefs into grievances. They look back behind them at old land, lost, that "a thousand generations have tilled." Poets—this line is from Ivor Gurney, in "Brown Earth Look"—write elegiacally about lost ways of life. Unhappy are the countries that need elegies. Unwittingly, the world loses the old farmers' expertise, their storytelling, their music—all the values that Wendell Berry vividly recalls in "Farmland without Farmers."[46] And how can they themselves, and the still-burgeoning populations they served, and distant eaters in cities, do without the food they might have produced?

The Plights of Aging Green

"Age is becoming in the country," Emerson wrote, presumably not alluding to the failed Transcendentalist farming experiment of Fruitlands, but to the Roman gentry turning to their country estates in old age to write pastorals about the amours of shepherds. The facts of aging green on a working farm are more unsettling. Outside of farm fiction, typically centered on one family, the truths remain to be told. Around the world, old people surviving on the land need literary scribes who feel that these farmers are not subordinate characters but the main story. A literature of song and story—sad *rancheros* about leaving Papa behind, sentimental plays (of which one, *Senza Mamma*, is shown in the Little Italy theater scene in *The Godfather*, Part II)—narrates the sorrow of separation.[47] But these speak from the point of view of those who left to seek their fortune, bravely and guiltily. Where are the laments of the elders? Theirs is a story of amazing, mostly unapplauded, resilience.

Old people are a minority of all nations' populations, even Japan's, so the fact that over half live in rural areas is disproportionate. The farmers among them are trapped there at a time of mounting, indeed ominous, crises around land, water, and food itself. The social transformations that still stun farm families in the United Kingdom, Western Europe, or the United States (the departure of the young, the end of legacy farming) have been going on for centuries, but in some places they now occur within a single lifetime. Sudden demotions can be the most bewildering; long foreseen but unavoidable losses, the most tragic.

If no children of working age are present, the aches of old age or malnutrition don't end the workload. There is no age limit when farmers must retire, and rarely any nonfarming income to provide leisure. People work (staving off dependency on adult children) until they can't. In China, 41 percent of rural people over sixty rely on income from their own labor, and those who receive some family support also work.[48] Julian Chavez, a sixty-eight-year-old Nicaraguan widower I interviewed in his front yard, a stroke victim, showed me proudly how he stills plants seeds. He stood to mime the rhythmic gesture of hoeing weeds, using his good right arm. His strapping son, Carlos, thirty-seven, who was sprawled on a chair listening, does the plowing. In some societies, one or more adult children stay to help the parents.

Mainland China has a new contributory pension system for farmers, though it covers relatively few. A Hong Kong paper headlined its story, "Pension now covers 143m[illion] farmers, just 757m to go." In 2011 China paid out US$8.61 a month (55 yuan) to these peasant farmers,[49] much less than urban retirees get. Some countries have a good policy on paper, but, a sixty-six-year-old Tanzanian woman observes, "There is nobody to implement it. It is just there in books." Paper cannot blush.[50]

On the Planet of the Abandoned Fields and Mines, when the young leave behind their old folks and sometimes their own children, they may send money back and return for visits, or not. Reciprocity may well remain a longed-for value, but filial norms of caregiving are often betrayed by economic pressures and geography. Then parents have no one to whom to convey the precious lore that took a lifetime to acquire.

Some old folks raise their grandchildren. Migration can be a family survival strategy, so it often results, not surprisingly, in increased support from older parents to adult children in the form of domestic, agricultural, and childcare work.[51] Women are often most responsible for caring for their grandchildren, some of whose parents, in areas affected by HIV and AIDS, are sick or have died.[52]

The elders go on despite debility or lack of filial protection. Younger people may disrespect them. In some countries, the old remember a more harmonious age system where their own parents did not have to beg. When women get old, one sixty-seven-year-old Tanzanian woman explained, referring to the line waiting at a well to draw water, younger women say, "We are not the ones who made you old, it is God; so you must wait until we all finish."[53] If the older women become too disabled to walk to the well, or lose access to water in other ways, they are doomed. Lack of electricity and running water make hygiene, care of the sick, and end-of-life care harder. In advanced countries too, health care, transportation, and social care may be inadequate. In Canada, around 30 percent of rural old people live in communities that lack a physician or pharmacy.[54] Isolation may be a serious issue.

Some older farmers, trying to adapt to climate change, know it is better with little rain to diversify, to cultivate low-water crops or raise animals instead of row crops. But the training and the chicks and piglets tend to skew young, to coax young transplanted urbanites back to the farm. One Zimbabwean, aged sixty-four, raising four grandchildren, wants to learn. Education stops, but not by his choice. "Even these young men and women who have been told why there are so many droughts these days have no time to explain these things to old people like me." *I am still human; try me.* The Zimbabwe Commercial Farmers Union president, Wonder Chabikwa, says that, although some of the elderly are included in agricultural services, most are shunned: "It is as if the aged don't exist, yet many households out there are under their care and guidance."[55] Experts from the University of Kwa-Zulu note that with 40 percent of the African population below the age of fifteen, the elderly are crowded out of national policies.[56]

So on top of everything else, there is often ageist neglect. Officials do not appreciate the contributions of older people, think they can't learn new tricks, cruelly believe they won't want to travel to extension classes (ignoring the likelihood that they don't have the necessary bus fare). Medical personnel, where available, may send the old and disabled away. *They have lived long enough.* In advanced economies, austerity reduces welfare provision in rural areas that didn't get much to begin with—"perpetuating the invisibility of poverty among older groups," a researcher writes, summarizing four Welsh studies.[57] In Spain, EU programs target various interest groups; "rural aging" is studied, and data show that most rural people over sixty-five are women. But regional training courses (in rural tourism, restoration, computers, handicrafts) that try to attract "women" may not include older women. In general, such programs also fail to create associations, or improvements in the marketing networks, that might help both older people and younger stay in agriculture together and resist exploitation.[58]

In nations that have legal rules regulating the government for the benefit of the elderly, these rules are scattered, not systematically related to each other as "elder law." One Korean legal scholar points out frankly that, "Unlike rights-to-freedom claims, social-rights claims cannot create governmental actions as [one] wishes—these claims are highly subject to governmental discretions that are at the mercy of financial situations. . . . The elderly are essentially powerless within this legal framework."[59]

Confronting the stubborn facts of globalization and climate charge, the expert elders in farming populations soldier on without much notice or relief. If the young don't want to, or can't, farm, and the old must, where does it make sense to put the agricultural development dollar? The oblivion is transnational. In varied ways, ageism dirties the whole system.

AGROPOLIS

One unexpected hope for food, and for some older farmers and their life-giving relationships with younger generations, lies in urban farming. In the concrete and cinderblock agglomerations, many who want cheap, healthy food decide they need to grow it themselves, however unpropitious the circumstances. Countries doing food censuses often exclude urban areas, but they are becoming important.

In places where urban gardening is organized, it goes on in schoolyards, "pocket parks," on civic rooftops, on college campuses. Where there are community allotments, a city may provide permits and clean water. People receive plots that may be crowded or small, but are temporarily theirs. My son met his wife-to-be in a pocket park in Alphabet City, Manhattan. When people squat on land they don't own, they plant wherever they can—next to the dwelling, under power lines, beside sewage ditches, alongside highways. In a dense slum in Nairobi, residents plant "vertical gardens" of kale and spinach in recycled bags of soil and rocks. The guerrilla gardeners use run-off water, often polluted, on worn-out, rubble-filled soils.[60] Such vacant spaces in cities are the latter-day paradises of our new era on the Planet of Slums.

Such spontaneous, not to say anarchic, food happenings spread internationally in the twentieth century. They continue to do so, now with more notice taken. In *agropolis* (the handy neologism of L.J.A. Mouget), people of all ages satisfy hunger. Agropolis the concept doesn't focus on age—as etymology suggests, the focus is on food production in conurbations. But some of the best gardeners are midlifers or old women and men, bringing in skills and resourcefulness from the country. As in New Orleans and in Minnesota's cities, gardening communities attract immigrants and natives of all ages. When my husband and I were young landless renters who had moved to Boston and obtained a plot in the Fenway Victory Gardens, a talented Korean man who seemed elderly to us helped us start out. From his lush space, he gave us tips on soil and the raspberry plants we still harvest. Tennessee's statute gives priority when allocating garden plots to older people, low-income families, and school-age children. Detroit (a city with 100,000 vacant lots) gets recognized for its "grannie porches," decks on which people sit to rest and watch gardening activity.[61]

One way or another, agropolis is widespread, much more so than people imagine. There are some 200 million urban farmers in the world, supplying food to 700 million people, about 12 percent of the world population. (Agropolis provides 50 percent of vegetable consumption in Karachi and an astonishing 85 percent in the sprawl of Shanghai, population 16 million. Some 50 percent of Asian urban households were involved, the FAO stated, in 1996.[62]) The Cuban government, in its "Special Period in Time of Peace," had to abandon fuel- and chemical-dependent farming; by 2012, its 380,000 urban farms supplied 70 percent of all fresh vegetables consumed in Havana and other Cuban cities.[63]

Community gardens, often initiated by women, nourish the old implicit needs: for a closer connection to nature, for the chance to teach younger people, for produce that couldn't be more local, for camaraderie and social trust. They regenerate empty lots. In some cities—in the Victory Gardens in Boston—with neat little sheds for tools, a pergola, wisteria, they become tourist destinations. They may achieve 501(c)(3) nonprofit status and win grants. Some give food away; others sell it. Such initiatives are healing gardens. They conscientiously counter obesity, chemical inputs, and limited access to healthy and reasonably priced food. In effect, they also fight ageism, the isolation of elders, xenophobia, government disinvestment, juvenile delinquency, crime, poverty, and the hot dry airless concrete of cities. As in Detroit, many vacant urban lots could, with appropriate legislation, be dedicated to food gardening and social justice. One-fifth of all land in American cities in 1998 was classified as vacant.[64]

The FAO believes that "One of the major efforts of the next 25 years must therefore be to develop urban farming systems, which can supply much of the food cities require without expensive transport costs."[65] This trend doesn't help old people laboring in the countrysides, but it has the potential to prevent urban famine and to lower rates of malnutrition.

FOOD PRODUCTION IN CRISIS TIMES

As the world population of mouths rises steadily, and Big Farma expands, the global food supply, in both quantity and quality, is becoming a supranational concern. For "consumers"—people who buy what they eat, which means everyone except subsistence farmers, at all class levels—the current crises start with dramatic rises in the prices of food. These have sparked protests in Mexico, Morocco, Senegal, Indonesia, Cameroon, Egypt, Haiti, and at least twenty other countries.[66] ("Raise food prices, deal with a revolution," is what dictators must say to one another over cocktails.) The costs of foodstuffs rise with the prices of the inputs (seeds, fertilizers, irrigation equipment), which are controlled by agro-industry. Transporting fresh food from distant places uses petroleum, a dangerous and expensive resource. Aside from cost, there are other crises. In some regions, nourishing food is scarce, and there are food deserts in low-income neighborhoods ignored by the giant supermarket chains. Available food may be contaminated by E. coli or salmonella. Canned food is high in sodium or sugar and may contain pesticides. The outcome in many countries is lessened access to adequate calories. Underlying all is the mother crisis, global warming. Older people, whether urban unemployed with low incomes, or producing on subsistence farms, are more vulnerable in any conditions of scarcity.

Widespread hunger and famine are the danger. In the Anthropocene, the perils are also human-made. Cormac McCarthy's terrifying postapocalyptic novel, *The Road*, about a father who must feed himself and his son in an ash-covered America where nothing grows any longer, can be read allegorically, as dread that the crises involving global food scarcity cannot be solved.

FARMERS' MARTYRDOM DAY

Nine out of ten farms worldwide (more than 500 million) are family farms.[67] They're small, the vast majority under five acres. The stubborn hundreds of millions who stick to basic food production for the poorest, in these deteriorating conditions, deserve respect, especially those in later life, increasingly the die-hards doing it.

Pulling back to look at structural problems makes the grim fates of current older farmers in many countries understandable. Lakshmi's story, from India, typifies some of the problems.

> To Asia's biggest cotton mandi [Hindi for trading hub] comes 60-year-old
> Lakshmi, a Lambadi tribal woman from Vardhamapet village. Her three
> sons have left home. She planted 2 acres cotton. Twice she dug a bore
> well but couldn't hit water even at 200 feet. . . . . Now she has to pay back
> Rs 10,000 . . . , plant a new crop in June, and meet living expenses till Octo-
> ber when harvest brings fresh income. She desperately needs credit but no
> bank will touch her because the land is not in her name.[68]

Farmers unable to get credit go into unpayable debt. But women farmers are
"worse off than the most hapless male," in the headline of an article from *India
Times*. Everywhere, patriarchy may limit women's access to land, cash, credit.
Women household heads tend to have smaller, less well capitalized holdings.[69]
Widows may lose land through misogynistic laws and predatory deals while
paying off their husbands' debts.

Ram K., a reader of *The Hindu*, knowledgeably lamented the broader historical contexts of deprivation: "Dwindling public investment in developing
agri infra[structure] and near absence of extension services and failing R&D
[research and development] institutions coupled with soil degradation and
dwindling water tables are making farming a burden and youngsters do not
want to continue in farming."[70] Prodded by supranational market ideology
from the 1980s on, including the International Monetary Fund's "structural
adjustment" policies and the World Trade Organization, and by their own
major exporters, many nations, far from defending small farmers, were forced
to scuttle their support. Credits, extension teaching, price subsidies, input provision (not just fertilizer but seeds), and marketing services became things of
the past. The needs of this key profession are unlikely to result in additional services wherever governments are geared in colonial fashion to buy foreign food
or sell staple food crops; lack technical expertise to acquire new information or
design programs, can't collect taxes or honestly dispense revenues, or haven't
instituted pensions. National governments may delay providing farmers with
secure land titles, or take land through eminent domain or for back taxes. Corrupt developers, politicians, and usurers prey on small-holders.

In the United States, subsidies to Big Farma wreak havoc on small farmers,
crowded out by industrial agriculture. "Redneck" became a term of scorn for the
remaining (white) small-holders and day laborers who were often unorganized,
less well-educated, and powerless. A miniscule program—$20 million worth
in the 2014 Farm Bill—to help small farmers and elderly low-income people

simultaneously gives out fresh-food coupons worth no more than $50 a year per person, in the forty-two states that accept the program.[71] Imperious countries subsidize their own producers while fighting tariffs. Northern farmers dump agricultural goods on foreign markets at prices so low that nonsubsidized farmers cannot compete. In Mexico, the NAFTA treaty has meant that US farmers could sell corn for tortillas, a staple of life, more cheaply than could Mexican family farmers. Failure was inevitable. The many younger people trying to cross the border are partly the result of trade policy. Older people, as we know, stay.

The weaker rural remnant often subsists on worn-out soil (worsened by monoculture) in climates that are increasingly menaced. Globally, trees are cut down for fuel or lumber; then more topsoil blows away. As Ram K. observed, water tables then drop. In Nicaragua, the wells dry up even in the "rainy season" in some years. The mayor in our town sends water trucks to the villages for drinking and washing, but not for irrigating. Desertification makes a home place unlivable, makes droughts inevitable, makes planting crops impossible. With adult children gone, the labor—the entire enterprise—may eventually become too hard, or impossible. Not seeing this, not reckoning with the cumulative problems dumped on older farmers, adds ageism to the list of transnational failures to provide food security.

Around the world, being a small-scale farmer is a risk not only to health but to life. Farmers' suicide rates are the highest of any occupation. In India an estimated 270,000 farmers, lacking state support amid the disaster of falling agricultural prices, have committed suicide since the mid-1990s, according to India's National Crime Records Bureau. M. D. Nanjundaswamy, an Indian farmer, lawyer, and campaign leader, organized an annual World Farmers' Martyrdom Day to bring attention to the causes. American farmers have three times the suicide rate of the rest of the US population. Rural suicide rates in Australia are among the highest in the world: At least two-thirds of farmer suicides occur in older groups, mainly those over the age of fifty-five. Australia has half the number of farms it had in the 1960s. Current farmers feel "their cultural identity and national relevance [is] questioned." British farmers, too, commit suicide at a higher rate than do urbanites. "They feel they mustn't be the first generation that fails," one commentator observes.[72] Like long-term unemployed blue-collar and middle-class people, they don't realize failure is not their fault. Can these people be rescued in time, if global eaters develop a heightened sense of their relevance? Sometimes it seems as if every day in some part of the world is farmers' martyrdom day.

REPAIR

In 2002 the United Nations recognized the plight of rural elders, in the Madrid International Plan of Action on Aging, pointing to the neglect of older farmers in national and regional planning. Wise social policy, determined political action, and enormous economic inputs could conceivably solve the food crises created by the convergence of corporate agriculture and its proprietary seed market, the nation-states' disinvestment, and even some aspects of global warming. The next step after top-down multinational proposals (how well did the Kyoto treaty work to slow warming?) is for each national government to take responsibility for its part of the dilemma. They have a good security reason to try: food sovereignty can be closely tied to national sovereignty. A country that imports much of its food had better be not only rich but politically and militarily secure.

The Taiwanese government, recognizing how interrelated such problems are, is trying to lure younger people back to the farms while simultaneously keeping the all-important older growers surviving and working there. Some economists imagine that old farmers must be "inefficient"—too close to the end of working life to buy new technology or learn new techniques. Taiwan, however, apparently not having gotten this ageist memo, trusts them. It gives subsidies to farmers over sixty-five, and also to those who rent land to farmers under the age of fifty-five.[73] In Brazil, Lula da Silva's administration passed a law requiring that 30 percent of school lunch funds be spent on food provided by family farmers, with preference given to indigenous farmers, descendants of slaves, and beneficiaries of agrarian reform.[74] But Taiwan and Brazil, taking some responsibility for their small-holding food producers, seem exceptional.

BACK TO THE LAND

"We must get back to our land!" "We must hold on to our land!" are the cries of a new agricultural movement. It is inspired by the injustices of the past, by collective need, and by the specter of many more becoming Past Farmers of the Planet. After a famine, in 2005 a new president of Malawi made "a very bold decision to provide subsidies for seeds and fertilizers over the objections of the development partners," the vice-president of the UN's International Fund for Agricultural Development said, noting that during one meeting with senior Malawian officials a furious representative of a donor country had stormed out of the room, "But the government stood its ground." Harvests improved, and Malawi had extra grain to sell.[75]

What is taking place, mostly under the radar, is a wide-ranging revolution, a sign of outrage at the current badly organized food system, Frances Moore Lappé believes. Transnational advocacy is needed to combat international corporate actions and supranational governmental policies. Via Campesina, perhaps the largest nonreligious organization on the planet, a collection of 150 groups that calls itself "the International Peasants' Voice," represents about 200 million of them.[76]

Control is the keyword. "People around the world are acting to take control of their food or, rather, to re-take control," writes Nora McKeon, a friend who spent decades working to open up the FAO to small-scale producers' organizations. These collectives began by organizing nationally; now they have reached a global level. McKeon is optimistic, without denying the power of the opposition. "After all, locally centered food systems were a basic part of the texture of human society until three decades ago, when liberalization and globalization opened the door to a corporate takeover of what we grow and what we eat. Today, a rich and powerful range of alternatives to the corporate food system is coming up locally in all regions of the world."[77]

With the help of Via Campesina and national groups like the Brazilian Movimento Dos Trabalhadores Rurais Sem Terra (the Landless Workers' Movement), farmers have been organizing against the giant forces. In her essay in *Food Movements Unite!* McKeon explains. "Under the auspices of the new Committee on World Food Security [which reports to the UN General Assembly], . . . authoritative and eloquent representatives stand up to governments and the CEOs of agribusiness multinationals and win recognition that they merit the support of national agricultural policies and investments."[78]

Senior activists earned their authoritative knowledge of the lay of the land. Vandana Shiva, the Indian author of *Stolen Harvest*, was brought up by a father who was a conservator of forests and a mother who was a farmer. Dolores Huerta, who promoted the first legislation in the United States allowing farm workers to organize (only in 1975), was the daughter of a farm worker and union activist. The passion of such leaders comes from intimate knowledge of socioeconomic oppressions, gained through family and work, over a life's time.

Lee Kyung Hae, mentioned earlier as the organizer of a nationwide South Korean Young Farmers group, was an admired farmer-activist whose advocacy became even more fervent when prices dropped, the bank called in his loans, and he, like so many others, lost his land. At the Cancun meeting of the World Trade Organization in 2003, he committed suicide to protest decades of farm policy, which in his last writing he called "inhumane, environmentally degrading, farmer-killing, and undemocratic. It should be stopped immediately. Otherwise the false logic of neoliberalism will wipe out the diversity of global agriculture and be disastrous to all human beings." He was fifty-six. After he died, the *Guardian* reported, "Cancun echoed with thousands of voices, chanting: 'We are all Lee, we are all Lee.'"[79] Most of the farmer-martyrs are nameless, but Lee is remembered all over Asia.

THE END OF THE SESSION

For many traumas, we may rightly feel we can do nothing to help, except whatever follows from listening and understanding. One reviewer of multiple books on food/farm crises concludes, with foreboding, that the world needs "very large outcomes, well beyond an individual's control or even that of a single society."[80] Even democratic nation-states may not be able to control the biggest capitalist players.

Nevertheless, our acts on the consumer end, inspired by new information, empathy (and tastes), count. As organic locavores and sustainable eaters, we can buy more fresh food from CSAs (community-supported agriculture), farmers' markets, and farm stands; donate to food banks; advocate for government programs that distribute fresh food and make land available for victory gardens, and insist, like Brazil, School Food Focus, and Real Food Challenge, that produce for schools come from local farmers. If we have some land or planters, we can grow food organically, thus learning to admire the pros. As food ethicists with some disposable income, we can be willing to pay more if cultivators get a bigger share of it. Otherwise, we can support agricultural unions modeled on Cesar Chavez's, and urge politicians to take small-hold regenerative farming and reforestation seriously. If wealthy, we can divest from institutions that grab land and pollute. With the "green revolution" oversold, our world needs reform at all levels. Governments with such a movement behind them could better protect small farmers, and implement proven strategies for remedying world food insecurity. Not food banks, or food as a market commodity, but *a right to food*, and to healthy food, should be a societal and global demand.

What can be done to help the elder producers on those half-billion farms, a majority of them women, holding on in the difficult circumstances described? None of these actions, valuable as they are, or others that are urged on us, aid *older* farmers directly. Typically, state remedies target the best-identified groups and issues, not necessarily the more precarious subgroups hidden within. Whatever we do, we can hold in mind and heart a new visual icon, the poster elder. For me that would be Julian Chavez, with his withered left arm and his determined right hand, dragging a hoe. Via Orgánica in Mexico trains farmers in regenerative agriculture—minimum tillage, cover cropping, rotation of crops, composting, carbon sequestration in soil. National programs that educated Julian and his son together would dignify both generations, improve yields, and help reverse climate warming.[81]

A universal pension for farmers would help, if it included women. It might seem a utopian dream for countries low on the UNDP's Human Development Index, but two countries that rank low on that index—Lesotho (138th) and Nepal (142nd)—have introduced such plans successfully. China's new system, meager as it is, may have good effects. Larry Willmore, an economist with the UN Secretariat for twenty-six years, says, "Even a small pension transforms an aged person from a burden into an asset for his or her family."[82] Self-esteem reinforces anti-ageism.

A movement in which a seasoned organizer kills himself as a form of principled protest, and in which others are willing to go to jail, and still others, without an organization behind them, take their own lives out of hopeless distress, spotlights the urgency of resistance and the need for protection. Like many Westerners, I had long focused my admiration on the gardens of the tasteful rich and the energetic backyard gardens of my friends, on the high art and big cash outlays of garden design from Capability Brown to Frederick Law Olmsted to the New York High Line of Diller-Scofidio+Renfro. Those complacent elite biases left me ignorant of the grandeur of the half-billion peasants and small and medium farmers who feed much of the world from humble underserved plots. But it is they, many of them old and frail, themselves often ill fed, who currently, for as long as they last, stabilize the food supply for the neediest. They are the stoic heroes of the vulnerable Earth we all depend on.

CHAPTER 5

(

THE ALZHEIMER'S DEFENSE

"FAKING BAD" IN INTERNATIONAL ATROCITY TRIALS

PART ONE: THE MALEFACTORS

Delay, Evasion, Lies, Impunity

After decades of impunity, Ray E. Davis, a retired US Navy captain in his mideighties, was finally charged with providing intelligence to the Chilean secret police that led to the abduction and execution of two American journalists, Charles Horman and Frank Teruggi, in 1973. Soon after the military coup that overthrew Chile's president, Salvador Allende, on September 11th of that year, Davis, then commanding the U.S. Military Group in Chile, reported to the killers that Horman was "subversive." Given Davis's "coordination with Chilean agents during the Pinochet coup d'état, the U.S. commander had been in a position [to] prevent the murder" but failed to take any action. Horman's murder "happened during secret operations against American citizens and was part of Ray E. Davis's intelligence activities."[1]

The charge of accessory to murder against Davis was handed down in 2011 by a Chilean judge, Jorge Zepeda. For almost forty years, few would have bet on any indictment ever coming out of the CIA-backed coup. Peter Kornbluh, an activist who has long been collecting evidence about it, reported that the long-awaited indictment by Judge Zepeda "stunned the families and the world."[2]

The young men—Horman was thirty-one, Teruggi, twenty-four—were working in Chile at the time. Horman, a screenwriter for the state film company, had been on the coast, possibly to investigate secret links between the military plotters and the CIA.[3] His widow, who has spent her life trying to learn what befell him, believes that he uncovered them. "Basically, what Charles encountered in Viña del Mar was a group of American military personnel that were boasting about the smooth operation of the coup, and taking credit for it."[4] Horman was "disappeared," like thousands of others—taken from his home, tortured, and executed.

Getting Ray E. Davis to testify under oath was important, Zepeda knew. Davis, who had also been on the coast, gave the two a lift to the capital, Santiago, shortly before they were arrested. The two men may have talked too trustingly to a fellow American. A State Department memo of 1976, released long after, implicates Davis.[5] The indictment opened the possibility of learning what had really happened to Horman and Teruggi, and meting out a posthumous judgment on General Augusto Pinochet, who engineered the coup and reigned as dictator for seventeen years. Bringing Davis to trial, or even forcing him to undergo a competency hearing, would have been part of a much-deferred dream of justice for the families of the regime's victims, the survivors, and the friends of Chile around the world. Revealing the historical truth of US involvement in Chile might also prevent future international tragedies by guiding foreign policy.

What is most important to age studies, as well as to Americans, Chileans, and international justice, is what happened next, after the indictment of 2011. Although Davis, who had denied involvement in the murders in 2000, was in his mid-eighties, there is no statute of limitations on murder. Davis's wife, living in Niceville, Florida, immediately told the press that her husband had "dementia" and was living in a nursing home. That single word connotes the scariest behaviors linked to end-stage Alzheimer's disease (A.D.): speechlessness, aggression, psychosis, as well as total failure of memory retrieval. Country songwriter Glen Campbell's song addressed to his wife, "Best of all, I'm not gonna miss you," sung at the Academy Awards in 2015, is the standard "dementia" trope that the public has memorized. "Dementia" attracts terrifying metaphors: zombies, life-in-death—all the "horrors" of deranged posthuman existence. Two cultural critics, Mark Schweda and Aagje Swinnen, correctly observe, "The concept of dementia is no longer limited to expert biomedical discourse, but is now functionally integrated into public imagination and popular culture." This means that, for many, "the social construction of A.D. patients as zombies has infused stigma with disgust and terror," as Susan Behuniak, a political scientist, reports.[6] The term "dementia" as a synonym for A.D. is also misleading. Many people who are considered "demented" (an even more harmful locution) speak, respond, long retain memories and affects, and may never become psychotic or aggressive.

What made the news about Davis's condition grimly intriguing was watching his wife deploy what I call the Alzheimer's Defense. Just as a witness emerged—an insider, an agent—the tiny hope of truth was smashed again. "Dementia" had remarkable power. It permitted Patricia Davis to stonewall reporters. She refused to say where Davis was, making it difficult to find and interview him to verify the story. Aversion and ignorance of the range of conditions meant that no reporter pushed her despite Davis's importance as a witness. The symptoms she described to allege his "dementia" functioned better than an alibi to put Davis beyond the reach of media curiosity and the law. Nothing could be discovered about his cognitive status or willingness to testify. We'll never know. As it turned out, Davis was not in the United States at all.

Davis is only one case, and rather a cold case at that. But the allegation of "dementia" alerted me to a story.[7] The knowledge I had gained by then about the problems of diagnosing Alzheimer's and using "dementia" as a synonym for it, made this silence about Davis's whereabouts and mental condition compelling. This curiosity was going to ramify and deepen in unexpected ways. I soon discovered that aging dictators and gangsters increasingly try the Alzheimer's Defense when the law catches up with them. It was about then that my connection to international criminal law became transformed from a world citizen's interest in redress into a cause, or a set of causes, that I, for professional, political, and, ultimately, personal reasons, seemed particularly well suited to undertake.

Americans know a good deal about Charlie Horman and that Chilean coup, compared to the little we usually know about other Cold War interventions, such as the overthrow of President Arbenz in Guatemala in 1954 or President Mossadegh in Iran in 1953. In 1973, millions saw the burning of the Presidential Palace and heard with shock of Allende's suicide. Like the 1950s, the 1970 and 1980s were scoundrel times. Costa-Gavras's award-winning movie *Missing* (1982) tells the harrowing story of Horman's father and his wife, Joyce, searching for Charlie in the chaos after the round-up of dissidents in the Santiago sports stadium. Jack Lemmon plays the patriotic American who slowly becomes disillusioned about his country's role in his son's ghastly execution. The embassy knew of Horman's arrest while he was still alive.

My friends and I discussed the role of the United States in the coup, and then the revelations in *Missing*, with compassion and outrage. The coup deprived a country of its democracy and was responsible for the deaths of three thousand Chileans and for the exile and imprisonment of hundreds of thousands, as well as for terrorist murders in Washington, DC. The crimes were never forgotten. For much of the world, Chile 1973 is *the* September 11th. Was Davis acting as a vigilante, or doing as ordered from Washington?

With Zepeda's indictment, politics and age issues converge. Aging matters in historical judgments or high-level criminal cases for layered reasons, some not obvious. The life review, a concept first developed by Dr. Robert Butler in 1963, is the thoughtful look back that anyone can take in later life, reevaluating motives, coping with pain, relishing successes.[8] There can also be a politics, or perhaps ethics, of the life review. In old age, some major perpetrators—retired, no longer being paid to lie, unable to return to power, or for other reasons— feel free to describe the crimes they were able to get away with. One stone-cold set of hands-on killers, men who had committed some of the Indonesian government's atrocities in 1965–1966, shamelessly reenacted the murders for filmmaker Joshua Oppenheimer's documentary *The Act of Killing*, until they realized he meant them no good. Some intellectual architects of war crimes become morally capable of expressing some of their less humiliating regrets. (Robert McNamara, deeply responsible for the Vietnam War, was given such a chance by Errol Morris for his film *The Fog of War*.) Henry Kissinger, however, impenitently declared, about his and Richard Nixon's role in supporting the disastrous Chilean coup, "In the Eisenhower period, we would be heroes."[9]

Once the Chilean Supreme Court asked for Davis's extradition from Florida, where they had been led to believe he was living, if Barack Obama's Department of Justice (DOJ) had then had any interest in opening the Cold War case, its first step would have been to conduct its own investigation into the matter, as extradition treaties permit. This can be an alternative or a preliminary to deporting an accused person. But his wife's allegation of Davis's A.D. stifled any public outcry that might have forced the DOJ to respond to charges they and the State Department apparently did not want to face. Whatever resolution or revenge might have been obtained through legal means was foreclosed.

It now appears that Davis was secretly already living in Chile. He would not have needed to be extradited. Reporters might have interviewed him. He was admitted to a Santiago nursing home, possibly around the time of his indictment in 2011. He allegedly died there in 2013. Joyce Horman asked the US Embassy to provide proof of the cancellation of his captain's pension.[10] The results of using that one word, "dementia," were amazing. Davis's wife's uncorroborated Alzheimer's Defense, rather than his death a few years later, stymied truth and justice.

Playing the Alzheimer's Card

Eventually charged with crimes against humanity and extradited back to Chile, General Pinochet himself tried to use mental incapacity as his defense. He kept the Chilean courts busy arguing over his alleged dementia for years. Then a few days after he was finally put under house arrest, he escaped ignominy by dying, age ninety-one. In Guatemala, Umberto Mejía Victores, the ex-general and minister of defense, was finally accused of genocide forty years after the Guatemalan government's savage extermination of two hundred thousand indigenous people. By then it was 2012, and the court found him, in his eighties, unable to testify due to a stroke. His boss, US-backed ex-dictator Efraín Rios Montt, had boasted about his good health and willingness to testify, but in 2015, when he was tried on genocide charges at age eighty-nine, his lawyer pleaded that he was mentally unfit, and the National Forensic Institute concurred. "Their continued freedom is a mockery of the dead," Pamela Yates, the director of *Granito* (*Every Little Grain of Sand*) says in her moving documentary about the futile attempts to bring the guilty to trial.[11]

In Africa, Laurent Gbagbo, former president of the Ivory Coast, aged sixty-six in 2011 when he was finally accused of responsibility for crimes against humanity and solicitation of rape and murder, was offered three expert examinations after his defense argued he had suffered medical, psychological, and cognitive losses. In Asia, a former Khmer Rouge social affairs minister, Ieng Thirith, was facing charges of crimes against humanity, genocide, homicide, torture, and religious persecution in a special court established to bring the dictators of that country to trial. The Khmer Rouge caused the deaths of at least 1.7 million people, during only four years of rule, 1975–1979. In her mid-seventies, Thirith was declared *compos mentis* in 2007, but when the trials finally began in 2011, she too alleged dementia.

Long delay to trial is typical everywhere that courts confront world-historical crimes.[12] Delay is the result first of the putative perpetrators' long impunity; then of the torturous negotiations needed to establish the courts in the first place, then the ordeal of finding witnesses unafraid to speak, then patient and expensive sleuthing to locate documents or forensic evidence of murders that have been long concealed. Lawyers then have to prove that crimes occurred, follow the liability evidence trail to particular commanders, and then connect them to those who did the deeds, so the ringleaders cannot argue they were ignorant. How painstaking and even life-threatening this work is, can be seen in Yates's riveting *Granito*. All of this means that the indicted, unlike the people they allegedly tortured and murdered, have often lived comfortably enough to become old and enjoy a luxurious retirement. They may die before they can be overtaken by public shaming and ignominious imprisonment.

Old age in itself is no defense, as the world has seen in the prosecution of Nazis for the Holocaust. German courts are sending ninety-year-olds to prison. Frailty is no excuse. People can be tried from wheelchairs. They can be tried from gurneys. But elite lawyers around the world know that, if their clients are old enough to make it plausible, the dementia card, the last card in the deck, is available to prove unfitness for trial and maintain impunity to the end of life. So "old age," the definition of which has great cultural diversity, is a coordinated sine qua non for such defendants.

Once a trial finally starts, further delays are occasioned by the need to prove or disprove the alleged dementia. Merely being chronologically old (despite the correlations the media constantly report) is not legally acceptable as evidence of cognitive loss. Through delay, if in no other way, the lawyers often win. Then clients walk out on the courts of justice without offering the survivors, their long-suffering communities, and hardworking victim advocates, a chance to hear any of the hidden truth. Although international courts lack "universal jurisdiction," at least they hold out the promise of justice at last, somewhere on the globe.[13] Countries like Cambodia, Guatemala, the former Yugoslavia, and Chile have endured so much lawlessness, so much high-handed, hard-hearted devastation and shameless impunity, that the mere institution of courts must seem like a miracle. A dubious miracle, like a saint's face seen in a pat of butter.

Alleging "Dementia"

The rise of this historic legal expedient has, by a bitter historical irony, coincided with a historical situation that I, along with other scholars, call the Age of Alzheimer's.

Naming a historical period after its prime mental illness can imply many things, but to begin with it means that by now many people believe that A.D. is becoming more prevalent, that it is difficult and expensive to care for, and that, dreadfully, it "steals the mind." A *New Yorker* cartoon illustrating a serious Jerome Groopman article about the failures of medical research to find a cure shows a white-haired man with large holes cut out of his head and shoulders, the pieces lying on the floor near his feet. After a decade in which President Ronald Reagan showed increasing signs of memory loss that were mostly ignored by the press, a book appeared with the title *Alzheimer's Disease: Coping with a Living Death* (1989). "Living death," in regard to a range of conditions (some not incompatible with being the head of the Free World), entered common parlance.

As Susan Behuniak says, the tropes of disidentification, disgust, and fear undermine empathy and respect for people with the illness. In 2014 the UK Alzheimer's Society held what it chose to call a Zombie Evacuation Race: "You will not only be tackling muddy covered obstacles, you will be dodging the zombies. They are hungry to stop you finishing the race alive—run faster or become one of them!"[14] Here, from people who should be experts in consideration, is the language of cannibalism, metamorphosis into "one of them," and urgent alienation. People overestimate their likelihood of getting A.D., based on conflicting but often exaggerated projections of how many will contract it by a particular year (e.g., 2035) or age (eighty-five/ninety-five). Many lay people think they can correctly recognize the symptoms, on the weak basis of actors' performances in film or hyberbolic descriptions in media articles and fiction.

If you contract "dementia," your age per se is no longer the issue. You can be in your forties, healthy and active. The label overrides your age, capacities, or resilience, your character, and even your title to be considered human. There is increasing evidence that people fear A.D. more than cancer. Shame may accompany a diagnosis, and embarrassment the mere acknowledgment that one is losing memories. People joke about Oldtimer's Disease but hide what they think of as potential symptoms. One person is widely known to have committed a preemptive suicide. Sandra Bem, a highly regarded feminist psychologist, after receiving a diagnosis of A.D., postponed the day of her dying for many years, but eventually followed through. Her family had celebrated her life shortly before. Despite some remonstrance from other family members, her former husband seems to have suggested the day. On that day, he had to help Bem twice when she confused which glass was wine and which was the lethal beverage. He rested beside her as she breathed her last.[15]

"We disown the feelings of weakness and vulnerability that arise at every stage of life, and transfer them instead into older people," Anne Karpf writes in *How to Age*. "With such a heavy load of fragility to bear—their own and that belonging to the rest of us—no wonder they're always shown with walking sticks and walkers."[16] Many thinkers argue there has always been a flight from old age, from debility, and from mental illness. In the twenty-first century, aversion to the conjoint conditions seems to be taking more violent forms. People have told me intently that they intend to commit suicide if they contract A.D. They don't say it in the careless jocular tone in which people say, "Shoot me if I get like that!": they have plans, albeit often vague. (Being the recipient of such confidences is one of the occupational hazards of being known as an age critic in the Age of Alzheimer's.) The feared conditions appear to overlap, not despite, but because of, our much-touted longevity.

In short, that anyone would want to feign this feared illness—pass himself off as a "zombie"—at first sight seems incomprehensible. A layperson logically concludes that no one would lie about it. So, if the question arises whether a person indicted for crimes against humanity should be excused from trial simply because he or she has received a diagnosis of A.D., the answer might seem obvious: *Of course.* A kind of soft ageism can make people sentimental about the unrepentant old, even though they have committed mighty evils. Judge Juan Guzman, in Chile, while he was pondering whether to indict General Pinochet at ninety, at first hesitated, thinking the ex-dictator must be like Guzman's own dear mother at ninety.

Although prosecutors sometimes callously disregard other mental illnesses of criminal defendants, an allegation of A.D. seems more genuine, more worthy of attention. It lacks associations with criminality. If it does not connote innocence, it connotes exculpation. This defense might even be able to evoke a kind of empathetic anticipatory terror in bystanders, jurors, or even judges: how could I, if I had dementia, endure a trial? Perhaps the mere mention of a potentially devastating mental loss elicits a sense of vicarious helplessness: how could Y or Z with dementia possibly remember his or her crimes, monstrous though they were?

One problem with letting the indicted go free is that some suspects fake symptoms. These are not comic TV characters like Uncle Junior, a Mafia killer who is advised to fake forgetfulness in *The Sopranos*, or Betty White's character in *Hot in Cleveland*, also advised (by her roommates) to act confused when being tried for possession of stolen property.[17] The dementia wannabes in criminal cases are real, once powerful abusers of human rights, instigators of civil wars, *génocidaires* whose alleged heinous crimes often were committed over years or decades. They assert A.D. because they prefer the mere stigma of cognitive loss to the abasement of hearing their crimes described by victims, being publicly condemned by authorities, and ending life in prison.

Geriatrics, forensics, and clinical or caregiving experience should cause us to question any naïve or sentimental assumptions. Alzheimer's is hard to

diagnose. A 2011 study found that half of those autopsied who had been identified as having A.D. had been misdiagnosed in life.[18] And people who died
having had no symptoms have been found to have brains with the plaques or
tangles taken to be identifying markers. Even when a clinician's determination
seems correct, A.D. takes different courses. The cognitive capacity of a person
may be indistinguishable from yours or mine for many years. People with A.D.
have written books about it. Suzanne England, a social worker and humanistic age critic acutely aware of decline stereotypes, was surprised that her aunt,
although depressed, did not show other symptoms that England had thought
universal: "There was no steady decline but rather a plateauing."[19] In some situations, the metaphor of a swooping mountain range might be more apt. Experts
know that people who have lost memories may have at the same time plenty
of terra firma of recall, astuteness, and capacity for fraud. People with A.D.
can have a memory loss one day and remember with sharply etched details on
another. We are misled if we think the course of any case of A.D. is like another.
In any case, people who play the A.D. card may have other cognitive or psychiatric problems, or none.

The Psychiatric Expert Circus

If the data and stories about psychiatric misdiagnoses and symptom variability
do not make one reluctant to believe attributions of dementia, the history of
the Alzheimer's Defense in criminal prosecutions in atrocity trials might succeed.[20] Feigning memory loss is highly motivated: it may gain sympathy from
grand juries or judges. In private life, concealing true losses may be hard, but,
in criminal cases, feigning cognitive impairment—"faking bad" on tests, as
it is called—is a not infrequent ploy. Successful play-acting might ultimately
mean incarceration in a locked mental health facility, but it always produces a
desirable delay—by, in the words of two Dutch researchers, Kim van Oorsouw
and Harald Merckelbach, setting in motion the "psychiatric expert circus."[21] In
high-profile cases, defense lawyers shop for neuropsychologists to administer a
battery of tests in hopes of getting the desired expert decision.

Ordinary criminal defendants try this. A Mafia don named Vincent (Chin)
Gigante, who often wandered around Greenwich Village in bathrobe and slip-
pers, mumbling, got his lawyers to contend that he was mentally impaired.
It took seven years of legal battles over competence before he stood trial for
racketeering and conspiring to kill another mobster, and until a judge finally
imposed a twelve-year sentence. In another Mafia case, as told by Selwyn Raab,

"a thorny conspiracy indictment" against Tumac Accetturo was initially upset when he found psychiatrists who classified him as unfit to stand trial. Then the diagnosis was shown as a fraud: " 'I slipped and banged my head in the shower and the Alzheimer's went away,' he told friends."[22]

How can attempts at evasion be detected when they serve as the defense in major international atrocity cases? This is an unexpected, difficult, and absorbing question that has been confronting justice systems in many venues. It has not been of interest before to age critics, who have missed its relevance to our concerns.

Pinochet was faking, exploiting the stereotype of the doddering demented. A vain man and a publicity hound, however, he let his guard down on a TV show. Many malefactors do very much like to chat about their record. In Chile, Judge Guzman heard Pinochet making moral distinctions and cleverly defending himself.[23] Guzman stopped thinking he was indicting his mother and went ahead with the charges. It behooves judges to be a priori skeptical about the Alzheimer's Defense.

Courts have a duty to investigate the claim. And the questions of how A.D. functions as a defense are complex. The issue is not the agent's impairment at the time of the crimes, perhaps decades earlier, but fitness to stand trial now. Jurisdictions vary in how they decide a claim of incompetence. The case of Pavle Strugar, who was tried by the International Criminal Tribunal for the former Yugoslavia (ICTY) in 2004, demonstrates the careful procedures the ICTY thought necessary. In this instance, both the prosecutors and the defense administered tests to Strugar. The prosecution interviewed his nurse, viewed videotapes of the accused interacting with judges, observed him during a court session, and conducted a forensic examination that lasted two days. This thorough review took time. In Strugar, the ICTY Appeals Chamber ruling upheld the Trial Chamber's finding that "an accused claiming to be unfit to stand trial bears the burden of so proving by a preponderance of the evidence."[24] Studies over time, although they should not be unduly prolonged, can bring experts' conflicts to light. After reading the reports, the judges decided that Struger was capable enough and went ahead with the trial. Strugar was convicted. Standards defined by the ICTY in this case are often cited.

In the Cambodian Khmer Rouge trials, the standard is that an accused, in order to effectively exercise his or her rights, must be able to "meaningfully plead, testify, instruct counsel, understand the nature of the changes, the course of the proceedings, the details of the evidence, and the consequences of the proceedings." This standard must be interpreted. In the trial of Laurent Gbagbo, when his psychologist in the Hague testified that he was "the mere shadow of his former self," the Chamber of the ICC tartly responded, "The question is not whether Mr. Gbagbo is at present in full possession of the higher or better faculties he may have had in the past but whether his current capacities are sufficient for him to take part in the proceedings against him."[25]

When Ieng Thirith was freed in 2012 on the grounds of cognitive unfitness, it shocked the survivors who had experienced Pol Pot's murderous sidekicks' deathly campaigns. Millions have watched the trials on television or online. Thirty thousand attended between 2006 and 2014, many of them high school and university students, and the trials continue. "Civil parties," permitted to file alongside the prosecution, sit in the public gallery. Each morning and afternoon, ordinary villagers clamor to be admitted. Many weep on hearing testimony. In these haggard halls only the guilty seem to be above it all. "The court should speed up their work and finish their duty before the two defendants die," says Svay Sophoan, fifty-five, who lost his father and several relatives during the reign of terror.: "I need justice, a justice that comes from a fair trial, because these Khmer Rouge leaders have killed millions of people, not taken just two or three lives."[26]

Many Cambodians considered Thirith's release a mockery of justice. How did this release come about? The Cambodian trial chamber of five judges, the Extraordinary Chambers in the Courts of Cambodia (ECCC), does not work on the same adversarial system as the ICTY, according to Nushin Sarkarati, an advocate for the victims. She told me that the judges had chosen a single geriatrician, John Campbell of New Zealand, to provide the first tests of Thirith's fitness in 2011. Campbell's report was not made public. The only tests mentioned in the media were a simple test of logic and drawing hands on a clock to indicate the time. Clock drawing, part of a brief test called the mini-mental, is possibly the easiest test to fake. Campbell concluded that Thirith had a "moderately severe dementing illness, most probably Alzheimer's disease."[27]

Later, four psychiatrists examined Thirith. One, a Cambodian woman, Dr. Chak Thida, disagreed with the others. She found that Thirith had sufficient mental capacity when questioned by a Cambodian woman in a sensitive way. The civil parties supported Dr. Thida's contention that Thirith was fit enough. The prosecution supported the other doctors. After reading the conflicting reports, the court first decided that the medical evidence of Thirith's condition was "not conclusive." The judges ordered her kept in provisional detention, to try reducing her antipsychotic medications and to receive whatever treatment "may help improve her mental health to such an extent that she becomes fit to stand trial," according to the BBC.[28]

The experts considered whether Thirith was deceiving them and agreed it was unlikely. But the judges disagreed among themselves on her future mental health. The three Cambodian judges felt there was a chance she might improve; they wanted treatment. The two international judges thought there was no basis to think she might recover and thus no basis for medical treatment. Cultural presuppositions about decline in cognition, mistrust in current medicine, or political considerations may have played a role in these disparate results.

In 2012 Thirith was freed into her daughter's care, on condition that she be tested again annually. In line with other trials of accused with terminal illness or cognitive impairment, the charges were not withdrawn; there was no finding of guilt or innocence. The Trial Chamber "undertook to consult with experts every twelve months to ascertain if new treatment options or therapy have been discovered which are likely to restore the Accused's cognitive capacity."[29] Thirith died in 2015.

In Guatemala Judge Carol Patricia Flores also ordered that Umberto Mejía's health be reexamined, with the case to be reopened should his speech improve. Given the passions involved, leaving some slight possibility of trial was a prudent political decision but has left little hope that Mejía will ever testify.

When Ray Davis's indictment came through, his wife averred that Davis "doesn't open his eyes. He doesn't speak. . . . He doesn't recognize me. I don't count anniversaries anymore."[30] But spousal testimony, even if veracious, is not adequate proof in the absence of the accused and absent a variety of functional tests administered by specialists who are alert to the signs and methods of feigning. The rule in jurisprudence is, as it should be, grave caution in evaluating the assertion of Alzheimer's.

Distinguishing the Bluffs

Malingering can actually be improved by getting coaching or modeling one's behavior on Internet research findings about cheating better. Kim van Oorsouw and Harald Merckelbach stress, however, that "intentional poor effort" can sometimes backfire, because people who simulate brain injury tend to perform *more poorly* on tests than do those in brain-damaged control groups. The dissimulators overdo it. On some tests, research would suggest not trying to get a suboptimal score, since some patients diagnosed with A.D. obtain perfect scores. No single test can be reliably used in isolation. Oorsouw wrote me that malingered A.D. might be detectable on several tests, including a 75-scale test called Structured Inventory of Malingered Symptomatology, which has an amnesia subscale to assess feigned memory problems and a section that detects illogical or atypical neurological symptoms. There are other clues. Some defendants demonstrate abilities that are not usually spared at the level of loss they claim (reading a foreign-language newspaper with comprehension might be an example). Their self-report is suspiciously detailed about their losses. They display active agency. By contrast, "genuine amnesia is usually gradual and blurred in onset and termination, contains 'islands of memory', and fades as time passes. Feigned amnesia is often described as sudden in onset, limited to the crime or the events preceding it, and full blown" or total.[31] People who feign A.D. have a luxurious choice: they can either fake total absence or have convenient recalls.

Pamela Merchant, formerly the executive director of the Center for Justice and Accountability in San Francisco, believes that few of the indicted slip through. Merchant, also a former prosecutor in the US Department of Justice, explained to me, "As prosecutors, we would do everything we could to detect and uncover fraudulent claims of dementia or diminished capacity. International courts and tribunals are quite sophisticated and I am confident that they would be able to weed out false claims of incompetency by human rights abusers."[32]

Unfortunately, to date Strugar's is the only major human rights case my CJA informants can recall in which a killer who pleaded dementia was judged competent and then, once found guilty, spent any time in prison. Pinochet died. John Demjanjuk, found guilty on twenty-eight thousand counts of being an accessory to murder at the Sobibor extermination camp, was diagnosed with "bouts of dementia" and died in a nursing home. In Cambodia, Nuon Chea, like Thirith, may slow the legal process long enough to die before being globally dishonored.[33] Sandra Bem, perhaps to avoid being a burden, kills herself. But none of the excused criminals—loathed by compatriots, probably guilty of heinous crimes, and judged to be suffering from conditions that will end more or less as Bem thought hers would end—chooses suicide.

The dementia defense, however necessary in law and clement in principle, turns out in practice to be another obstruction to justice in these already long overdue trials. Individuals charged with war crimes numbered in the high two hundreds as of the end of 2010.[34] Hundreds of thousands of trials are yet to come in the former Yugoslavia, in Africa, and in Latin America. As secretary of state on September 11, 1973, Kissinger stands out as a person of interest. Like Pinochet, in televised conversation he appears to have undiminished capacity. If he were indicted by Judge Zepeda, however, he, too, now in his late eighties, might claim forgetfulness. Many of the accused will evade retribution, for various reasons. A false dementia defense should not be one of them.

The Politics of the Trials

Age and disability politics converge with justice interests in evaluating these trials. Since determination of fitness is necessary, if the Department of Justice had agreed to a hearing when Chile requested Davis's extradition, then he would have been tested by both sides. An assessment would have achieved several worthy objectives. On the political side, it would have shed light and discredit on the Nixon administration's intervention in Chile, educated the public about what happened to Charles Horman and Frank Teruggi, and raised respect for human rights in the present, when, as in the cases of Anwar al-Awlaqi and Samir Khan, the Obama administration arrogates to itself directly killing American citizens without trial. Given that Obama announced the end of the Cold War in 2016 in Cuba, it is high time for a presidential apology to the Horman and Teruggi families and the Chilean people for American's deadly and pointless anticommunism.

Another worthy ethical objective is to decide whether the accused should be tried even if judges conclude they have A.D. Survivors, many of them old, and having endured the long impunity, want to see the defendants in the dock. The survivors and younger members of their families want answers to historic questions that to them have never grown less urgent—any kind of testimony or regret. Many are frustrated, riven by impatience, grief, and rage. Some want retaliation. In the years when Pinochet's dictatorship seemed perpetual, a middle-class Chilean woman, Clemencia Isaura, then in her seventies, felt lost "in the wasteland of her late-life frustrations." In Gabriel Garcia Márquez's telling, Isaura said that she had discovered her true vocation: conspiracy and armed struggle. "Better than dying in bed . . . I'd prefer to go out in a street fight against the cops with a bellyful of lead."[35]

Even if Davis, Ieng Thirith, Kissinger, or others were to lack total recall, that might matter less than whatever facts and feelings they could still supply. Some of the guilty might express remorse, assuaging the agony of the people in the courtroom, people seeking corroboration of their memories and historical truth. At a minimum, they want the guilty to have to listen to hearing their crimes treated as detestable rather than heroic. But under most current legal regimes, requiring an alleged criminal who has been excused to be a witness (even if he or she wanted to testify) is impossible.

PART TWO: THE INNOCENTS IN THE AGE OF ALZHEIMER'S

This special session is about two kinds of justice, one legal, one interpersonal. It is a painful intimate irony that Ieng Thirith, an accused *génocidaire*, received cautiously monitored medication and the most alert psychiatric attention to her ability to function, while our good mothers and fathers, at the first signs of memory deficiency, may be treated to automatic prescriptions of useless or harmful or expensive drugs, and to social irritation, indifference, disdain, shunning, medical abandonment, or incitements to kill themselves.

An investigation of Ray Davis's mental fitness, carried out in the United States, would have provided incalculable cultural benefits, over and above the political ones. As a nation terrified about memory loss, ours would benefit from watching lawyers in a fair and high-stakes contest trying to sort out the vast array of conditions scrambled together under the label "Alzheimer's." An A.D. defense, probed in front of the world, might prove how wide the spectrum of cognitive deficits is. Neatly dividing "us" from "them" doesn't work. We need "binary defiance" workshops, like those that trans people have held to convince us that a spectrum of sexualities exists. Better informed discussion of Asperger's humanized the autism spectrum. The same conversation might help with this set of cognitive impairments.

Problems arise of measuring accurately, when precise measurement matters—whether for criminal justice or for human decency and dignity. Some think they will "recognize A.D. when I see it." For caregiving purposes, a diagnosis may be useless. One set of markers in spinal fluid can supposedly indicate A.D. long before symptoms appear. ET scans showing beta-amyloid plaques have little predictive power, Jerome Groopman reports. MRIs, which can identify brain lesions or activity, "reveal little or nothing . . . in terms of levels of impairment across cognitive, emotional, and behavioral spheres," according to Daniel A. Martell, a neuropsychologist. A radiologist, Dr. James Katz, confirmed to me that an image "evaluates anatomy, not physiology. It shows what thinks look like, not how they function." Between 1998 and 2013, there were 101 unsuccessful attempts to develop a treatment for A.D.[36] There are no vaccines or cures, and the drugs supposed to delay symptoms work, if they do, only for a short time.

A riveting public assessment of fitness in a major tribunal—like Thirith's, but covered by the media blow by blow—could demonstrate how test results conflict, and how experts can disagree about them. Before deciding that Strugar's level of impairment was only mild, the judges in the ICTY observed the accused closely for a period of five months. They noted that Strugar was capable of raising concerns with his counselor and with the court, thus participating in the process. Most significantly for everyday contexts, the judges criticized Strugar's defense expert for emphasizing diagnosis—what labels could be applied—and "the possible effects of such disorders" rather than focusing on "actual effects" and "relevant capacities."[37] Actual functioning is what not only foreign courts, but loved ones and caregivers, nursing home staff and policy makers, op-ed writers and novelists, ought to focus on.

A.D. Diagnoses and Precursor Diagnoses

Beyond Pavle Strugar, Ieng Thirith, Ray Davis, and Vincent Gigante lie intimate and societal questions that matter urgently to all of us who are not criminals. In normal life, in kitchens, and around the water cooler, what does a label of impairment mean, aside from a stigma that may immediately affect all of our human relations, many for the worse? Will people around us talk to us normally without prejudice? Or will some, guided by fear for themselves and dread for us, anticipating the most drastic possible impairment, treat us to baby talk, or avoid us, find us a burden to come, wish us out of the way? In stark contrast to the torturers and executioners on trial, we have a powerful interest in proving that a wide range of abilities remains after a diagnosis has been pronounced.

Who determines whether we have a pejorative label applied to us? In the Age of Alzheimer's, the medical model means that physicians and psychiatrists assume they will decide. From their point of view, the earlier a label is applied, the better.

The MCI label (mild cognitive impairment, as it used to be called) is often taken as a precursor of A.D. As such, it has been increasingly criticized. The reasons are methodological, clinical, philosophical, social, and ethical. In the UK, the National Screening Committee decided against mandating universal testing in people over sixty-five because the test is unreliable. The committee found that out of one hundred people tested, twelve would be told they had "dementia" when they did not, and one case would be missed. Clinicians recognize the "clinical heterogeneity of individuals labelled with MCI," as Kevin Peters and Steven Katz point out in an issue of *Dementia* dedicated to these concerns. Further, a meta-analysis of many well-designed studies, by A. J. Mitchell and M. Shiri-Feshki, reports that even after ten years, more than 60 percent of people with mild impairment will not convert to Alzheimer's. A metasynthesis of studies of people diagnosed with MCI concluded, "It remains uncertain whether fact and fiction have yet been distinguished even in the expert discourses of research and medicine."[38]

Elizabeth Milwain, a psychologist at the Oxford Project to Investigate Memory and Ageing (OPTIMA), pointed out with lucid exasperation in the *Lancet* that the question of whether MCI is a useful diagnostic category is equivalent to asking if "all healthy elderly people with a memory complaint who score below 1.5 standard deviation from the mean in a memory test share a neurological disorder,, which is clearly unreasonable." Summing up the situation, Peter Whitehouse, the co-author of *The Myth of Alzheimer's*, and Harry Moody, the co-author of *Aging: Concepts and Controversies*, conclude that MCI shows a "hardening" of categories, is a dangerous label, and should not be used clinically.[39]

Although MCI is medically baffling and the use of the term controversial, to say the least, some mental health professionals have empowered themselves, godlike, to reify by naming. The *Diagnostic and Statistical Manual of Mental Disorders* (DSM)—"a taxonomy whose importance to the field of mental health cannot be overstated," according to Dr. Marcia Angell—tells psychiatrists what counts as a mental illness and how to diagnose it. Angell, the former editor of the prestigious *New England Journal of Medicine*, points out in the *New York Review of Books* that "not only did the DSM become the bible of psychiatry, but like the real Bible, it depended a lot on something akin to revelation. There are no citations of scientific studies to support its decisions."[40]

This controversial guide is intended to be a tool to help avoid misdiagnosis. In 2013, its diagnostic categories grew. A new section of the DSM-5 lists *mild neurocognitive disorder* without mentioning MCI, adding further confusion. Psychologists and social workers say the category is necessary to permit them to receive payment for providing therapy, instead of medication, to worried people. They are helping one person at a time—someone who might not need therapy if not for the trauma of receiving the label. Given how hard MCI is to define, it may not make sense to burden many millions with inaccurate, anxiety-producing, and stigmatizing testing.

Many wise heads argue against the diagnostic creep of the DSM-5 because it escalates our social risks. Margaret Price, an English professor at Spelman College, points out that "often the very terms used to name persons with mental disabilities have explicitly foreclosed our status as persons." Dr. Paula Caplan, the lead editor of *Bias in Psychiatric Diagnosis*, told me,

> It is a good idea to notice when someone we love has even a mild cognitive impairment, in order to consider whether accommodations are needed to make their and our lives easier, but that is very different from making the often-erroneous assumption that if a mild impairment is identified, there is any medical treatment that will be helpful, and it carries the danger of unwarranted pathologizing of the person, that is, treating them as though they are mentally ill rather than as though they are having mild problems of memory or thinking.[41]

The clinical terms "MCI" or "mild neurocognitive disorder" shrivel the imagined distance between normal memory loss, on the one hand, and the dreaded, zombiefied end of the A.D. spectrum.

If you or I begin to lose recall of proper nouns and source memory—common complaints that may start in middle life—we might well do a cost-benefit analysis of getting tested neurologically. On the pro side, according to the boosters for testing, is the possibility that after taking complex tests we will be told we have nothing to worry about. Or that we have something treatable, such as benign brain tumors, strokes, metabolic problems, medication effects, alcoholism, or hydrocephalus.

Or the worried forgetful, weighing current stigma against the potential ability to receive reimbursed treatment for adjusting to the stigma, might eschew the old MCI and the new DSM-5 labels. They might look to their internist for other etiologies—anxiety, depression, the shaming of people aging toward old age (feelings which exaggerate all supposed symptoms)—and treat that issue while waiting to see how any symptoms resolve. One by one, constructing a less stigmatizing nation makes more sense right now than obeisance to a new category of mental illness.

The Essence That Remains

By the time my mother was nearing her mid-nineties, her engaging midlife geriatrician had decided she did have Alzheimer's. He gave her no test—no clockface, no counting back from 100 by 7s (which she would have aced)—and he didn't tell her. He squatted on his heels next to her chair, listened to her, and appreciated her character. "The more you start with, the more you retain," he said, acknowledging the role of education and work-sharpened abilities in later-life cognition, and, in her particular instance, her rationality, wit, and language skills. My own verdict was still vascular events, since I had been present for a transient ischemic attack. "It's not Alzheimer's," I told my mother, marveling at her Scrabble prowess. We continued to call it "moderate memory loss."

Warm, charming, and encouraging to all she met, in her assisted living residence she chatted alike with the cognitive elite and the residents they tried to avoid (which began to include her). She told well-crafted Jewish jokes, gossiped about relatives, recalled heroes she and I shared, like Paul Robeson, John Dewey, and Maggie Kuhn. She was Heritage Central. Some people dismiss repetitiveness as a boring tic. I was enjoying her jokes, historical allusions, and precious family stories more than ever. I needed to hear her tell them again and again because I was memorizing some.

I've kept her closest secrets and I maintain her dignity posthumously. But she wouldn't mind my telling the following details, although some are intimate. She wanted her life to be useful.[42]

For years, focused elsewhere, I was not alert to her memory losses. But she was. She made observations about her cognitive processes as if she were a neurologist. "I have no frame of reference," she stated factually, about people she recalled having known well. She, with her recently great executive abilities, reported, "I have lost initiative." I was already wary of labeling and its nefarious effects on self-esteem and social relations. "You're over ninety, after all," I told her. "Old age is a factor." Sometimes she was saddened, saying "My memory is an abyss." Other times she said serenely, "My memory is my worst enemy and my best friend." She had short crises of confusion and anger, but they were rare. She seemed less frightened than I was.

Listening to her, even when she gossiped or sang "Avanti Popolo," I was often angry at first, exhausted by the steepness of my learning curve and by holding on to a few old conflicts. For my own sake I started reading the work of brilliant gerontologists who engage with the memory-impaired. They convinced me that I was right to overcome my anxiety by focusing her and myself on her strengths. My mother was living, often contentedly, on those solid islands of land around the lagoons of loss. I made a decision to live with her there. As always, I turned to her for advice. In her living room, I started to take notes. "Who knows, Mum," I said happily, "maybe this can go into another book."

(Some does, in chapter 7.) Having been a first-grade teacher for twenty-five years, she was accustomed to being admired. Posthumous recognition is a cheerful thought. She enjoyed that. I did too. There's not much you can give back after receiving a lifetime of gifts.

Truth is, forgetfulness seemed to make my mother more pithily quotable. Much mind is left as various memories depart. When people have appreciative listeners, what they can produce improves. I wrote up her biography so the aides would know what to talk to her about aside from themselves. It described her values as a teacher, feminist, union member; her preferences in clothes, food, music, activities. The aides could read aloud excerpts from my books, where she figured as a model, and restore her selfhood in moments when she felt it had abandoned her. When hospice aides eventually took shifts at the apartment, I made sure they too read the short bio. Conversation, I said firmly, was part of the job description. As my mother weakened, I asked the aides to start a second log, not for meds, but for recording her witticisms, songs, and the advice she gave them. Actual subjectivity—in all its winding, unexpected courses (some revealed first-hand in A.D. memoirs)—was what I was after. The medical logs I later jettisoned. But these others I saved, because they confirm how much she remained Betty Morganroth deep into cognitive impairment, macular degeneration, and physical weakness.

This was our time to reciprocate and make her as happy as possible. She steadily enjoyed my husband and me, music, singing, talk, visits from her great-granddaughter and grandson. Nothing cheered her like stories of our successes—true for so many parents. Maintaining her self-esteem in newly disorienting frailty, she sometimes said, "I am doing my best."[43] Hugging her, I'd repeat warmly, "Your best is very good indeed." How good was my best? I was often anxious, grieving for my future loss prematurely, hiding that as best I could. I had to solve problems, some of which surged up with calamitous speed.

We want to play our parts in the conversation as long as we can before the final silence, don't we? Until days before she died, I could count on my mother for repartee. As an unknown writer puts it, she lost nothing of "her essence, the expression of her most beautiful qualities." When her words didn't quite make sense, I knew what she meant and could respond. Her last words to me, as I left one evening, were "Bye, baby." I was with her in her last hours. Every story of A.D.—and this is true of any terminal illness—must be different. If you say my mother and I were lucky, I won't argue much. We had five close years together, off and on our best and our worse, before she died, at ninety-six, in July 2010.

In 2011, when Ray Davis's wife played the Alzheimer's Defense, I was ready to follow that story into any courtroom that would pursue the vestiges of cognition with a vengeance.

Dignity

A woman in her seventies was caring for her older husband, "Bart," with advanced A.D. He had been admired as a professor, scholar, and poet. One day Bart said to her, wide-eyed, "I don't know who I am."

"You are my beloved."

A pause. "I can understand that."

This kind woman tells her husband directly that one of his last and most important self-identities is a relationship she prizes. Without social inclusion, individuals lose whatever selfhood they have, as the professor knew even at that point.

Carrying appreciation of what remains out of the courtroom setting, we see freshly how important it is to observe our loved ones carefully, to respond to their best intentions. We can listen at least as hard as international prosecutors for sense-making and sensibility. Our charge is to slow down, noticing what abilities are spared: language, art-making, humor, emotional intelligence, loving kindness. Untrained people can learn rewarding lessons about what maintaining someone else's personhood requires. Better relationships will result. Tom Kitwood, whose books on personhood lead a movement to listen to people diagnosed with A.D., teaches us manners when he notices that people who can barely speak can perfectly well understand mocking or intimidating or affectionate tones of voice. Anne Basting, who has done theater with people with A.D., thinks we overvalue remembering: *Forget Memory* is the title of her influential book. When speech fails, caregivers keep communication going, perhaps more warmly, by touch and tone. People who have been fearful of terminal illnesses from afar, by providing person-centered care may transcend much of what is irrational, narcissistic, frightened, or overwhelming in the actual situation and the discourse that frames it.

In a chapter about people in the final stages of memory loss, at the time when they can no longer socially reciprocate, Ronald Dworkin writes, "Every person has moral standing, such that it is intrinsically, objectively important how his [*sic*] life goes." Dworkin, a philosopher, goes on with delicate exactness. "We mark his continued moral standing . . . by insisting that nothing be done to or for him that, in our community's vocabulary of respect denies him dignity."[44] Deciding acts that meet this criterion may be hard, but we can support the effort.

The stories of my mother and Professor Bart are anecdotal additions to the "vast literature demonstrating the meaningful lives such individuals continue to live," as Renée Beard and Tara Neary write.[45] In *A Separation*, an Iranian film directed by Asghar Farhadi (2011), the wife, Simin, bitterly rebukes her husband, Nader, for his devotion to his invalided, cognitively impaired father, which prevents him from fleeing the country with her. She says, as if that ended discussion, "He doesn't remember who you are."

Nader retorts, "But I remember that he is my father."

We uphold our own dignity, too, by our treatment of others.

Working for Our Defense

Closely observing the medico-legal uncertainties of a fitness assessment enlightens us about cognitive impairments among the innocent. When prosecutors and the defense set up a legal battle over a client's mental status, it is actually a battle about what counts as evidence, and how competence is defined. A defense team, like Strugar's or Gbagbo's, seeking as a last-ditch stand to prove their clients' deficiencies, often prefers test results, keeping clear of actual functioning. They try to shrink the distance between drawing clock hands awry and such signs of real mental absence as speechlessness, confusion, or hallucinations. So do we shrink that distance, in jest, when we utter the formulaic "Oldtimer's disease" just because we forget a date or name.

A true judge, by doubting paper-test results and waiting patiently to discover competencies, is symbolically on the side of all of us: to wit, anyone growing past youth with visible memory loss and all neuro-atypicals of any age. Our true defenders are those attentive to the million ways in which we remain ourselves. In the UK, according to the first two statutory principles of the Mental Capacity Act (2005, 2007), the presumption is in our favor. "A person must be assumed to have capacity unless it is established that they lack capacity." Perhaps even more importantly, "A person is not to be treated as unable to make a decision unless all practicable steps to help him to do so have been taken without success."[46]

The innocent, unlike criminal defendants, have a stake in envisioning cognitive abilities as a very broad spectrum, widening the distance (in years and capabilities) from mere forgetfulness to full-fledged A.D. or other disease. On the other side of this conceptual wall, although they are unlikely to see it this way, are those whose interests lie in locating our failures as early as possible in the life course, and are believed when they prognosticate the worst case scenario as our eventual state. Alva Nöe, a neuroscientist and a professor of philosophy, sums up the critique. "Like teenagers, neuroscience is in the grip of technology; it has a grandiose sense of its own abilities."[47] Most of neuroscience's good intentions around memory reside, as it were, in mice. Others on the far side of the wall include researchers seeking precursor markers, the pharmaceutical companies looking to commercialize our minds by hyping their drugs, the authors of the DSM-5 who invented the new label, even the Alzheimer's associations when they reify A.D. and spread the fear of longevity.

Public resistance could also critique well-meaning protective policies that fall short. In a funded program called "Dementia Friendly America," communities are training police and volunteers to relate politely and cordially to signs of confusion and agitation in strangers. Since people who are or seem mentally ill can be shot by untrained police, good training is certainly worth the money. But this effort, although applauded at the 2015 White House Conference on Aging in 2015, calls strangers who appear confused, if they are older, "persons with dementia," "dementia sufferers."[48] The assumption is wrong. They might just be lost, and Siri unhelpful. The continued use of the designation does not reduce fear or aversion on the street or in the family. I eschew the term "dementia." To be truly friendly, we would find another word about those we want to cozy up to.

THE END OF THE SESSION

Normal life—the ability to feel "connected with his [sic] past and moving toward a creative-productive future"—can continue, writes Heinz Kohut, the self-psychologist, "only as, *at each stage in his life*, [a person] experiences certain representatives of his human surroundings as joyfully responding to him, as available to him as sources of idealized strength and calmness, as being silently present but in essence like him, and, at any rate, able to grasp his inner life more or less accurately so that their responses are attuned to his needs."[49] To Laurence Nolan, a professor of Law, "Having a sense of belonging means that the older person . . . is an insider, not an outsider. A sense of belonging includes feeling secure, being able to participate, being recognized and valued by others, and fitting in with one's environment."[50] To Nolan, ageist ableism is rejection. I believe its opposite, social integration, is a human right. It cannot be enforced by law, but we should respect it enough to confer on others. I fear I need to add that, instead of planning suicide, we ought to try to calm our own anticipations. Do unto ourselves as we would do unto others is the rule of self-compassion.

This chapter takes a fresh if indirect route to awaken interest in problems of measurement and stigma, to recruit caregivers into the revolutionary personhood movement of A.D. or deepen the commitment of those already in it. If this transnational story of dementia claims, impunity, and testing has a lesson in it, it is this: we must do justice to the innocent who are cognitively impaired, or are imagined to be. Since there are so many more innocents, and they are so close to us—indeed, they *are* us—the argument of justice becomes more compelling.

But, as Margreet Th. Bruens notes, improving "care culture does not mean that dominant opinions about organizational care and people with dementia will also change."[51] Especially for people who believe that memory impairment leads inevitably to A.D., either diagnosis or misdiagnosis carries predictable sequelae of shame and dread—as well as, of course, the whole admirable human range of resilient philosophical, psychological, practical, and spiritual responses to uncertainty and loss.

In the 1980s, it was HIV that terrified the world. "Mild cognitive impairment" was in fact first widely used in relation to people with HIV. HIV, considered a precursor diagnosis, was thought to lead infallibly to AIDS. The stigma had a choke-hold on society. The Age of Alzheimer's has obvious parallels with that period, in terms of bad jokes, scientific ignorance, rumors, apocalyptic writing in the media, stereotyping and avoidance of sufferers—a pile-on of stigma. If scientists learn the cause of A.D., it may no longer prove to be a biological fate. But uncensured dehumanization makes it, now, a social fate. Aversion from the victims of A.D. and hostility toward their existence endanger the very lives of the people to be protected.

Over the shouts of "crisis" from the public square, we can rarely hear resistant voices. Anything that helps us become more rational about people with memory loss and more closely connected to them would be a healthy leap forward for American society, and, given the influence of our science and our media abroad, for the globalized world as a whole.

CHAPTER 6

☾

OUR FRIGHTENED WORLD

FANTASIES OF EUTHANASIA
AND PREEMPTIVE SUICIDE

Examine carefully the behavior of these people:
Find it surprising though not unusual
Inexplicable though normal
Incomprehensible though it is the rule.
. . . Ask yourselves whether it is necessary
Especially if it is usual.

                          —Bertholt Brecht, Prologue, *The Exception and the Rule*

In photography, "shooting" old people is a metaphor, which hints that the click of the shutter sometimes has disgust or pity behind it. But shooting can also be literal. A book that starts with a metaphor now reckons with loaded guns.

This special session collects a troubling variety of current discourses and situations which, as they become common, increase estrangement from disabled older people. Alienation from designated minority groups raises a burning question about *age*: How far toward violence (real killing or incitement to suicide) does social exclusion carry a society?

KILLERS IN REAL LIFE, THE MEDIA, AND THE LAW

In the circumstances of later-life illness, some old men kill old women who could scarcely be more closely related to them—their wives. John Wise, the Ohio man mentioned in chapter 1, shot his wife as she was dying in the hospital. Another man, Dan Crabtree, age eighty-four, who was beginning to exhibit signs of Alzheimer's Disease, shot and killed his wife, Carol, who was severely arthritic and wheelchair-bound but otherwise unimpaired. His killed his son's wife, Rita Delehanty, age sixty-two, who had early-onset A.D. He and Carol had been caring for their daughter-in-law during the day. Then Dan shot himself.

The media like sensation. The *Today* show featured this dreadful crime for a report on caregiving, titled "Alzheimer's Extracts a High Price on Caregivers Too."[1] "Too" implies that we know enough about the victims' sufferings; time to empathize with these overworked "carers," even when they kill. Caregiving is "tough," we are told, as we are invited to imagine the horrors of caring for the disabled. Society has a "ghoulish interest [in] the extremities to which dementia can lead," writes Hannah Zeilig, a British humanist gerontologist.[2]

Among the addled "extremities" is *Today*'s sympathy for the son. Although homicide and suicide can be devastating for surviving children, Jim Crabtree, who has just lost his entire family, tells his support group calmly, "It sounds like a horrible violent end, but in actuality it was a euthanasia that my father did. It was a great gift that my father was able to give me. He ended my Alzheimer's and elder-care issues at once."[3] No one on the show criticizes Jim's stance that the murders were "mercy killings" rather than acts of derangement, or notices that this way of ending "elder-care issues" involves killing elders. If caregiver stress were the main problem, why didn't Dan Crabtree, John Wise, and others end their distress by killing themselves? Homicide-suicide among old people has become an emerging public health concern. A killing occurs once every two weeks in Florida alone.[4] The perpetrators are mostly male, although 63 percent of caregivers for chronically ill adults are women.[5] Wife-killers almost invariably use guns. There are firearms in 40 percent of households headed by someone age fifty or older.[6] (Older women do sometimes kill their spouses, or try to, but usually in retaliation for abuse.) Incidence of murder-suicide is low but rising among male caregivers over fifty-five, according to Julie Malphurs and Donna Cohen. As with police killings of African Americans, the crisis is marked by a pattern of deadly violence in a relationship that should be protective.

Understanding the grave troubles of unpaid family caregivers is urgent. The United States has particular problems coping with chronic and end-of-life care. Hospice is inadequately funded. In forty-five states, assisted dying—which I voted for in Massachusetts after many hesitations[7]—is unavailable. Without national long-term care insurance, with pensions disappearing, late-life care is drainingly exhausting and expensive. Most people who accept the responsibility, whether out of love or out of necessity, are untrained.[8] People may spend all their waking hours, and some that should be dedicated to sleep, in giving care. Anxiety about end-of-life care (whether giving it or receiving it) spreads far beyond these overworked millions. Contextualization of the right kind would be welcome.

But isn't any pity pass for a murderous "caregiver" misplaced? In Oregon, where a doctor helping someone end his or her life is legal, the decision involves a deliberative process. People diagnosed with six months to live must make a request twice in writing, over a two-week period.[9] Prescribed pills, not a bullet, end their lives. Even when relabeled "euthanasia," shooting your wife is clearly distinguishable from treatment refusal, treatment withdrawal, and assisted dying, by the absence of consent. It is illegal and reprehensible.

Others sometimes speak posthumously for the corpse, alleging that "she wanted to die." This may be the worst form of "speaking for." The victim having said so is not implausible, but if true would be insufficient. Victims may not have felt hopeless. In news articles occasionally, we hear a plaintive daughter's voice: "My mother *liked* her life." My mother did too, even when her memory losses were compounded by growing blindness. An affiliate of the international group of disabled people, Not Dead Yet, explains, "Sometimes conditions mislabeled last stages are far from last, and sometimes conditions mislabeled terminal are merely incurable, like many of our own conditions."[10] Oregonians with six months to live, who receive prescriptions for hastening death, do not always use them.

Healthy people are not good at imagining how they will feel about living-with-dying.[11] People who say, "Shoot me if *that* ever happens" often feel, after the shock of discovery, a strong desire to prolong life. *Life Itself* (2014), an intimate documentary about the film critic Roger Ebert, who had throat cancer, reports that he said once, "I want to die." But a person may thus express a state of intense suffering rather than be formulating a clear positive wish for someone to end it. Caregivers might be moved to express loving sorrow, as Ebert's wife was, without being moved to homicide. Ebert, living with the loss of his lower jaw , insisted that the documentary show his suction machine as well as his ability to communicate and engage with family. "Much of the capacity to resist the process of objectification derives from the exercise of personal agency and the capacity to display a socially recognized intent," Chris Gilleard and Paul Higgs write, about overcoming abjection.[12]

Killers do not always terminate themselves afterward, but the law is lenient to an old man with a gun (who is typically white). The legal system, usually hard on homicide, often swerves toward mercy for the uxoricide. George Sanders, eighty-six, was arrested after killing his wife, Virginia, eighty-one, who had long had multiple sclerosis. (A.D. is not the sole cause of the alleged need for "mercy killing.") At the trial, Sanders's son, sobbing, affirmed, "My lifelong hero is my dad."[13] George Sanders says his wife "begged" him to kill her shortly before she was to be admitted to a hospital. Did the prosecutor ask for an advance written request?

News reports lack any sense that up-to-date consent is an issue. Yet no one, we assume—however pained, sick, or brain-injured—wants to be shot.

When his patient is dying "too slowly," some men do not feel high urgency about asking her what she wants as end-of-life care. Sanders was allowed to plead guilty to manslaughter and was sentenced to two years of unsupervised probation.[14] Although over one in ten elderly people who live at home experience abuse each year, journalists don't ask whether these killers had a rap sheet or a history of impatient rage; whether they were depressed, alcoholic, taking drugs with violent side-effects.[15] Journalists can be quite romantic about them. "Did he just not want to go on without her?" a caregiver blog speculated sentimentally, about another high-profile murder-suicide.[16]

Journalists reviewing the conviction of John Wise observed, "The shooting leaves authorities in a dilemma some experts say *will happen with greater frequency as the baby boom generation ages*—what is the appropriate punishment when a relative kills a loved one *to end their suffering?* More often than not, a husband who kills an ailing wife never goes to trial and lands a plea deal with a sentence that carries no more than a few years in prison, research has shown. In some instances, there are no charges."[17] Autism is becoming more common too, but a mother who kills her severely autistic child gets the book thrown at her. Wise first received a life sentence, but his prosecutor too reduced the charge to manslaughter.[18] Not Dead Yet argues that the consequences for murdering one's disabled spouse or child should be equal to killing people without disabilities. But prosecutors often act as if femi/senicide is a victimless crime. Use of the term "mercy killing" takes the pain and violence out of "killing." Age may factor in. Like *génocidaires*, the accused killers are "old." The truism that "old people are going to die anyway" may help justify the trolls' hate speech, homicide, and legal leniency. D.A.s, accustomed to prosecuting stereotypical "young black male shooters," on seeing an atypical "old white man with a gun," may simply think "Daddy."[19] Not even the will of the state to deter, by inflicting punishment after an irreversible crime, operates reliably here.

Frail elderly or chronically ill people and their paid caregivers used to be invisible in American popular culture. And when care means concern, consideration, communication, conversation, comfort, or cash support, invisibility still reigns. But when Alzheimer's is at issue and violent death results, ethical issues blur. The law often colludes with men's Wild West independent problem-solving. Lethal acts can be stamped merciful. And the news media circulate a message of impunity and "understanding."

If getting old is synonymous with being female (because more women live to be eighty or one hundred, and "dementia" is becoming synonymous with getting old), A.D. is increasingly a woman's disease. As media discourses relentlessly pound the expensive demographic catastrophe under way, despite admiration for longevity in the abstract, the risks of living "too long" are becoming more severe: it's bad of women with A.D. to live on, and, unlike some *génocidaires*, they are never faking.[20] Now, for this extra reason, A.D. can be a woman's fear. This unsuspected war on defenseless women could be another motive for backing gun reform. When I mentioned the Florida homicides to a girlfriend married twenty years, she said, "We better watch our backs."

"In a moral account of harm-doing, some allowance can be made for those who act wrongly under duress," writes my friend A., the philosophy professor, who prefers to be anonymous. About those who end their caregiving via "euthanasia," A. suggests, "They did not want to be flawed or distressed. They wanted to react with some accomplishment. But it's as if their preparation didn't dovetail with the foreseen inevitable events, some lapse in life's education." A significant question—whether these men, as caregivers, could afford aides, or were receiving any support from the extended family—is rarely asked. Respite care is available to family caregivers but varies tremendously by state.[21] Is Florida, a neoliberal state, offering below-par services? Were any of the perpetrators being treated for depression? As in the film *Amour*, discussed later in this session, men may not seek help for themselves. Help would be merciful to the desperate husband and to the dependent wife as well, providing her with freshly patient faces and activities.

Meanwhile, must popular culture valorize any old man who "takes charge" by reaching for a weapon? Should they be forgiven because they never got the training in patience that many women get, their "lapse in life's education"? Are wife-killers even to be admired, as long as assisted dying and long-term insurance are unavailable?

NOT DEAD YET

The assumption that people who "have" Alzheimer's, or who merely believe they do, will want to die preemptively is part of the American terror and cultural sickness about this disease. How that assumption is spreading—beyond criminals to normal folk and influential writers and film directors—is the gist of this session. For the slaughter of old women to be repudiated legally and morally, a cultural critic must not only bring it to notice but show how ageist emotions of aversion and disgust are sustained or aggravated. For instigations to suicide to be challenged, we need to witness how a preemptive desire to die is made increasingly plausible. Suicide can be a private option without becoming a social fate.

In almost all femi/senicides, media sympathy that is transferred posthumously to the perpetrator might more usefully go to the woman who died atrociously. The functional abilities of the silenced victim, not to mention her feelings, go unmentioned. Her right to live is ignored. Like news articles about the murders, "Mainstream films [such as *The Savages, Away from Her,* and *Iris*] frequently concentrate on the plight of the carers and reinforce medical models of the condition [A.D.] as obscure and impenetrable."[22] The activists of Not Dead Yet should not have to anticipate that one reaction to its name might be an irritable "Why *not?!*"

I write here as a woman of a certain age, a former unpaid caregiver, and a potential "social burden" (a not uncommon location) as well as an age critic and social philosopher. The typical crime stories about wife-killing seem ignorant and morally obtuse; the judicial outcomes, cruelly biased. Losing one's memory little by little, living with a dreaded terminal illness, and struggling to find pleasantness in everyday life—these may be hard enough without being treated as "socially dead" and finding one's caregiver distressingly impatient, not to say nasty, argumentative, or violent. The prevalence of abuse in private, and increasingly abusive language in public, is traumatizing. *These* are burdens we scarcely hear about.

When many anticipate with dread needing care or providing the duty of care, what is missing from our cultural imaginary, deep below the terror, is the goodness of ordinary life. AARP writes admiringly, "Every day, a silent army of Americans performs a great labor of love: caring for aging [or disabled] parents, spouses, brothers, sisters, aunts, uncles, friends."[23] Most of the older male family caregivers (who are disproportionately Asian, Latino, African American) are capable, nurturing, adaptable, and innovative. They feel they are protecting their wives, repaying years of being cared for.[24] If fear of other people's helplessness and mortality went as deep as some analysts think, all this would be impossible. The United States may be predominantly heartland after all, while the discourses I am tracking foul the public air.

Louis Theroux's documentary *Extreme Love: Dementia* seems influenced by the person-centered care movement. Theroux interviews a family living in "circumstances that can be among the strangest and most challenging imaginable," meaning, dealing with A.D.[25] Selina is in her forties. Doing the clock test, she is embarrassed, not knowing where to put the numbers. In her presence, her husband says that "in two years she won't recognize her daughter." In front of the staring camera, Selina has no option but to laugh. Said privately, this would be mean. Said before a stranger, it is rude, disempowering, falsely scientific, and treacherous.[26] This husband hasn't learned that he can no longer unload his fears on his wife, now that they are *about* her. When Selina says she wants to see her daughter grow up, Theroux generously responds, "There's plenty of time." Selina nods, relieved that someone, even a stranger, is not counting down her days of consciousness. "Slow and sweet," the nine-year-old daughter reminds her father, about how best to treat that perennially embarrassed woman who is his wife.

Constructing "the Burden"

We need to hear and appreciate examples of loving kindness that supports dignity (Selena's daughter, Nader, the professor's wife) because the label "dementia" marks a category change into something like no longer being human. People used to say, admiringly, about a person living "somewhere near the end": "Still going strong." "Bless his heart." Some still do. But others think, "He lived long enough." Or even, "She's lived too long." The slide from one of these vocabularies to the other is becoming normalized. "A Life Worth Ending" was the title of an article in *New York* magazine by a midlife son about his mother.[27] In the millennial history of dying, many adult children have fervently prayed for a parent's swifter death. Many do still, silently. But some feel entitled to shout out their futile wish to four hundred thousand readers. Once they might have been ashamed to openly deny their parent a life-prolonging treatment. Now editors can be found to publish their death fantasies.

The femi/senicide stories expose murderous impatience at caregiving. The media's burdensome "burden" stories edge toward justifying such feelings. If irritated impatience toward suffering parents comes out of a filial relationship that should be protective, what value can old lives have for strangers? In her classroom in chapter 3, Sofi introduced the term "burden" to her students, but not its history. Formerly, using that word could be justified as a way of empathizing with neglected caregivers. In the past few years, however, the mainstream media have been shifting the term's meaning: from hard caregiving work to the person for whom the work is done. *She* is the burden. *They* are expensively "dying." The frustrated, accusative shift has come about with striking rapidity. The trope of "the burden" derives in part, writes anthropologist Sarah Lamb, from "[a] burgeoning discourse on the topic of 'successful aging,'" alternatively labeled "active," "healthy," or "productive."[28] This individualistic and impossible ideal is endorsed by medicine, psychology, and public health, and is prevalent in popular conversation and self-help books. National austerity politics underwrites it. Those who are sick and old, or disabled and old, are felt to have failed.

The *Atlantic Monthly* permitted Sandra Tsing Loh to tell, at length, "Why Caring for My Aging Father Has Me Wishing He Would Die."[29] Writers regularly invade their parents' privacy to reveal their weaknesses and humiliations. Joe Klein, in a *Time* issue whose cover promises advice about "How to Die," begrudges his mother a heart-valve operation (an example of Medicare's "unnecessary expenditures") that cost $100,000, even though she lived a full decade longer.[30] The *New York Times'* sidebar description of its long-lived blog, "The New Old Age," explicitly stated that caregiving for our parents is a "burden": "Thanks to the marvels of medical science, our parents are living longer than ever before. Most will spend years dependent on others for the most basic needs. That burden falls to their baby boomer children."[31]

"Most basic needs" is winking code here for diaper-changing and spoon-feeding. It doesn't say that caring for a *husband's* "basic needs" is a burden. Its formulation, "our parents," in fact insultingly excludes an eighty-year-old caring for her life partner or helping amortize the kids' mortgage. The intended audience is midlife offspring. (The midlifers can be maligned as "greedy" all-powerful "Boomers,"[32] but when their parents are Othered as here, the younger cohort gets only sympathy for their trials.) Writing the genre of the burden memoir, will our adult children feel it obligatory, as Philip Roth and others have done, to include the first sight of our naked penises or vaginas, the scene of the shit they have to clean up?

When midlife adults turn to major media outlets for authoritative information about the economy, they learn about their tax burden and the nation's
"entitlement" deficits. When they go to learn about health, they're smacked
with their parents' diseases and their own risks of dementia. "Statistical pan-
ics," as Professor Kathleen Woodward terms them, often have doubtful bases in
fact.[33] Risk assessment and misinformation (whether about the future percentage of A.D. sufferers, or about the causes of budget deficits) come laden with
emotion construction.

Even experts collude in creating terror. Although some pursue a "dementia-
friendly" society, other so-called bioethicists have called for "setting limits" to
life for people who suffer from some combination of age, physical frailty, and
mental disability. Their particular human situations come labeled as if they
described a stage of life, like toddlerdom or adolescence: "the Fourth Age."
Many critical gerontologists dislike the term, but others persist in using it. (A
fuzzy but reifying and dehumanizing category, it is avoided in this book.)

Neither doctors nor the media appropriately emphasize *undertreatment*,
although people are terrified they can't get the care that might help: "the SOL—
shit-out-of-luck—people," as the daughter of a Floridian bitterly described
her mother. As noted in chapter 1, many surgeons would act on their belief
that a patient's age justifies denying treatment. Previously healthy women with
stage IIA breast cancer, the *Oncologist* reported, would be likely to receive less
therapy if they are seventy-five than if they are sixty-three, although the older
women, covered by Medicare, might be eligible for the same benefits.[34] This
is undertreatment.

Although many Americans abhor the idea of removing tubes from coma-
tose patients, the killing of old and sick people, especially those with some
cognitive impairment, may be moving into a different moral/conceptual/emo-
tional space. As I learned when researching an earlier book, the image of "the
old Eskimo on the ice floe" appeals to many people who don't object to—or
notice—the socially coerced nature of that mythical form of killing.[35]

Adults are increasingly overt about wanting to avoid the much-advertised
specters of dependency for themselves. Can anyone seriously fantasize about
dying young to avoid old age? Well, yes. Some, in print. Dr. Ezekiel Emanuel writes at length in the *Atlantic* essay, quoted by Sofi in chapter 3, about
why he "hopes" to die by seventy-five. His father, since his heart bypass at
seventy-seven, is barely *living*: "as my father demonstrates, the contemporary
dying process has been elongated."[36] Emanuel père, however, dares to say he is

happy. No doubt, as Emerson knew, what "does not decay" in him feels "central and controlling."

Ezekiel, once chief of clinical bioethics at NIH, wants to reason readers, some certainly seventy-five and over, into feeling that it's not worth living after that age. This bigot sets a high threshold for wanting to try to live: not just absence of disability, but productivity, animation, speed! Add cognitive impairment: Who would be so selfish as to inflict their reduced selfhood on their offspring? But people way over sixty-five are often sturdy, disease-free; they are wanted as organ donors.[37] Their good health is the reason they enjoy longevity. And were they to live longer than they might want, they cannot die by willing it.

Doctors having "The Conversation" (as it is called, as if it superseded all others) about end-of-life care sometimes discuss with their patient the reasons for deciding to stop treatments. This sounds like common sense: another option. But incentives from "fee for service" are weakening. A label of MCI or A.D. might factor into the options a physician lays out. Anyone over sixty-five might worry about undertreatment when they hear adult children publicly doubting the value of their parents' prolongevity, on top of pundits saying the nation can't afford to save them. Too many sources repeat with alarming frequency how expensive "old people" are to treat, how unwanted "overtreatment" is. It doesn't create trust.

The statements I have highlighted are irrational; one-sided, cruel, apparently unconscious of bias. Why are they widespread? I am unsure. Some gerontologists think we should follow the money. The Boomer children will inherit a windfall as their Great Generation parents, who were scrimpers, die. Roz Chast, the graphic novelist admired for her frankness about her parents' last years, avows an "admittedly selfish bitterness about how much less there would be left for me when they died."[38] Another explanation is psychological. Children hurt by their parents' greater and sometimes malign power may remain angry deep into adult life. Borrowing from Shelley's anti-imperialist poem, "Ozymandias," Dr. Eugene Halpert suggests some children felt their parents were omnipotent. Now, for these adult offspring, "Two vast and trunkless legs of stone / Stand in the desert," still showing "a sneer of cold command."[39]

Younger or healthier people's fears for themselves as declining subjects can be disowned by being projected onto the age/disability class. In this "unconscious phantasy . . . unwanted or unmanageable aspects of the self are split off and located in someone else who is then identified with those aspects of the self," Paul Terry, a clinical psychologist, suggests.[40] (Remember the stereotypes

Young Judges acquire: *Old people are dependent, alone, confused, in misery. Not me in any way. They* must *want to die.* This is not pity.) Frightened by their misconceptions of the life course, some Young Judges act, as Melanie Klein might say, on this projective identification. The ageist aggressively dumps his load of unwanted emotions onto the Other. The abuser harms and the killer eliminates the abjected object he himself has sullied.

Like fear of death, fear of growing old and sick fluctuates historically. Now it is surging at this nexus of disability and longevity. In "aging nations," people are taught to be frightened of living with too many old people, in a nation whose "health" is said to be in jeopardy from the minority who are old and the minority of those who are also sick. Even gerontologists can't keep themselves from repeating the A.D. data projections, dangerous as doing so is now, with irresponsible punditry insinuating that dependent old people are an insoluble problem.

Suicidal and parricidal fantasies (*I would want to die, and so must they*) are hard to extricate. At younger ages, people can become alarmed that they may come to be considered burdens by their adult children or society or, worse, both. Most of the life course is not memory but our anticipated narrative. As Rüdiger Kunow convincingly theorizes, "the [speculative] future is always already there, requiring action in the here and now." Preempting "aging" as decline used to involve only youthfulness: fitness regimes, plastic surgery, "anti-aging" products as they become available. Even "choice"—a value feminism has widely instilled, without always noticing the irrational pressures that might influence a lethal choice in later life—supports what Kunow calls "the preemptive imagination."[41] Few observers expect "required actions" to go beyond what are lightly called "enhancements." But "dementia" makes fear of growing old worse than fear of dying. With big voices combining to strengthen the feeling that there is a generalized duty "not to be a burden," "preempting aging" can now include self-conferred death. By our own choice and for our own sakes.

Out of this overdetermined panicky culture of feeling, new characters who are old and ill are emerging into literature and film. Two action figures emerge in the next half of the chapter: the person with cognitive impairment who wants to commit suicide (in a film, *Poetry*, and in a Tony Kushner play), and the caregiving "mercy" killer who gets "understood" (in the film *Amour*). Serious writers are linking *the will to kill* or *the desire to die* with age. Is the figure bearing burden-shame becoming a literary fixture? Will the figure of hysterical lethal distress become more common? Cultural analysis must try to factor in all the ageisms, starting with the loaded gun, the dead women in the coroners' offices, the prosecutors' lenient charges, the access to the media given to tendentious adult children, backed up by the neoliberal determination to evaporate government responsibility for long-term care. What about works of art? Can we trust artists with this anguished material? Do writers have any responsibility to understand their conditions of production? These are our next questions.

EMPATHY CAN BE DANGEROUS

Empathy is powerful and literature is one of the major ways we experience it. George Eliot put this beautifully: "The greatest benefit we owe to the artist, whether painter, poet, or novelist, is the extension of our sympathies. . . . A picture of human life such as a great artist can give, surprises even the trivial and the selfish into that attention to what is apart from themselves, which may be called the raw material of moral sentiment."[42] Empathy of the right kind leads to intersubjectivity, psychologists tell us, and thus opens the way to community building. But empathy can also be dangerous. Not only because it overrides reason and objectivity, as Bertolt Brecht argued.[43] My quarrel with particular empathetic texts aims to bring to the surface their hidden agendas. Empathy, precisely, for whom? Against whom? On what ethical grounds?

Reading, Toni Morrison writes, requires "being alert and ready for unaccountable beauty, for the intricateness or simple elegance of the writer's imagination, for the world that imagination evokes." But it also requires, Morrison continues, in her insightful book of cultural criticism, *Playing in the Dark*, "being mindful of the places where imagination sabotages itself, locks its own gates, pollutes its vision."[44] I heard Morrison give the original lectures on how whiteness imagines blackness. I was irritated to be told, even ever so nicely, that I had missed the racism when reading Henry James and other canonical writers. Rushing home to search favorite texts, I was chastened. "Morrison is right!" She had given me new impetus to read writers vigilantly for any of their inchoate, fearful projections.

How is the reader being positioned in texts when younger writers imagine disabled old age? For this campaign of discovery, we need a more nervy, freewheeling, and wide-ranging critique to confront unexamined bias: *Playing in the Dark*, meet Jonathan Cobb and Richard Sennett's *The Hidden Injuries of Class* (1993); meet Kate Millett's *Sexual Politics* (1969); meet age studies. When writers imagine age in our time, they are rarely as enlightened as they are about otherness generated by racism, classism, sexism, or homophobia. Age is often unexamined otherness.

The bellwether texts I single out next are not blatantly ageist or ableist. They are rich in empathic concern for (some) older characters. But these works are written, produced, and received amid the widespread panic over A.D. and aging-as-decline, in a culture in crisis from top to bottom. Empathy, doled out selectively in literature, obscuring relevant facts or adjacent persons, can lead to affective conclusions that are (touchingly) wrongheaded. A writer can be like a frightened child given a doll, who tears off its pink plastic arms. So with playwrights and directors who choose to pick up the Alzheimer's doll, and wind up smothering it or stuffing pills down its throat or drowning it. Watching them artfully play with the disease of the century leaves this age critic somber.

Poetry, Pathology, Pathos

Many characters in recent plays or film become, or think they will become, "demented." Cognitive weakness is suddenly glued to being the oldest person in the dramatis personae. Boston theater has had a few such characters. One London season (2011–2012) had several.[45] I focus on works that are highly regarded, either because they win prizes or because the writer is so distinguished that his work claims critical attention. In Chang-dong Lee's film *Poetry*, his protagonist Mi-ja is over sixty. In a play by Tony Kushner, Gus Marcantonio is seventy-plus. In Michael Haneke's film *Amour*, Georges and Anne are in their eighties. Suicide is demonstrated in the first two as an appropriate response to a level of cognitive impairment far lower than the vulgar concept of "dementia." Murder is made understandable in the third.

Poetry was seen by many more people than usually see South Korean art films, because it was nominated for an Academy Award as Best Foreign Film. This film focuses on an older woman, a gentle spirit who drowns herself soon after being told she has Alzheimer's. Viewers are expected to recognize that the medical diagnosis is true merely because Mi-ja forgets a single word ("station") when she leaves the hospital after receiving the terrible news. A wiser doctor, in a different genre, would have warned her about "anxiety amnesia" or depression after a traumatic revelation about her health.

Mi-ja has another, nonmedical, risk factor for suicide. She is placed in a grim ethical situation in which she feels her honor is at stake. Her teenage grandson was part of a group of students who raped a classmate repeatedly. The girl drowned herself in the river. The parents of the other boys want to give the girl's family money, and Mi-ja finds herself paying her daughter's share and then reporting her grandson to the police. In a shame culture with strong hierarchical responsibilities, erasing his dishonor through destroying herself is not an impossible motive for a matriarch. Her life has few crumbs of comfort besides writing poetry. When the policeman comes, she can foresee losing her entire family. Neither her daughter nor her grandson will forgive her.

Mi-ja is lonely and strikingly honorable, but to the point of taking her life? (The ending is a long take of the same brimming, fast-flowing river. Some Western viewers, not wanting her to die, doubt that this shot implies her drowning.) The plot of A.D. seems to be brought in to solidify the implied suicide of the ending. A film script as impenetrable about Mi-ja's feelings, and as weak on evidence for her condition, needed to multiply her motives.

It's worth focusing on the "precursor diagnosis." As I pointed out in "Faking Bad," DSM-5 disease-mongering means clinicians might provide MCI or A.D. diagnoses to millions of people, a hefty percentage of which will be inaccurate. Yet MCI, doubtful as a diagnostic tool, is known to create hopelessness in people said to have it, some of whom see it as a precursor to A.D. Might diagnoses, true or false, lead to preemptive suicides? *Poetry* softens the jarring leap to death with emotional restraint and cinematographic beauty. Might *Poetry* have been welcomed because it represents sorrow and regret for a predicament—family abandonment and suicide—that some currently foresee as destiny? You and I will still have a duty to die, but someone will cry about it. That's elegy.

Failure to Rescue

When AIDS became the most feared disease in the country, and people with HIV were shunned, and dementia was one of the terrifying AIDS symptoms, some of the infected killed themselves. In response, Tony Kushner came to the rescue with the dazzlingly hopeful and aggrieved *Angels in America*. "And then in a shower of unearthly white light, spreading great opalescent gray-silver wings," an angel, crying "Greetings, Prophet; The Great Work begins," descends to protect the sick; a gay man who abandons his stricken lover is corruscated with scorn; Ethel Rosenberg haunts Roy Cohn when he is alone, also dying of AIDS.[46] Revenge heroically abounds. By the end of the play, divine and human companionship surround the ailing.

Kushner is no new kid on the block where medical conditions crudely entangled with social issues are concerned.

But now it's twenty years later. And with Alzheimer's the most feared disease in the country, Kushner writes *The Intelligent Homosexual's Guide to Capitalism and Socialism, with a Key to the Scriptures*, about a seventy-two-year-old widower who tells his children that he is planning to kill himself that weekend because, he says, he has A.D. "The action, like that of *The Cherry Orchard*, begins with the arrival of the extended family and ends . . . with their departure."[47] Toward the end, Gus Marcantonio, sitting in his dark kitchen, awaits the delivery of a bag of lethal drugs. Shelle, the widow of a fellow longshoreman, arrives when Gus is wrung out, offering the remains of a stash her husband used to end his suffering from amyotrophic lateral sclerosis. Far from being told how best to survive adversity, viewers (who included me in New York City in 2011) are told exactly how to die in a presumably failsafe way, how not to regurgitate or panic. Those who believe in rational suicide praise Kushner for including such a scene, although anyone has been able to find the information (now on the Internet) since Derek Humphrey's *Final Exit* (1991).

Gus hasn't seen a neurologist, and calls what he has only incipient. In the first act, he becomes desperate at a lapse, being unable to remember the year his father died (he does, minutes later). "Blank spaces, not like forgetfulness, but like *trying to remember* has become this dangerous thing, it . . . pulls me into the blank space, I'm . . . I become the irretrievable, I go away."[48] This totalizing statement has memorable plausibility, as if it were snatched from poetic autobiography rather than fiction. When I forget a proper name, I don't heighten my sense of peril by metaphors implying that blankness becomes the only me. In life, Gus might have mild cognitive impairment. Or not. In our current toxic atmosphere, "trying to remember" has become dangerous. Those who know the unreliability of MCI labeling can be appalled at Kushner's making a plot depend on it.

How is it possible that Kushner, a visionary who rallied so courageously on behalf of people with HIV-AIDS in the early 1990s, fails to find a way of defending people with MCI or early A.D. when this is the new self-despising illness? Kushner knows AIDS history. People wrote testimonies; they acted up. Drugs emerged to treat the disease.[49] The stigmas lessened. Talking about slavery, Kushner had wisely described "a kind of deep, interior damage that's done to any people who are told they don't belong to themselves."[50] People are told that if they get A.D. they will no longer "belong to themselves." Unless Kushner now believes that HIV sufferers should have sought death early instead of writing as they did—giving instructions about how to live better longer[51]—he of all people should not have written this plot, that scene, with that big bag of pills.

What turned the Angel into a death-dealer? Is it the way Kushner, who was fifty-three when he started writing the play, feels about later life? Can he not identify with sufferers who are no longer potential love objects? Does he not recognize the "interior damage" wrought on people aging-past-youth? Only a writer, having examined his own blind spots, can say. "I find this particular play very frightening," Kushner said while writing it, "because I don't feel in control. . . . It's about old-fashioned Freudian things like death drives: things that are antithetical to progress and hope. But I have to explore it—not to get rid of it but to give it its full voice and power."[52] For a writer who believes in history, social support, and economic determinants, the "death drive" (in Freud, an internal, universal, essential drive) makes no sense.

The New York Times's reviewer dismissed the diagnosis. Ben Brantley argued that Gus's "truer motivation may be a loss of faith. A former longshoreman and union activist . . . he feels that he now lives in a post-Marxian world that has given up and given in." "What you call progress, I call the prison rebuilding itself," Gus tells his daughter, M.T.[53] As a union leader, Gus was forced to put up for a vote a painful labor contract: older members would keep their salaries but the next generation would not benefit. Such votes epitomized the weakness of unionism since 1975. Politically savvy, Gus could know that capitalism ground down millions by such cruel exercises, victimizing two generations and crushing seniority for future generations as they would age. But Gus thinks he personally failed; he is burning the papers that document his union efforts.

Could Gus's suicidal misery have been conveyed without giving him MCI and a creepy public service announcement about methods? Why not? He had slit his wrists a year earlier, before his self-diagnosis. All three children abandon him on the very weekend of his bitter life review, obsessed by their own passions. At one point of head-aching disintegration, Gus starts clapping loudly to drown out their acrimony. Shamed, despairing, his daughter says, "We're helping him do it, we'll drive him to his . . ." (Act Two, Scene 4).

Gus's bitter regret at having betrayed the principle of union, his state of being guilty while guiltless, a man needy for solidarity left in ghastly solitude, an alien to the polis—these reasons for despair are sufficiently heartbreaking. Gus comes from a lineage that pledged money in 1904 to help a noble regicide, Gaetano Bresci, cross the ocean from Paterson, New Jersey, to Italy to kill the brutal king Umberto I, who had fired into a famished crowd rioting for bread. The last scene, where Gus explains his grandfather's long-hidden funding pledge, contrasts Gus's useless suicide to Bresci's heroic self-sacrifice a hundred years before. This moving scene should have been all the play needed to demonstrate the spiritual declension Gus feels so viscerally. His real illness is the impotence of radical activism, individual or collective.

More political than *Death of a Salesman*, with a protagonist admirable in self-knowledge, capable of passing values to his children, *Guide* without A.D. could have been tragic, a play only Kushner could write. Audiences still hurting from the Great Recession, educated by Occupy, might be thought capable of prizing work and resistance as they watched jobs vanish, might understand the sorrow of Gus's life projects wasted, might feel what he feels, "the unbearable enraging injustice of the world that's triumphant now" (Act 4, Scene 2). But by 2011, with the economy apparently improving, Kushner perhaps doubted there was a theatrical market prepared to struggle against the corrosions of capitalism.

In tragedy, a character's self-immolation (Brutus, Antony, Cleopatra) needs an urgent proximate cause. It was a hard task Kushner set, eliminating every possibility of renewal for a protagonist who is eloquent and vital in failure and only seventy-two. Intractable pain wouldn't have worked: his children could not then abandon him. A.D.—actually, mild memory loss with anxiety—was roped in to clinch the hopelessness. Yet a suicide of frightened anticipation seems implausible for a man of such character.

In fact, when elevating Gus's character, *Guide* comes close to attaining the solemn beauty of elegiac loss. But a claim to elegy is undermined by Gus's obstinate resolution. Arguing at his children over hours of stage time, he savages the value of everything: the family house he raised them in, his own life's work, and finally, his daughter's belief that there is no single day on which capitalism is definitively proven omnipotent and uncontestable. To his Cordelia he sets a masochistic Lear-like test: *How much do you love me? Can I drive you away?* His daughter, M.T., the last to leave, honors him until, distraught at failing to dissuade him, she curses the despairing decisiveness that negates her own life project. Like M.T., audiences need Gus Marcantonio to want to live. The more we have shared Gus's values, the less value adheres to him by the end.

Kushner might have saved Gus's character and his play's genre, and obviated agewise viewers' objections, with a few equivocal words. Gus gets his youngest, Vito, out the door only by promising not to kill himself. It appears to be a lie. Gus might add, as if forced to honesty, "I'll do it, Vito, eventually. Not now. It's too soon." In the dim final scene where Gus is left asking a male prostitute what the boy would charge to stay with him, he might be imagined as thinking not how to die, but *whether*. He, and his politics, could be rightly mourned.

Homophobia, a capacious bias, once had disease-terror built into it. Now it is ageism, equally capacious, that carries this terror. It is possible for viewers, like authors, not to notice that MCI is the new HIV, A.D. the new AIDS. The latest word in death sentences.

Explaining Euthanasia

Michael Haneke's *Amour* received an exceptional degree of adulation for a film in which a husband smothers his frail, helpless wife. It won the Oscar for Best Foreign Language film. Although some reviewers hinted that Jean-Louis Trintignant's perfect caregiving as the husband Georges would go sour, most avoided giving away the shock ending. They praised it. The *Boston Globe* praised the film's "hard, hushed sanctity." The *Guardian*, mentioning the "eventual stench of putrefaction," gushed that the husband copes in his own "mad, heroic way."[54]

That a strange film explaining elder homicide-suicide has been highly acclaimed while remaining almost unexamined ethically is worrying. The major implicit conviction of Haneke's plot is that even a loving and patient unpaid caregiver will crack under the strain of caring for a stroke victim, his wife. Since marital caregiving is a scenario lived by millions, this is a visual document whose signature event ramifies into many lives. Georges is so devoted and stoic that only two scenes prepare for his emotional breakdown. One is when he slaps his ailing wife. The other is a dream foretelling violence: Georges is walking down his hallway, which is filling up with water, when he is attacked from behind by a hand covering his nose and mouth. Who would not retaliate to such a brutal home invasion, which is what Anne in her changed state now represents to his unconscious? This scene foreshadows his sudden decision to suffocate her rather than letting her die as she is doing, by refusing food and water.

Anne never repeats her early wish to die, which Georges had then movingly refused to abet. No crucial conversation puts such a wish beyond a reasonable doubt. But despite Anne's struggles as she is suffocating (also clearly shown), viewers may feel they understand Georges and not notice how the film treats *her*. A French friend, viewing Anne empathetically, found the deck stacked against her. "Right away, you are frightened by her circumstances. The husband is very hapless and ignorant, thinking his wife is making fun of him when she is having a minor stroke. . . . You feel that he will be very fragile, more than her."

Some see *Amour* as a beautiful tragedy.[55] This view avoids considering how moral disasters can be prevented. In life we want to learn how to avoid having thoughtful attention turn into exasperation, despair, and slaughter. In *Amour*, Georges first seems to be giving good instructions about the unaccustomed work of nursing. Viewers may feel grateful. But experts—nurses, gerontologists, disability activists—might warn that Georges is *too* dedicated, *too* private. Why don't critics and viewers know more about this body of knowledge, decades into the epidemic? Because of the risks of ill health and depression, and now the temptation to murder, caregivers are advised to get respite care and provide social life for themselves and their loved ones. In Haneke's plot, every claustrophobic choice of independence makes Georges's isolation, and Anne's, greater. His haughty declaration that Anne refuses to be "shown" is ill advised. A more resolute daughter might have persuaded her mother, for as long as possible, to get out for walks in a wheelchair, get her gorgeous haircut, visit a friend. People are no less human because they see themselves as deformed. Their shame should not lead to self-exclusion. Smiles and conversation can convince them they are still likeable.

End-of-life care can need expertise even more than chronic care. Georges doesn't train the obtuse aide; he self-righteously fires her. Grandiosity is a risk for some solitary caregivers: *I can do it all, I can stay the course.* Haneke shows that this is murder: that suffocation means air hunger, a dreadful death. But he omitted a compassionate option. Since 2005, France permits assisted dying. (Euthanasia is illegal.) A doctor who makes house calls, as does their family doctor, Bertier, could have provided adequate pain medication. In an A.D. horror film, alleviations—practical solutions, consoling information—go underreported.

Amour ends with suicide as Georges lurches, left alone, psychically disintegrating. After dressing Anne's body, he seals her room, stalks a bird, hallucinates that Anne speaks, puts on his overcoat, vanishes. Distinct risk factors for murder-suicides, we have seen, include untreated depression and being an older male caregiver.

Insofar as the film engages any character's interior life, the screenwriter seems identified with the male caregiver. Haneke at seventy knew one instance of that role close up. A ninety-two-year-old aunt who had raised him asked him for help in dying. He couldn't do it. When she tried to kill herself, he found her and brought her to the hospital.[56] Haneke seems to have exorcized this trauma through Georges. As a director rather than a nephew, Haneke may also have felt that a long film about patient marital nursing needed violence because otherwise it would be monotonous. It's hard to see how Vienna's Society for Geriatrics and Gerontology could have awarded Haneke a prize for this film.[57]

My father died in 1974 of Lou Gehrig's disease; I helped my mother care for him at home until the end. No statistical panic exaggerated the horror, no compassion for us dared ignore his sufferings, no public voice pressed him to be "still Marty" and save money.

Hidden Wishes

Fantasies express impossible wishes. Impossible can mean dangerous, impractical, illegal, irrational, or guilt-provoking. Writers, too, entertain them. *Amour* may be interpreted as Haneke may have *consciously* meant it to be, given his intimacy with his loving aunt. In this light, it implies a desire to rescue flawed, exhausted, isolated, and bewildered caregivers; support long-term-care reforms and hospice; and legalize assisted dying, hedged with careful precautions.

The fantasies of *Amour*, I daresay, exceed any desire for a more perfect social system. Then what wishes are hidden here? A wish, given the horror, the horror, of Anne's straits, to be a victim of such "mercy"? I doubt it. Merely hearing about the ending of *Amour* pains some members of Not Dead Yet. They seek equal access to suicide prevention, as well as judicial convictions of people trying to leave them dead.

One of *Amour*'s few early critics, the *New Yorker*'s Richard Brody, thinks the writer/director brought viewers into complicity through an overwhelming preponderance of mitigations.[58] I agree. The victim's gender is one. Anne and Georges were played by well-known stars, Emmanuelle Riva and Jean-Louis Trintignant. If Riva had been cast as the caregiver of Trintignant, and had smothered her bedridden husband in a fit of madness, would this film have been embraced by the industry and reviewers? Could Trintignant be shown as Riva is, with his old heavy male body stripped in a shower, uttering humiliating cries? Killing an old woman who has been seen naked is conceivably more acceptable.

The impossible wish, I speculate, is to show a man driven mad enough to eliminate his scruples and end his ordeal. This film details Anne's decline so cruelly and Georges's caring so respectfully that it becomes hard to disagree with his choice or even notice his cruel breakdown. There are at least two fantasies involved. A fantasy is a wish made precisely in "the absence of the object," Anne Anlin Cheng writes.[59] Georges's wish—phrased gently as "I wish I could have helped her die"—is presumably what critics praised, ignoring his wife's lack of consent.

The wish is still forbidden. The ethical argument against killer "caregivers" like Crabtree and Georges is summarized by A., the philosophy professor: "The most salient feature of their state is that they are not at risk of death, so they don't have to act to save themselves." The film deals with this by giving Georges the nightmare of being attacked: The surreal hand smothering his face, the most highly charged image in the movie, is arguably more harrowing than the medium shot of Anne's leg pumping as she is *literally* smothered. Georges's punishment, blurry as it is, is another mitigation. Wishful fantasies of "getting away with" the prohibited thing "are often surprisingly abbreviated," Adam Phillips, a psychoanalyst, observes: "the story of satisfaction is the story we don't know how to tell."[60] Haneke's film expresses a kind of prayer that a tortured murderer be forgiven, for his prior compassionate care and because of the nonbeing he deals himself. Confronted by a homicidal perp, a grand jury of film buffs might see instead the sad, hollow-eyed Trintignant.

Anxiety about caregiving (perhaps worse among those not caring for anyone) embeds fear in the psyche. Georges's breakdown heightens this fear by illustrating the dire consequences of being devoted. Haneke's fantasies, the terrifying and obscure last acts of his film, are especially dangerous to our cultural health. Warmth toward Georges's dedication, carrying him beyond reasoning or self-care, is empathy gone awry. Uncritical "understanding" of Mi-ja's and Gus's wishes for suicide suggests that, besides lacking knowledge of how to help people who are living with lessened competence, frailty, and/or disability, society fails to value them. I don't know a word for this overlapping bias, *ageist ableism*, but we need one. The failures ramify into the arts, nursing, psychiatry, philosophy, law, social policy, and, of course, the home.

These creative works are different from the frustrated or subtly furious articles by adult offspring quoted earlier. Only for Haneke is the illness by itself, worsening, sufficient reason to wish for a death. For Lee and Kushner, the diagnosis is not distressing enough without other deeply wounding causes. All three describe children's abandonment without attributing it to fear of dementia: the offspring are merely preoccupied. One way or another, the duty-to-die will be lonely.

Some people might feel grateful that major artists are choosing to explore the nexus of age and mental disability, long ignored. But making a character's desire for suicide plausible or justifying "mercy killing" is not resistance. Writers may be disowning fears by projecting them, or be captured by preemptive pity for themselves. In an era that is medically baffling, psychologically distressing, commercially tantalizing, and discursively overwrought, this literary development is dangerous. When "repetitions of a mass imaginative failure" become common, Adrienne Rich observed, they may stun even good writers.[61]

THE PILE-ON

Anton Chekhov laid down a rule of foreshadowing: if there is a gun in the first act, it will have gone off before the end of Act 3. Nowadays, if there is A.D. in the first act, there will very likely be a suicide attempt (or a fantasy of murder) by the last. In Peter M. Floyd's play *Absence* (2014), Helen's suicide is only accidentally foiled. Helen, whose language problems are brilliantly staged (the other actors talk fluent and emotional gibberish to her, and the audience is as bewildered as she is), goes to the kitchen looking for a knife and runs into her horrified granddaughter. In *Blackberry Winter* (staged in many regional US theaters in 2015–2016), in her near breakdown toward the end, the loving caregiver says she fantasizes taking her A.D.-impaired but ambulatory mother, whom we never see, out to a wood and braining her with a rock.

Competition for eyeballs creates literary pressure to escalate. Future filmmakers may not feel the need to provide a second motive: Mi-ja's shame, Gus's despair, Georges's madness. They may follow *Still Alice*, which provides only a few degrading symptoms to help viewers understand the allure of suicide. The filmmakers show Julianne Moore lost and dismayed, having peed herself. In *Away from Her* (an A.D. movie from 2006), a caregiver slaps on domestic labels ("refrigerator"). Ads sell "disposable briefs," which makes incontinence private. Yet no one on the team of *Still Alice* thought viewers would think it odd that Alice's family members, with full cognition, had omitted to label the bathroom door for her or provide absorbent panties.

In *Poetry* (in 2011), shame was wordless. In *Still Alice* (2015, only four years later), it results in a video of Alice leaving death instructions for her later self. She becomes placid about living on, having lost the self-estrangement required to kill herself. Anne Tyler has a character, Abby Whitshank, think calmly about her memory problems in *A Spool of Blue Thread*: "It's like when you're drifting off to sleep and a gear sort of slips in your head. . . . It's just tiredness, I imagine."[62] But finding her video by chance, Alice obeys orders. They don't mention dying. Suddenly she is credited with enough executive ability to follow them: she carries her laptop upstairs, finds the pills and the correct icons to replay the instructions, and manages to open one of those tricky child-proof pill bottles. (A reviewer in the *Gerontologist*, who fails to mention the suicidal intention, praises the film for "the accuracy of its details."[63]) The robotic attempt fails. But an undying will to suicide (on the part of people if they are "still" themselves) could scarcely be shown more strongly.

A.D., as portrayed, "symbolizes the overall horror that is assumed to be a part of the aging process," notes Sally Chivers, a film critic in age studies.[64] Soon, I suspect, other diseases linked to later life will be deposited in a first act—ALS, Parkinson's, whichever ailment the writer is most frightened of or thinks his audience might be—and an "understandable" attempt on the targeted life will ensue. Hate speech on the Web, revealing vague fantasies of our disappearance, can perhaps be dismissed; perhaps the criminals who shoot their wives will remain too few to matter. It is much harder to dismiss the heavyweight artists, the arbiters of wisdom.

I fear it is coming to be taken for granted that people with such conditions want to die. I have friends with Parkinson's. They might stumble upon films or a novel, such as Sue Miller's *The Distinguished Guest* (1995), that make them feel uneasy about going on as long as they want. In our frightened world, many people are made to understand that others feel their lives are worth ending. Ageist ableism is becoming a storm of wrong, while the countervailing forces are low-voiced. That is my reluctant conclusion. I hesitated about voting for assisted dying because of such pressures.

My worry extends to all generations. Offspring may feel less urgency about asking sick old parents if they prefer interventions. "Well, well, she has lived long. There must come an end to everything," as the medical assistant says in Chekhov's story "Rothschild's Fiddle." Our culture cannot keep us from grieving. (My mother died in 2010. Recently I broke into tears when the phone rang. I had some news that no one but she could properly appreciate, and it couldn't ever be she who was calling. Grief seems so inevitable that I am amazed the duty-to-die writers don't anticipate it publicly. Like their editors, they imagine an insensitive readership.) In this cold world, an adult child may insist to herself, "I love my mother; I will care well for my mother." Still, a bit of ice may have lodged in her eye. Offspring may be less likely to converse properly—proposing alternatives, offering more care—if a parent or spouse with MCI/A.D. says she or he is collecting lethal pills. If asked to help, how will they respond?

People in good health, not needing to plan their dying, are also being prepared to think more favorably about a future of letting go quickly, docilely, and cheaply, in more yet-to-be-named circumstances. Do you wonder whether culture has already skewed the intimate decisions you may need to make at the end of life? I do. Choice is the keyword. Will my loved ones and I have the mental freedom necessary for autonomous end-of-life decision making? The huge weight of public opinion could press on the backs of afflicted people. Those who want life-prolonging treatment may feel they are bucking a remorseless tide. If I get a diagnosis of A.D., will the correct protocol be for me to offer to die prematurely? Wouldn't that be kinder all round? What defense would I propose if I have a terminal illness but do *not* choose suicide or hospice? In this new script, how would the dialogue with my loved ones go? The writers and directors who provide suicide plots are leading us toward a future we may, helplessly, detest.

Aversion takes flight when it can, to escape from fear—which means whenever no new emotional education intervenes. Who, at this crossroads, with so much in favor of death, is imaginatively helping us want to live?

Passion Is Contagious

"Conscience is the least reliable of our intellectual organs," says Ruth Kluger, a Holocaust survivor who speaks with authority.[65] But since conscience is an organ of emotional intelligence, if not stifled it can grow. Literary empathy can do much. Arthur Kopit's *Wings* is a brilliant play about a former aviatrix locked into aphasia, whose thoughts are worth hearing though only the audience can hear them.

Bring your fear of Alzheimer's and old age to a heartening film based on a true story: *Still Mine* (2012), written and directed by Michael McGowan. The sex scene early on made me want to get in the sack with my husband. We're told the couple have racked up sixty years together.[66] They are awfully attractive: Geneviève Bujold as the petite, witty wife, Irene, who is becoming dangerously forgetful, and James Cromwell as Craig Morrison, six-foot-seven-inches of craggy manhood. Craig is supposed to be eighty-five. Bujold looks younger, with her lined but flawless skin, tilted smile, and that mane of white hair. It's night time, and she is already in a delicate white nightgown.

"Let me see your body, old man," Irene orders unexpectedly, straight-faced.

To her, he is *both* old *and* desirable. Morrison drops his trousers with dispatch; Irene pulls up her nightgown, revealing lovely breasts. The camera shows them naked to just below the waist, and I dare anyone to say it is not a pretty sight. They cling to each other. We see his charmed beaky face. He says, "Sorry."

"For what?" she asks.

The next instant, he declares, "Nothing."

Cut to them lying in bed close together, wearing only each other and "the lineaments of gratified desire," in the words of the poet William Blake. "We have always been good in the passion department," she says.

It's not as if the movie is all about sex. This is only one scene, which I could wish longer, if only by a few seconds. Every second gouges a longed-for hole in the ageist slag that sullies our vision of old people. Older people are told to be ashamed of their bodies; younger people are told sexuality wanes after youth; some scholars say "elderly sex" is characterized in our culture by its "unwatchability." Meanwhile, in private (it appears) something else is going on. Here, we are privileged to watch.

The basis of this marriage must also have been conversation. The couple flirt and talk. Craig, an articulate version of the stereotypical laconic farmer, can be tetchy with others, including their children, who don't match the standards of sly good sense that Irene sets. He counts on her for these qualities even though she won't remember to turn off the stove. When she falls down the stairs, he is the one who says glumly, "I think we're on the downward slope."

Irene is the one who reassures, objecting vigorously, "I don't think so."

"Oh really? How do you figure that?" he inquires, his head cocked toward her, waiting.

"By all rights, I should have broken my hip," she says gleefully, enjoying winning the point against him and holding their luck solid. She hadn't (yet) broken anything at all.

Unlike others who think *Alzheimer's!* and stop treating the person as normal (Selina's husband in *Extreme Love*) or even as "living," Craig waits for Irene's responses; and, like others similarly treated, she mainly rewards good expectation. Irene's canny bridge game infuriates the opposing husband in their foursome. Come to think of it, she is "vigorous, animated, astute, funny, warm, loving." Craig, keeping up with her limitations, doesn't nudge her to remember something forgotten, as the wife in *A Song for Martin* (2002) does. When Craig makes mistakes, he rues them. He is an example of best practices, naturally. His adult offspring wise up to the aptness of his behavior. His trouble with the law comes from his insistence on building his wife a house, easier to navigate, with his own hands.

Viewing the sex scene, younger people might reflect, admiringly, *So this is what sex looks like later on. I can live with that.* Barbara Marshall and Stephen Katz, sociologists of aging, observe that "the biomedical focus on sexual function has added it as another key indicator of successful aging."[67] *Still Mine* is bold in conferring successful desire on a woman with cognitive impairment. As opposed to politicians who abandon "damaged" wives, Craig is possessive. *Still Mine* tops most youthful rom-coms by showing a man who protects his long-loved partner even at the risk of going to jail.

Empathy need not be a zero-sum game. The last atypical achievement of McGowan's superb film is, if I may speak personally, that I identified with both people, enthralled both ways. I could be the one offering patience-centered care, who enjoys carpentry and obstinately finds a way around authority. And I could also be the witty older woman who delights in her husband and continues to cut his hair, and is going to be properly cared for as long as he lives.

A fantasy? Heaven help us if this is not a true story.

The Last of the Five Special Sessions

More than ever, we need the companionship of such stories on the long steep road where affection for a parent or romance with a lover, or, for that matter, self-love, runs headlong into worsening disability. This last session on the traumas of ageist ableism may be the saddest. The pile-on of the duty-to-die ideology works across genres to reach its widening audiences, moving rapidly from marginal voices toward social acceptance, via Internet spew to bloody tabloids, to network news and op-eds, to journals of opinion, to arthouse theaters, to renowned stages of New York, London, Boston, and Berkeley, to reviewers who equate A.D.- suicide fantasies with realism.

I have argued that duty-to-die discourses, when public and shared, seem not far removed from incitements to suicide. The targeted groups (old frail people, older women with mental impairments, people with terminal illnesses) are easily identifiable. Although the group is sometimes pitied as well as demeaned, either feeling creates an atmosphere of dread (for oneself) or avoidance (of others). Incitement—influencing the will to self-harm—can be considered morally wrong even if no action follows. Goading someone to suicide should be taken with the utmost seriousness, just as it is when adolescents yell or text "Jump, Jump" to a peer contemplating suicide. "Concern is not merely with the occurrence of harm but also with its prevention."[68]

The issue here is not proving any instigator's evil intentions, but of raising consciousness about how abject subjects are constructed. Imagine being "a potential dementia patient": as Felicia Nimue Ackerman asks, "Who isn't?"[69] On top of our possible vague notions of memory loss or incontinence are piled extra, specific, threatening cultural weights: the potential violence of husbands; the legal indifference to consent; the obtuseness of crime-beat reporters; the aversion of (some) adult offspring to their frail elders; (some) physicians' and surgeons' prejudices, ignorance, and malpractice; certain writers' tendency to sensationally escalate our fear; government cost-containment efforts; lack of compassionate provision for those who, sure they are free of coercion, do wish to die; weakening respect for those choosing medical treatment. And driving deep into us, the subject of the next chapter: shaming about growing old at a time when "aging" typically means decline.

Still Mine is one antidote. If our time comes, we do not want to fail; we want to be good people, caring for our loved ones with accomplishment. If we wisely anticipate disability, we hope to be cherished in turn. Pass cherishing forward. Be the better angel.

The cultural terrorizing around longevity's ailments will dwindle. No one knows precisely how, but I have faith that it will. Perhaps because I can't bear living in a society that goes further this way. It must. It may well get worse first. The call to action seems plain. What could be nobler than lessening the national terror of A.D., now coterminous with aging, and crushing the ideology of the "duty to die"? Exposed to our broadly streaming culture of death, let us judge it with insight, wrench ourselves away, and demand new expansions of the moral imagination.

CHAPTER 7

❨

INDUCTION INTO THE HALL OF SHAME AND THE WAY OUT

Two More Birthday Parties

Camilla is a sophisticated woman, a well-known writer whom our mutual friend Elinor describes as slim, athletic, and beautiful. Camilla called her to say, "I want to invite you to my sixtieth birthday party . . . [pause] five years late." Her sixty-fifth birthday was coming up, a milestone inscribed in life in these United States because of Social Security. Elinor, who is ten years older, wondered, was Camilla going to pretend to be sixty, or was that a joke?

Camilla broke out, "Oh Elinor, I am getting so old! I'm so ashamed!"

The pleasure Camilla might have derived from enjoying a celebration of herself was obliterated. Although the party hadn't occurred, she vividly imagined it. Having passed as younger for so long, she miserably took for granted that she would lose face. "Notice, then," philosopher Martha Nussbaum observes, "that shame is far from requiring diminished self-regard. In a sense, it requires self-regard as its essential backdrop. It is only because one expects oneself to have worth or even perfection that one will shrink from or cover the evidence of one's nonworth or imperfection." Notice that Nussbaum thinks that verifiable evidence is in question, rather than an *imputation* of imperfection.[1] This is a common error. To correct it, we need to move insistently from *shame*, an internal feeling, to *shaming*—what others are doing to us that makes us vulnerable.

When aging serves as the trigger for ageism, shaming is its weapon.

Through shaming or expected shaming, the self is moved from being its own vital center into being an object, unkindly observed. The problem is not anything one has done, as in *guilt*, but who one *is*. "Shame may be viewed as [one's sense of] living in the minds of others as an undesirable self."[2] Shaming hyperfocuses like a clown mirror. Having sabotaged Camilla's good feelings, like glee at festivities, the funhouse mirror inflates whatever she lacks, blocking the worth she possesses, for herself and others. Shame erases from her mind all those who might not bother about her age one way or another.

Shame can be felt at home alone, but "figures in most social interactions," one astute psychologist, Thomas Scheff, believes. Members of a society may constantly anticipate it, Erving Goffman, one of the great symbolic interactionists, implied. Perhaps age-shaming figures any time we suspect that we might be less wanted than heretofore. Ezekiel Emanuel's father may worry that none of his brilliant sons will want to visit him, now that the whole world knows one son will remember him as "lethargic." Shame may include fear—of being ignored or viewed with contempt, or of enduring the humiliations of violent physical, verbal, or psychological abuse. Whenever ageism is even unconsciously expectable, the self anticipates a *world* of critical others. Suffering can be imagined with age peers or younger people, at any future encounter. A date. A college reunion after years apart. A stressful meeting with adult children. A boss's frown. Public speaking. Occasions of shaming in later life are like occasions of sin: potentially everywhere, since all adults within a wide span of decades are considered old by the majority coming behind.

Shaming linked to "aging" can undermine quite solid identities. It usually does. Without necessarily being conscious of the sources, enlightened people rich in self-compassion, purpose, and companionship can be caught inside the cult of youth and the disgust at age and disability, whirling around us like exhaust fumes in tunnel gridlock. What makes this a crisis or trauma is precisely that it is "an event that does not reflect any of an individual's prior life experiences," as Christin M. Jungers and Leslie Slagel write, offering "Special Considerations for an Aging Population."[3] The anxiety that precedes interactions in later adulthood can be far worse than the age anxiety of middle life, which, in my case, struck early, in my mid-thirties.[4] Then I was wary of the shamers and able to toss them off, *knowing* I was really young. Now I have to agree: I am not young. (That concession is not, of course, the last word. *So what?*)

Feeling ashamed of what we now call "aging" isolates. Even an older feminist, clever about group identities, intersubjectivity, and interpretation, agentic in many areas, furious at her ability to boil herself in shame—even she may think of "aging" as private, innate, asocial, ahistorical, inevitable losses of self: *my* problem (even if shared with friends), *a story about the misery that is me.* Then suddenly, as in a twittery world, my lessened worth goes public. Dignity and self-esteem wounded, valued identities ignored: this won't stop. Ageism fixes each of us as "old" in a bad sense, a dominating new identity we cannot exit from and that nevertheless, in hostile cultural contexts, is considered our *fault.*

Ageism, not aging per se, threatens public exile from all the major age identities one has actively dedicated oneself to: the selves with which we have sturdy, story-worthy histories over a long term. I once chose the formulation "the embodied psyche, in culture, over time," to describe this thick, changing age identity. Considering age-related fear and trauma, I see the formula as too individualistic, unemotional. If we do know to grieve being subject to ageism, it is partly at losing the precious, formerly intact *selfhood-in-relation.*

Threats to the social bonds can injure us along a pain register of duration and intensity delineated by Thomas Scheff, from embarrassment to shame to humiliation and mortification.[5] This chapter focuses on the devastating end of the spectrum of affects that age-oppression provokes, rather than the micro-aggressions. (The micro-aggressions remain perplexing. Our bewildered astonishment rarely goes beyond "How dare they?" Retorts do not spring to mind. Our helplessness burns.) Describing what shame feels like to Brené Brown, who was studying shame-resilience, people used words like *devastating, noxious, consuming, excruciating, diminished, trapped, powerless, isolated.* Brown concludes, "The experience of shame has been revealed to potentially hold the same properties as traumatic events involving intrusions, flashbacks, strong emotional avoidance, hyperarousal, fragmented states of mind, and dissociation." Lodging in many different souls, aging-related shocks can result in self-blame, envy of the younger, avoidance of others, or silence. Self-suppression may follow, along with psychosomatic illness, grief, mourning, and depression.[6] Ageist shaming at its worst, as this book has shown, results in murder and suicidal ideation.

However intense a victim's feelings are, they have been considered "sub-disorder" levels. People who suffer from other socially inflicted attacks, like racism or sexism, are often able to acknowledge their feelings. As we'll see, some victims of ageism barely acknowledge pain.

Ageism probably will lurk in many situations. At an academic gathering, some untenured people are thinking, about a senior scholar: "He'll retire soon, leaving an opening." The collegial setting can now be understood, without cynicism in the age of adjuncts, as a scene of age-tinged envy, Schadenfreude, or generational hatred. Will there be younger people at Camilla's party thinking, "Sixty-five. She's going to eat my Social Security. It won't be there for *me*"? (After years of hearing this drastic policy failure asserted as confidently as if it had already happened, I regard some younger people's witless belief in the propaganda as an enraging certainty.) If Camilla anticipates negative behaviors—The look! Or the looking away—and then notices them, it's not because she "just imagines" that behavior. Or is it? *Have I stupidly misrepresented as ageism someone's innocent sentence/behavior?* (They look innocent because they don't know they are doing wrong.) This maddening doubt must suffuse many encounters, as it could not have done earlier in our lives.

Chloe Zerwick (her real name) told a related birthday party story to the *New York Times*: "In my upstate community . . . I had deliberately concealed my age. However, when I turned ninety, I decided it was time to come out of the closet and had a ninetieth-birthday party attended by what I thought were my nearest and dearest. It was a lovely evening two years ago. And I haven't been invited over by any of them since."[7] Zerwick survived the dawning surprise and isolation of rejection resiliently. In old age it isn't only the death of friends but the unkindness of the living that may leave you lonely. By coming out as ninety-and-abandoned to the entire audience of the *New York Times*, she was courageously using the public power of the long finger of shame to point to the guilty parties, the partygoers.

Zerwick had been able to pass for younger for such a long time, I hypothesize, not only because of her good looks or health but because, *and only as long as*, she hadn't made her age the most salient fact of her identity. People turning thirty-five may hang black balloons to jokily mourn having aged out of the prized eighteen-to-thirty-four commercial demographic, but they do not suffer social abandonment. In late adulthood, however, a "big" birthday can have the effect of stripping us of other accumulated identities to leave us with the one. Of course the hypertrophied salience of age wouldn't matter if aging-into-old-age were impressive and desirable, like, say, turning "double digits." However, the day of the powdered wig for thirty-five-year-olds is long over.

I had managed to avoid identity-stripping on my seventieth birthday, although foregrounding my age, by pointedly asking guests not to bring age-related material to read. It turned out to be easy to separate chronological aging, a cause of celebration, from ageism. The motto "Aging is the process that serves as the trigger for ageism" furnishes a fresh definition of "aging" that works for resisters rather than for detractors. Aging should have nothing to do with shame, and shame should have nothing to do with aging.

Recognizing the Ageism in Shaming

How does aging operate as a trigger in American subcultures? A frank and fearless anti-ageist in her lithe early sixties tells a story on herself. A keynoter, Ashton Applewhite was attending an Art and Science of Aging conference.

> My chiropractor's been giving me balance exercises, so I attended a conference session about preventing falls through better balance. . . . I also learned that I'm still ageist, even in public. When presenters Nancy Mason and Julie Lake asked everyone who was worried about falling to raise their hands, I didn't. Falling is for *older* people, I rationalized in the moment, older than me. That's age denial—and when we're stuck in denial, nothing changes. I did cop to my lapse, sheepishly and out loud, and I hope it made for a teachable moment for someone besides me.

Applewhite, who has been honing her consciousness and ours since 2008 through her blog "Yo! Is This Ageist?" copped to her lapse publicly in her online newsletter. She has written a free downloadable booklet, "Who Me, Ageist?" to help people develop ageism consciousness in groups, and published a major manifesto called *This Chair Rocks* (2016).[8]

In fact, it was disability that Applewhite was identifying with, not aging. Identifying herself as a person with a physical impairment took guts. Recognition that this could be a teachable moment for others made her recovery from passing instantaneous. Applewhite did the opposite of competitive ableism, where people of impressive upper ages boast about skydiving, marathon walking. May her behavior start a new fad of solidarity for pro-aging disability-oriented progressives.

Applewhite's moment of psychic imbalance suggests how difficult it is to make even tested resistances count at moments associated with shaming. If we are not ideologically savvy enough to 'fess up and stand with the reviled group (as Applewhite did), how do we commonly respond to situations where shaming is possible? At this perilous crossroads, shame gives nothing but bad advice.[9] Two responses, although contradictory, coexist.

One is mocking oneself by pointing to one's deficits, the meme I call "I Hate

My Neck." This is often done as a round-robin: "*I* hate my stomach." "*I* hate my . . ." Young Judge, the bully inside, wins.

The other response is the effort that many midlife and older people—including those who never reach for a single "anti-aging" product, not even hair dye—expend to pass for younger. I do it. We enter a room of potential ageists with *the same* presence, speak with *the same* rapidity. Performing ourselves as we have always done avoids, we hope, ageist interactions that will irritate us and embarrass the other, or worse. Passing might cover anything—from clothing, athleticism, tech purchases, vocabulary, ways of walking—by means of which we "mime the dominant" we have long been. We feel intact. Most passing of this kind is slight and (unlike Botox or surgery) fairly harmless.

I mention this not to provoke defensiveness. I want instead to focus on the distinctly dangerous settings and individuals who might startle us into ageist self-consciousness and shame. Does my interlocutor, after a single look (that age glimpse, again), expect that I will drop proper nouns? I am alerted by anxiety. Ethically, I judge him: it is cruel for a younger person to watch an older person (or a child, or anyone considered inferior) with a latent conviction that *this person will fail*. But I may not have the listener's malice uppermost in my mind as I watch him watching my lips. I may have my own lips and brain, exertion and risk, *my age*, foremost in mind. I hesitate. Self-presentation falters. Shaming starts small, but its consequences may be grave.

Mimicking youth too obviously marks the strivers' age, to both parties, as the strivers' primary identity. To be seen to try too hard is to fail at being authentic. The majority age group learns to censure. An earlier chapter in this volume, How (Not) to Shoot Old People, about disrupting the youthful age gaze, noted how expertly trained the gaze is to pick out tiny signs of failure. The young don't like their tastes or lifestyles mimicked, psychologists Michael S. North and Susan T. Fiske report. In fact, some hate it. It spoils their fragile in-group identity. Everyone knows that passing for younger is difficult (and often expensive and demeaning), but these psychologists explain why it is *impossible*. Writer Vivian Gornick, in the tough mode we admire her for, advises that "Instead of pleading with the gentry to be let in—'Look, I can do you to perfection'—those born on the wrong side of the cultural divide must harden their hearts against the hope of inclusion."[10]

Exclusion—the sudden "failure" to be accepted as the self that one has long been—reminds us of Emerson's men, their lip "made up with a heroic determination not to mind it." I may lose my outward composure through the inner earthquake of sudden demotion. Exclusion then produces "the burden of having to reconstitute one's self-identity under 'post-traumatic' conditions."[11]

Moreover, damage to one victim, like a communicable disease, may infect others. As happened to me, in fact, after merely hearing a story told by a woman I will call Violet, who was suffering a post-traumatic state.

DAMAGE

I had a nightmare, the very day after giving a keynote that was enthusiastically applauded at a performance and age-studies conference. My subject lay close to my heart; at times I felt comfortable enough to speak with passion. In my dream, however, I am exhaustedly trying to teach a mass of students in an awkwardly wide room filled with ambient howling like wind or turbulent crowds. I am swinging my head left and right to see them all, shouting a question. In the dreamscape some students answer in reluctant monosyllables, but I can't hear them. The nightmare, full of frustration, is obviously a teacher's scenario of humiliation about losing authority over younger people whom she had hoped to enlighten.

The day after being applauded at the groundbreaking conference, I shouldn't have suffered a nightmare about no longer being listened to. But I instantly understood the proximate cause. Vicarious suffering. At the conference, a strikingly beautiful actress my age with short springy white hair had told a story about a barbaric rehearsal process for *King Lear*. Violet had been the only older person present one day, and no one had picked up on any ideas she offered, although she herself, an admired character actor, was going to play Lear. Violet then kindly decided she would have to go silent the next day to let the young actors speak. They did speak. To borrow a street term used also in psychoanalysis, they dumped on her. On her ideas. "They said they were bored."

"I felt destroyed," she frankly told us. They had publicly stripped her of a major identity as an experienced theater professional. After that, she had barely been able to get through another speech, this time one spoken by the Duke of Gloucester, who stands, as he thinks, above the cliffs at Dover. "Paralysis," she said, overtook her. She labored through Gloucester's suicidal lines of farewell to the gods.

This world I do renounce, and, in your sights,
Shake patiently my great affliction off.

It took her forever to get through it. Shaming typically undoes some vital parts of us. If we stay wordless, it may cause somatic symptoms: from nausea, acid reflux, vomiting, to paralysis. Violet didn't mime *this*; we didn't see a submissive downcast gaze, broken speech, sobs, shaking. Firmly she recounted how she forced her way through her task after the crushing demotion.

But then she said the cast's meanness was her "fault," "for being old." Violet felt she was wrong, rather than that she had *been wronged*. For Camilla, shame about "aging" was a fearful anticipation, but in Violet it flares up from external violence. She was thrown by the affect in the rehearsal air (as my late friend, author and philosopher Teresa Brennan, called it). That affect had to have been the younger people's irritation at her (female) authority, at her grand voice from under her energetic spray of thick white hair, and their giddy pile-on as Young Judges.

It took bravery to tell us. Violet had forged a public space at the conference for reporting this violence. But by making the "mistake" of blaming herself, she gave everyone present—future writers and actors, age critics in literature, filmmaking, playwriting—her impression, which she conveyed in her actor's passionate performative way, that age was a crime that deserved punishment. I had felt intense sympathy for her paralysis. Now, although silent, I became agitated. Violet didn't undermine only herself. She was teaching shame. People are no longer told to be ashamed of cancer; they know it's not their fault. "Ageism," when misconstrued by its victim, is shameogenic.

How could Violet overlook the youthful spite that had paralyzed her? Like Camilla, she is an active professional woman—one of the many New Women of our time. Yet it was precisely her professional chops that younger colleagues faulted. Previously, Dr. Paul Terry described "projective identification" on the part of younger people against older people. This has a terrorizing aspect, Terry argues: "the recipient of the projection often is induced to feel what is projected into them [e.g., the worthlessness of their lives] but mistakenly experiences such feelings as his or her own."[12] "If I am not aware that there are affects in the air, I may hold myself solely responsible for them," writes Brennan, in her evocative book *The Transmission of Affect*.[13] Not unlike rape victims, ageism's victims may recognize that another person is involved, even at fault, but they assume the shameful "charges" must be accepted..

Brennan has no hesitation about marking shaming, linked to self-accusation, as traumatic: "The tendency to self-blame and related shame (survivor guilt) that marks all trauma, in the theory offered here, is another mark of the death drive, insofar as it is (I suggest) the mark of what the body experiences as an alien deposit. . . . In such cases, trauma (originally, a piercing of the brain) becomes a piercing of the psychical shield as well as a dumping. But it does not fade . . . with time or distance, [even] if the intersubjective context alters."[14] Brennan interprets "the death drive" not as an intrapsychic motive but, quite otherwise, as an alien "piercing," with long-term consequences.

Exposed to other people's stories of trauma (of being abused, raped, having watched a murder), some lawyers and social workers develop symptoms like PTSD, including insomnia and bad dreams. This is vicarious vulnerability. Therapists, according to psychoanalyst Richard Reeve, may feel nauseated listening to clients who feel deep shame.[15] Empathy for Viola's paralysis also explains why my subconscious put me that same night in a windy outdoor classroom that guaranteed failure as a teacher. It is *my* mission that is at risk, *my* entire life project that may falter. (Shades of Gus Marcantonio, a union leader without a union.) Therapists, physicians, and philosophers tend to talk about what they consider the normal, predictable limitations and losses that come with growing old. But shaming should not be one of them. I can't predict and don't yet fear physiological declines, but ageism already terrifies me. *Ageism* seems predictable. My nightmare underscored that difference.

If we grip our demotions as personal failures, as Violet did, feeling stricken and alone, then the perpetrators are misrecognized—not seen as alien occupiers stupidly reciting ageist propaganda. The conference might have provided Violet with a safe forum in which to disrupt the rehearsal trauma by naming a grievance. But Violet said the conference made her feel "passé." She might also have feared our compassion. No one wants to be pitiable. Kindness can break down defenses, bring tears, reinstate victimhood. In any case, she was unable to perceive good forces. "Feelings are thoughtful, and affects are thoughtless," Brennan explains.[16] Shame thick as a burqa prevented Violet from feeling potentially healing currents. Shame is an autoimmune disease of the psyche.

Accepting that feeling ashamed is *our mistake* may be hard, when aging is seen as the decline of *my lone body* rather than a life process rife with social entanglements. The cognitive side of this mistake derives from a weakness in theories of mind: the belief that individuals are autonomous rather than suggestible. Brennan observes in *The Transmission of Affect* that, though we may "accept with comparatively ready acquiescence that our thoughts are not entirely independent, we are, nonetheless, peculiarly resistant to the idea that our emotions are not altogether our own."[17] Elena Ferrante, the Italian novelist, expresses it more vividly: "To be alive mean[s] to collide continually with the existence of others and to be collided with, the results being at times good-natured, at others aggressive, then again good-natured."[18] With Violet's experience, we are flung far from Emerson's protective bell jar.

Let's not aggravate the mistake. Where "shame" was, let "shaming" or perhaps, shameless "shamer," more often be. *Shame theory* ought to be renamed *shaming theory*.

Is the affect ubiquitous? Presumably not, given the heterogeneity of life experiences, personalities, subcultures, and the unequal distribution of wealth, privileges, and protections. I am willing to posit that the majority of older adults have some positive self-images. Still, strengths developed from having an age identity well fortified by struggles and recoveries can coexist (as I argue later) with feeling shame over aging-into-old-age. Strength makes falls more humbling.

Many might find something to confess to an open-ended question like that posed by David Crossley and Kirk Rockett, "As you have grown older, what [if any] are the sorts of things you have tended to feel a sense of shame about?" In this UK study of forty outpatients, men and women, whose average age was seventy-seven, only two listed "needing psychiatric care" first. To thirteen (the highest response), the appearance of agedness was worse. "I'm ashamed of losing my hair, even though it's not my fault," respondent number 40 said.[19] Two did say they felt less sense of shame than when they were younger, an important longitudinal benefit that we must not forget. Social scientists often ask older subjects the wrong question; they are not offered the chance to say whether they notice or endure ageism.

Studying this pernicious self-blaming is not best approached, however, as an empirical issue of prevalence. And, even for women, it is not always about the body. Not only midlife women with premature balance issues are led into attempts to conceal physical declines. Not only Alzheimer's patients like Serena in *Extreme Love* are forced into embarrassment, before a deeper state of humiliation ensues. Nor is it only actors forced into acute intergenerational distress— true abjectness, the harsh feeling of paralysis—who blame themselves. Anne in Haneke's *Amour* is too ashamed to accept visitors. Shame linked to age-shaming and disability-shaming is everywhere.

People may not die of shame, as the expression goes, but they may wish they could. People whose adult offspring highhandedly tell them they can't keep their car keys may thereafter, like the Grandmother in Jansson's *The Summer*

Book, fail to thrive. Shaming can kill. Old farmers driven off their ancestral land and men driven out of the workforce, facing desperate economic straits in an economy that demands independence, losing their pride and their family's livelihood, commit suicide. Shame presumably had a role in the suicide of the Baltimore steelworker in chapter 1 (#Still Human), who found himself unemployable after his factory closed. Other recent male midlife unemployed suicides couldn't hear, "It isn't your fault, it's the system." If there are more A.D. suicides, anticipated shame (although they might also anticipate they would not feel shame later) may drive them. The aging survivors of tyranny, as in Chile or Cambodia, seeing the new courts fail to bring perpetrators to judgment, may be ashamed of their powerlessness to get revenge for their beloved dead. Much of this book about ageism has had shaming as its subtext. Shame is not rational. The innocent experience it.

If you have been waiting to see how the perpetrators of ageism get away with it—why ageism consciousness does not get continually raised, why no great rights-and-justice movement has swelled, why outrage finds so little expression—it is not because older people are innately apathetic, or stupid, or tired. (It is certainly not because all our issues have been resolved.)

How does shaming inflict impotence? The accumulated ageisms dislodge vulnerable older people from any superior position they might enjoy in the age-status hierarchy of the Long Midlife, and remove them to a subaltern one at the very moment (as gerontologists keep futilely anticipating) when they finally have mature powers to fight back. This eviction should not be so easy. If the midlife extension is fairly secure and enjoyable, if old age still confers some undeniable advantages and commands any respect, wouldn't resistance be ferocious?

No. It isn't. In this country at this time, the Great Demotions, ever more powerful, suppress it. This is the capsule insight of this chapter and this book.

Decline ideology, the oppressive system to blame for the ageisms, is responsible for the insidious culture of age-shaming. Its vociferous agents, carelessly active, if told the harms they accomplished, would mostly be unashamed of inducing shame. Power works, making ageism widely misunderstood, trivialized, and uncensored. Anti-ageism, unlike antiracism or antisexism, is embryonic. This lack means that trauma related to ageism is not a familiar concept. It can be ignored. Like any similarly inflicted distress, it operates where the iron of practices and cultural representations slams against our soft microsubjectivity.

THEORIZING THE AGEIST COMPONENT OF SHAMING

Ending Ageism is witness to the fact that becoming old in the twenty-first century has newly insufferable aspects. Shame at "aging" is an affect—a painful, wordless sensation of being wrong, foisted on members of the minority age-classes by hostile exterior forces. I now believe that the average expectable environment of older adults may include increased indifference or neglect, social rejection, disdain, or even aversion, aggression, contempt, ostracism, sadism. Not all assaults produce trauma, not all traumas produce shame. But sadly, shaming can be reconsidered as a "normal," predictable harm incident to aging, a psychosocial risk—not unlike osteoporosis or arthritis, but more common.

Trauma theory, once it becomes imbued with ageism consciousness, can finally make visible the damages that dominant society keeps invisible. Theory needs to take that leap. Trauma has been ethnicized, as in the Holocaust, the Nakba, the Turkish genocide. It has been gendered, as in rape, domestic violence, and war crimes. It has been racialized, as in lynching and police violence. Feminist theory, broadening the experiences to be considered traumatic, urged that what is "deemed traumatic" be determined by the target rather than by an observer.[20] Each of these understandings has been hard won and contested. Expanding the term further may still prove controversial.

If ageism is not yet deemed trauma-inducing, this is partly because scholars haven't looked hard at its darkest effects and affects. We have not had enough accounts, or adequately contextualized accounts, of age-related shaming.

Like other affects, shame is neither static nor universal. I suspect that age-shaming now occurs in all developed countries chained to the epithet "aging." But it would once have been stranger to hear the word "shame" used in an American context. Anthropologists used to teach that the United States is a guilt-based (Protestant) culture, not an other-directed shame-oriented culture like Japan or Korea, where people may commit suicide because they feel morally at fault. Experts now assert almost the opposite. Although so many bold-faced names are patently shameless, Thomas Scheff among others believes that shame is, in his words, our "master emotion."

If so, why then is the evidence I present here underobserved? One familiar answer, Scheff explains, is that the term "shame" is itself taboo. People would rather admit to guilt. But this gross taboo can't be the final answer. Over the past two decades, the emotions have become a well-examined subject, not only in therapeutic but also in academic circles. Scholars study guilt, mourning, anger, melancholy, grief.

My answer is that public conversations about "self-conscious emotions" like shame are rare *in connection with the subgroups or identities that specifically suffer from them.* When emotions about being racialized are explored, this self-examination, once infrequent, is rightly considered brave. The same is true for memoirs of disabilities. Since shaming about age seems to be so buried, any new revelations, even as limited as half-statements or anecdotes, deserve respectful attention.

Age matters. From the first psychoanalytic writings of the twentieth century, shame was age-graded by being centered in childhood, linked to repression. The focus on children's shame long blocked analysis of shaming over the life course. In practice, shame was gendered female. Since feminists made the critical turn to the body, writers including Susan Bordo, Julia Kristeva, and Elizabeth Grosz have highlighted devastating affects foisted on women.[21] But shame-work seems to have in mind mostly adolescents or younger women, not older women or, for that matter, older men.[22]

Cultural criticism that focuses heavily on the uglification and dysfunction industries may neglect other fierce projectors. The sociopolitical, economic, neuro-based stereotypes ooze into social encounters and public discourse, professional and even, alas, family life, with their overlapping allegations of the deficits of older people. In these contexts, shaming gets honed sharper. Shame research and theory that disregard ageist assaults can become illegible—beside the point and unhelpful. Anthropologists, feminists, and writers who have made the turn to the cultural and social politics of the emotions potentially do better. Starting from generalizable traumatic experiences, they analyze "how social and institutional structures, and political and economic power, shape and produce individual and collective experiences of suffering and trauma."[23]

Shame theory suffers from another anachronistic conceptual weakness, which is to link shame to morality. Thus, when one has failed to meet others' standards of what is appropriate or desirable, one is being rightly judged. (The model is perhaps the shaming of children: but that too is now counterindicated for promoting learning or morality.) If you think that members of certain groups deserve humiliation, try bringing specific social sources of shaming into the dialogue: gay-baiting, race-taunting, Boomer-bashing, the "duty to die." The antidiscrimination movements, one after another and combined, should have taught everybody that being the target of an -ism is not the fault of the target. Our *character* is not what determines their contumely.

Aging-into-old-age is unquestionably no one's fault, and merits no self-reproach. Ageism, while certainly predictable, is not normal, produces unwarranted pain, and should not be tolerated. Let the ageist perps hang their heads. Their shaming provides no moral compass, leads to no reparative action. Martha Holstein, Jennifer Parks, and Mark Waymack, three philosophers who understand the critical turn in the ethics of aging, rightly call shame "antithetical to the central value of human dignity."[24]

Even now, I believe, theory needs to go deep into later-life shaming, providing historicized, culturally up-to-date, accurately intersectional, full-life-course accounts of how ageism works. This chapter aims to start filling some gaps. A step toward excavation comes from explaining why the awful shaming inflicted on us in childhood can be more readily overcome than can that of late adulthood.

The Afterlife of Childhood Shame

When adults look back they may remember, perhaps more strongly than other feelings, experiences of being publicly humiliated. I was not abused in childhood. But being a protected child still left me with burning instances of shame. I could summon them up any night and be scalded, no matter how long it had been since the events occurred. Hell nights. The first had to do with my third-grade teacher scolding me. She caught me reading a chapter book under my desk while the class was reading some assigned baby book. In a sharper voice than I had ever heard addressed to me, a model student, she ordered me to close the book and pay attention.

For decades, I could summon up the original scorching feelings. College added new shames. I was not a Brahmin. I was Jewish! Lower middle class! Not a man! From the wrong end of Brooklyn! As I aged past youth, however, I began to notice that life was not adding additional episodes. Marriage, raising a child, getting a Ph.D. seemed to insulate me from new frame-ups of self-derision. The tremendous grinding gears of history—feminism, the Holocaust—made some of my identities speakable, acceptable, minor, ignorable, sources of pride. And Mrs. O'Brien had been proud of my reading well; what a hypocrite! As indignation weakened the shameful bits, hell nights dimmed. Like survivors of serious childhood traumas, I could measure my emotional strength by the lessening damage I could do myself nightly.

All these—the reflective revisionist side of shaming-reduction, the attack-dog side—are maturity dividends, as thinkers from Anna Freud on have claimed. Resilience can be strengthened like a muscle. And self-reproach can be used up like a *shmatta* worn thin through overuse. Eventually we may have no critical superiors, at work or on the telephone. Our parents, if they were critical, die; and their voices, once heard loudest in their absence, fade. Adam Phillips writes in his beautiful essay "Against Self-Criticism," "Freud's superego is the part of our mind that makes us lose our minds, the moralist that prevents us from evolving a personal, more complex and subtle morality."[25] Maybe the superego, if that is what it is, gets a little flabby or forgetful about that hazy, long-ago material? The nasty yammering gets crowded out by pleasanter voices. We may even refresh our childhood memories. *These*, we are happy to share.

Humiliations make being a powerless child painful. But children usually look forward to escaping authorities and gaining more power in the age hierarchy. *It gets better.* In our culture, however, past a certain age point it may not. Suddenly, aging—beyond youth, or beyond the middle years, into old age, or into frail old age—brings a rotten switch in expectation. The shame of becoming old may batten on earlier experiences of shame; therapists would say the affect re-infantilizes. I agree. I nevertheless still want to theorize that some large part of age-related shaming, coming as it does unexpectedly much later in life, feels freshly sharp, a shiv into delicate skin. Shame feels worse when it is a "global and stable self" that is considered wrong.[26] Ageism makes the late-life self feel it has lost control that it once possessed over the outside world, the way illness or accident may lead one to feel the body is gone out of control.

Improving Shaming Theory with a Life-Course Lens

My shaming theory needs to accommodate the fact that many people who live long enough enjoy increased well-being, or happiness. James J. Gross and Laura L. Carstensen and their colleagues write in "Emotion and Aging": "Our preferred interpretation of these findings is that older participants' greater control of emotion permits them to selectively enhance positive emotions and selectively dampen their experience of aversive negative emotions such as sadness, anger, and fear."[27] Such findings are well established. But there has not been much study of the development of the "self-conscious" emotions, guilt and shame, over time.[28]

One rare large cross-sectional survey does examine shame over the life course. Its results, in conjunction with these robust life-course development findings, have influenced my hypotheses here. The authors, Ulrich Orth, a professor of psychology at the University of Bern, and two colleagues—using the responses of twenty-six hundred Internet users, 69 percent women, most Americans—found that shame decreased from a high in adolescence, sloping down into middle adulthood, bottoming out around age fifty. Their graph is vivid: up to age fifty, shame followed the resilience and maturity pattern.[29]

That shame in particular lessens up until about age fifty can be explained socioculturally. By midlife, many people have attained some ego ideals, enjoy a certain self-regard. The stigma of menopause has lessened. (Once women's health activists and researchers proved the uselessness and harm of hormone "replacement," pharmaceutical companies discarded much stigmatizing advertising and "informational" packets formerly sent to women's magazines and news outlets.) Writing about agency, Maureen McHugh summarizes other widespread gains for female cohorts over fifty. They are better educated than women in any previous historical period: "Many women have spent their entire adult life in paid employment . . . in a variety of fields including technical, corporate, and government work. Women aged 45 to 64 are a growing segment of the workforce, and their participation impacts [improves] their current and future financial and health status."[30] Studying longitudinal data on college-educated women ("within-individual change") Abigail Stewart and Joan M. Ostrove learned that, in their fifties, "identity certainty, confident power, and awareness of aging were all rated even higher than they were in the[ir] 40s."[31]

Age-improved qualities, men's or women's, do not necessarily depend on privileges like higher education, money, social class, whiteness. They can derive from life competence: overcoming childhood traumas, surviving troubles, raising children, doing better at impression management, overcoming sexual shame, holding jobs, behaving well as a friend—whatever an individual can be proud of having added to the selfhood of youth or deleted from its weaknesses. Selfhood, even threatened by adversity (job loss, death of parents, divorce) can seem fairly stable by, say, fifty. Exposed to growing ageism, the so-called Boomers were also the "first major population to grow up with positive images of aging," writes Dr. Gene D. Cohen, an exponent of the creativity that comes with the years.[32] Although we don't know how well pro-aging discourses and images psychologically protect people who receive them—this is an unexamined correlation—or how many in the Boomer age cohort received these messages, older people may learn self-compassion, treating ourselves with the kindness, patience, and encouragement that we direct to others.[33]

People of color and people with early disabilities, exposed to discriminations, may develop extra resilience. Having learned that their differences (skin color, shape of nose, shape of eyelid, prosthesis) can't be made invisible, many learn how to resist humiliations early on in life. In a national survey, almost 40 percent of LGBTQ respondents aged forty to sixty-one believe that the challenges of coming out helped them prepare for "aging" (I read, *ageism*). Hispanic (51 percent) and African American respondents (43 percent) were more likely than the sample as a whole to agree.[34]

Many women are said to suffer from "feeling there is an irremediable disparity between who one is and who one appears to be," because one's lined face doesn't seem to "match" one's inner qualities.[35] But that sense of disparity, too, may weaken. As T. S. Eliot wrote, "There will be time, there will be time / To prepare a face to meet the faces that you meet." By midlife, some women enjoy a pleasant internal peace with our faces and bodies. As ethicist Martha Holstein dryly speculates, "If women have throughout their lives suffered from multiple oppressions, having an 'old body' may not rank among the worst."[36] Older people may like their bodies better than they did when younger, when they were hypercritical.[37]

So far, so good. But to their surprise, Ulrich Orth and his colleagues unexpectedly found shame starting to increase again in the 578 people aged fifty and over. Unlike sadness, anger, and fear, emotions that become regulated, shame *rose* from age fifty on up to age eighty-nine. It rose to the high levels seen first among teenagers. All of the other trends from adolescence through middle age are consistent with the maturity principle. The shame trend is not.[38] I suggest the cause is ageist assaults. The Great Demotion undermines a midlife status that has been accumulated, feels earned, and should be stable.

Elinor had commented to me, about Camilla's outburst, "There are these liminal states of awakening to aging that are very shocking."[39] The metaphor of "awakening" needs to be qualified. Camilla ("intelligent," "professional") had not been fully asleep. No more than the rest of us. To age past youth takes a long time. Aging-past-midlife is already a disaster foretold. As we saw in the chapter on college students, people learn young the insults and bad attitudes that older others are subjected to. At some point, we must vaguely suspect that it may someday be our turn. Ageism's battery is thus both expected and unexpected. Camilla was probably one of the hyper-alert. "Is that day come?" is the shock. The move from *maybe-not-me-yet* to *me*.

The other shock is the disempowering realization that vaguely forewarned is not internally prepared. Unlike purveyors of racism or sexism, age-shamers latch onto something new in embodied selfhood that is seen or felt as irreversible. Most body novelties are harmless and could be considered trivial (graying hair, lines, baldness, a less jaunty step, lower metabolism). But even if a walker, a motorized chair, a hearing aid may feel to us, their new owners, like sorrowful aging-related changes, they could still go unremarked or acknowledged with ready accommodations. They would be *nondefining* in a better educated, more humane society that refused to shove the weak to the wall on behalf of greedy or ignorant elites. Some imputations are imaginary, like the younger actors' belief that Violet, a seasoned actor, had nothing more to say about theater. (Nobody had her back at the time. One person might have made a difference.)

Developmental psychologists look mostly at self-esteem, and psychotherapists focus on shame. Theorists of age-shaming, by contrast, in order to understand the late-life affects from ageism, need to understand growth and demotion as a *sequence*. The decades-long sense of rising inner worth crunches up against the sudden or repeated confrontation with allegedly shameful self-aspects. Life-course shaming theory is able to see how ageism shoves its victims into the new unwanted identity described earlier—undignified, belittled, self-swallowing—as a reduced "old person." (Note: none of the people telling their stories in this chapter is frail or impaired or in pain. "Aging," stereotypical physical aging, is not their problem.)

All these women have had some exposure to resistances like feminism. Unable to see the trauma as inflicted or collective, the targets may, as Brennan says, "incorporate the very structure of abuse . . . which keeps the trauma current by repeating it in the imagination."[40] Is this only a more troubled sense of self-presentation, intermittently still successful? Or is it a never-ending wrong, in the terminology of Erving Goffman: a *permanent* breakdown in our confidence that we provide a good-enough self to the world out there? At worst, the new normal might be subject to further erosions described and anticipated by the decline narrative of aging. At best, new accessions of respect, new insights and resistances, might mitigate the individual's pain.

The see-saw alternation over the life course suggests that shame is best observed not in a quick snapshot of youth or a snapshot of old age, but, ideally, longitudinally through agewise autobiographies that acknowledge ample historical contexts. What does contemporary history have to do with Orth's strange down-and-up curve? As it happens, all of those 578 people were aging between 1965 and 2005, during the two-faced era of Longevity. This is the period in which Medicare and Medicaid saved many, while the cult of youth built taller temples, and respect for the middle years and old age was crumbling, while well-paying jobs for people over fifty-five were disappearing along with secure pension plans, while inequality was growing, and toward the end of which the discourses of "burden" and cognitive failure were proliferating like wildfire. Feminism developed, but with little anti-ageism. In other words, in those years, for people of those ages, in at least one large sample, the rich maturity advantage was overwhelmed. Age-shaming seems to be rising in later life, not only because age critics may notice it more now, but in tandem with historical changes we may not be aware we endure.

ERADICATING OTHER SHAMERS?

What makes this discovery that shame may be rising in late adulthood more disturbing is the observation that during the very same historical period social shame from other sources was becoming less likely, *less* widespread. North American shaming, always culturally contingent, has a strange and turbulent recent history.

A few sources of culturally inflicted shame that used to be too common in the mid-twentieth century are dwindling. Social, body-based categories that used to be considered worthy of being hidden or downplayed (being gay, being female, being nonwhite, being adopted, being disabled) are now a bit better shielded from the shame-throwers. Some once-offensive epithets are usable in special ironic, in-group, or theoretical contexts ("queer" "crip," the "n"-word). In the 2016 election, to be sure, the abusive right wing resumed hate speech that progressives had thought buried. Still, movements, laws, higher sensitivity now lend the people in vulnerable categories some protection, even some pride. Racism doesn't disappear, and can be lethal, but shame about racialization can now be recognized and perhaps abjured. Sexism doesn't vanish, and in some ways may get worse, but being a woman can be flaunted. Some biases can be recognized and called out in classrooms, living-rooms, boardrooms.

This modest success in resisting the systems should be encouraging to anti-ageists. Like a vaccine, aging past young adulthood into fuller consciousness

may be protective. As shaming category after shaming category gets represented positively on a protest tee shirt in liberated subcultures, isn't shame, an
internalized bias of subalterns, weakening?

Not where aging is concerned. There (despite a tee shirt proclaiming "Old Is
the New Black"), shaming appears to be growing.[41]

Ninety-year-old Chloe Zerwick, publicly denouncing the ageists who
snubbed her, seems to shed a bright brave light through the fog of prejudice.
But the story of Camilla, a woman professional in the twenty-first century—
admitting that she felt "so ashamed" and reporting this to a friend who, being
older yet, might feel *more* ashamed—was to me so surprising, so little attuned
to contemporary revisionist sensibilities, and thus so revelatory, that it seemed
important to open the chapter with her. It was not a pessimistic choice so much
as a tactical one. Camilla is wounded in ways that should no longer be possible. Violet and outpatient number 40, like others who appear earlier, have
brought us sharply back to unfiltered, unnamed age trauma, subjectively felt.
They hark back all the way to Emerson's men on the trolley who didn't guess the
dirty atmosphere that choked them. Emerson succeeded in describing what he
sensed, more or less named it, and correctly laid a little blame. That we haven't
done much better is a mighty set of failures to persist in the twenty-first century. We ought to be able to do better.

Breaking the Oppression of Silence

It becomes urgent to envision how best to overcome age-shaming, if mature
emotional intelligence fails to protect and historical revisions of other once-
inferior categories do not get translated into anti-ageism.

The way forward is to start from the darkest toxic space where targets dwell.
They don't know what hit them, the reality of the violent event, the violence of
the reality. Traumas of sudden onset like ageism (unlike those long endured)
may be "shattering." *They think this is the real normal me.* Trauma may force
a bewildered suppression of some details even when someone recalls other
details perfectly.[42] *What just happened?* Anxiety amnesia can stand in the way
of remembering who precisely caused it. *Was it X or was it Y who jeered? Am I
hurt, angry? Indifferent?* If we can figure out our feelings, shame keeps us from
voicing them. *Should I retort? How?* The assault, so brief and normal: it seems
futile to contest. *Does this signal the new backdrop of a lesser life?* Grinding on
about this being a private crisis, shame is leagues away from allocating the

blame to a system that tolerates and exacerbates it. The affects caused by ageism remain harder to talk about than feelings inflicted by homophobia, racism, sexism, or ableism.

By layering the incomprehensions, ageism internalized as private shame of aging is active and mystifying. Kathleen Woodward, examining representations of racialized shame, argues that *confusion* itself is "central to the analysis of the phenomenology of shame in terms of oppression" (her emphasis).[43] In *The Melancholy of Race*, Anne Anlin Cheng describes such confusion as "shock mixed with expectation, anger with shame, and yet again shame for feeling shame."[44] Shame about aging obstructs the recognition of ageism with four or five different thicknesses of confusion. I will try to separate the layers.

The first obstruction is the targets' silence. (Calling it "stoicism" gets us nowhere.) Violet, "destroyed" by the irresponsible hostility of her auditors in rehearsal, was speechless. Walter White of *Breaking Bad*, insulted in his menial second job, stifles any response to his boss; he seeks a dangerous world of crime, where (who knows?) he may dominate. The Baltimore suicide had nothing to say to an economy that repulsed him. Nothing to say, no hope. Judith Butler lists some outcomes: "A loss in the world that cannot be declared enrages, generates ambivalence, and becomes the loss in the ego that is nameless and diffuse and that prompts . . . self-beratement."[45]

Utterance enables affects to come to consciousness, Teresa Brennan writes. "For our purposes here, I define feelings as sensations that have found the right match in words." The way forward may start by focusing on the "transmission of affect" by the perpetrators.[46] *"They made me feel . . ."*

Sharing "the right match" in words with intimates, the first outlet, serves as a landmark recognition that silence is not agency or consolation. But such confidences don't meet all psychic needs. A victim may feel permanently muted because she anticipates the larger culture is likely to be tone-deaf to the grievance. Silence, like speech, has in mind a shadowy imagined interlocutor. The shock of an assault isolates, suggesting there is no one willing to understand. *Is my grief too slight to be heard?* Margaret Stetz writes, about voicing troubling speech, "Much of what we call 'silence' is in fact speech that someone does not wish to hear, it is present, yet has gone unregarded or has been disregarded. The problem that this alleged 'silence' raises is not one of failure on the part of the vocalizer, but of denial on the part of the auditor, who has not yet taken up the responsibility to pay heed."[47] Many heedless are unwilling to accept that age bias causes grief. Their sensitivity is untrained. (I saw this in the Boston College classroom where the youngish man said that if he thought Web death wishes were addressed to him, he would just laugh.) Some reject the ethical hoop of wondering whether they are perpetrating forms of ageism and might need to stop. They need cushioning in social bias to feel blamelessly normal.

Anne Anlin Cheng writes, profoundly, "Public grievance is a social forum and luxury to which the racially melancholic minorities have little or no access."[48] Old people, a differently "melancholic" minority, have little or no access either to airing this unspeakable grief or turning it into a grievance. "Are they ashamed of being alive?" is a question some therapists dare ask, about people who might feel irrationally guilty for having survived collective trauma. To me, this is a not implausible question to ask about some victims of ageism. The midlife suicides. Anyone with a supposedly shame-worthy condition like cognitive impairment.

Age-shaming begets psychic confusion precisely (I summarize here) because its application to *me* is felt, obscurely, as something fiendishly new in my life course; because the appearance of agedness cannot be undone and I am helpless to deny the isolating demolishing "facts"; because no big voice tells offenders that the assaults are wrong; and because no social movement has taught us how we can successfully respond.

Speaking Bitterness, Speaking Indignation

Ah, the luxury of public comprehension. To heal and teach, the target must eventually tell "not only the reality of the violent event but also the reality of the way that its violence has not yet been fully known," writes Cathy Caruth in her aptly titled *Unclaimed Experience*.[49] It might take a therapist to help with this, but not just any. There are asymmetries of power even without the therapist, who is younger, feeling either flooded with unwanted emotion or youthfully invulnerable.

Some therapists try to convince ageism's targets that their losses, failures, and rejections are shared by younger women. Having *been* younger, older clients know in their bones that these particular abuses were not inflicted on them earlier. Asking them to agree that "This is a moment of suffering. . . . Suffering is a part of life," is like denying racism to a woman of color, comments my current Brandeis undergraduate intern, Danielle Rock. Older clients may feel that "there is no safe space in which to discuss their experiences without them getting hijacked."[50] "Acceptance therapy" can emphasize accepting aging as if it were the utterly natural acultural ahistorical phenomena this book has worked to demolish.

Why don't the wronged "fully know"—this is quite an exact phrase—the violence? Perhaps a prior question had better be, *How can we listen better, to hear what they are saying?* The concept of "idioms of distress," in the plural, has "refined global understanding of psychological, social, and somatic expressions of distress, while providing a blueprint for researchers and clinicians across countries to account for the phenomenology of distress specific to [diverse] cultural settings," writes Dr. Sotheara, who gave two days of testimony as an expert witness at the Cambodian war crimes' tribunal.[51] The search for idioms of age-related woe argues for interviewing people who might never say they are the victims of ageism, much less traumatized by it, but who can openly say they are ashamed of aging.

Here is one last story, about half-knowing. An essay by Emily Fox Gordon called "At Sixty-Five," chosen for reprint in *Best American Essays 2014*, opens, "Over the past few years, I've really begun to feel age." Even if she thus evades the word "old," "age" can mean only "old age" and thus inexorably refers to the *body-at-risk*. Fox Gordon has little to impart on this score—she enjoys good health—but starts anyway with the physiological report. "Check me out" is now the obligatory hook from a not-so-very-old writer. *This is what is required if you write old. You have to expose, chortle, emote, entertain.* For "aging" news ("I Hate My Neck"), editors expect an audience. Even readers uncomfortable with tattling on their own corporeal self may accept this voyeurism. The oppression of speech exists right alongside the oppression of silence.

Gordon now can get to the heartfelt point that she couldn't use as her lead, although there it would have had more impact. It turns out that she receives mean assaults from others, and not only from strangers. She then repeats her odd statement, "feeling age": "But as I say, I'm feeling age. I feel it in my invisibility to strangers. . . . I'm not at all sure I like this new kind of anonymity, which is an absolute dismissal. Even in contextualized situations like readings and receptions, eyes slide past me; internal shutters fail to click."

She has much more to say on this mournful theme. "Being interesting is getting harder." In a "cynical" mode, she confesses, "More and more I feel that I'm here on sufferance. If I don't want to be left out on an ice floe, I'd better try to be pleasant." Most of her essay relates strategies devised to ingratiate herself by altering her demeanor. "But instead of growing bolder and more heedless, I seem to be growing more circumspect, more nervously observant of the proprieties, more conscious of other people's feelings." Jean-Paul Sartre is relevant again. Like "the Jew" in an anti-Semitic society, a person who cannot help but be old learns the particular modes required for impression management: "he has learned that modesty, silence, patience are proper to [this] misfortune, because misfortune is already a sin in the eyes of men."[52]

Fox Gordon, without knowing it, is post-traumatic. Having suffered hurtful situations and retained the pain, like Violet, she has recognized some sources (unlike Violet), yet she has still been unable to point a complaint. Her essay, so vivid in some ways, is frustrating. She has evaded confrontation even where it is safe, on the printed page.

Maxine Greene, like other philosophers and social critics, suggests that oppressed individuals often need to be "helped to become indignant" about the injustices done to them and others like them.[53] How might one advance beyond this state of post-trauma? I want to put Gordon in imagined dialogue with a concerned and understanding peer. The Rumanian saying comes to mind: "If you don't have elders, buy one!"

I have one. Best of all, my mother in her old age. Betty Eisner Morganroth was an instinctive anti-ageist. There is such a thing. Living to ninety-six, despite some forgetfulness and gathering blindness, she never felt embarrassed about getting old. She would have been amazed that anyone does. Her reproofs of ageism (or any ism) came to her spontaneously, with naïve indignation. She didn't back away because an interlocutor was unready to listen; she restated patiently. She had not read Virginia Woolf, Alison Jagger on "outlaw emotions," or Kathleen Woodward justifying political anger in later life. She lived them. Her words about anger in the dialogue below come from notes I took in 2009 when I got her talking about wisdom. Now, by channeling her kind, plain-speaking, decent voice here as best I can, I may find the right tone for this predicament. She represents "the Elder within" that we may hope to create in ourselves if she/he doesn't yet quite exist.[54]

BETTY

Dear Emily, "nervous," "circumspect"—and feeling close to the "ice floe." Oh dear, this is no way to learn to be old. "Adjustment," they used to call it. It may be practical, although I doubt it. But self-defeating, sad.

EMILY

[Any words in quotation marks are taken from her essay.]

"I also notice an age-related touchiness, an increased sensitivity to slights and insults to my dignity."

BETTY

You *deserve* dignity. You are a thoughtful person. *Age-related* touchiness! How can you notice such nastiness and then "forget" to conclude that those who slight and insult you are the precipitating cause of "feeling age"? You blame your own "sensitivity" rather than their rudeness. Should we lower our expectations of decent behavior? Recognizing our "mistake" starts by observing that others have acted badly. You wiped the perpetrators out of the picture. I don't see their faces. Male? Female? Why not get mad at *them*?

EMILY

"What I feel now instead of a straightforward rage is a quivering, querulous outrage that I have no choice but to conceal behind a tight smile."

BETTY

Yes. You aired some grievances many older people share. Passive suffering and concealment are detrimental to our mental health. You do have a choice. There has to be a place for anger. It's a motivating thing, it helps us to function, do the right thing. It gives us strength to react. Anger helps fight injustice, it certainly does. How can you feel "outrage," even concealed, without at least contemplating the need to change something in the environment?

EMILY

"I can't deny that often I am depressed, but I also find myself in the grip of an inalienable stoicism. Even when my moods are acutely painful, I no longer try to force my way out of them through explosion or confrontation or drinking." How in the world can I change the world as it is?

BETTY

Best Essays gave you the attention of the world. Human social life is not always impervious. Let us help one another. Can you trust in change? My daughter has had calling cards printed up that read, "You just made an ageist/ableist remark or behaved in an ageist/ableist way. Perhaps you didn't know it. Permit me to bring this to your attention." Such remarks and conduct demean individual targets. They have a political impact like that of racism and sexism: they marginalize, silence, and deform an entire class of people (the old). Ageism degrades our social world. It will bring you a more bitter old age. Thank you for reading this.

EMILY

(*silent for a beat*)

I dare you to hand them out, Betty, strong as you are.

BETTY

We are each weak individually. I wouldn't do it alone. But if we organized an ageism consciousness-raising group, as others are doing, we might show the card to get our conversations started. Teachers could hand them out. Some already do; they ask their students to write up the attacks they see— in classrooms, dorm rooms, at home, on the street.[55] The students need not be bold enough to hand-deliver them, but they immediately start noticing, *Who merits the card?*

FROM ZERO TO HOPE

Why do people alter their persona and their relationships, let confusion dominate, rather than turn on the shame wielders when they get a chance? If you already know the answers, you are more agewise than I was before writing this book. I had to work my way toward understanding my own vulnerability to ageism. In the first chapter, I considered whether, to avoid having to consider myself a victim, I might have kept myself unconscious of being a target: *Agentic older woman, agile at raising my voice. Only five-foot-four but nobody bumps into me.* What changed? Not Violet's story, but committing myself, as I listened to her, to answer by writing an essay on shame: this chapter. That unconscious decision to fight back brought on the dream of the howling classroom. Before that, I was confused about immunity. Writing this was a milestone for me.

Pondering my bravado, Camilla's wail, Alix's shout, and Ashton's admission, I ask, "Why are people more ashamed to admit suffering ageism than to acknowledge declining physiologically?" They seem to be. Some with a new physical weakness or disease may be embarrassed, but they can tell friends how they cope: It is not considered a great demotion. *This is life.* I thought victims of ageism would be willing to share these inflictions, if only to escape the repetitious self-defeating topic of bioneurological aging.

"Fear ageism, not aging," I am wont to say. "Defy ageism. Name the shaming of older people as a 'public crisis,' rather than dealing with it quietly through whatever solitary defense mechanisms, strategies of intactness, and creativity you possess." My thought was that, like other resisters, the targets might feel active, engaged, agitating for progress.

Some, however are still thinking, *It must be my fault that now I am being ignored/ struck/derided/avoided shunned. And this woman wants me to offer a ghastly public confession!* I might as well have been demanding, "Show your wound." Rationally, if I suffer an assault, that is somebody's else failure of perception and sensitivity. Shame on them. Irrationally, however, when an outer aggressor pounces, a moment of terrorized identification may occur, via that inside voice and age gaze, Young Judge. At such moments, unwillingly accessing a junior self, current selfhood finds it contains, like a dirty thorn buried in putrid flesh, that dismissive youth-identified ageist. That self, undead (the real zombie), plugging us into the perps, complicitly sharing their hostility, *understands* why we deserve ignominy. Some reaction like this mutes any call the host self may feel to outrage and activity. Miming youth, silence, emotional blockage, scapegoating, depression, or suicide, cannot remain the only possible responses to age-shaming. "[Don't] assume that good politics can emerge only from good feelings; feeling bad might, in fact, be the ground for transformation," Ann Cvetkovich suggests.[56] With shaming too, one must confront the grimmest affects. It is a primitive place, but healing occurs. A theory called "post-traumatic growth" finds evidence that survivors of even the worst traumas—the Holocaust, the Cambodian genocide—do not always succumb.

However alone and helpless each of us may feel, the target is our entire group. Millions. Eschewing personal blame for "aging" is a prerequisite for growth and social change. In Simone de Beauvoir's unitary theory of identity, *I* am what has been damaged *and* the weapon inflicting the damage. "Within me it is the Other—that is to say the person I am for the outsider—who is old: and that Other is myself."[57] But my theorizing starts from a concept of multiple and longitudinal identities, which can change over time. Some become ripe for eviction. "Young Judge" can be viewed as another juvenile deluded anachronism. (I earlier cast out my "boy- crazy" and "female-despising" selves.) By envisioning Young Judge as a poisoned thorn, I can revise Beauvoir's horrifying description of an immovably internalized, ageist doppelganger, constrained to robotically repeat earlier ideological attitudes.

Current Self, our longest-living identity formation, is then no longer inertly identifying with the aggressor. She becomes an agent. Standing on the solid ground that our epidermalization is his bullying pretext, and leaning on the knowledge that she has ejected other early socializations, she can pull out the infected thorn. As soon as ageism is designated a foreign fragment, the memories are no longer flesh of her flesh. De-internalization may not happen in a flash. But Current Judge, relishing her strength, might eventually ball up her knuckles and strike.

In my temporal theory, Current Judge, the Elder within, deploys resiliences developed over the life course and through decolonizing ideas. Defenses can be dormant, held like unused tools in an armoire until hope and enlightenment call upon them. "Inactive" rather than "immobile" is the keyword. We can haul our resources over to the undefended part of the castle.

But nota bene. If I have noticed that aging is the trigger for ageism, then other individuals must, as well. Suppose people dread aging-into-old age before they approach it, not exclusively because of fear of pain or illness or loss of friends, but because they fear demotion as a social fate? As I do. We cannot underestimate the nature of this infection. But we *can* prepare for ageism— through empowering fantasy, energizing speech, acts that accompany freedom, and demands for social change.

Awakening

Envision true awakening, the deep stretch of long inactive muscle. We need our own recognition scenes. Racism consciousness, homophilia, have many such. The "Aha!" moments of the women's movement came from speaking and listening sessions, where no one belittled "bad" feelings and where others acknowledged similar experiences. Discoveries suddenly came in cascades of clear water flushing away filth. "I let him abuse me," led to "I am not alone."

Ageism consciousness follows similar trajectories. "We are not alone." Wide-eyed, someone asks, "Do you have to feel aging-shame at all? *Do we?*" That question can resolve the blur in one jolt of mental reorganization.

"*That* was what made me feel inferior."

"*They* are all part of a system."

"I am so angry."

"*We* judge."

"The system can be brought down."

"Let's go."

((

REDRESS

HEALING THE SELF,
RELATIONSHIPS, SOCIETY

The End of Ageism is the goal. It is not close. Achieving a post-ageist world would require momentous changes across numerous domains, including (as Neal King and Toni Calasanti somberly anticipate) "a massive redistribution of wealth and esteem."[1]

Many organizations already oppose decline ideology in their separate spheres; they forcefully represent the interests of our vulnerable minority to the majority. More groups are springing up in the United States as I write. Old or new, they focus, rightly, as in an emergency, on the essential and increasingly threatened first-generation services: on maintaining Medicare as a right, on expanding Social Security, hospice, and community-based long-term care, on housing homeless elders, and on making sure low-income old people get enough to eat. These worthy agencies are siloed by their particular mandates (health, housing). The second-generation ageisms are harder yet to overcome, as every earlier chapter has indicated. I wrote this book out of the stern realization that the prerequisite for action and the accompaniment to action is success in warning the people about the ageisms polluting later life.

Not even the most influential organizations—the UN General Assembly, pursuing a convention on the Rights of Older People, say, or HelpAge International's grassroots organization, Age Demands Action[2]—believes its efforts can weaken the relentless macro forces of oppression. Consider: these include neoliberalism shrinking welfare states, the courts' undermining of what's left of later-life job security, and capitalism's invisible hand squeezing the globe, through its efforts to eliminate seniority and unions, drive midlife workers toward the bottom as low-wage labor, hypocritically idealize youth, and commodify the deregulated commons of water, air, earth. These disasters, harsh as they are for everyone in the bottom 99 percent, often strike those in middle and later life with disparate impact. Close observers see a mass of latent forces and indefatigable efforts to counter the powers that be, but no unifying movement on the horizon able to, as it were, Occupy Old Age.

We must know the worst to know what to wish for. *Ending Ageism* makes a contribution to knowing the worst. The right question is not, then, grandiosely, "What is to be done?" but the pragmatic "What comes next for individuals?" And, finally, what demand can come from a future mass collective?

In Fantasy Begin Responsibilities

Reconsider revenge. Might revenge seem tempting, for those confusedly grasping, like a handful of writhing snakes, the conditions in which we live? "Redress" starts with revenge fantasies. This book promised to describe the affects of ageist ideology and, doing so, has ended with shaming and shame. It would be incomplete if, after discerning this array of traumas, it sidestepped an array of reactions. Out of confusing affects, fantasies produce definite feelings. Some of the wishes fantasy lets loose were described earlier, negatively, as potentially dangerous, illegal, irrational, or guilt-provoking. But knowing one's feelings can start a long, strongly empowering process. There is a place for revenge fantasies in anti-ageist hearts and a social justice movement.

Other groups seeking justice, who had readier access to their wrath, gave it a threatening aspect: the thousands who resisted at the Stonewall Uprising, the Black Panthers in their period of open-carry. They stood up to the police. Old people do not, however, represent danger to the state nor (yet) attract others by our militant passion. Old age, in man or woman, is stereotyped as weak. The fear of age does not extend to fear of militancy from people who look old. Yet, leaders of a cause—think of Nelson Mandela and Aung San Suu Kyi—and martyrs can be of any age. #OldStrong.

When the ferocious resentment of some old people was represented in a movie, "worldwide audiences embraced [its] cinematic envisioning." In the film *R.E.D.*, about a group of retired black-ops agents banding together for a mission, a young man wielding a shoulder-fired missile calls Marvin, one of the main characters, "old man" to his face. Spat out, "old man" is as insulting as the "n" word. Marvin (played by fifty-six-year-old John Malkovich) responds, "Old man, my ass!" and kills him. This thriller justified lethal vengeance by a team of older male stars plus Helen Mirren, in return for a micro-aggression. Here's a new meaning for "successful aging," embodied in a violent collective.[3]

"All thoughts of revenge are born of the pain of helplessness," an analyst writes in Siri Hustvedt's novel *The Blazing World*. "And let us not lie. Vengeance is invigorating. It focuses and enlivens us, and it quashes grief because it turns the emotion outward. In grief we go to pieces. In revenge we come together as a single pointed weapon aimed at a target."[4] Quashing grief, trouncing shame, becoming whole, all sound like acceptable motives for this mental exercise.

By fantasizing revenge or readiness for retaliation, people wounded by their helplessness wield power. Recall Ezekiel Emanuel's father: after reading that this son thinks he is "dying" slowly, not really alive, did the senior Dr. Emanuel not feel even an instinctive second of wishing to disinherit him? Daniel, the gentle former NGO chief whose life was irrevocably changed by being pushed down the subway stairs: did he never, for an instant, wish to hurl that unseen assailant over a precipice? The elegant woman with perfect posture, who fears a sidewalk encounter as the young hustle obliviously on their pursuits: doesn't she imagine herself swishing a cane threateningly as she saunters down Main Street? A cane: not a sign of frailty but an open-carry weapon.

Parents with cancer or mild cognitive impairment who don't want to forgo treatment or commit suicide, forced to imagine explaining to younger family members *why*: do they never envision spending down the estate while living as well as possible? If you have good cause to anticipate your husband turning violent if you become memory-impaired, doesn't divorcing him and taking the house cross your mind? If you are an old farmer about to lose your drought-ridden land, doesn't garroting the banker seem more appealing than poisoning yourself, as Indian farmers are doing? If your mother was starved to death by a tyrant who decades later is using an A.D. defense to avoid prison, does blowing yourself up next to his limousine while he is in it never occur to you? There must be outlets for these traumas.

Revenge, even if we don't want it, will come to the coarse young Manhattan biker during his own life course in this guilty century. According to the Baltimore Longitudinal Study of Aging, the biker will suffer from signs of cognitive impairment sooner than someone who doesn't know the words "old hag." "Those holding more negative age stereotypes earlier in life had significantly steeper hippocampal volume loss and significantly greater accumulation of neurofibrillary tangles and amyloid plaques, adjusting for relevant covariates."[5]

(A scholarly article can wield putative power and implicitly threaten revenge.) Even without future impairment, if this man does not overcome his elder-hostility and help to change his culture, his future is Dantean—as in the level of *Inferno* in which the evil you never repudiated becomes your own fate. In our contemporary hell in the eyes of others, he may become in time, and not so very long a time, a superannuated midlife worker unemployed long enough to eat his savings, a "codger," a "geezer," an "old fart." An old man. One truth of aging: if ageism can't be mitigated, it sooner or later strikes the only-temporarily young.

Why dwell on the theme of revenge if retaliation is impossible, self-defeating, or takes too long? It feels good. Dislodging the demoted from a state of dumb acceptance, revenge fantasy proves to anyone who feels stifled by ageism that they are capable of righteous anger. The innate wish to be recognized as persons of equal worth cannot be suppressed entirely. A psychoanalyst I will call Clare tells me how good it feels to "express your violent side." Another analyst recently taught Clare a karate jab, punched out into the air. She acted it out for me. The jab is a quick forth and back, which tenses muscles of the upper arm and whole body in a powerfully free way. It involves emitting a grunt, reaching out widely to embrace a huge space above and around, and then "entering into the shape of a punch." There's a twist on the end, capable of delivering the imagined fatality. "The gift he gave me," Clare said, "is that it is okay to own the feeling, to let it forth. I have the stature to do that. The strength not to wilt."

The sense of possessing strength in reserve is liberating, enlarging thought and freeing speech. Clare, age seventy-four, finds this sense of strength good in professional meetings where peers, including women and feminists, ignore her. This is another "invisibility": although older women have many contributions to make, they can be as disregarded as a child, or as a parent. Clare doesn't want to invent surly rebuttals in the watches of the night. Prepared with new strength, she now sometimes prefaces her utterances with a bit of her life-course résumé: "From working with such patients for over thirty years, I learned . . ." Sometimes Clare finds a colleague to repeat her idea while crediting her. "As Clare said, and I agree . . ."

My point is not that old people have an inherent bad-ass core. The good folks I encountered researching this book have been resilient, not (as far as I can tell) resentful, nonviolent in the face of the violences they are subjected to. Many would be better off being more aggressive. Not our character but circumstances, that is, may provoke unexpectedly intoxicating images of using force.

If my evocation of power scenarios teases your interest, a self within you resents injustice—if not for yourself, for peers. We want the ninety-pound weakling to best the bully. We want the world to be fair. In her classic essay "Against Wisdom," Kathleen Woodward, arguing that old people need to let themselves feel angry rather than mimicking "wise" placidity, writes that "anger can be a sign of moral outrage at social injustice, at being denied the right to participate fully in society. Such anger is a judgment, or more strongly, an indictment."[6] Dwelling in anger is like lying in a cesspool, but a short sojourn in the land of the unthinkable refreshes.

Thus fortified, some leave anger and fantasy behind; others use anger forever as fuel. In any case, the power honored by admitting a hankering for revenge is wisdom to locate the *source* of ageism outside of one's self. Agewise anger knows its sources. Enlightenment comes from naming the macro causes. If you feel an urgent ability to speak up or act, good again. Individually, you and I can't disinherit the billionaires or feed all malnourished elders. So, jab a fist; then use that rush of adrenaline to blame ageist targets. We need to word the indictments comprehensively. Defining our grievances frees up options for practical rebellions. Just for starters, we might, through scorn and satire, push out of public discourse the obeisance to the ideology of scarcity, "burden" language, and the careless use of "dementia." Phone-banking, we might dump congressional representatives bent on snatching the Social Security trust fund. Voting, we might get the Supreme Court to reinstate the age-proxy doctrine.[7] I have a usable fantasy of a nonviolent collective, a Billion Person March across the round globe, where people of all ages and conditions carry urgent signs: "#StillHuman," "Take Back the Sidewalks," "Medicare for All," "Feed me, I'm 64," "Treat me, I'm 75," "Bank Credit for Old Farmers," "Uppity Elder," "Unashamed of Aging." There, the only shame might be staying away.

RECONCILIATION

Acts of oppression cannot unhappen. But survivors may reconstruct the world they live in. Consider again the Grandmother in Tove Jansson's novel *The Summer Book*, whom we met in chapter 1. Her enduring trauma was life-threatening, not unlike the aftermath of rape. What might she have done to resume her pleasant life after her son unexpectedly tossed her pell-mell into alienated old-lady-hood? A novel gives insight into the pain of injury when real-life survivors cannot put their hearts into their mouths.

At the time, as stupefied as a real-life victim, the Grandmother doesn't reproach him. What she feels is inexpressible except through a silent metaphor, being treated like "a potted plant." Offspring taking one's car keys is a more common example of this attitude. A woman of ninety with some signs of memory loss is abruptly told not to drive. A friend from her assisted-living building tells me, "A son came and took her car away without asking permission. Eventually he returned it, but the rupture has not healed easily." Everyone in the building who knew her empathized. Losing mobility, autonomy, and authority at one blow, she was ashamed of her impotence, but the cause was her son's harsh appropriation. Who rebukes such people? Who educates them?

Careless ageism drives the stake of evasion and disrespectful subordination into relationships. The story of the car keys is rarely told from the parent's point of view, so powerful are the youngers, publicizing it as *their* problem. A woman on NPR used "taking the car keys away" from her grandmother as another acceptable example of a horrid "leadership" responsibility that cannot be refused. In a Brandeis anthropology class, which I canvassed about that granddaughter's attitude, students first gave examples of their grandmothers' bad driving, as if they agreed that female incompetence was the issue. A woman then added that her grandfather felt diminished when he relinquished his car, given the hardship of poor public transportation. Adding an example involving a *man* ended the incompetence discussion. Eventually an African American woman offered the word "dialogue" as an alternative to surreptitiousness and mistrust. Older people, I added, referring to research, drive rarely, carefully, short distances. Far riskier situations arise from Americans over fifty, armed and dangerous, having the highest gun ownership rates. States do require driving proficiency, but "the idea of enacting such competency tests for gun owners hasn't proven popular."[8]

In *The Summer Book*, the Grandmother's friend Verner is a fellow victim of "Nasty relatives. They tell him what to do without asking him what he wants, and so there's really nothing at all he really does want." She advises him "to think of some way to outwit them."[9] The advice "to outwit" is a milestone for her, imagining for another a strategy that she cannot envision for herself. The Grandmother and Verner are among the many newly made subalterns half rising. Frantz Fanon, a leading theorist of insubordination, describes the psychic activity involved in resentment. When consciousness feels a grievance and encounters opposition to its being recognized, he writes, the repressed self tastes "the experience of desire—the first milestone on the road that leads to the dignity of the spirit."[10] Dignity must be expressive.

With a group in Wellesley, Massachusetts, discussing ageism, I quoted from Jansson's novel. In discussion, the first speakers were indignant: they could never remain acquiescent after experiencing an adult child's neglect or disrespect. A woman I'll call Janet told us proudly how feisty her mother was about maintaining agency. When her mother turned eighty, Janet and her brother (at the brother's instigation) went to talk to her about moving to "a safer location." The mother saw them coming. They had barely sat down before she said firmly, "I have lived in this house for fifty-three years and I want to die here. If you two come here to try to get me to move, you are not welcome. You can walk right out the door." *Anticipated* threats to selfhood in peaceful home settings can be experienced as betrayals. Janet has told this story to her own children, probably more than once. By indirectly presenting her own determination to die at home, through her mother's voice, Janet gentled its point but made her point.

The group in Wellesley belongs to the national "village movement," which supports adults who prefer to age in their communities by offering referrals to vendors and volunteer support (e.g., rides, computer assistance, etc.). Their engaging motto is "Making neighbors into friends, making friends into family." The 120 villages in the United States probably draw on the most anti-ageist activists of any community. After Janet spoke, I asked, "Putting ourselves in the Grandmother's place—let's give her a name—what precise language might you or I suggest for *Ingrid* to say to her son? If he knew the effect of his behavior—that his mother lost her gusto for life—might he make the only apology that matters, reinstating her in a respectful embrace?"

The exercise mimics the college assignment in chapter 3, to address the troll effectively, but it imagines face-to-face encounters with loved younger adults, using sentences that an offended parent can feel comfortable saying. The concept of getting the wording right derives from Chaim Ginott's gnomic *Between Parent and Child*, and theories about healing interventions. "Were you thinking I am too old to be consulted about my own welfare?" might be too tart or self-pitying. An adult child might answer curtly, "Of course not." Few parents would risk such a blunt second dismissal.

Here are three responses, conceived by a group that became deeply engaged in the task.

"About that trip you want me to take to the Hansens'? Ask me directly, not through your little daughter."

"Son, you're fifty-five. If Sophia ignored *you* like that when *you* were eighty, how would you feel?"

"When you make plans to drop me at the Hansens' without consulting me, you make me feel like a dumb object to be moved this way and that."

The third sentence, the one baring his mother's true feelings, seems likeliest to lead to remorse. A fourth might be, "Going to the party without me? You've never done anything like this before, dear boy; why now?" The son may not know what's behind his new tactlessness. But feeling that his mother counts on him, and hearing her assume that this was a one-time oversight, he might make his apology warmer and restore some of her trust in him. And restore his own trust in himself as an equal adult friend and moral agent.

To heal, trauma needs to be experienced "as disappointing, enraging, diminishing, [and ithe expression of such feelings needs to be] directed to those in particular whom one expected to be loving and protective." This is the language of a psychoanalyst and sociologist, Jeffrey Prager, who studies post-conflict societies.[11] Struck by the social fate of agedness, if we cannot manage to touch known hearts in our families, is there much chance of coping with unknown hearts in the outside world?

The Wellesley discussants were using literature and their personal experiences not only out of self-interest, a laudable motive, but more broadly, to understand the dismal pervasiveness of decline. Discussions like ours make possible transfers of knowledge that can go far to modify and humanize our worlds. To avoid trauma, we can reflect on how to avoid being relegated to disregarded status anywhere: in medical situations, parties, streets, classrooms, courts, worksites, town meetings. We can rehearse effective responses and prepare to testify to the injury.

Interpersonal needs can be reinterpreted on a grander scale, worldwide. Although the fictional Grandmother and actual endangered small-hold farmers suffer for different reasons, the wide spectrum of grief and grievance links them. In common they suffer demotions of their true human worth where respect for their needs would be in order. For them to heal, their society must support them, getting the offenders to recognize and redress the wrongs. "Disappointment" is a keyword. It indicates that expectations of basic entitlements are reasonable and shared. People should rightly be able to expect their sovereign nations to be—not loving like a family, but—at least protective, throughout the life course. Our collective responsibility is to hold the nations to it.

Disseminations

Senexa, whom I designate the crone goddess of age studies, holds an enormous open book because educating global audiences is one urgent and necessary way forward.

Teaching through storytelling is a method favored by great writers of fiction and nonfiction. Storytelling about suffering and trauma is the core of this book, however much analysis and data, agency and alternatives, surround that core. The testimony from "Ingrid" led to stories provided by students themselves about other "potted-plant" plights of relatives. They had noticed the objectification. By reimagining such familiar scenarios from the older generations' points of view, they could empathize with the entire relevant age group while avoiding pity. No victimizable class wants to be associated with pity. What our age class wants is solidarity.

An ethical society prefers to prevent ageist behavior rather than to punish it. It therefore needs to disseminate unexecuted revenge fantasies. My formulating often unspeakable scenarios is an attempt to make the existence of such tough hidden wishes widely known. They educate, by showing that ageism can have devastating long-term effects, as rape does, and that it is deeply resented by silenced victims. This can come as a salutary shock to potential offenders. After being warned and gaining insight into the pain of others, people may make decent behavior habitual. White people work to repair the effects of their skin privilege. People of goodwill, youth-identified or wearing the shell of youth, can repudiate the systems that confer on them unearned power, and go for deeper changes. The fantasies of revenge that I imagined earlier can serve as an essential social backdrop, because they also imply the H-bomb of conscious potential resistance.

Education for anti-ageism has limits. Some malefactors in ageist systems may have to be sued, voted out, or exposed to judgment. Recognizing the harms that a tolerated system is capable of inflicting (as in racism and sexism) is the first milestone a nation reaches in its long march toward undoing gross injustices—including those toward elders.

Listening Protectively

Revenge, enacted, can fail to provide full justice. When Saddam Hussein and Osama bin Laden were murdered without trials, survivors were denied the opportunities to offer testimony, follow cross-examination, hear others in public, and witness authority figures condemning the crimes. As in Cambodia, their versions could expand the historical record and help historians decide truths. Retribution, political theorist Paul Muldoon argues, "lacks the complexity of vision shown by those who have embraced restorative, 'victim-oriented,' approaches."[12]

As in our own families, listening well to suffering may be healing even in harsh circumstances—even in atrocity trials that conclude with a dubious or corrupt verdict of mental incapacity. I suggested in "Faking Bad" that, for those declared unfit, the international criminal-justice community might invent a truth trial that has no penalty phase. If able to understand, up to the limits of their cognition, the "defendants" should be present. If willing to testify, they should be sworn in, with whatever safeguards about memory loss the prosecutor and the defense think the jury and the press need to hear. A person unable to defend himself or herself would not be forced to testify. Although a defendant would be held harmless, the trial phase might find him or her guilty and deliver a verdict. A verdict and a penalty phase are separable events.

The latest twist in the case of former dictator Efrain Rios Montt of Guatemala, once convicted but excused from retrial by reason of "dementia," approaches this solution. A court ruling, the Associated Press reported, "allows for a special trial where all evidence and witnesses will be presented behind closed doors with a representative of Ríos Montt. He can be found guilty or not guilty, but will not receive a sentence because of his health conditions."[13] The blatant flaw of this ruling is that the general, now eighty-nine, does not have to be present to hear his deeds recounted, and that testimony about the dirty war is given without journalists or survivors hearing it.

The traumas of aging witnesses need to be better broadcast. A trial that is respectful of their voices can facilitate a therapeutic process for them and reinstate trust. Jeffrey Prager would have us turn toward like-minded groups, because "recovery happens only in community, where expectations of lovingness and protectiveness can become reactivated."[14] To achieve an anti-ageist future for a culture on trial, the whole society needs to hear, in many media, not how wonderful or dreadful being old is, but how destructive ageism is.

INSERTING *AGEISM*

Dramatic social changes often arrive via single words, sentence by newly available sentence, idea by idea, in mind after mind. In my first college writing course, one assignment was a composition with an unfinished title, "I Wish I Were . . ." Did the professor expect some fantasy about otherness: I wish I were a chimpanzee, George Eliot, Mount Everest? Empty-headed, hunched over my typewriter, I smoked, drank bourbon, puzzled. Then I typed, "I wish I were a man," and the story of everything that was held tantalizingly out of my grasp poured out, copiously. Once again, fantasy started a process of liberation.

Years later, feminism named the force behind that impossible desire, and feminism taught me *why* it was bad. *Sexism.* Instead of disliking being a mere woman and fearing my future, stuck with the womanness said to be housed in my cells, I learned that womanness was institutionalized in my country's laws and customs and internalized in my head, standing between me and (male) advantages. What I came to dread was not my gender but sexism.

Naming and shaming go together. Use of the term "racism" disparages and drives out hate speech, housing and job exclusions, and other racializations. Calling out "homophobia" changes LGBTQ lives. Naming discrimination against people with disabilities as "ableism" changes the status and identity of people with disabilities. Targeting "ageism" instead of our own "aging" does heavy lifting on behalf of everyone alive, and positions old people to enjoy the accomplishment of making it so far so well.

"I wish I were . . . young" relates to the unstable illusion, described in chapter 3, that "being young" means "I can stay in this prized age class forever." This wish leads to forms of passing for younger that are destructive to selfhood and that stabilize prejudice, like trying to pass for straight or as white. A rapid uptake of anti-ageism will make "I wish I were . . . young" seem misguided, the worst wish possible to make in this domain. Other desires—"I wish I were treated economically like a younger person," "I wish I were farther from dying"—make rueful common sense. But to wish to be "young" is not merely impossible biologically, chemically, or surgically; it is another of culture's devilish psychological impositions.

Using the word "ageism" is no mere acquisition of vocabulary. It correlates with a development in mind, heart, and guts that may protect some solitary individuals from experiencing the full public force of a trauma, or help them recuperate and gain agency in the process. Speaking or writing, whatever "bears witness to the extreme experiences of solitary individuals can sometimes begin to repair the tears in the collective social fabric," two trauma scholars observe.[15] By using the term naturally and calmly, we teach better observation and encourage the sharing of abject experiences and recoveries. We make the epithet "ageist" (or "elder-basher," "shame-thrower," and other invectives) scathing. We raise consciousness, family by family, business by business. Seismic shifts can occur, vote by vote, march after march. The distinction between aging and ageism, which I initially said was rudimentary, will become indispensable. "Let me be young forever," will switch to "End ageism."

As we raise awareness and reduce bias, there will be less loss to mourn under the bell jar and less odium from the street. Knowing what's left to work for, we can envision a less burdened life course and a freer, better respected old age.

Demanding

The first chapter of this book began with the most modest imaginable request, to recall that people of a certain age are #StillHuman. Here at the end, before A Declaration of Grievances, is the place to declare the need for a utopian demand, nothing less than all. A utopian demand is a "political demand that takes the form not of a narrowly pragmatic reform but of a more substantial transformation of the present configuration of social relations. . . . In this sense, a utopian demand prefigures . . . a different world, the world in which the program or policy that the demand promotes would be considered as a matter of course both practical and reasonable."[16] History teaches us that recognition can bring collective demands for a better world. Demands raise consciousness, and consciousness more demands, in a virtuous spiral.

A society as warped by ageism as ours in the United States, or elsewhere, wherever grievous ageism is found, can be transformed only by a movement that attracts increasing numbers of passionate members. Meanwhile, no one should reach the hopeless point of believing that we can't censure capitalism and neoliberalism now, to begin to reeducate our frightened world. We must try though the goal is out of sight. People who care, heroically pursuing definite anti-ageist goals, can help many others rescue themselves from the mountainous traumas of ageism. Progressives are likely to sweep into this movement on a second wind. Art that is compassionate, knowledgeable, or merely instinctively resistant to decline culture steps up the pace of change. More statements of rights and progressive laws become guides to acting more responsibly toward others and more gently toward ourselves. Each one of us can do more, and together we can do much. This is the great coalition, yearning, observing, listening, pondering, teaching, complaining, explaining, judging, calling to account.

How the great movement will come to flourish we do not yet know, but with desire for it declared by a firm enough chorus of voices, it will. In our lifetimes, we may yet see vital activism on fronts that age activists now view skeptically. It is exhilarating to aim the arrow of history toward fairness and justice.

With Senexa as our female Virgil, we conclude this tour of our peculiar netherworlds by looking upward, through a small high aperture, toward our vision of the future. Dante wrote, *And thus we emerged to see at last the stars.*

O

A DECLARATION OF GRIEVANCES

This book began by citing the *Declaration of Independence* (1776) and the *Declaration of Rights and Sentiments* (1848), because both rhetorically confirm suffering through lists of substantial and deeply substantiated Complaints. Here at the end, in the same spirit that animated Thomas Jefferson and Elizabeth Cady Stanton, I offer a preamble of justification and a list of grievances. This list will surely prove preliminary. These charges are guided by a vision of social inclusion, well-being, and justice. This Declaration of Grievances is delivered in the choral voice of those in later life. Like earlier resolutions, it is addressed to all who are likely to corroborate the indictments and wish to correct the evils.

_____

When, in the course of human events, it becomes necessary for one portion of humankind to assume among the people of the earth a position different from that which we currently occupy, the one to which the laws of equality-in-diversity entitle us, a decent respect to the opinions of humankind requires that we should declare the causes that impel us to cast off our patient subjugation. Our portion consists of older human beings. "They" refers to agents of all ages who, knowingly or not, injure us or benefit from our subjugation.

_____

Through shameless age-shaming, they silence us. They destroy confidence in our own powers, lessen our autonomy, and make many accept, willingly or not, an unnecessarily dependent or abject life.

Through condescension, ridicule, and indifference, and through exaggerated deference to medicine and science, they make our own bodies foreign to us.

Through hate speech, they make contemporary media and the use of social media unpleasant to us.

Through depictions in the arts, they often distort our longings and agency and express fantasies noxious to our well-being.

In many ways, they make cultural participation, a human right, difficult for us.

Through careless bodily force, they sometimes make the public spaces of our land dangerous to us.

Disregarding our desires, talents, and abilities, they often exclude us from places of learning and power.

Disregarding our desire, talents, and abilities, they monopolize nearly all profitable employments and often entirely exclude us from meaningful work and necessary income.

Although we suffer from the disparate impact of laws, hostile behavior, and prejudicial discourses that undermine our ability to obtain or retain available work, the courts prevent us from having recourse to the governmental agencies that should help us to seek redress. The legislatures have refused assent to bills wholesome and necessary to our good.

By passing state statutes requiring forms of identification that many of us lack and some cannot obtain, they deprive many of us of the right to vote, rightly ours since our first coming of age, and basic to democratic process.

Through attested patterns of medical ignorance, neglect, or misconduct, they adversely impact our health outcomes, as if our well-being were worth less than that of others.

Through legal procedures lenient to evildoers, and in other ways, our lives, particularly if we are women and impaired, are held to be cheaper than the lives of others.

By treating us as burdens in public forums, and through the aforementioned medical and legal practices, many of those with power put in question our basic right to live.

May the blessings of the elders be apportioned to the deserving, and be heard and valued; and may their reproofs also serve as guidance to the generations.

ACKNOWLEDGMENTS

For the Romanian epigraph, "If you don't have elders, buy one!" I am grateful to Diana Manole, a Canadian theater director. She commented in an e-mail, "The word 'batrani' is a warm, rather tender one, w/o any reference to blood relations, and also gender neutral in its plural form. Thus, I chose 'elders' to translate it." George Katsiaficas suggested that "How Not to Shoot Old People" be the title of the book. It became the subtitle. Katherine Newman ended all debate by wisely suggesting the current title. After I found the photograph of Leda Machado I wanted for the cover, Trudi Gershenov produced the riveting cover design.

More people than I can reasonably name critiqued material in various drafts. For help with an early version of chapter 1, special thanks to the members of the Social Issues group at the Brandeis Women's Studies Research Center who commented insightfully, especially Smriti Rao, Helen Berger, Jan Freedman, and Maryline Kautzmann (whose praise, coming from a sister age critic from France, was particularly welcome).

Many thanks, for offering permission-free and digital versions of their photos for chapter 2, to the John Coplans Trust, Jeff Wall, Raymond Collet, David Gullette, Valerie Massadian, and José Parlá. The Tyre Fund at the Women's Studies Research Center at Brandeis gave me a grant to pay for copyright permissions and scans for the other art I needed to include. Thanks to Hannah Zeilig for inviting me to deliver a version as a keynote talk at the conference Mirror Mirror at the London College of Fashion, October 30, 2013. NEWIP, New England Women in Photography, invited me to speak, closer to home, to an intimate group of practitioners. Many photographers tendered examples of paradigm-breaking images of old people for my consideration, and I hope others will take up this good work. My research benefited from the International Photography Center's remarkable facilities in New York.

Chapter 3 on anti-ageist teaching was incisively read by Frances (Frinde) Maher, Elizabeth McKinsey, Judith Morganroth Schneider, Sarah Lamb (whom I interviewed about the program "Sages and Seekers)," and by some members of my Social Issues group (Nicola Curtin, Helen Berger, Phoebe Schnitzer, Jan Freedman). Their collective experience in the classroom probably amounts to over 150 years. Invitations to teach age studies came from Sarah Lamb, Erin Gentry Lamb, Terry Byrne, and others.

Brian Worsfold's invitation, from the Grup Dedal-Lit in the University of Lleida, to give a keynote address on farm fiction about old farmers at the October 2016 SIforAge conference, and the response there (in Barcelona), give me confidence that chapter 4 will find an audience and perhaps exert some influence.

Victor Wallis and members of the Social Issues group at WSCR gave me excellent comments on "Faking Bad." Pamela Merchant, Almudena Bernabeu, at the Center for Justice and Accountability, and Nushin Sarkarati, an advocate for Cambodian victims, answered questions about law and fact in Chile and Cambodia. Merchant commented on the legal concept I proposed in chapters 5 and 8. Andrea Petersen, a notable Massachusetts defense attorney, and Minna Schrag, a lawyer who worked as a senior trial attorney on the International Criminal Tribunal for the former Yugoslavia, commented on early drafts of chapter 5. Two transnational intersectional chapters, this and the chapter on old farmers, were begun in an inspiring "writer's retreat" in the guesthouse of Mounira and Douah El-Alami, my dear *Makhetunim* in Tangier.

In relation to the duty-to-die section of chapter 6, many audience members in Toronto at a conference, Theater and Age, in 2015, made wonderful remarks. Another section of that chapter, on a Tony Kushner play, expanded and published in *Modern Drama*, was skillfully edited by Marlene Goldman and Lawrence Switzky and an anonymous reader at that journal. *Modern Drama* also invited me to publish further remarks about my concept of "social fates." Thanks to the *Forward* for publishing an early version of the material about my mother's sense of her cognitive impairment, "Keeping the Conversation Going." *Age, Culture, Humanities* published the section on Peter Haneke's *Amour*, in an earlier version, in their first issue.

For help with chapter 7, thanks to Helen Berger and Frinde Maher for queries that sharpened several points, to Maher for the subtitle, and to Caroline

Cross Chinlund, Kathleen Woodward, and Elinor Fuchs for suggestions and commentary. Joyce S. Wadlington, executive director of Wellesley Neighbors, invited me to the discussion described in chapter 8. Ashton Applewhite helped with deft line readings and through her comprehensive knowledge of anti-ageist organizations. It was Connie Wilson Higginson's brilliant suggestion to put the Declaration of Grievances separately at the very end.

My Brandeis Scholar Partners, talented undergraduates all, have been exceptionally valuable assistants over the years. For help editing the chapter on photography, I am grateful to Madeline Rosenberg ('16). Lauren Katz ('13) helped with research on war crimes tribunals for "Faking Bad." Danielle Rock ('18), edited chapters 1 through 6 and checked the extensive references and endnotes and helped with the keyword index, a difficult job when trying to create an important teaching tool. Rock's wise critique is quoted in chapter 7. Editing by the Scholar Partners helped assure that all points were comprehensible to undergraduates and answered likely questions. This stimulus and assistance is not available to every writer and academic researcher; I am grateful to the Women's Studies Research Center for providing it to me for book after book. Indeed, my longstanding institutional relationship to the center under the directorship of Shulamit Reinharzer has been a fundamental identity, a source of collegial support and friendship, and a pleasure.

Sarah Lamb, who invited me to offer this book to her series, offered important suggestions about the structure as a whole at just the right time. Kimberly Guinta, my acquisitions editor, went beyond the call of duty (in my experience with acquisitions editors) by not only reading the book but also commenting on chapters in her thorough, amiable, and wise ways. I have evidence that Paula Friedman read not only every word but every letter, and she went beyond copyediting with some last-minute queries that I was glad to be given time to address. I am lucky that Rutgers has such editors. The book is better for it.

David Gullette has used his skills as an editor to improve *Ending Ageism* at every stage of its development and helped solve innumerable language questions, always in favor of the clearer and more forceful solution. Many members of the now widespread international age-studies community—a community of and for all ages—have been immeasurably helpful through their published writings, their willingness to answer my questions, and their support of my own work. Bless all the people who ever said, "You changed my thinking." You kept me going in moments of deep discouragement. Against the odds, age studies promises to be the enlightening intellectual revolution of this century.

To my close friends who have lived with me through the years that led up to this book, and to all those I didn't know well, or at all, who also told me stories of ageism and resilience (in conference hallways, over drinks, on the phone, via e-mail, on buses, in dirt-floored shacks, and in unexpected venues), I won't name you for privacy reasons, or because I never knew your names, but you are the impetus for this book and your stories are its soul.

NOTES

PREFACE

1. The Seneca Falls address (1848) was modeled on the Declaration of Independence and the analyses of abolitionists.

2. Emerson, "Old Age," 318. In his pioneering survey, *Old Age in the New Land*, Achenbaum quotes most of this passage on the age gaze (p. 36), but not the following passage on seeing dejection in the eyes of old men.

3. Emerson, "Old Age," 319–320, emphasis added.

4. I borrow from Fenstermaker and West, quoted in Kitzinger, "Doing Gender," 97.

5. Alison Jagger is quoted in Woodward, "Traumatic Shame," 216–217.

6. "Ageism is rarely equated with the most deleterious forms of discrimination; silence muffles the response to ageism, so it is usually left out of the debates about social justice even though *aging, the process that provides the catalyst for ageism*, is a noncontroversial, biological reality that links all human beings" (Davies et al., "Conversation," 96, my emphasis).

7. Bliss, cartoon, *Boston Globe*, May 19, 2014.

8. Robinson, *Death of Adam*.

9. Emerson, "Old Age," 328.

10. Wendy Lustbader, a gerontological social worker, wrote *Life Gets Better*. For a graph showing what "Ages 18–64 expect" versus what "Ages 65+ experience," see Pew Research Center, "Growing Old in America," 4.

11. Silke van Dyk, coining the term "Happy Gerontology," comments, "This approving stance more or less characterizes the mainstream of gerontology" ("The Appraisal," 93). Fishman, "It Gets Worse," reviewed Susan Jacoby's *Never Say Die*.

12. "A hopeless juxtaposition between the 'well-derly' and the 'ill-derly,' what psychoanalysts call 'splitting,' . . . leaves all of us impoverished," Harry Moody comments, personal communication, 2009. On the history of false dichotomies from the Victorian moralists on, see Cole, "The Specter," 31–33.

13. Although many scholars critique aspects of ageism, indices to books on aging rarely turn up many references to this invaluable keyword.

14. The number of journalists covering aging comes from Paul Kleyman, national coordinator of the Journalists' Network on Generations.

15. Data from Drèze and Sen, quoted by Farmer in "Who Lives and Who Dies," 18. Other rankings put the United States lower. Peter Orszag is quoted in Tavernese, "Disparity in Life Spans."

16. Wallis, "Intersectionality's Binding Agent," 610. His domains include jobs and entertainment.

17. Kohn, "Rethinking the Constitutionality," 217–227. *Massachusetts Board of Retirement v. Murgia* (1976), *Gregory v. Ashcroft* (1991), *Kimel v. Florida Board of Education* (2000) are some of the decisions legal scholars find detrimental.

18. "The High Costs of Middle Ageism," in Gullette, *Aged by Culture*.

19. Scharf and Keating, "Social Exclusion," 6.

20. Meek is satirizing British neoliberalism but his fable, "Robin Hood in a Time of Austerity," is applicable elsewhere.

21. Social Security Administration, "Fact Sheet."

22. Chief Justice Kennedy's used the state's aim to provide "dignity and purpose" in his decision ruling against the Defense of Marriage Act.

23. "In the scientific and popular literature recently there has been a widespread call for classifying normal aging as a disease, so that it can be 'manipulated, treated, and delayed.' " Biogerontologist David Gems is quoted in Nieuwenhuis-Mark, "Healthy Aging as Disease?"; Harry (Rick) Moody generously researched the data for me on the board-certified practitioners, and the members of the American Academy of Anti-Aging Medicine, who cannot be board-certified, as of March 2011: 26,000 non-board-certified practitioners touting unapproved substances versus 8,913 geriatricians and geriatric psychiatrists.

24. Cruikshank, *Learning*, 3, summarizing Julia Rozanova.

25. Robinson, *Gilead*, 142, 143–144.

26. Kohn, "Rethinking the Constitutionality," 236.

27. Scheiber, "The Brutal Ageism of Tech."

28. Bureau of the Census, "U.S. Population Projections," 30. The global median barely moves up.

29. Sartre, *Anti-Semite and Jew*, 89.

30. John Rawls uses the term "test of justice."

CHAPTER 1. #STILL HUMAN: INTO THE GLARE OF THE PUBLIC SQUARE

1. "Sexism" first appeared in print in *Vital Speeches of the Day*, November 15, 1968 (Shapiro, "Historical Notes," 3–16). The first use of "ageism" occurs in Dr. Robert Butler's landmark essay, "Age-ism, Another Form of Bigotry," in 1969.

2. In 2015 *Generations* devoted an issue to ageism: http://asaging.org/blog/pernicious-problem-ageism. Eight aging organizations organized a report whose title doesn't use "ageism," also in 2015 (*Gauging Aging*, by Eric Lindland et al.). Michael S. North suggests that "ignoring the study of ageism might represent a bias in and of itself" ("Ageism Stakes Its Claim").

3. In 1983, under Ronald Reagan, retirement age was raised gradually from sixty-five to sixty-seven, ignoring high later-life unemployment and people unable to hold full-time jobs.

4. Bill Bytheway uses the term "service-oriented" in his book, *Ageism* (43), which surveyed the field in 1995.

5. I wrote about this in *Agewise*, 75–76.

6. Gullette, "Oh. *America.*"

7. "Political Notebook," *New York Times*, A8.

8. Eric Holder quotes Ginsburg in Toobin, "Holder v. Roberts," 48.

9. See data from the Center on Aging and Work at Boston College, at http://capricorn.bc.edu/agingandwork/database/browse/facts/fact_record/5656/all. CDC, "Suicide among Adults," table 2; see Gullette, "What Do the Suicides . . . Reveal?"; Hopkins, "Sparrows Point." Economists consider "prime age" to be 25–54. With increasing longevity and health, perhaps they should raise the upper age limit. I use "midlife workers."

10. See Allen, "Ageism," 4, 1; also Martinson and Berridge, "Successful Aging," 63–64. *The Gerontologist* 55, no. 1, deals with "Successful Aging."

11. Woodard et al., "Older Women."

12. Gorman, "Diagnosis Unprepared."

13. Quoted in Stripling et al., "College Students."

14. Gilleard and Higgs, "Ageing Abjection," 140.

15. Coyne, "John Wise"; AP, "Prosecutor."

16. Brody, "Evaluating," 21, describing unexpected assaults on education.

17. Lorde, *Sister Outsider*, 123.

18. In 1965, Lyndon Johnson's secretary of labor, in *The Older American Worker*, said ageism in employment, although rampant, "did not appear to result from dislike of or intolerance toward the aged" (quoted in Kohn, "Rethinking," 234n105). It is harder to overlook dislike and intolerance now.

19. The term "the affective dimensions of ideology" comes from Gil, "Culture and Subjectivity," 442.

20. Baars et al., *Aging*, 4. "Macro" can be defined as definite issues that laws can address, but here I like this definition, pointing to the amorphous and occluded.

21. Judith Herman's *Trauma and Recovery: The Aftermath of Violence, from Domestic Abuse to Political Terror* (1992) expanded trauma studies.

22. Dittman, "Fighting Ageism," 50.

23. Emling, "Aging," about an AARP study.

24. Clarke, "A Memoir."

25. Jansson, *The Summer Book*, 37.

26. Ibid., 126, 127.

27. Ibid., 133.

28. Ibid., 129; Forna, *The Memory of Love*, 380.

29. Gullette, "Losing Lear."

30. Post, "In Response to Margaret M. Gullette" (emphasis in original).

31. Shulman, "Half Full."

32. Terry quotes the analyst, Hinze, in "Ageism and Projective Identification," 157.

33. I borrow this terminology from Walzer, "Imaginary Jews," 31. For an in-depth look at how difficult it is to determine "When Old Age Begins," see O'Rand's homonymous article.

34. Butler, "Critically Queer," 18.

35. Karpen quotes Shinoda Bolen in "Golden Girls." See also Pickard, *Age Studies*, 5–7, 13.

36. Leni Marshall, "Ageility Studies," and e-mail exchange, April 5/6, 2015.

37. John Lindemann Nelson, "Death's Gender," 113–129.

38. Angell, "This Old Man."

39. Men's early illnesses, including cardiovascular disease and cancer, require expensive reparative in-patient care. Men have more chronic illnesses. Harvard Men's Health Watch, "Mars vs. Venus."

40. Meyers, "Miroir," 32, 38.

41. Sebelius, "Secretary Sebelius Letter."

42. Cruikshank, *Learning*, 4.

43. Hightower, "Time," 14.

44. Gullette, "Creativity, Aging, Gender," 45–46. The term "Age Studies" was first adopted as the name of a book series edited by Anne Wyatt-Brown for the University Press of Virginia from 1993 to 2001. Kathleen Woodward presciently used "Age" rather than "Aging" in the title of an important collection of feminist essays, *Figuring Age* (1998). The first book with the title *Age Studies* is by Susan Pickard (2016).

45. Horsfield, "Statement," 206.

46. Emerson, "Circles," 319.

47. "Blame ageism, not aging" is an Ashton Applewhite slogan. "Fear ageism, not aging" and "Blame ageists" are mine.

CHAPTER 2. HOW (NOT) TO SHOOT OLD PEOPLE:
BREAKING AGEIST PARADIGMS THROUGH PORTRAIT PHOTOGRAPHY

1. To problematize this further, see O'Rand, "When Old Age Begins" and Overall's radical "Old Age."

2. Baudelaire, *Le Peintre*, 39–40.

3. Phu and Steer, "Introduction," 235.

4. The cover of Sophie Calle's *M'as-tu vue?* shows a woman with her hand covering one eye.

5. Daston and Galison, *Objectivity*, 188.

6. "The Work of Art in the Age of Spectacular Reproduction" is the title of a *Nation* article (August 31/ September 7, 2015, 36). "Still and mute," comes from Galassi, "'Bursting,'" 44.

7. Quoted in Bogan, "Ashton Applewhite, Part 3," around minute 2:20.

8. The term "age gaze" appears first in "Face-Off" in my 1997 book, *Declining to Decline*, 67; Woodward, "Performing Age," 164, emphasis added; 167.

9. Cruikshank, *Learning*, 151.

10. Ribbat, "Out of It?" 68, 68–69. He too curates a set of images he likes.

11. Bytheway, *Ageism*, 65.

12. "Funny Old People," accessed August 6, 2010, http://www.you-can-be-funny.com/Funny-Old-People.html. Ridiculous old People, accessed August 6, 2016, https://www.google.com/search?q'ridiculous+old+people&espv'2&biw'999&bih'727&tbm'isch&tbo'u&source'univ&sa'X&ved'oahUKEwjb5eG10a30AhWElR4KHVZHBnsQsAQIGw. Ornstein, "Nursing Home Workers," covers the crimes.

13. This terminology comes from Walzer, "Imaginary Jews," 31.

14. Dorfman, "Portrait."

15. Cristofovici, *Touching Surfaces*, 4–5, my emphasis.

16. Quoted in Rosenberg Foundation for Children, "Art, Activism, and the Rosenberg Fund for Children" (video, minute 4:09).

17. Stallabrass, "Cold Eye," 151.

18. Gullette, "Caitlyn Jenner."

19. For Topaz's "SILVER: A State of Mind," go to www.womenonaging.com/main.php#/VIEW%2.

20. Chapter 1 of Gullette's *Aged by Culture* discusses photographic ways of doing justice to selfhood, using Jo Spence's concept of auto-photography and Hans-Pieter Feldmann's very different "series," *A Century.*

21. Bytheway, "Visual Representations," 32.

22. Machado is visible, as is the original Havana mural in color, at minutes 26:24 and 26:28 of a video, *Wrinkles of the City*, by Social Animals and Parlá Studios, June 12, 2014. i, https://www.youtube.com/watch?v=BD2VWmxW1nk. Accessed December 2, 2016.

23. Hall, "Stuart Hall." Hall did not discuss narrative.

24. McFadden, "Teaching the Camera."

25. *Saveur*, 86.

26. Kathleen Woodward curates a small collection in "Performing Age," 167.

27. Woodward, *Figuring Age*, 155.

28. Arbus's Guggenheim application.

29. Silcoff, "Why Your Grandpa."

30. Bajac, "A View," 59.

31. Bright, "Motherhood Reimagined."

32. Pollock, "Missing Women," 234.

33. Cristofovici discusses *Giant*, critiquing (ageist) readings, in *Touching Surfaces*, 23–27.

34. Twigg is quoted in Pickard, "Biology as Destiny?" *Agewise*, 110.

35. Wall, email.

36. Shapiro, "Interview."

37. Quoted in Cristofovici, *Touching Surfaces*, 26n2.

38. Seventh comment in McLaren, *The Photographers' Gallery.*

39. Certo, "The Unconventional," 12.

40. Coplans, "John Coplans Memorial."

41. Angier, *Train Your Gaze*, 33.

42. Coplon, "Description."

43. Ribbat, "Out of It?"

44. Go to http://farm5.staticflickr.com/4061/4656970973_001f108964.jpg.

45. Linnecar, "A Discourse Analysis."

46. Quoted in Anon, "Book Review."

47. Quoted on Peters, "Richard Avedon's Letter."

48. Danto, *What Art Is*, 106, 105.

49. Sultan, "Pictures from Home," 9, 10, 12, 13.

50. Quoted in Dwoskin, "Age Is . . . ," presskit.

51. Sontag, "Photography within," 66.

52. Kunhardt, "On Gordon Parks," n.p. The genealogy of Parks's photo may include a classic Walker Evans photo of objects on a Depression-era bureau.

53. hooks, "In Our Glory," 62.

54. Ruohomaa's biographer, Deanna Bonner-Ganter, writes me that the caption reads: "On a child's swing near the picnic grounds Edward Rogers Castner, who ran a general

store in Damariscota, Maine, for 60 years, gives his wife (Lillian) a fine ride. Both husband and wife are eighty and have been married 60 years." Bonner-Ganter, email. TMI.

55. Stallabrass, "What's in a Face?" 73.

56. Quoted in Woodward, "Assisted Living," 11.

57. Michael Lessac said this after a Boston showing of his fascinating film *Truth in Translation*.

58. Sontag, *On Photography*, 178.

CHAPTER 3. THE ELDER-HOSTILE:
GIVING COLLEGE STUDENTS A BETTER START AT LIFE

1. Stripling et al., Poster presentation.

2. Levy et al., "Facebook"; Levy, quoted in Shelton, "Yale Study Finds Bias."

3. D'Onfro, "Facebook Employees"; Conner, "Hello."

4. Buckels et al., "Trolls," 97, 98, 100.

5. Stripling et al.; Mead, "The Troll Slayer," 33.

6. Harris, "Young Thug Says."

7. MacLaine, "Youth Wanted."

8. Frick, "How Old?"; Chittum, "Audit Notes"; Rejuvenation Center, "Is Ageism Causing?"

9. See North and Fiske, "An Inconvenienced Youth?" 984–990, and North and Fiske, "Act Your (Old) Age."

10. *The Male in the Head* is the title of a 1998 book by Janet Holland et al.

11. Ruiz, "Why Women Should Stop."

12. Isaacs and Bearison, "The Development"; see also Aday et al., "Changing Children's Perceptions."

13. Cottle and Glover, "Combating Ageism," 511.

14. American Press Institute, "How Millennials Get News."

15. The AARP article that published these gloomy facts is gaily headlined "Intergenerational Conflict? Think Again!"

16. Marshall, email.

17. The Fraboni statements I use come from Wurtele and Maruyama, "Changing Students' Stereotypes."

18. See Gullette, *Agewise*, 141–158. A related genre is called "auto-ethnography."

19. On "postmaternity," see Gullette, "Postmaternity," 553–572; "Wicked Powerful," 107–139.

20. Umphrey, email communication.

21. Parker and Satkoske, "Ethical Dimensions," 7.

22. Andreoletti et al., "Gender, Race, and Age," say few studies look at compound stereotypes.

23. Marshall, "Teaching Ripening," 56, citing Ellis and Morrison. An array of other possible assignments can be found on Marshall's Website, www.aging.org.

24. AARP/USC Report; Calasanti, "A Feminist."

25. Hotchkiss, "Researchers."

26. Williams, "Cruelty," 11.

27. Lamb, Erin, "Polyester Pants"; Siegal and Kagan, "Teaching."

28. Pierce, "Poststructural Feminist Pedagogy," 43.
29. Seligman et al., *Living with Difference*, 105.
30. Dunbar and Molina, "Opposition," 94.
31. Proctor et al., "Woman."
32. Nelson, "Ageism."
33. Gullette, ed., *The Art and Craft of Teaching*; all my writers had taken Christensen's famous course.
34. Freire, in Freire and Macedo, "Rethinking Literacy," 355; Seligman et al., *Living with Difference*, 98 and n8.
35. Collier and Foster, "Teaching Age."
36. Banaji and Greenwald, "Interview."
37. Quoted in Kennedy and Whitlock, "Introduction," 253.
38. Proctor et al., "Woman."
39. In 1997, people over fifty-five made up only 1.6 percent of undergraduates (Bratrud, "The Lived Experience," Appendix K1, 248).
40. Email from "Linda Serenata," December 2013.
41. DeMille, "Age Discrimination," B2.
42. Scholle and Denski, *Media Education*.
43. When teaching midlife literature at the Radcliffe Seminars, I started a weekly "barometer" of age-related items that students brought in.
44. Siegel and Kagan, "Teaching," 23.
45. Rampell, "The Burden," emphasis added.
46. Williams, "Cruelty."
47. Ozeki, *All Over Creation*, 172.
48. Chand et al., "Teaching," 17; see also 10, table 1.
49. Meek, "The Millennial-Boomer Alliance."
50. Lamb, "Polyester Pants."
51. Marshall, "Teaching Ripening."
52. Lamb, "Polyester Pants"; de Medeiros, email.
53. Lamb, "Polyester Pants."
54. Except for the first sentence, this speech comes from a student in Kate de Medeiros's course at Miami University of Ohio, fall 2015. De Medeiros offered an optional assignment, to report on instances of ageism that students observed. Many responded.
55. Discussing professional videos has been shown to reduce ageism. Making videos themselves, as students do in Erin Lamb's course, must be even more valuable.
56. The Association for Gerontology in Higher Education endorsed this, May 18, 2016.
57. Chekhov, "Rothschild's Fiddle."
58. In 2013, there were 15.8 million undergraduates. US Census Bureau, "College Enrollment Declines."
59. Umphrey and Robinson, "Negative Stereotypes," 316, is a study of "other-person perceptions" and social distance.
60. Levy et al., "Longevity Increased."
61. Barnett, "Focusing," 91.
62. Private communication from Sarah Lamb; see also Sages and Seekers website, "The Eight-Week Program."

63. Emily is at minute 2:57 of Sages and Seekers, "3-Minute University Video."
64. Biggs, "Aging in a Critical World," 118–119.
65. Katz, "What Is Age Studies?"
66. Quoted in Barnett, "Focusing," 92.

CHAPTER 4. VERT DE GRIS: RESCUING THE LAND LOVERS

1. The Vietnamese saying is from VEGGI Farmer's Cooperative, "Ăn Quả Nhớ Kẻ Trồng Cây."
2. Lawson, *City Bountiful*, 281.
3. Carlisle, "Education," 23.
4. Baldacci, "The Origins," 3.
5. Wozniacka, "Woodlake Pride."
6. George et al., "A Model," 389–404.
7. Gray, "Black Farmers' Lives Matter."
8. Romer, "The Radical Potential," 12.
9. Data in McKenna, "Planting New Farmers."
10. The "human ecology perspective" is an exception: see Keating and Phillips, "A Critical Human Ecology Perspective," 1–10. I am writing an essay on US farm fiction's few old people.
11. Mitchell et al., "The Aging Farm Population," 97; International Network, "Why?"
12. One exception, including interviews with "stoic" women, some former farmers, is Eales et al., "Age-Friendly," 109–120.
13. Harding, "What We're about to Receive."
14. Lappé, "The Food Movement" and "Farming for a Small Planet"; McKibben, "The Pope," 42.
15. Data about the percentage of women farming is hard to find. Japanese data: Jöhr, "Where?" 9, 11. UK data: UK Agriculture, "Crisis"; American data: Imhoff, "Farm Bill 101," 28; USDA Census 2012, "Census Highlights," figure 2.
16. Beales, "Tackling."
17. USDA, "2012Census of AgricultureHighlights."
18. Baldacci, "The Origins," 3. In Europe, travel brochures display "wrinkled older rustic faces" (Giarchi, "Older People," 716).
19. Gessler, "Macon Fry."
20. Quest-Riston, "The Best."
21. Thoreau, *A Writer's Journal*, 171, 145; Dolan, *Beyond the Fruited Plain*, 72–73.
22. Bhatti, "'When I'm in the Garden,'" 322.
23. Waring, *If Women Counted*, 84.
24. Rao, "Indicators," 4.
25. Pomrehn et al., "Ischemic Heart Disease."
26. Pollak, "Vital Signs"; Anderson, "Longevity." Social and productive activities like volunteering resulted in similar health and longevity benefits.
27. Westermarck, *Wit and Wisdom of Morocco*.
28. Giarchi discusses opportunities for part-time older workers in Europe and England ("Older People," 709).
29. Robertson, *The Orchard*, 7.

30. Zuckerman, "Constant Gardeners," 31.

31. Guyer and Salami, "Life Courses," 211.

32. Ibid., 212.

33. Holt-Giménez, "From Food Crisis."

34. Imhoff, "Farm Bill 101."

35. Keizer, "Getting Schooled," 181.

36. Koutsou et al., "Present or Absent," 411.

37. Of 445 of our graduates surveyed, 56 percent have come from rural backgrounds. See https://sanjuandelsursistercityproject.wordpress.com/adult-education/.

38. On Greeks keeping land in the family, see Koutsou et al., "Present or Absent," 404–419, esp. 416.

39. GRAIN, "Seized!"

40. Grant et al., "Black Farmers United."

41. Quoted in Bowens, *The Color of Food*, 39–40.

42. Pantic and Miljković, "Regional Differences," 30.

43. IRIN, "Zimbabwe's Neglected."

44. Cook and Liu, "Can 'Distant Water . . . ?'" 34; see also 36.

45. Bhatti, "'When I'm in the Garden,'" 333–334.

46. Gurney, "Brown Earth Look," 25; Berry, "Farmland without Farmers."

47. A Mexican song about "leaving Papa." https://www.facebook.com/ajuchitlandel progreso/videos/396551120515015/?fref=nf.

48. Jiang et al., "Bequest Motives," paragraph 2.

49. Zuo, "Pension Now Covers," 5.

50. Glasgow, "Poverty among Rural Elders," 311; "non-blushing paper" comes from Spitzer and Mbeyo, *In Search of Protection*, 116.

51. Cook and Liu, "Can 'Distant Water . . . ?'" 37.

52. Beales, "Tackling the Food Crisis."

53. Spitzer and Mbeyo, *In Search of Protection*, 99, also 100.

54. Edmondson and Scharf, "Rural and Urban Aging," 414; Scharf and Bartlam, "Ageing and Social Exclusion," 99.

55. IRIN, "Zimbabwe's Neglected"; see also Spitzer and Mbeyo, *In Search of Protection*, 116–119.

56. Pillay and Maharaj, "Population Ageing," 12. Kate de Medeiros led me to Pillay and Maharaj's book containing this.

57. Milbourne, "Austerity, Welfare Reform, and Older People," 86–87.

58. Gómez Garcia and Rico Gonzales, "Rural Development," data on 9, 11; 22.

59. Chang, "Korean Elder Law," 37.

60. Zuckerman, "Constant Gardeners," 28, 30–31.

61. Schukoske, "Community Development," 378, 390n249.

62. FAO, "Feeding the Cities."

63. Schultz, "Food Sovereignty," 128.

64. Schukoske, "Community Development," 378, 390n249.

65. FAO, "Feeding the Cities," xxxiv.

66. Holt-Giménez, "From Food Crisis to Food Sovereignty."

67. 2014 study for the FAO, Lowder et al., "What Do We Really Know?" 3–24, ii.

68. Srinivas, "Women Farmers Are Worse Off."

69. On US women in agriculture, see Allen and Sachs, "Women and Food Chains."

70. Ram K., letter in response to "Elders Seek Special Session."

71. National Sustainable Agriculture Coalition, *Senior Farmers' Market.*

72. International data from Kutner, "Death on the Farm"; on Australia, National Rural Health Alliance, *Fact Sheet 14*, and Perry, "Drought"; on USA, Berry, *Bringing It to the Table*, 16; on UK, BBC News, "Farmers More Likely."

73. *Taipei Times*, "President Ma Details Increase."

74. Huber, "Slow Food Nation," 23.

75. Fleshman, "A Harvest of Hope."

76. Romer, "The Radical Potential," 8.

77. McKeon, "Now's the Time," 257.

78. Ibid.

79. Watts, "Field of Tears."

80. Harding, "What We're About to Receive."

81. Kastner, "Hope," especially 168–170.

82. Willmore, Review of *Intergenerational Support and Old Age in Africa*, 2.

CHAPTER 5. THE ALZHEIMER'S DEFENSE:
"FAKING BAD" IN INTERNATIONAL ATROCITY TRIALS

1. Kornbluh, "Letter," 26; Van Auken, "Chilean Prosecutor."

2. For the full text of the charge, see Zepeda, "Second"; *Notes on the Americas*, "An Extradition Request"; CIA, "CIA Activities in Chile"; Kornbluh, "Chile"; Associated Press, "Chilean Court."

3. Yapp, "Chile Requests Extradition."

4. CNN, "Joyce Horman."

5. National Security Archive, "Chilean Judge Requests."

6. Schweda and Swinnen, "Call"; Behuniak, "Living Dead?" 75, also 84–85.

7. Kaczor et al., "Wife"; Kornbluh, "Chile."

8. Butler, "The Life-review."

9. Kissinger is quoted in Kornbluh, "Letter," 26.

10. Associated Press, "Chilean Court"; Bonnefoy, "Chile Hunt for Justice."

11. NISGUA, "Genocide Cases"; Reuters, "Guatemalan Ex-dictator"; Yates, in Kinoy et al., *Granito.*

12. *Notes on the Americas*, "The Slow, Slow Pace."

13. "Universal jurisdiction" is a controversial or misleading term. The United States has given immunity to its military, exempting itself.

14. Groopman, "Medical Dispatch"; Alzheimer's Society UK, "Zombie."

15. Henig, "The Last Day."

16. Karpff, *How to Age.*

17. England, "Performing."

18. Dickerson et al., "MRI-derived."

19. England, "A Personal Note," 18.

20. David Scheffer's rationale for the term "atrocity crimes," *All the Missing Souls*, 426–435; see especially 428.

21. Oorsouw and Merckelbach, "Detecting."

22. Raab, "Vincent Gigante"; Raab, *Five Families*, 12.

23. The film that describes Guzman's reversal is *The General and the Judge*, produced by Westwind Productions. http://www.westwindproductions.org.

24. Weiner, "Fitness Hearings," 188.

25. KRT Trial Monitor, "Monitoring Program," section III B; "Burden of Proof"; on Gbagbo, ICC, "Pre-Trial Chamber I."

26. Viewer data from Chansok, "Can Khmer Rouge Survivors Get Justice?"; Fawthrop, "Cambodia"; Seiff, "Khmer Rouge Tribunal."

27. Campbell's conclusion can be found on KRT Monitor, "Case OO2: Special Report," 2 and n7; UPI.com World News, "Court Orders Treatment." On the court's deciding Thirith's appeal, see Reaksmey, "Ieng Thirith"; on the clock hands test, "Specialist."

28. On Dr. Thida, KRT Monitor, "Special Report," 14; on the "not conclusive" finding, see Sheridan, "Cannibalism"; BBC News Asia, "Khmer Rouge 'First Lady' "; KRT Monitor, Part II, "Summary."

29. Al Jazeera, "Cambodia to Free"; ECCC, "Decision," 14.

30. Kazcor, "Wife."

31. Email communication with Oorsouw, March 22, 2012; see also http://www.psych assessments.com.au/products/302/prod302_report1.pdf ; Oorsouw and Merckelbach, "Detecting Malingered Memory," 107.

32. Merchant, personal communication.

33. NISGUA, "Genocide Cases."

34. Scheffer, *All the Missing Souls*.

35. Márquez, *Clandestine*, 108.

36. Groopman, "Medical Dispatch"; Martell, "Forensic Neuropsychology," 316; Dickerson et al., "MRI-derived . . . Atrophy"; Personal communication with Dr. James Katz, of RiverBend Medical Group, Chicopee, MA; Flinn, "Dementia Care Costs."

37. Weiner, "Fitness Hearings," 196–197.

38. Public Health England, "Recommendation against"; Peters and Katz, "Voices," 186; Mitchell and Shiri-Feshki, "Rate of Progression"; Gomersall et al.. "Living with Ambiguity," 909.

39. Milwain, "Mild Cognitive Impairment"; Whitehouse and Moody, "Mild Cognitive Impairment."

40. Angell, "The Illusions."

41. Price, "Mental Disability," 118; Paula Caplan, email communication. "Having said that, it is of course essential to have a neurological workup if there is reason to think that the person has an actual brain tumor or neurological disease, but none of this belongs in a manual of mental disorders."

42. When I wrote my last book, *Agewise*, my mother was still alive. "The Essence That Remains" fills in some of the rest of our story. Much of this section originally appeared in Gullette, "Keeping."

43. The concept of "successful frailty" was developed by Wendy Lustbader, *Counting on Kindness*, 15.

44. Dworkin, *Life's Dominion*, 236, 237.

45. Beard and Neary, "Making Sense," 141.

46. UK Department of Constitutional Affairs, *Mental Capacity Act*, 19.

47. Nöe, *Out of Our Heads*, 7.

48. Thielking, "Efforts Spread," A1, A6.
49. Prager quotes Kohut in "Healing from History," 413.
50. Nolan, "Dimensions," 319.
51. Bruens, "Dementia," 87.

CHAPTER 6. OUR FRIGHTENED WORLD:
FANTASIES OF EUTHANASIA AND PREEMPTIVE SUICIDE

1. Carroll, "Alzheimer's Extracts." The NBC story was sent me by Kate de Medeiros.
2. Zeilig, "Dementia."
3. Carroll, "Alzheimer's Extracts."
4. Malphurs and Cohen, "A Statewide Case-Control Study." See also Eliason, "Murder-Suicide: A Review."
5. Data from Sanders and Power, "Roles," 41.
6. Data from Reese, "Murder-Suicide Disturbing Trend," and Malphurs and Cohen, "A Statewide Case-Control Study"; on guns, DiFilippo, "Armed and Aging."
7. Gullette, "Why I Hesitated." This issue of *Feminism and Psychology* focuses on autonomy.
8. Gullette, "Florence Nightingale—Dammit." Many feminist gerontologists write feelingly about the difficulties of caregiving.
9. Oregon Public Health Division.
10. Smith, "Q and A."
11. See Gullette, "How We Imagine."
12. Gilleard and Higgs, "Ageing Abjection," 139.
13. Skoloff, "Arizona Man, 86."
14. Ibid.
15. Lake, "Bullying Is Ageless."
16. Reese, "Murder-Suicide Disturbing Trend."
17. Sheeran and Seewer, "Ohio Hospital Shooting."
18. AP, "Lighter Term."
19. Eberhardt, "Seeing Black."
20. Kate de Medeiros made this ironic point in a private communication.
21. AARP tries to improve access to each state's unique respite care program, for family caregivers.
22. Zeilig, "Dementia," quotes Cohen-Shalev and Marcus.
23. AARP, "I [Heart] Caregivers."
24. Sanders and Power, "Roles," 41–42.
25. Theroux, *Extreme Love.*
26. Tom Kitwood identified seventeen "malignant" practices used against the helpless (*Dementia Reconsidered*, 46–47).
27. Wolff, "A Life Worth Ending."
28. Lamb, "Permanent Personhood," 42.
29. Loh, "Daddy Issues."
30. Klein, "The Long Goodbye."
31. *New York Times*, http://newoldage.blogs.nytimes.com/. The sidebar used to begin, "Adults over age 80 are the fastest growing segment of the population. . . ."

32. Gullette, "'The Boomers' vs. 'the Xers.'"
33. Woodward, *Statistical Panic.*
34. Foster et al., "How Does Older Age?"
35. The Inuit are cited as putting their elders out on ice floes to die: see Gullette, *Agewise*, chapter 1, on the forms this takes, from joke to recommendation.
36. Emanuel, "Why I Hope to Die."
37. Span, "Over 65?" D5.
38. Chast, *Can't We Talk*, 144.
39. Quoted in Flinders, "The Internal Struggles of Aging," 262.
40. Terry, "Ageism."
41. Kunow, "Preemptive Biographies"; on the "preemptive imagination," see 104–112.
42. Eliot, "Natural History," 198–199.
43. Brecht, *On Art and Politics*, 196, 197, 200–201, 227, 229, 230.
44. Morrison, *Playing in the Dark*, xi.
45. Moore, "Depth," 166–168. In Tim Price's *Salt, Root and Roe*, seventy-year-old twins, one of whom "has dementia," drown themselves. In Ben Power's *A Tender Thing* (2009), a couple "journey towards euthanasia" (167). Moore lists others (168).
46. Kushner, *Angels in America, Part One*, 118–119; 729. Although he doesn't discuss *Guide*, age, or MCI, Kornhaber's essay ("Kushner at Colonus," 733–739) has been helpful.
47. Savran, "Kushner's Children."
48. Kushner kindly gave me access to the unpublished 2009 manuscript, and permission to quote a few lines. The play may have changed since 2009.
49. NIH funding for HIV/AIDS research is twenty-three times that for Alzheimer's research. Five times as many Americans have Alzheimer's as have HIV (Bright Focus Foundation, "Alzheimer's Facts").
50. Itzkovitz, "Lincoln," 88.
51. Tougaw, "Testimony," 167–168.
52. Green, "The Intelligent Homosexual's Guide."
53. Quoted by Brantley, "Debating Dialectics"; *Guide*, Act Two, Scene 1. http://nymag .com/arts/theater/profiles/68994/index1.html.
54. Burr, "*Amour* Bears Witness"; Conrad, "Haneke." The *Guardian* also published my own critique, "*Amour.*"
55. Desmond O'Neill, a geriatrician, also wondered sadly if "the final events might be construed as noble or beautiful in this context" ("*Amour*").
56. Conrad, "Haneke."
57. "Gerontology Prize."
58. Brody, "Michael Haneke's."
59. Cheng, *Melancholy of Race*, 164.
60. Phillips, *On Balance*, 199.
61. Rich, *What Is Found There*, 204.
62. Tyler, *A Spool*, 161.
63. Hepburn, "Still Alice" [review]. Lisa Genova, the author of the novel, also omits the word "dying": "Then get in the bed and go to sleep" is the final instruction, as if the former self were trying to trick the later self (271).
64. Chivers, *Silvering Screen*, 73.
65. Kluger, *Refus de Témoigner*, 226; my translation, my italics.

66. James Cromwell was only seventy-two in 2012, Geneviève Bujold seventy-one.

67. Marshall and Katz, "The Embodied Life Course," section 4.

68. Timmermann, quoting A. Ashworth, "Incitement," 826.

69. Ackerman, Letter to "The Conversation."

CHAPTER 7. INDUCTION INTO THE HALL OF SHAME AND THE WAY OUT

1. Nussbaum (*Upheavals of Thought*, 196) is writing not about adults, but of shame in children.

2. Crossley and Rockett, "The Experience of Shame," 368.

3. Jungers and Slagel, "Crisis Model," 92.

4. I discuss age anxiety and identity-stripping in *Declining to Decline* (1997).

5. Scheff, "Shame," 254. His bibliography concerns shame in general (rather than ageism-related, racialized, etcetera, or shamings in the plural).

6. The italicized language comes from Brown, "Shame Resilience Theory," 45; Womersley et al., "The Construction of Shame," 876.

7. Zerwick, "Ageism in Our Society."

8. Applewhite, "What I Learned in Grand Rapids." The booklet is at http://passiton network.org/wp-content/uploads/ConciousnessRaisingBooklet.pdf.

9. To avoid this form of ageism, Stephen Katz suggests mixed-age physiotherapy classes ("Hold On!" 204n54).

10. Cheng, "The Melancholy of Race," 55; North and Fiske, "Act Your (Old) Age"; Gornick, "Delmore's Way."

11. Eric Santner, a literary scholar who writes on psychoanalysis, is quoted in Berger, "Trauma and Literary Theory," 574n5. Santner is not talking about old age, mourning youth, or passing for younger.

12. Terry, "Ageism," 156.

13. Brennan, *Transmission*, 6.

14. Ibid., 200n17; 47–48.

15. Reeve, "Shame."

16. Brennan, *Transmission*, 116.

17. Ibid., 2.

18. Lagioia, "Writing."

19. Crossley and Rockett, "The Experience of Shame," table IV, 371. Ten subjects did not volunteer anything to feel ashamed about. ("If any" is my addition.)

20. Root, "Reconstructing the Impact," 230.

21. Bouson's introduction to *Embodied Shame* provides a good overview of feminist and other theories.

22. "Limited research exists that has explored the frequency and impact of interpersonal trauma across the life span," write Clarke, and Griffin, "Body Image and Aging." They do not focus on ageist shaming.

23. Kennedy and Whitlock, "Introduction," 252.

24. Holstein, Waymack, and Parks, *Ethics, Aging, and Society*, 54.

25. Phillips, "Against Self-Criticism," 14.

26. Wong and Tsai, "Cultural Models," 210.

27. Gross, Carstensen, et al., "Emotion and Aging," 597; see also 591.

28. Orth et al., "Tracking the Trajectory," 1069.

29. Ibid. The twenty-six hundred were aged from thirteen to eighty-nine.

30. McHugh, "Aging, Agency, and Activism."

31. Stewart and Ostrove, "Women's Personality in Middle Age."

32. Achenbaum, "Gene D. Cohen," 246.

33. Kristin Neff, a scholar who studies self-compassion, distinguishes it from self-esteem, which may be supercilious, narcissistic, or bullying (TedX talk). www.youtube .com/watch?v=IvtZBUSplr4.

34. MetLife, "Out and Aging," 42, 53.

35. Meyers, "Miroir," 32.

36. Holstein, *Women in Late Life*, 59.

37. Swedish sociologists found that older people report greater body satisfaction than younger people. Cited in McKee and Gott, "Shame and the Aging Body," 75.

38. Orth et al., "Tracking the Trajectory," figure 3.

39. Elinor Fuchs, email.

40. Brennan, *Transmission*, 47–48.

41. A woman wearing this tee shirt appears on Ari Seth Cohen's site, Advanced Style.

42. Radstone refers to Dori Laub and Caruth on the phenomenon of "an event without a witness," "Trauma Theory," 12. Her analysis helped me refine the concept of the Current Self, the Elder within, later in this chapter .

43. Woodward, *Statistical Panic*, 95; see 95–97. Woodward builds on the work of Sandra Lee Bartky.

44. Cheng, *Melancholy*, xi.

45. Butler is quoted in Kahane, "Gender and Patrimony."

46. Brennan, *Transmission*, 5.

47. Pierce quotes Stetz in "Poststructural Feminist Pedagogy," 49.

48. Cheng, *Melancholy*, 174.

49. Caruth is quoted in DeFalco, "Dementia, Caregiving, and Narrative."

50. Dougherty et al., "Assisting Older Women," 24, emphasis added; Rock, email.

51. Sotheara, "A Qualitative and Quantitative Investigation," 28.

52. Gordon, "At Sixty-Five," 34, 36, 38; Sartre, *Anti-Semite and Jew*, 109.

53. Pierce quotes Greene in "Poststructural Feminist Pedagogy," 43.

54. Moody quotes Brugh Joy on the concept of the "Elder Inside," "Human Values."

55. Kate de Medeiros gave these cards to her students in a Fall 2015 class at Miami University of Ohio. They were to write about whatever they observed and post the comments on a communal blog. It makes interesting reading.

56. Cvetkovich, *Depression*, 3.

57. Beauvoir, *Coming of Age*, 284.

CHAPTER 8. REDRESS: HEALING THE SELF, RELATIONSHIPS, SOCIETY

1. King and Calasanti, "Empowering the Old," 152.

2. For how nations participate in Age Demands Action, see http://www.helpage.org/ get-involved/campaign-with-us/ada-global/.

3. Vitols and Lynch, "Back in the Saddle," 14, 16.

4. Hustvedt, *Blazing World*, 112.

5. Levy, "A Culture-Drain Link," abstract.

6. Woodward, "Against Wisdom."

7. Accepting the age-proxy doctrine, as Congress intended, would overturn *Hazen Paper Co. v. Biggins* (1993), which decided that an employer's termination of a sixty-two-year-old man to avoid vesting his pension, which he was weeks from achieving, did not constitute discrimination *by age*. A more liberal Congress might pass something the "Protecting Older Workers Against Discrimination Act," which recognizes employers' "mixed motives" as possible ageism. Querry, "Rose," 531.

8. DiFilippo, "Armed and Aging." In California a judge can give a person of any age a restraining order, taking away his guns for up to a year.

9. Jansson, *The Summer Book*, 135.

10. Fanon, *Black Skin*, 169.

11. Prager, "Healing," 411.

12. Muldoon, "The Moral Legitimacy," 304.

13. Associated Press, "Guatemala Court."

14. Prager, "Healing," 415.

15. Miller and Tougaw, "Introduction," 3.

16. Kathi Weeks's definition is quoted in Coyle, "Review," 344.

BIBLIOGRAPHY

AARP. "I [Heart] Caregivers." Accessed September 20, 2014. https://act.aarp.org/iheart caregivers/?autologin=true&CMP=EMC-SNG-ADV-CARE-111314.

AARP Press Center. "Intergenerational Conflict? Think Again!" November 22, 2004. Accessed April 5, 2016. http://www.aarp.org/about-aarp/press-center/info-2004/aging _1.html.

Achenbaum, W. Andrew. "Gene D. Cohen, MD, PhD: Creative Gero-Psychiatrist and Visionary Public Intellectual." *Journal of Aging, Humanities, and the Arts* 4 (2010): 238–250.

———. *Old Age in the New Land: The American Experience since 1790.* Baltimore: Johns Hopkins University Press, 1978.

Ackerman, Felicia Nimue. Letter to "The Conversation." *Atlantic,* July/August 2013. Accessed December 8, 2016. http://www.theatlantic.com/magazine/archive/2013/07/ the-conversation/309406/.

Aday, R. H., Kathryn L. Aday, Josephine L. Arnold, and Susan L. Bendix. "Changing Children's Perceptions of the Elderly." *Gerontology and Geriatric Education* 16, no. 3 (1996): 37–51.

Al Jazeera. "Cambodia to Free Khmer Rouge 'First Lady.'" *Al Jazeera,* September 13, 2012. Accessed March 7, 2016. http://www.aljazeera.com/news/asia-pacific/2012/09/ 2012913105425114170.html.

Allen, Julie Ober. "Ageism as a Risk Factor for Chronic Disease." *The Gerontologist* 55 (January 23, 2015): doi:10.1093/geront/gnu158.

Allen, Patricia, and Carolyn Sachs. "Women and Food Chains: The Gendered Politics of Food." *International Journal of Sociology of Food and Agriculture* 15, no.1 (December 2006): 1–16. Accessed February 9, 2016. http://www.ijsaf.org/contents/15–1/allen/ index.html.

Alzheimer's Society, UK. "Zombie Evacuation Race." Accessed May 5, 2016. www .alzheimers.org.uk/site/scripts/documents_info.php?documentID=2257.

American Press Institute. "How Millennials Get News: Inside the Habits of America's First Digital Generation." March 16, 2015. Accessed March 21, 2016. https://www .americanpressinstitute.org/publications/reports/survey-research/millennials-news/ single-page/.

Andreoletti, Carrie, Jennifer P. Leszczynski, and William B. Disch. "Gender, Race, and Age: The Content of Compound Stereotypes across the Life Span." *International Journal of Aging and Human Development* 81, no. 1–2 (2015): 27–53.

Angell, Marcia. "The Illusions of Psychiatry." *New York Review of Books*, July 14, 2011. www .nybooks.com/articles/archives/2011/jul/14/illusions-of-psychiatry/?pagination=false.

Angell, Roger. "This Old Man: Life in the Nineties." *New Yorker*, February 17, 2014.

Angier, Roswell. *Train Your Gaze: A Practical and Theoretical Introduction to Portrait Photography.* Lausanne, Switzerland: AVA, 2007.

Applewhite, Ashton. *This Chair Rocks: A Manifesto against Ageism.* 2016. https://this chairrocks.com/book.

———. "What I Learned in Grand Rapids." *This Chair Rocks* newsletter, March 4, 2015. Accessed December 3, 2016. http://us6.campaign-archive1.com/?u=b7e45e0548&id= e83f9957dd.

Arbus, Diane. "Plan for a Photographic Project." *Orange Mercury.* Accessed February 6. 2014. https://orangemercury.blogspot.com/2009/03/diane-arbus-american-rites -manners-and.html.

Associated Press (AP). "Chilean Court Links US Intelligence to 1973 Killings of Two Americans." *Guardian*, July 1, 2014. Accessed March 11, 2015. http://www.theguardian. com/world/2014/jul/01/chile-us-intelligence-1973-killings-americans.

———. "Guatemala Court." *Guardian*, August 25, 2015. Accessed December 8, 2016. http://www.theguardian.com/world/2015/aug/25/guatemala-rios-montt-genocide -trial-not-sentenced.

———. "Lighter Term Offered in Slaying Case." *Boston Globe*, November 15, 2013.

———. "Prosecutor Seeks Break in Ohio Hospital Shooting." CNSnews, November 14, 2013. Accessed June 21, 2016. http://www.cnsnews.com/news/article/prosecutor -seeks-break-ohio-hospital-shooting.

Baars, Jan, Dale Dannefer, Chris Phillipson, and Alan Walker.. "Introduction: Critical Perspectives in Social Gerontology." In *Aging, Globalization, and Inequality: The New Critical Gerontology.* Amityville, NY: Baywood, 2006.

Bajac, Quentin. "A View from a Judgment Seat: Quentin Bajac in Conversation with Philip Gefter." *Aperture* no. 213 (Winter 2013–2014): 59.

Baldacci, David. "The Origins of *Wish You Well.*" Accessed February 2016. http://david baldacci.com/wp-content/uploads/2013/11/The-Origins-of-Wish-You-Well.pdf.

Banaji, Mazharin. "Project Implicit." Accessed December 8, 2016. https://implicit .harvard.edu/implicit/takeatest.html.

Banaji, Mazharin, and Anthony Greenwald. "Interview." *Edge: The Third Culture*, 2008. Accessed May 1, 2013. http://www.edge.org/3rd_culture/banaji_greenwald08/banaji_ greenwald08_index.html.

Barnett, Barbara. "Focusing on the Next Picture: Feminist Scholarship as a Foundation for Teaching about Ageism in the Academy." *NWSA Journal* 18, no.1 (Spring 2006): 85–98.

Baudelaire, Charles. *Le Peintre de la vie moderne, variétés critiques* II. Paris: Bibliothèque Dionysienne, 1924.

BBC News. "Farmers 'More Likely to Be Suicidal.'" February 25, 2003. Accessed December 8, 2016. http://news.bbc.co.uk/2/hi/health/2793533.stm.

BBC News Asia. "Khmer Rouge 'First Lady' Ieng Thirith Will Be Detained." December 14, 2011. Accessed September 16, 2015. http://www.bbc.co.uk/news/world-asia-16173009.

Beales, Sylvia. "Tackling the Food Crisis." *Ageways: Practical Issues in Ageing and Development* 76 (February 2011): 4–5.

Beard, Renée L., and Tara M. Neary. "Making Sense of Nonsense: Experiences of Mild Cognitive Impairment." *Sociology of Health and Illness* (January 2013): 130–146.

Behuniak, Susan. "The Living Dead? The Construction of People with Alzheimer's Disease as Zombies." *Ageing and Society* (January 2011): 70–92.

Berger, James. "Trauma and Literary Theory." *Contemporary Literatur* 38, no. 3 (Autumn 1997): 569–582.

Berry, Wendell. *Bringing It to the Table: On Farming and Food*: Berkeley, CA: Counterpoint Press, 2009.

——. "Farmland without Farmers." *Atlantic* online, March 19, 2015. Accessed August 4, 2015. http://www.theatlantic.com/national/archive/2015/03/farmland-without -farmers/388282/.

Bhatti, Mark. "'When I'm in the Garden I Can Create My Own Paradise': Homes and Gardens in Later Life." *Sociological Review* 54, no. 2 (May 2006): 318–341.

Biggs, Simon. "Aging in a Critical World: The Search for Generational Intelligence." *Journal of Aging Studies* 22 (2008): 115–C119.

Bliss, Harry. Cartoon. *Boston Globe*, May 19, 2014.

Bogan, Sheila. *Ashton Applewhite: Part 3*. Video. Accessed December 8, 2016. https:// www.youtube.com/watch?v=P3LdG-LtNa8.

Bonnefoy, Pascale. "Chile Hunt for Justice Winds Up as Enigma." *New York Times*, September 26, 2013. Accessed December 8, 2016. http://www.nytimes.com/2013/09/27/ world/americas/chile-hunt-for-justice-winds-up-as-enigma.html?_r=0.

Bonner-Ganter, Deanna. E-mail communication, May 19, 2016.

Bouson, J. Brooks. *Embodied Shame: Uncovering Women's Shame in Contemporary Women's Writing*. Albany: State University of New York Press, 2009.

Bowens, Natasha. *The Color of Food: Stories of Race, Resilience, and Farming*. Gabriola Island, British Columbia: New Society Publishers, 2015.

Brantley, Ben. "Debating Dialectics and Dad's Suicide Plan." *New York Times*, May 5, 2011.

Bratrud, Shirley Ann. "The Lived Experience of Attending College as an Older Adult: The Phenomenological Perspective of Students Age 60 and Older." PhD diss., Texas Tech University, 1999.

Brecht, Bertolt. *On Art and Politics*. Edited by Tom Kuhn and Steve Giles; translated by Laura Bradley, Steve Giles, and Tom Kuhn. London: Methuen Drama, 2003.

Brennan, Teresa, *Transmission of Affect*. Ithaca, NY: Cornell University Press, 2004.

Bright, Deborah. *Dream Girls* (1989–1990). Accessed June 12, 2016. http://www.deborah bright.net.

Bright, Susan. "Motherhood Reimagined." *Time* online, October 17, 2013. Accessed December 2, 2016. http://lightbox.time.com/2013/10/17/motherhood-reimagined-by -susan-bright/?iid=lb-gal-moreonno.11.

Bright Focus Foundation. "Alzheimer's Facts and Statistics." May 13, 2016. Accessed May 5, 2016. http://www.brightfocus.org/alzheimers/article/alzheimers-disease-facts-figures.

Brody, Howard. "Evaluating the Humanities." *Academe* 99, no.1 (January–February 2013): 19–23.

Brody, Richard, "Michael Haneke's Sterile *Amour*." *New Yorker*, January 4, 2013. Accessed May 5, 2016. http://www.newyorker.com/culture/richard-brody/michael-hanekes -sterile-amour.

Brown, Brené. "Shame & Body Image." *The Mothers Movement Online*. Undated. Accessed December 8, 2016. http://www.mothersmovement.org/features/body_image/b_brown_body_shame_2.htm.

———. "Shame Resilience Theory: A Grounded Theory Study on Women and Shame." *Families in Society: The Journal of Contemporary Social Services* 87, no.1 (2006): 43–52.

Bruens, Margreet Th. "Dementia: Beyond Structures of Medicalization and Cultural Neglect." In *Ageing, Meaning, and Social Structure: Connecting Critical and Humanistic Gerontology*, ed. Jan Baars, Joseph Dohmen, and Amanda Grenier, 81–96. Bristol, UK: Policy Press, 2014.

Buckels, Erin E., Paul D. Trapnell, and Delroy L. Paulhus. "Trolls Just Want to Have Fun." *Personality and Individual Differences* 67 (February 2014): 97–102. Accessed December 8, 2016. http://scottbarrykaufman.com/wp-content/uploads/2014/02/trolls-just-want-to-have-fun.pdf.

Burr, Ty. "'*Amour*' Bears Witness to an Awful—and Intimate—Truth." *Boston Globe*, January 17, 2013. Accessed May 15, 2016. https://www.bostonglobe.com/arts/movies/2013/01/17/amour-bears-witness-awful-and-intimate-truth/NEooUorEUSsDBIFaOs6ehM/story.html.

Butler, Judith. "Critically Queer." *GLQ* 1 (1993): 17–32.

Butler, Robert N. "Age-Ism, Another Form of Bigotry." *The Gerontologist* 9 (1969): 243–246.

———. "The Life Review: An Interpretation of Reminiscence in the Aged." *Psychiatry* 26 (1963): 65–76.

Bytheway, Bill. *Ageism*. Buckingham, UK: Open University Press, 1995.

———. "Visual Representations of Later Life." In *Aging Bodies: Images and Everyday Experience*, edited by Christopher A. Faircloth, 29–53. Walnut Creek, CA: AltaMira, 2003.

Calasanti, Toni. "A Feminist Confronts Ageism." In *Coming of Age: Critical Gerontologists Reflect on Their Own Aging, Age Research, and the Making of Critical Gerontology*, edited by Ruth E. Ray and Thomas R. Cole, Special Issue, *Journal of Aging Studies* 22, no. 2 (April 2008): 152–157.

Caplan, Paula. E-mail communication, March 22, 2012.

Carlisle, Julia. "Education from the Ground Up." *Hobart Mercury* (Australia), September 30, 2011, 23.

Carroll, Linda, "Alzheimer's Extracts a High Price on Caregivers, Too." NBC News, Health/Aging, September 5, 2013. Accessed May 15, 2016. http://www.nbcnews.com/health/aging/alzheimers-extracts-high-price-caregivers-too-f8C11070658.

Centers for Disease Control and Prevention (CDC). "Suicide among Adults Aged 35–64 Years—United States, 1999–2010," Table 2, May 3, 2013. Accessed June 11, 2016. www.cdc.gov/mmwr/preview/mmwrhtml/mm6217a1.htm?s_cid=mm6217a1_wno.tab1.

Chand, A., J. Clare, and R. Dolton. "Teaching Anti-Oppressive Practice on a Diploma in Social Work Course: Lecturers' Experiences, Students' Responses and Ways Forward." *Social Work Education* 21, no.1 (2002): 7–22.

Chang, Cheoljoon. "Korean Elder Law for a Reasonable Development, Based on New Constitutional Jurisprudence." *Journal of International Aging Law & Policy* 6 (2013): 34–49.

Chansok, Lak. "Can Khmer Rouge Survivors Get Justice?" *London Review of Books*, May 30, 2014. Accessed July 22, 2016. http://thediplomat.com/2014/05/can-khmer-rouge-survivors-get-justice/.

Charles Horman Truth Project. Accessed December 8, 2016. http://www.hormantruth .org/ht/.

Chast, Roz. *Can't We Talk about Something More PLEASANT?* New York: Bloomsbury, 2014.

Chekhov, Anton. "Rothschild's Fiddle." In *Anton Chekhov's Short Stories*, edited by Ralph E. Matlaw. Translated by Marian Fell. New York: W. W. Norton, 1979.

Cheng, Anne Anlin "The Melancholy of Race." *Kenyon Review* 19, no.1 (1997): 49–61.

———. *The Melancholy of Race: Psychoanalysis, Assimilation, and Hidden Grief.* New York: Oxford University Press, 2001.

Chittum, Ryan. "Audit Notes." *Columbia Journalism Review*, March 31, 2014. Accessed December 6, 2016. www.cjr.org/the_audit/audit_notes_sex_bias_and_arbit.php?page =2no.sthash.uHapMjQO.dpuf.

Chivers, Sally. *The Silvering Screen: Old Age and Disability in Cinema.* Toronto: University of Toronto Press, 2011.

CIA (Central Intelligence Agency). "CIA Activities in Chile." September 18, 2000. Accessed July 28, 2016. https://www.cia.gov/library/reports/general-reports-1/chile/ index.htmlno.6.

Clarke, Brock. "A Memoir Whose Value Is in Telling, Not the Tale." *Boston Globe*, February 23, 2014.

Clarke, Laura Hurd, and Meredith Griffin. "Body Image and Aging: Older Women and the Embodiment of Trauma." *Women's Studies International Forum* 31, no. 3 (May–June 2008): 200–208.

CNN. "Joyce Horman on the Death of Charles Horman in Chile." CNN, June 18, 2000. December 8, 2016. http://www.cnn.com/COMMUNITY/transcripts/2000/6/19/ horman.

Cohen, Ari Seth. *Advanced Style.* Accessed July 17, 2016. http://advancedstyle.blogspot .com/2015/02/old-is-new-black.html.

Cole, Thomas. "The Specter of Old Age: History, Politics, and Culture in an Aging America." In *Growing Old in America*, edited by Beth B. Hess and Elizabeth W. Markson, 23–37. 5th edition. New Brunswick, NJ: Transaction Publishers, 1995.

Collier, Elizabeth, and Celeste Foster. "Teaching Age and Discrimination: A Life Course Perspective." *Nurse Education in Practice* 14, no. 4 (August 2014): 333–337.

Combs, Michelle. "What Not to Wear After Age 50: The Final Say." *Huffington Post*, February 11, 2015. Accessed December 8, 2016. http://www.huffingtonpost.com/michelle -combs/what-not-to-wear-after-ag_b_6656902.html.

Conner, David Michael. "Hello From the Other Side: A Message to Davey Wavey About Older Gay Men." *Huffington Post*, February 1, 2016. Accessed December 8, 2016. http://www.huffingtonpost.com/david-michael-conner/hello-from-the-other-side_ 1_b_9119432.html.

Conrad, Peter. "Haneke: There's No Easy Way to Say This . . ." *Guardian*, November 3, 2012. Accessed May 16, 2016. www.theguardian.com/film/2012/nov/04/michael -haneke-amour-director-interview.

Cook, Joanne, and Jieyu Liu. "Can 'Distant Water . . . Quench the Instant Thirst'? The Renegotiation of Familial Support in Rural China in the Face of Extensive Out Migration." *Journal of Aging Studies* 37 (2016): 29–39.

Coplans, John. "John Coplans Memorial." Video. Cooper Union, NYC, 2004.

Coplon, Jennifer. E-mail communication, September 21, 2012.

Cottle, Nate R., and Rebecca J. Glover. "Combating Ageism: Change in Student Knowledge and Attitudes Regarding Aging." *Educational Gerontology* 33 (2007): 501–512. doi: 10.1080/03601270701328318.

Coyle, Eugene. "Review of Kathi Weeks's *The Problem with Work*." *Review of Radical Political Economics* 48, no. 2 (2015): 342–344. Accessed July 18, 2016. doi: 10.1177/0486613415574472.

Coyne, John P. "John Wise Convicted of Shooting Wife in Ohio Hospital." *Huffington Post*, November 8, 2013. Accessed June 11, 2016. http://www.cbsnews.com/news/john-wise-ohio-man-gets-6-years-in-wifes-mercy-killing/.

Cristofovici, Anca. *Touching Surfaces: Photographic Aesthetics, Temporality, Aging*. Amsterdam: Rodopi, 2009.

Crossley, David, and Kirk Rockett. "The Experience of Shame in Older Psychiatric Patients: A Preliminary Enquiry." *Aging & Mental Health* 9, no. 4 (July 2005): 368–373.

Cruikshank, Margaret. *Learning to Be Old: Gender, Culture, and Aging*. 3rd ed. Lanham, MD: Rowman and Littlefield, 2013.

Cunningham, Imogen, and Margaretta Mitchell. *After Ninety*. Seattle: University of Washington Press, 1977.

Cvetkovich, Ann. *Depression: A Public Feeling*. Durham, NC: Duke University Press, 2012.

Dale, David C. "Poor Prognosis in Elderly Patients with Cancer: The Role of Bias and Undertreatment." *Journal of Supportive Oncology* 1, Supplement 2 (2003).

Danto, Arthur C. *What Art Is*. New Haven: Yale University Press, 2013.

Daston, Lorraine, and Peter Galison. *Objectivity*. New York: Zone Books, 2010.

Davies, R., Judi Hirsch, and Gloria Graves Holmes. "Conversation: Unearthing Hidden Curriculums." In *Six Lenses for Anti-Oppressive Education, Partial Stories, Improbable Conversations*, edited by Kevin K. Kumashiro and Bic Ngo, 95–103. New York: Peter Lang, 2007.

DeFalco, Amelia. "Dementia, Caregiving, and Narrative in Michael Ignatieff's *Scar Tissue*." *Occasion, Interdisciplinary Studies in the Humanities* 4 (June 15, 2012). Accessed December 4, 2013. http://arcade.stanford.edu/sites/default/files/article_pdfs/OCCASION_v04_Woodward_053112_0.pdf.

DeMille, Barbara. "Age Discrimination in Higher Education Is Both Overt and Subtle." *Chronicle of Higher Education*, June 7, 1989: B2.

Dickerson, B. C., L. A. Beckett, D. A. Bennett, L. de Toledo-Morrell, C. Forchetti, I. Goncharova, M.P. Sullivan, et al. "MRI-derived Entorhinal and Hippocampal Atrophy in Incipient and Very Mild Alzheimer's Disease." *Neurobiology of Aging* 22 (2001) 747–775.

Di Certo, Alice. "The Unconventional Photographic Self-Portraits of John Coplans, Carla Williams, and Laura Aguilar." *Art and Design Theses*, Paper 4, Georgia State University, 2006.

DiFilippo, Dana. "Armed and Aging: Should Seniors Face Tighter Gun Controls?" *New America Media*, August 18, 2016. December 8, 2016. http://newamericamedia.org/2016/08/armed-and-aging-should-older-americans-face-tighter-gun-controls.php.

Dittman, Melissa. "Fighting Ageism." *APA Monitor* 34, no. 5 (May 2003): 50. Accessed June 12, 2016. http://www.apa.org/monitor/may03/fighting.aspx.

Dolan, Kathryn Cornell. *Beyond the Fruited Plain: Food and Agriculture in U.S. Literature, 1850–1905*. Lincoln: University of Nebraska Press, 2014.

D'Onfro, Jillian. "Facebook Employees Get 'Zero Credit' for Their Titles." *Business Insider*, December 26, 2014. Accessed November 9, 2015. http://www.businessinsider.com/what-its-like-working-at-facebook-2014-12.

Dorfman, Elsa. "Portrait of the Portrait Photographer." Accessed September 2013. http://www.elsadorfman.com/categories/2-essays/albums/41-portrait-of-the-portrait-photographer.

Dougherty, Elizabeth N., Nancy Dorr, and Richard T. Pulice. "Assisting Older Women in Combatting Ageist Stereotypes and Improving Attitudes toward Aging." *Women & Therapy* 39, no. 1–2 (2016): 12–34. http://dx.doi.org/10.1080/02703149.2016.1116308.

Dunbar, Edward, and Andres Molina. "Opposition to the Legitimacy of Hate Crime Laws." *ASAP (Analyses of Social Issues and Public Policy)* 4, no. 1 (2004): 91–114.

Dworkin, Ronald. *Life's Dominion. An Argument About Abortion, Euthanasia, and Individual Freedom*. New York: Vintage, 1993.

Dwoskin, Stephen. "Age . . . Is." *House on Fire*. Accessed December 8, 2016. http://houseonfire.fr/content/age-is/?lang=en. Link broken.

Eales, Jacquie, Janice Keefe, and Norah Keating. "Age-Friendly Rural Communities." In *Rural Ageing: A Good Place to Grow Old?* Edited by Norah Keating, 109–120. Bristol, UK: Policy Press, 2008.

Eberhardt, Jennifer, Paul G. Davies, Phillip Atiba Goff, and Valerie J. Purdie. "Seeing Black: Race, Crime, and Visual Processing." *Journal of Personality and Social Psychology* 87, no. 6 (2004): 876–893. Accessed October 2014 doi: 10.1037/0022-3514.87.6.876.

ECCC (Extraordinary Chambers in the Courts of Cambodia). "Decision on Immediate Appeal against the Trial Chamber's Order to Unconditionally Release the Accused Ieng Thirith." Accessed July 26, 2016. http://www.eccc.gov.kh/sites/default/files/documents/courtdoc/2012-12-17%2015:46/E138_1_10_1_5_7_EN.pdf.

Edmondson, Ricca, and Thomas Scharf. "Rural and Urban Ageing." In *Handbook of Cultural Gerontology*, edited by Julia Twigg and Wendy Martin, 412–419. London: Routledge, 2015.

Eliason, Scott. "Murder-Suicide: A Review of the Recent Literature." *Journal of the American Academy of Psychiatry and the Law* 37, no. 3 (2009): 371–376. Accessed May 6, 2016. http://www.jaapl.org/content/37/3/371.1ong.

Eliot, George. "Natural History of German Life: Riehl" (1856). In *The Writings of George Eliot*, 194–242. Boston: Houghton Mifflin, 1909.

Emanuel, Ezekiel. "Why I Hope to Die at 75." *Atlantic.com*, September 17, 2014. Accessed December 8, 2016. http://www.theatlantic.com/features/archive/2014/09/why-i-hope-to-die-at-75/379329/.

Emerson, Ralph Waldo. "Circles." In *The Complete Works of Ralph Waldo Emerson: Essays, First Series*, 301–322. Boston and New York: Houghton Mifflin, 1929.

———. "Old Age." In *The Complete Works of Ralph Waldo Emerson: Society and Solitude, and Poems*, 315–336. Boston and New York: Houghton Mifflin, 1929.

Emling, Shelley. "Aging: Well-Being Improves As People Get Older, Despite Physical or Cognitive Decline, Study Says." *Huffington Post*, December 7, 2012. Accessed June 12, 2016. www.huffingtonpost.com/2012/12/07/aging-getting-older-and-feeling-better_n_2245026.html.

England, Suzanne. "Performing Age-Related Dementia in Popular Culture" (2012). Accessed August 18, 2015. https://www.academia.edu/2030546/Performing_Age-Related_Dementia_in_Popular_Culture._Paper_for_ASTR_2012.

England, Suzanne. "A Personal Note." 2012 ms., sent by author.

Fanon, Frantz. *Black Skin, White Masks*. New York: Grove Press, 1967.

FAO (Food and Agriculture Organization of the United Nations), Natural Resources Management and Environment Department. "Feeding the Cities, The Role of Urban Agriculture." 1996. Accessed December 8, 2016. www.fao.org/docrep/x0262e/x0262e22.htm.

Farmer, Paul. "Who Lives and Who Dies." *London Review of Books* 37, no. 3 (February 5, 2015): 17–20.

Fawthrop, Tom. "Cambodia: Trial Gives Killing Fields Survivors a Chance of Justice." *Guardian*, July 16, 2009. Accessed October 26, 2015. www.theguardian.com/world/2009/jul/16/cambodia-killing-fields-genocide-trials.

Fishman, Ted. "It Gets Worse." *New York Times*, February 25, 2011.

Fleshman, Michael. "A Harvest of Hope." *African Renewal*, October 2008. Accessed August 7, 2016. http://www.un.org/africarenewal/magazine/october-2008/harvest-hope-african-farmers.

Flinders, Susan. L. "The Internal Struggles of Aging." *Journal for the Psychoanalysis of Culture and Society* 8, no. 2 (Fall 2003): 258–262.

Flinn, Ryan. "Dementia Care Costs Reach $109b, and Are Expected to Double." *Boston Globe*, April 5, 2013, A6.

Forna, Aminatta. *The Memory of Love*. New York: Grove Press, 2011.

Foster, J. A., L. L. Casebeer, D. Mansell, G. D. Salinas, and J. C. Williamson. "How Does Older Age Influence Oncologists' Cancer Management?" *Oncologist* 15, no. 6 (2010). Accessed June 12, 2016. doi: 10.1634/theoncologist.2009–0198.

Freire, Paolo, and Donald Macedo. "Rethinking Literacy: A Dialogue." In *The Critical Pedagogy Reader*, edited by Antonia Darder, Marta Baltondano, and Rodoflo D. Torres, 354–364. New York: RoutledgeFalmer, 2003.

Frick, Walter. "How Old Are Silicon Valley's Top Founders? Here's the Data." *Harvard Business Review*, April 3, 2014. Accessed May 3, 2016. https://hbr.org/2014/04/how-old-are-silicon-valleys-top-founders-heres-the-data/.

Fuchs, Elinor. E-mail communication, March 2, 2015.

Galassi, Peter. "'Bursting with Meanings and Emotions.'" *New York Review of Books*, October 24, 2013, 44.

García Márquez, Gabriel. *Clandestine in Chile: The Adventures of Miguel Littín*. Translated by Asa Zatz. New York: Henry Holt, 1986.

Genova, Lisa. *Still Alice: A Novel*. New York: Pocket Books, 2009.

George, Daniel, Catherine Whitehouse and Peter Whitehouse. "A Model of Intergenerativity." *Journal of Intergenerational Relationships* 9, no. 4 (2011): 389–404. Accessed August 4, 2015. http://dx.doi.org/10.1080/15350770.2011.619922.

"Gerontology Prize for Michael Haneke." *Austrian Times*, March 20, 2013. Accessed October 5, 2013. No link.

Gessler, Anne. "Macon Fry: Gathering Tree Collective–New Orleans, Louisiana." *Cooperative Oral History Project*, June 10, 2012, 1–12. Accessed February 23, 2016. http://coophistories.files.wordpress.com/2012/07/macon-fry-transcript.pdf.

Giarchi, George Giacinto. "Older People 'on the Edge' in the Countrysides of Europe." *Social Policy and Administration* 40, no. 6 (2006): 705–721. Accessed December 10, 2016. DOI: 10.1111/j.1467–9515.2006.00528.x Gil, Rosalind. "Culture and Subjectivity in Neoliberal and Postfeminist Times." *Subjectivity* 25 (2008): 432–445.

Gilleard, Chris, and Paul F. D. Higgs. "Ageing Abjection and Embodiment in the Fourth Age." *Journal of Aging Studies* 25, no. 2 (2011): 135–142. Accessed October 3, 2015. doi: 10.1016/j.jaging.2010.08.018.

Glasgow, Nina. "Poverty among Rural Elders: Trends, Contexts, and Directions for Policy." *Journal of Applied Gerontology* 12 (1993): 302–319. Accessed December 8, 2016. http://www.sagepub.com/moody6study/study/articles/controversy8/Glasgow.pdf.

Gomersall, Tim, A. Astell, A. Hwang, A. Mihailidis, L. Nygård, and A. Sixsmith. "Living with Ambiguity: A Metasynthesis of Qualitative Research on Mild Cognitive Impairment." *Gerontologist* 55, no. 5 (2015): 892–912. Accessed April 17, 2016. doi:10.1093/geront/gnv067.

Gómez Garcia, Jesus Maria, and Margarita Rico Gonzalez. "Rural Development, Population Aging and Gender in Spain." Paper presented to the 44th European Congress of the European Regional Science Association, Oporto, August 25–29, 2004. Accessed December 27, 2015. http://www-sre.wu-wien.ac.at/ersa/ersaconfs/ersa04/PDF/379.pdf.

Gordon, Emily Fox. "At Sixty-Five." In *The Best American Essays 2014*, edited by John Jeremiah Sullivan, 34–40. Boston: Houghton Mifflin Harcourt, 2013.

Gorman, Anna. "Diagnosis Unprepared: Elderly Patients Arrive Sick, Often Leave Disabled." *New American Media*, August 20, 2016.

Gornick, Vivian. "Delmore's Way." *The Nation*, June 12, 2015.

GRAIN. "Seized! GRAIN Briefing Annex. The 2008 Landgrabbers for Food and Financial Security." October 24, 2008. Accessed December 8, 2016. https://www.grain.org/article/entries/93-seized-the-2008-landgrab-for-food-and-financial-security.

Grant, Gary R., Spencer D. Wood and Willie J. Wright. . "Black Farmers United: The Struggle against Power and Principalities." *Journal of Pan African Studies* 5, no. 1 (March 2012): 3–22. Accessed December 8, 2016. http://www.jpanafrican.com/docs/vo15no1/5.1BlackFarmers.pdf.

Gray, Heather. "Black Farmers' Lives Matter: The Significant Contributions of Black Farmers in America." Federation of Southern Cooperatives Press release, October 14, 2015. Accessed December 8, 2016. http://www.federationsoutherncoop.com/press/pr2015/October%2014,%202015.htm.

Green, Jesse. "The Intelligent Homosexual's Guide to Himself." *New York Magazine*, October 17, 2010. Accessed December 8, 2016. http://nymag.com/arts/theater/profiles/68994/index1.html.

Groopman, Jerome. "Medical Dispatch: Before Night Falls." *New Yorker*, June 24, 2013. Accessed December 8, 2016. http://www.newyorker.com/reporting/2013/06/24/130624fa_fact_groopman.

Gross, James J., Laura L. Carstensen, A.Y. Hsu, M. Pasupathi, C.G. Skorpen , and J Tsai. "Emotion and Aging." *Psychology and Aging* 12, no. 4 (1997): 590–599.

Gullette, Margaret Morganroth. *Aged by Culture*. Chicago: University of Chicago Press, 2004.

——. *Agewise: Fighting the New Ageism in America*. Chicago: University of Chicago Press, 2011.

——. "Aging Is *NOT a Collection of Diseases*." *WIMNS' Voices: A Group Blog*, August 6, 2008. Accessed November 29, 2016. http://www.wimnonline.org/WIMNsVoices Blog/2008/08/06/aging-is-not-a-collection-of-diseases/.

——. "Amour." *Guardian*, February 28, 2013. Accessed December 8, 2016. www.the guardian.com/film/filmblog/2013/feb/28/amour-advert-for-euthanasia.

Gullette, Margaret Morganroth, ed. *The Art and Craft of Teaching*. Cambridge, MA: Harvard University Press, 1984.

———. "'The Boomers' vs. 'the Xers': A Contrived War." In Margaret Morganroth Gullette, *Aged by Culture*, 42–60. Chicago: University of Chicago Press, 2004.

———. "Caitlynn Jenner: The Messages in the Image." *Silver Century*, June 22, 2015. Accessed June 24, 2016. www.silvercentury.org/polBlogs.cfm?doctype_code=Blog& doc_id=967no..VcuNO_lViko.

———. "Creativity, Aging, Gender: A Study of Their Intersections, 1910–1935." In *Aging and Gender in Literature: Studies in Creativity*, edited by Anne M. Wyatt-Brown and Janice Rossen, 19–48. Charlottesville: University of Virginia Press, 1993.

———. *Declining to Decline: Cultural Combat and the Politics of the Midlife*. Charlottesville: University of Virginia Press, 1997.

———. "Florence Nightingale—Dammit—Still Shows the Way." *Womens eNews*, March 28, 2013. Accessed December 8, 2016. http://womensenews.org/2013/03/florence -nightingale-dammit-still-shows-the-way/.

———. "How We Imagine Living-with-Dying." *Salmagundi* (Summer 2016).

———. "Keeping the Conversation Going," *Forward*, September 28, 2012. Accessed December 9, 2016. http://forward.com/articles/163585/keeping-the-conversation-going/.

———. "Losing Lear, Finding Ageism." *Journal of Aging, Humanities, and the Arts* 1, no. 1–2 (2007): 61–69.

———. "Oh. *America*. How Obamacare Finished Off *Breaking Bad*." *Silver Century*, June 10, 2016. Accessed June 21, 2016. http://www.silvercentury.org/polBlogs.cfm?doctype_ code=Blog&doc_id=4098&Keyword_Desc=no..V21K6fkrIdU.

———. "Postmaternity as a Revolutionary Feminist Concept." *Feminist Studies* 28, no.3 (Fall 2003): 553–572.

———. "What Do the Suicides of Fifty-Year-Old Men Reveal? The Public Health Emergency Exposes an Economic and Existential Crisis." *Tikkun* (Spring 2014): 21–24, 59.

———. "Why I Hesitated about 'An Act Relative to Death with Dignity' and Then Voted for It." *Feminism and Psychology* 25, no.1 (February 2015): 118–123.

———. "Wicked Powerful: The Postmaternal in Contemporary Film and Psychoanalytic Theory." *Gender and Psychoanalysis* 5 (2000): 107–139.

Gurney, Ivor. "Brown Earth Look." In *Field Days: An Anthology of Poetry*, edited by Angela King and Susan Clifford, 25. White River Junction, VT: Chelsea Green, 1999.

Guyer, Jane, and Kabiru K. Salami. "Life Courses of Indebtedness in Rural Nigeria." In *Transitions and Transformations: Cultural Perspectives on Aging and the Life Course*, edited by Caitlin Lynch and Jason Danely, 207–217. New York: Berghahn Books, 2013.

Hall, Stuart. "Stuart Hall: On Photography." Video interview with Sunil Gupta, 2001. Accessed June 4, 2016. http://multimedia.autograph-abp.co.uk/video/51527926.

Harding, Jeremy. "What We're about to Receive." *London Review of Books* 32, no. 9 (May 13, 2010): 3–8. Accessed February 23, 2016. http://www.lrb.co.uk/v32/n09/jeremy -harding/what-were-about-to-receive.

Harris, Christopher. "Young Thug Says Jay Z's Too Old to Rap." HipHopDX, February 4, 2015. Accessed December 8, 2016. http://www.hiphopdx.com/index/news/id.32403/ title.young-thug-says-jay-zs-too-old-to-rap.

Harvard Men's Health Watch. "Mars vs. Venus: The Gender Gap in Health." January 1, 2010. Accessed June 12, 2016. http://www.health.harvard.edu/newsletter_article/mars-vs-venus-the-gender-gap-in-health.

Henig, Robin Marants. "The Last Day of Her Life." New York Times, May 14, 2015. Accessed May 18, 2016. http://www.nytimes.com/2015/05/17/magazine/the-last-day-of-her-life.html?_r=0.

Hepburn, Kenneth. "Still Alice" [review]. The Gerontologist 55, no. 2 (2015): 328–329. Accessed December 28, 2015. doi: 10.1093/geront/gnv017.

Hightower, Jim."Time for a Populist Revival." The Nation, March 24, 2014.

Hirsch, Marianne. "Connective Histories in Vulnerable Times." Presidential Address 2014, PMLA 129, no.3 (May 2014): 330–348.

Holland, Janet, Caroline Ramazanoglu, Sue Sharpe, and Rachel Thomson. The Male in the Head: Young People, Heterosexuality, and Power. London: Tufnell Press, 1998.

Holstein, Martha B. Women in Late Life: Critical Perspectives on Gender and Age. Lanham, MD: Rowman and Littlefield, 2015.

Holstein, Martha B., Jennifer A. Parks and Mark H. Waymack. Ethics, Aging, and Society: The Critical Turn. Thousand Oaks, CA: Springer, 2010.

Holt-Giménez, Eric. "From Food Crisis to Food Sovereignty: The Challenge of Social Movements." Monthly Review 61, no. 3 (July 1, 2009). Accessed February 16, 2016. http://monthlyreview.org/2009/07/01/from-food-crisis-to-food-sovereignty-the-challenge-of-social-movements/.

hooks, bell. "In Our Glory: Photography and Black Life." In Art on My Mind: Visual Politics, 54–64. New York: The New Press, 1995.

Hopkins, Jamie Smith. "Sparrows Point: A Year after Collapse, Unsettled Lives." Baltimore Sun, June 8, 2013. http://data.baltimoresun.com/stories/sparrows-point-a-year-after-bankruptcy-unsettled-lives/.

Horsfield, Craigie. "Statement." In Documentary, edited by Julian Stallabrass. London: Whitechapel Gallery, 2013.

Hotchkiss, Michael. "Researchers Chart New Path for Study of Ageism." Medical Xpress, April 22, 2013. Accessed April 6, 2016. http://medicalxpress.com/news/2013-04-path-ageism.html.

Huber, Bridget. "Slow Food Nation." The Nation, August 15/22, 2016.

Hustvedt, Siri. The Blazing World. New York: Simon and Schuster, 2014.

ICC (International Criminal Court). "Pre-Trial Chamber I, Decision on the Fitness of Laurent Gbagbo to Take Part in the Proceedings Before This Court." November 2, 2012. Accessed July 27, 2016. http://www.icc-cpi.int/iccdocs/doc/doc1501444.pdf.

Imhoff, Daniel. "Farm Bill 101." The Nation, October 3, 2011.

International Network on Rural Ageing. "Why Is Rural Ageing Important?" International Journal of Ageing and Later Life 7, no.2 (2012): 17–51. http://www.icsg.ie/sites/www.icsg.ie/files/personfiles/why_is_rural_ageing_important_1.pdf Link broken.

IRIN. "Zimbabwe's Neglected Elderly Farmers." September 2, 2014. Accessed November 20, 2014. http://www.irinnews.org/report/100566/zimbabwe-s-neglected-elderly-farmers.

Isaacs, L., and D. Bearison. "The Development of Children's Prejudice against the Aged." International Journal of Aging and Human Development 23, no.3 (1986): 175–194.

Itzkovitz, Daniel. "Lincoln and the Radicals." Transition 12 (January 2013): 79–98.

Jansson, Tove. *The Summer Book*. Translated by Thomas Teal. New York: NewYork Review Books, 2008.

Jiang, Quanbao, Marcus W. Feldman, and Xiaomin Li. "Bequest Motives of Older People in Rural China: From the Perspective of Intergenerational Support." *European Journal of Ageing* 12, no.2 (June 2015): 141–151. Accessed February 24, 2016. http://link.springer .com/article/10.1007%2Fs10433–014–0330–z.

Jöhr, Hans. "Where Are the Future Farmers to Grow Our Food?" *International Food and Agribusiness Management Review* 15, Special Issue A (2012).

Jungers, Christin M., and Leslie Slagel. "Crisis Model for Older Adults: Special Considerations for an Aging Population." *ADULTSPAN Journal* 8 no. 2 (2009): 92–101.

Kaczor, Bill, Eva Vergara, and Jack Chang. (AP). "Wife: US Official Accused in Chile Has Alzheimer's." Boston Globe, December 1, 2011. Accessed December 15, 2016. http:// archive.boston.com/news/nation/articles/2011/12/01/wife_us_official_accused_in_ chile_has_alzheimers/.

Kahane, Claire. "Gender and Patrimony: Mourning the Dead Father." *differences* 9, no. 1 (Spring 1997): 49.

Karpen, Ruth Ray. "Golden Girls: Rediscovering the Crone." *The Blue Review*, December 16, 2013. Accessed June 12, 2016. http://thebluereview.org/golden-girls-crone/no.sthash .maX13ex5.dpuf.

Karpf, Anne. *How to Age*. London: Pan Macmillan, 2014.

Kashi, Ed, and Julie Winokur. *Aging in America: The Years Ahead*. New York: power-House Books, 2003.

Kastner, Rachel. "Hope for the Future: How Farmers Can Reverse Climate Change." *Socialism and Democracy* 30, no.2 (July 2016): 154–170.

Katz, Stephen. "Hold On! Falling, Embodiment, and the Materiality of Old Age." In *Corpus: An Interdisciplinary Reader on Bodies and Knowledge*, edited by Monica J. Casper and Paisley Currah, 187–205. New York: Palgrave Macmillan, 2011.

———. "What Is Age Studies?" *Age, Culture, Humanities* 1 (2014). Accessed June 13, 2016. http://ageculturehumanities.org/WP/what-is-age-studies/.

Keating, Norah, and Judith Phillips. "A Critical Human Ecology Perspective on Rural Ageing." *Rural Ageing: A Good Place to Grow Old?* edited by Norah Keating, 1–10. Bristol, UK: Policy Press, 2008.

Keizer, Garrett. "Getting Schooled." In *Best American Essays 2012*, edited by David Brooks, 176–192. Boston: Houghton Mifflin, 2012.

Kennedy, Rosanne, and Gillian Whitlock. introduction to Special Issue: "Witnessing, Trauma, and Social Suffering: Feminist Perspectives." *Australian Feminist Studies* 26, no. 69 (2011): 251–255.

King, Neal, and Toni Calasanti. "Empowering the Old: Critical Gerontology and Anti-Aging in a Global Context." In *Aging, Globalization, and Inequality: The New Critical Gerontology*, m edited by Jan Baars, Dale Dannefer, Chris Phillipson, and Alan Walker, 139–157. Amityville, NY: Baywood: 2006.

Kitwood, Tom. *Dementia Reconsidered: The Person Comes First*. Buckingham, UK: Open University Press, 1997.

Kitzinger, Celia. "Doing Gender: A Conversation Analytic Perspective." *Gender and Society* 23, no. 1 (February 2009): 94–98.

Klein, Joe. "The Long Goodbye." *Time*, June 11, 2012. Accessed December 10, 2016. http:// time.com/735/the-long-goodbye/.

Kluger, Ruth. *Refus de témoigner: Une jeunesse.* Translated by Jeanne Étoré. Paris: Éditions Viviane Hamy, 1997.

Kohn, Nina A. "Rethinking the Constitutionality of Age Discrimination: A Challenge to a Decades-Old Consensus." *UC Davis Law Review* 44, no. 1 (2010): 213–282.

Kopit, Arthur. *Wings: A Play.* New York: Hill and Wang, 1978.

Kornbluh, Peter. "Chile: Judgment Day on the U.S." *The Nation*, December 26, 2011.

———. "Letter from Chile." *The Nation*, September 23, 2013.

Kornhaber, David. "Kushner at Colonus: Tragedy, Politics, and Citizenship," *PMLA* 129, no.4 (2014).

Koutsou, Stavriani, Maria Partalidou, and Michael Petrou. "Present or Absent Farm Heads? A Contemporary Reading of Family Farming in Greece." *Sociologia Ruralis* 51, no.4 (October 2011): 404–419.

KRT Trial Monitor. "Case 002: Special Report, Ieng Thirith's Fitness to Stand Trial, November 2012." Accessed July 24, 2016. https://krttrialmonitor.files.wordpress.com/2012/11/special-report-it-ftst_-final.pdf.

———. "Monitoring Program Case 002: Update no.4, Fitness to Stand Trial II." War Crimes Study Center, University of California, Berkeley, October 20, 2011. Accessed July 2015. Link broken. http://wcsc.berkeley.edu/wpcontent/uploads/documents/4.Fitness%20to%20Stand%20Trial%20II_19–20oct2011.pdf.

Kunhardt, Philip B., Jr. "On Gordon Parks." In *Gordon Parks: A Poet and His Camera.* New York: Viking Press, 1968.

Kunow, Rüdiger. "Preemptive Biographies: Life and the Life Course in the Age of Security Administration." In *Alive and Kicking at All Ages: Cultural Constructions of Health and Life Course Identity*, edited by Ulla Kriebernegg, Roberta Maierhofer, and Barbara Ratzenböck, 101–116. Bielefeld, Germany: Transcript, 2014.

Kushner, Tony. *Angels in America: A Gay Fantasia on National Themes. Part One: Millennium Approaches.* New York: Theatre Communications Group, 1993.

———. "The Intelligent Homosexual's Guide to Capitalism and Socialism, with a Key to the Scriptures." Unpublished ms., 2009.

Kutner, Max. "Death on the Farm." *Newsweek*, April 10, 2014.

Lagioia, Nicola. "Writing Is an Act of Pride: A Conversation with Elena Ferrante." *New Yorker*, May 19, 2016.

Lake, Nell. "Bullying Is Ageless: Conflict and Violence Widespread in Nursing Homes, Study Finds." WBUR CommonHealth, November 14, 2014. Accessed May 9, 2016. http://commonhealth.wbur.org/2014/11/conflict-and-violence-in-nursing-homes-study.

Lamb, Erin Gentry. " 'Polyester Pants and Orthopedic Shoes': Introducing Age Studies to Traditional-Aged Undergraduates." *Age, Culture, Humanities* 1, no.1 (2014). Accessed June 10, 2016. http://ageculturehumanities.org/WP/polyester-pants-and-orthopedic-shoes-introducing-age-studies-to-traditional-aged-undergraduates/.

Lamb, Sarah. "Permanent Personhood or Meaningful Decline? Toward a Critical Anthropology of Successful Aging." *Journal of Aging Studies* 29 (2014): 41–52.

Lappé, Frances Moore. "Farming for a Small Planet: Agroecology Now." *Great Transition Initiative*, April 2016. http://www.greattransition.org/publication/farming-for-a-small-planet.

———. "The Food Movement: Its Power and Possibilities." *The Nation*, September 14, 2011.

Lawson, Laura. *City Bountiful: A Century of Community Gardening in America.* Berkeley: University of California Press, 2005.

Lee, Chang-dong, director. *Poetry*. Film. 2011.

Levy, Becca R., L. Ferrucci, S. M. Resnick, M. D. Slade, and A. B. Zonderman. "A Culture-Brain Link: Negative Age Stereotypes Predict Alzheimer's Disease Biomarkers." *Psychology and Aging* 31, no. 1 (February 2016): 82–88.

Levy, Becca A., Pil H. Chung, Talya Bedford, Kristina Navrazhina, "Facebook as a Site for Negative Age Stereotypes." *The Gerontologist* 54, no. 2 (2014): 172–176.

Levy, Becca R., Martin A. Slade, Suzanne R. Kunkel, Stanislav V. Kasl. "Longevity Increased by Positive Self-perceptions of Aging." *Journal of Personality and Social Psychology* 83, no. 2 (2002): 261–270.

Linnecar, Corinne. "A Discourse Analysis of Annie Leibovitz's Louise Bourgeois." http://corinnelinnecar.blogspot.com/2012/03/discourse-analysis-of-annie-leibovitzs.html.

Loh, Sandra Tsing. "Daddy Issues: Why Caring for My Aging Father Has Me Wishing He Would Die." *Atlantic Online*, March 2012. Accessed August 20, 2016. http://www.theatlantic.com/magazine/archive/2012/03/daddy-issues/308890/.

Lorde, Audre. *Sister Outsider: Essays and Speeches*. Trumansburg, NY: Crossing Press, 1984.

Lowder, Sarah K. Jakob Skoet, and Saumya Singh. "What Do We Really Know about the Number and Distribution of Farms and Family Farms Worldwide?" Background paper for *The State of Food and Agriculture 2014*. Agricultural Development Economics Division (ESA) Working Paper No. 14–02. Rome: FAO, 2014. Accessed December 20, 2016. http://www.fao.org/docrep/019/i3729e/i3729e.pdf.

Luminous Light blog. "Book Review." February 27, 2012. Accessed December 10, 2016. http://luminouslight.wordpress.com/2012/02/27/book-review-roswell-angier-train-your-gaze/.

Lustbader, Wendy. *Counting on Kindness: The Dilemmas of Dependency*. New York: Free Press, 1991.

Life Gets Better: The Unexpected Pleasures of Growing Older. New York: Tarcher/Penguin, 2011.

MacLaine, Kerry. "Youth Wanted: The Rampant Ageism in Silicon Valley." *Appealing Studio*. November 6, 2015. Accessed December, 10 2016. http://appealingstudio.com/youth-wanted-the-rampant-ageism-in-silicon-valley/.

Maher, Frances Aldrich, and Mary-Kay Thomson Tetreault. *The Feminist Classroom*. New York: Basic Books, 1994.

Malphurs, Julie, and Donna Cohen. "A Statewide Case-Control Study of Spousal Homicide-Suicide in Older Persons." *American Journal of Geriatric Psychiatry* 13, no. 3 (2005): 211–217.

Márquez, Gabriel Garcia. *Clandestine in Chile: The Adventures of Miguel Littin*. New York: Henry Holt, 1987.

Marshall, Barbara, and Stephen Katz. "The Embodied Life Course: Post-ageism or the Renaturalization of Gender?" *Societies* 2, no.4 (2012): 222–234. Accessed October 17, 2014. http://www.mdpi.com/2075-4698/2/4/222/htm.

Marshall, Leni. "Ageility Studies: The Interplay of Critical Approaches in Age Studies and Disability Studies." In *Alive and Kicking at All Ages*, edited by Ulla Kriebernegg, Roberta Maierhofer, and Barbara Ratzenböck, 21–40. Bielefeld, Germany: Transcript, 2014.

———. "Teaching Ripening: Incorporating Lessons on Age Identity, Aging, and Ageism into the Humanities Classroom." *Transformations: The Journal of Inclusive Scholarship and Pedagogy* 19, no. 2 (Fall 2008/Winter 2009): 55–80.

———. "Thinking Differently about Aging: Changing Attitudes through the Humanities." *The Gerontologist* (July 5, 2014): 1–7. doi:10.1093/geront/gnu069.

Martell, Daniel A. "Forensic Neuropsychology and the Criminal Law." *Law and Human Behavior* 16, no. 3 (1992): 313–336.

Martinson, Marty, and Clara Berridge. "Successful Aging and Its Discontents: A Systematic Review of the Social Gerontology Literature." *The Gerontologist* 55, no. 1 (2015): 58–69.

McFadden, Syreeta. "Teaching the Camera to See My Skin." *BuzzFeed*, April 2, 2014. Accessed June 4, 2016. https://www.buzzfeed.com/syreetamcfadden/teaching-the -camera-to-see-my-skin?utm_term=.ayyrr9Z2gXno..wxRDDygenB.

McHugh, Maureen C. "Aging, Agency, and Activism: Older Women as Social Change Agents." *Women and Therapy* 35, no. 3–4 (2012): 279–295. Accessed April 7, 2015. doi: 10.1080/02703149.2012.684544.

McKee, Kevin J., and Merryn Gott. "Shame and the Aging Body." In *Body Shame: Conceptualisation, Research and Treatment*, edited by Paul Gilbert and Jeremy Miles, 75–87. Hove: Brunner-Routledge, 2002.

McKenna, Maryn. "Planting New Farmers for the Future of Food." *National Geographic*, December 14, 2015. Accessed February 24, 2016. http://theplate.nationalgeographic .com/2015/12/14/planting-new-farmers-for-the-future-of-food/.

McKeon, Nora. "Now's the Time to Make It Happen: The UN's Committee on Food Security." In *Food Movements Unite!* edited by Eric Holt-Gimenez, 257–274. Oakland, CA: Food First Books, 2011.

McKibben, Bill. "The Pope and the Planet." *New York Review of Books*, August 13, 2015. 40–42.

McLaren, Janice. "29 Results for 'Giant.'" *The Photographers' Gallery*. http://janice mclaren.tumblr.com/search/Giant.

Mead, Rebecca. "The Troll Slayer." *New Yorker*, September 1, 2014, 30–36.

Meek, Ed. "The Millennial-Boomer Alliance." "Connections," *Boston Globe*, September 15, 2013.

Meek, James. "Robin Hood in a Time of Austerity." *London Review of Books* 38, no. 4 (February 18, 2016): 3–8.

Merchant, Pamela. E-mail communication. May 25, 2012.

MetLife. "Out and Aging: The MetLife Study of Lesbian and Gay Baby Boomers." *Journal of GLBT Family Studies* 6 (2006): 40–57.

Meyers, Diana Tietjens. "Miroir, Mémoire, Mirage: Appearance, Aging, and Women." In *Mother Time: Women, Aging, and Ethics*, edited by Margaret Urban Walker, 23–41. Lanham, MD: Rowman and Littlefield, 1999.

Middling, Sharon, Jan Bailey, Sian Maslin-Prothero, and Thomas Scharf. "Gardening and the Social Engagement of Older People." *Emerald Insight* 15, no. 3 (2011): 112–122. Accessed December 10, 2016. www.emeraldinsight.com/journals.htm?articleid= 1959184&show=abstract.

Milbourne, Paul. "Austerity, Welfare Reform, and Older People," In *Ageing Resource Communities: New Frontiers of Rural Population Change, Community Development, and Voluntarism*, edited by Mark Skinner and Neil Hanlon. Abingdon, UK: Routledge, 2016.

Miller, Nancy K., and Jason Tougaw, eds. "Introduction: Extremities." In *Extremities: Trauma, Testimony, and Community*. Urbana: University of Illinois Press, 2002.

Milwain, Elizabeth, "Mild Cognitive Impairment: Further Caution." *The Lancet* 355, no. 9208 (March 18, 2000): 1018. Accessed July 28, 2016. http://www.thelancet.com/journals/lancet/article/PIIS0140-6736(05)74764-4/fulltext.

Mitchell, A. J., and M. Shiri-Feshki. "Rate of Progression of Mild Cognitive Impairment to Dementia—Meta-analysis of 41 Robust Inception Cohort Studies." *Acta Psychiatrica Scandinavica* 119 (2009): 252–265.

Mitchell, Jim, D. Bradley, R. T. Goins, and J. Wilson. "The Aging Farm Population and Rural Aging Research." *Journal of Agromedicine* 13, no. 2 (2008): 95–109.

Moody, Harry. "Human Values in Aging." Subscription newsletter of the Arts and Humanities Committee of the Gerontological Society of America, April 1, 2016. http://www.hrmoody.com/human-values-in-aging-newsletters.

Moore, Bridie. "Depth, Significance, and Absence: Age Effects in New British Theatre." *Age, Culture, Humanities* 1 (2014): 163–195.

Morrison, Toni. *Playing in the Dark: Whiteness and the Literary Imagination*. New York: Vintage, 1993.

Muhlbauer, Varda, and Joan C. Chrisler, ed. "Women, Power, Aging: An Introduction." *Women and Therapy* 35, no. 3–4 (2012): 137–144.

Muldoon, Paul. "The Moral Legitimacy of Anger." *European Journal of Social Theory* 11, no. 3 (August 2008): 299–314.

National Rural Health Alliance [Australia]. *Fact Sheet 14. Suicide in Rural Australia*. May 2009. Accessed February 24, 2016. http://ruralhealth.org.au/sites/default/files/fact-sheets/fact-sheet-14-suicide%20in%20rural%20australia_0.pdf.

National Security Archive. "Chilean Judge Requests Extradition of U.S. Military Official in 'Missing' Case." Document 1: Department of State, SECRET Memorandum, "Charles Horman Case," August 25, 1976, Posted November 30, 2011. Accessed December 10, 2016. http://www.gwu.edu/~nsarchiv/NSAEBB/NSAEBB366/index.htm.

National Sustainable Agriculture Coalition. *Senior Farmers' Market Nutrition Program*. October 2014. Accessed December 10, 2016. http://sustainableagriculture.net/publications/grassrootsguide/local-food-systems-rural-development/farmers-market-nutrition-program/.

Nelson, John Lindemann. "Death's Gender." In *Mother Time: Women, Aging, and Ethics*, edited by Margaret Urban Walker, 113–129. Lanham, MD: Rowman and Littlefield, 1999.

Nelson, Todd T. "Ageism: Prejudice against Our Feared Future Self." *Journal of Social Issues* 61, no. 2 (2005): 207–221.

New York Times. "About." Sidebar to "The New Old Age." Accessed September 14, 2014. http://newoldage.blogs.nytimes.com.

Nieuwenhuis-Mark, Ruth Elaine. "Healthy Aging as Disease?" *Frontiers in Aging Neuroscience* 3 #3 (February 22, 2011). Accessed December 7, 2016. doi: 10.3389/fnagi.2011.00003.

NISGUA (Network in Solidarity with the People of Guatemala). "Genocide Cases: Ríos Montt to Testify, Mejía Victores Unfit for Trial." January 25, 2012. Accessed De-

cember 10, 2016. http://nisgua.blogspot.com/2012/01/genocide-cases-rios-montt-to
-testify.html.

Nöe, Alva. *Out of Our Heads*. New York: Hill and Wang, 2009.

Nolan, Laurence C. "Dimensions of Aging and Belonging for the Older Person and the Effects of Ageism." *Brigham Young University Journal of Public Law* 25, no. 2 (2011): 317–339. Accessed December 10, 2016. http://digitalcommons.law.byu.edu/jpl/vo125/iss2/8.

North, Michael S. "Ageism Stakes Its Claim in the Social Sciences." *American Society on Aging* blog, October 22, 2015. http://asaging.org/blog/ageism-stakes-its-claim-social -sciences.

North, Michael S., and Susan T. Fiske. "Act Your (Old) Age: Prescriptive, Ageist Biases over Succession, Consumption, and Identity." *Personality and Social Psychology Bulletin* 39, no. 6 (2013): 720–734.

———. "An Inconvenienced Youth? Ageism and Its Potential Intergenerational Roots." *Psychology Bulletin* 138, no. 5 (September 10, 2012). Accessed April 8, 2016. http://sk.sagepub.com/navigator/social-cognition/n42.xml.

Notes on the Americas. "The Slow, Slow Pace of International Justice." October 18, 2012; "An Extradition Request," April 21, 2012. Accessed August 7, 2016. http://notes ontheamericas.wordpress.com/tag/captain-ray-davis/.

Nussbaum, Martha C. *Upheavals of Thought: The Intelligence of the Emotions*. Cambridge: Cambridge University Press, 2001.

O'Neill, Desmond. *"Amour*, Ageing, and Missed Opportunities." *The BMJ* , November 23, 2012. Accessed May 15, 2016. http://blogs.bmj.com/bmj/2012/11/23/desmond-oneill -amour-ageing-and-missed-opportunities.

Oorsouw, Kim van, and Harald Merckelbach. "Detecting Malingered Memory Problems in the Civil and Criminal Arena." *Legal and Criminological Psychology* 15, no.1 (February 1, 2010): 97–114.

O'Rand, Angela M. "When Old Age Begins: Implications for Health, Work, and Retirement." In *The New Politics of Old Age Policy*, edited by Robert B. Hudson, 109–128. Baltimore: Johns Hopkins University Press, 2005.

Oregon Public Health Division. "Oregon's Death with Dignity Act—2011." Accessed December 10, 2016. http://public.health.oregon.gov/providerpartnerresources/evaluationresearch/deathwithdignityact/documents/year14.pdf.

Ornstein, Charles. "Nursing Home Workers Share Explicit Photos of Residents on Snapchat." *ProPublica*, December 21, 2015. Accessed December 10, 2016. www.propublica .org/article/nursing-home-workers-share-explicit-photos-of-residents-on-snapchat.

Orth, Ulrich, R.W. Robins, and C.J. Soto. "Tracking the Trajectory of Shame, Guilt, and Pride across the Life Span." *Journal of Personality and Social Psychology* 99, no. 6 (December 2010): 1061–1071.

Ortman, Jennifer. "U.S. Population Projections: 2012 to 2060." Bureau of the Census, Population Division. February 7, 2013: 34, "Median Age by Race and Hispanic Origin, 2012 and 2060." Accessed December 8, 2016. http://www.gwu.edu/~forcpgm/Ortman .pdf.

Overall, Christine. "Old Age and Ageism, Impairment and Ableism: Exploring the Conceptual and Material Connections." *NWSA Journal* 18, no. 1 (March 2006): 126–137.

Ozeki, Ruth. *All Over Creation*. New York: Penguin, 2003.

Pantic, Marijana, and Jelena Živanović Miljković. "Regional Differences between Rural Areas of Serbia in Population Aging and Agricultural Activities." *Spatium International Review* 22 (July 2010): 29–37.

Parker, Lisa S., and Valerie B. Satkoske. "Ethical Dimensions of Disparities in Depression Research and Treatment in the Pharmacogenomic Era." *Journal of Law, Medicine, and Ethics* 40, no. 4 (Winter 2012): 886–903.

Perry, Michael. "Drought Casts Suicide Shadow Over Rural Australia." *rense.com*, 2005. Accessed December 10, 2016. http://www.rense.com/genera166/dro.htm.

Peters, Kevin R., and Steven Katz. "Voices from the Field: Expert Reflections on Mild Cognitive Impairment." *Dementia* 14, no. 3 (2015): 285–297. Accessed July 27, 2016. http://dem.sagepub.com/content/14/3/285.full.pdf+html.

Peters, Robert L. "Richard Avedon's Letter to His Father." August 1, 2009. Accessed December 10, 2016. http://cumberbatchweb.tumblr.com/post/87535456589/benedict -cumberbatch-reads-a-letter-from-richard.

Pew Research Center. *Growing Old in America: Expectations vs. Reality*. June 29, 2009. Accessed June 13, 2016. http://www.pewsocialtrends.org/files/2010/10/Getting-Old-in -America.pdf.

Phillips, Adam. "Against Self-Criticism." *London Review of Books*, March 5, 2015, 13–16.

———. *On Balance*. New York: Farrar, Straus and Giroux, 2010.

Phu, Thy, and Linda M. Steer. "Introduction." *Photography & Culture* 2, no. 3 (November 2009): 235–240. Accessed March 11, 2016. doi: 10.2752/175145109X12532077132194.

Pickard, Susan. *Age Studies*. London: Sage, 2016.

———. "Biology as Destiny? Rethinking Embodiment in 'Deep' Old Age." *Ageing and Society* 34, no. 8 (September 2014): 279–129. Accessed December 10, 2016. doi: https:// dx.doi.org/10.1017/S0144686X13000196.

Pierce, Gloria. "Poststructural Feminist Pedagogy in a Post-Katrina World." *Feminist Teacher* 21, no. 1 (2010): 26–53.

Pillay, Natashya Kristanna, and Pranitha Maharaj. "Population Ageing in Africa." In *Aging and Health in Africa*, edited by Pranitha Maharaj, 11–51. New York: Springer, 2013.

Political Notebook. "Health Care Sign-ups Top 4.2 Million." *Boston Globe*, March 12, 2014: A8. Accessed June 13, 2016. http://www.bostonglobe.com/news/nation/2014/03/11/ almost-million-more-sign-for-health-coverage-february/IJgioswGj0D9HBLDvpk DJM/story.html.

Pollak, Michael. "Vital Signs." *New York Times*, August 24, 1999. Accessed February 23, 2016. http://www.nytimes.com/1999/08/24/health/vital-signs-longevity-stay-busy-live -longer-experts-suggest.html.

Pollock, Griselda. "Missing Women: Rethinking Early Thoughts on Images of Women." In *Over Exposed: Essays on Contemporary Photography*, edited by Carol Squiers, 229–246. New York: New Press, 1999.

Pomrehn, P. R., L. F. Burmeister, and R. B. Wallace. "Ischemic Heart Disease Mortality in Iowa Farmers: The Influence of Life-style." *JAMA* 248, no. 9 (September 1982): 1073–1076.

Post, Dr. Stephen G. "In Response to Margaret M. Gullette." *Aging, Culture, Humanities* 1, no. 1 (2014). Accessed June 13, 2016. http://ageculturehumanities.org/WP/in -response-to-margaret-m-gullette/.

Powell, Richard J. *Cutting a Figure: Fashioning Black Portraiture.* Chicago: University of Chicago Press, 2008.

Prager, Jeffrey. "Healing from History." *European Journal of Social Theory* 11, no. 3 (August 2008): 405–420.

Price, Margaret. "Mental Disability and Other Terms of Art." *Profession* (2010): 117–130.

Proctor, Jennifer, River E. Branch, and Kyja Kristjansson-Nelson. "Woman with the Movie Camera Redux: Revisiting the Position of Women in the Production Classroom." *Jump Cut* 53 (Summer 2011). Accessed December 10, 2016.http://ejumpcut.org/archive/jc53.2011/womenProdnClass/index.html. .

Public Health England. "Recommendation against National Dementia Screening." January 14, 2015. Accessed July 27, 2016. https://www.gov.uk/government/news/recommendation-against-national-dementia-screening.

Querry, Toni J. "Rose by Any Other Name No Longer Smells as Sweet: Disparate Treatment Discrimination and the Age Proxy Doctrine after *Hazen Paper Co. v. Biggins.*" *Cornell Law Review* 81, no. 3 (January 1996): 530.

Quest-Riston, Charles. "The Best of Gertrude Jekyll." *Country Life*, May 18, 2011. http://www.judithtankard.com/_pdf/contry_%20iifrev51811.pdf.

Raab, Selwyn. *Five Families.* New York: St. Martin's Press, 2005.

——. "Vincent Gigante, Mafia Leader Who Feigned Insanity, Dies at 77." *New York Times*, December 19, 2005. Accessed December 8, 2016. www.nytimes.com/2005/12/19/obituaries/19cnd-gigante.html?pagewanted=all.

Radstone, Susannah. "Trauma Theory: Contexts, Politics, Ethics." *Paragraph* 30, no. 1 (March 12, 2007). Accessed August 5, 2015. http://dx.doi.org/10.3366/prg.2007.0015.

Ram K. "Comment" to Gargi Parsai, "Elders Seek Special Session to Discuss Farmers' Suicides." *The Hindu*, December 16, 2011. Accessed December 10, 2016. http://www.thehindu.com/news/national/elders-seek-special-session-to-discuss-farmers-suicides/article2718296.eceno.comments.

Rampell, Catherine. "The Burden of Supporting the Elderly." *New York Times*, April 13, 2011. Accessed December 10, 2016. http://economix.blogs.nytimes.com/2011/04/13/the-burden-of-supporting-the-elderly/.

Rao, Smriti. "Indicators of Gendered Control over Agricultural Resources: A Guide for Agricultural Policy and Research." CGIAR Gender and Agriculture Network Working Paper No. 1, June 2016. Accessed July 27, 2016. http://pim.cgiar.org/2016/07/18/small-changes-for-big-improvements-criteria-for-evaluating-indicators-of-gender-gaps-in-control-over-productive-resources/.

Reaksmey, Heng. "Ieng Thirith Will Not Yet Be Released: Tribunal." *www.voanews.com*, December 13, 2011. Accessed July 27, 2016. http://www.voacambodia.com/a/ieng-thirith-will-not-yet-be-released-tribunal-135516428/1355305.html.

Reese, Diana. "Murder-Suicide Disturbing Trend among the Elderly." *Washington Post*, January 26, 2013.

Reeve, Richard. "Shame, the Invisible Affect." *Richard Reeve*, August 31, 2012. Accessed December 10, 2016. http://richardreeve.info/shame-the-invisible-affect/.

The Rejuvenation Center. "Is Ageism Causing an Increase in Cosmetic Procedures?" December 17, 2013. Accessed December 10, 2016. https://americanhealthandbeauty.com/articles/4866/is-ageism-causing-an-increase-in-cosmetic-procedures.

Reuters, "Ex-dictator Efrain Rios Montt Mentally Unfit for Genocide Retrial." *Guardian*, July 8, 2015. Accessed October 22, 2015. www.theguardian.com/world/2015/jul/08/ guatemalan-ex-dictator-efrain-rios-montt-mentally-unfit-for-genocide-retrial.

Ribbat, Christoph. "Out of It? Old Age and Photographic Portraiture." *Amerikastudien/ American Studies* 56, no. 1 (Winter 2011): 67–84.

Rich, Adrienne. *On Lies, Secrets, and Silence: Selected Prose 1966–1978*. New York: W. W. Norton, 1979.

———. *What Is Found There: Notebooks on Poetry and Politics*. New York: W. W. Norton, 1993.

Robertson, Adele Crockett. *The Orchard: A Memoir*. New York: Dial Press, 2005.

Robinson, Marilynne. *The Death of Adam: Essays on Modern Thought*. Boston: Houghton Mifflin, 1998.

———. *Gilead*. New York: Farrar, Straus, Giroux, 2004.

Rock, Danielle. E-mail communication, April 9, 2016.

Romer, Nancy. "The Radical Potential of the Food Justice Movement." *Radical Teacher* 98 (Winter 2014): 5–14. doi: 10.5195/rt.2014.78.

Root, Maria P. P. "Reconstructing the Impact of Trauma on Personality." In *Personality and Psychopathology: Feminist Reappraisals*, edited by Laura S. Brown and Mary Ballou. New York: Guilford Press, 1992.

Rosenberg Foundation for Children (producers). "Art, Activism, and the Rosenberg Fund for Children." Video. Accessed October 28, 2015. http://www.rfc.org/blog/ article/1984.

Ruiz, Michelle. "Why Women Should Stop Calling Themselves Old." *Vogue* online. Accessed November 1, 2015. http://www.vogue.com/13368217/why-women-should-stop -calling-themselves-old-ageism/?mbid=social_onsite_twitter.

Sanders, Sara, and James Power. "Roles, Responsibilities, and Relationships among Older Husbands Caring for Wives with Progressive Dementia and Other Chronic Conditions." *Health and Social Work* 34, no. 1 (February 2009): 41–51.

Sages and Seekers. "The Eight-Week Program," Accessed December 6, 2016. http://www .sagesandseekers.org/8-week-program.html.

———. "3-Minute University Video." Accessed December 6, 2016. http://www.sagesand seekers.org/what-they-say.html. *Saveur* no. 152 (September 2012): 86.

Sartre, Jean-Paul. *Anti-Semite and Jew*. New York: Schocken Books, 1948.

Savran, David. "Kushner's Children of the Revolution," *American Theatre* 26 #8 (October 2009): 42.

Scharf, Thomas, and Bernadette Bartlam, "Ageing and Social Exclusion in Rural Communities." In *Rural Ageing*, edited by Norah Keating, 97–108. Bristol, UK: Policy Press, 2008.

Scharf, Thomas, and Norah Keating. "Social Exclusion in Later Life: A Global Challenge." In *From Exclusion to Inclusion in Old Age: A Global Challenge*, edited by Thomas Scharf and Norah Keating, 1–16. Bristol, UK: Policy Press, 2012.

Scheff, Thomas J. "Shame in Self and Society." *Symbolic Interaction* 26, no. 2 (2003): 239–262. Accessed December 10, 2016. http://www.jstor.org/stable/10.1525/si.2003.26.2.239.

Scheffer, David. *All the Missing Souls: A Personal History of the War Crimes Tribunals*. Princeton, NJ: Princeton University Press, 2011.

Scheiber, Noah. "The Brutal Ageism of Tech." *New Republic*, March 23, 2014. Accessed June 13, 2016. http://www.newrepublic.com/article/117088/silicons-valleys-brutal-ageism.

Scholle, David, and Star Denski. *Media Education and the (Re) Production of Culture.* Westport CT: Greenwood Press, 1994.

Schukoske, Jane E. "Community Development Through Gardening: State and Local Policies Transforming Urban Open Space." *New York University Journal of Legislation and Public Policy* 3, no. 2 (2000): 351–392.

Schultz, Rainer. "Food Sovereignty and Cooperatives in Cuba's Socialism." *Socialism and Democracy* 26, no. 3 (November 2012): 117–138.

Schweda, Mark, and Aagje Swinnen. "Call for Abstracts: 'Popularizing Dementia,' Public Expressions and Representations of Forgetfulness." E-mail, June 4, 2013.

Sebelius, Kathleen. "Secretary Sebelius Letter to Congress about CLASS." October 14, 2011. Accessed December 10, 2016. https://www.ltcconsultants.com/articles/2011/class-dismissed/Sebelius-CLASS-Letter.pdf.

Seiff, Abby. "Khmer Rouge Tribunal Readies Way for Genocide Case." Associated Press, July 29, 2014. Accessed July 27, 2016. http://www.sandiegouniontribune.com/news/2014/jul/29/khmer-rouge-tribunal-readies-way-for-genocide-case/.

Seligman, Adam B., David W. Montgomery, and Rahel R. Wasserfall. *Living with Difference: How to Build Community in a Divided World.* Berkeley: University of California Press, 2015.

Shapiro, David. "Interview with Jeff Wall." *Museo Magazine,* 1999. Accessed December 10, 2016. http://www.museomagazine.com/JEFF-WALL.

Shapiro, Fred R. "Historical Notes on the Vocabulary of the Women's Movement." *American Speech* 60, no. 1 (Spring 1985): 3–16. Accessed June 13, 2016. http://www.jstor.org/stable/454643?seq=1no.page_scan_tab_contents.

Sheeran, Thomas J., and John Seewer. "Ohio Hospital Shooting: Mercy Killing or Murder?" *AP BigStory,* August 12, 2012. Accessed Mary 9, 2016. http://bigstory.ap.org/article/ohio-hospital-shooting-mercy-killing-or-murder.

Shelton, Jim. "Yale Study Finds Bias among Facebook Users against Elderly People." *New Haven Register,* March 30, 2013. Accessed December 10, 2016. www.mercurynews.com/nation-world/ci_22907563/yale-study-finds-bias-among-facebook-users-against.

Sheridan, Michael. "Cannibalism Sets Tone for Khmer Rouge Trial." *The Australian,* November 29, 2011. Accessed December 10, 2016. http://www.theaustralian.com.au/news/world/cannibalism-sets-tone-for-khmer-rouge-trial/news-story/e0dd7e1f85236-3983ebf5639d1501fe2.

Shulman, Alix Kates. "Half Full or Half Empty." *Women's Review of Books,* March–April 2014. Accessed December 10, 2016. http://www.wcwonline.org/Women-s-Review-of-Books-Mar/Apr-2014/half-full-or-half-empty.

Siegal, Brittany, and Sarah Kagan. "Teaching Psychological and Social Gerontology to Millennial Undergraduates." *Educational Gerontology* 38, no. 1 (2012): 20–29.

Silcoff, Mireille. "Why Your Grandpa Is Cooler Than You." *New York Times Magazine,* April 26, 2013.

Skoloff, Brian. "Arizona Man, 86, Gets Probation in Mercy Killing Case." AP, March 30, 2013. Accessed December 10, 2016. http://www.csmonitor.com/USA/Latest-News-Wires/2013/0330/Arizona-man-86-gets-probation-in-mercy-killing-case.

Smith, Eleanor. "Q and A: Not Dead Yet of Georgia." E-mail communication, April 2013.

Social Security Administration. "Fact Sheet: 2014 Social Security Changes." Accessed June 13, 2016. www.ssa.gov/pressoffice/factsheets/colafacts2014.html.

Sontag, Susan. *On Photography.* New York: Macmillan, 1977.

Sontag, Susan. "Photography within the Humanities." In *The Photography Reader*, edited by Liz Wells, 59–66. London, Routledge, 2003.

Sotheara, Chhim. "A Qualitative and Quantitative Investigation into Ethno-Cultural Framing of Trauma in Cambodia." Ph.D. diss., Faculty of Arts, Monash University, Melbourne, Australia, 2014.

Span, Paula. "Over 65? Hold On to That Organ Donor Card." *New York Times*, August 16, 2016, D5.

"Specialist." "KR [Khmer Rouge] Defendant Very Likely Has Alzheimer's." *Nation* (Thailand). August 30, 2011.

Spitzer, Helmut, and Zena Mnasi Mbeyo, *In Search of Protection: Older People and Their Fight for Survival in Tanzania*. Vienna: Drava, 2011.

Srinivas, Nidhi Nath. "Women Farmers Are Worse Off Than the Most Hapless Male." *Economic Times* [India], April 4, 2011. Accessed February 23, 2016. http://articles .economictimes.indiatimes.com/2011-04-04/news/29380209_1_bt-cotton-crop-insurance-farmers.

Stallabrass, Julian. "Cold Eye" (Review). *New Left Review* (November-December 1996): 147–152. Accessed December 10, 2016. https://newleftreview.org/article/download_pdf?id=2065.

———. "What's in a Face?" *October* 1, no. 122 (Fall 2007): 71–90.

Steichen, Edward, ed. *The Family of Man*. New York: Museum of Modern Art, 1955.

Stewart. Abigail, and Joan M. Ostrove. "Women's Personality in Middle Age: Gender, History, and Midcourse Corrections." *American Psychologist* 53, no. 11 (1998): 1185–1194.

Stripling, Alison, J. M. Calton, and Martin Heesacker. "College Students' Perceptions of and Responses to Internet Ageism." Poster presented at Gerontological Society of America meeting, Boston, November 19, 2011.

Sultan, Larry. "Pictures from Home." In *The Familial Gaze*, edited by Marianne Hirsch, 3–13. Hanover, NH: University Press of New England, 1999.

Tavernese, Sabrina, "Disparity in Life Spans of the Rich and the Poor Is Growing." *New York Times*, February 12, 2016.

Terry, Paul. "Ageism and Projective Identification." *Psychodynamic Practice* 14, no. 2 (May 2008): 155–168.

Theroux, Louis. *Extreme Love: Dementia*. BBC, 2012.

Thielking, Megan. "Efforts Spread to Aid Dementia Sufferers." *Boston Globe*, October 19, 2015, A1, A6.

Thoreau, Henry David. *H. D. Thoreau: A Writer's Journal*. Edited by Laurence Stapleton. New York: Dover, 1960.

TIAA-CREF Aging Workforce Series. "An Age of Opportunity." 2012. Accessed December 10, 2016. https://www.tiaa.org/public/pdf/aging_workforce_part1.pdf.

Timmermann, Wibke Kristin. "Incitement in International Criminal Law." *International Review of the Red Cross* 88, no. 864 (December 2006): 823–852.

Toobin, Jeffrey. "Holder v. Roberts." *New Yorker*, February 17 and 24, 2014, 42–49.

Topaz, Vicki. *Silver: A State of Mind*. Accessed December 2, 2016. www.womenonaging .com/main.php#/VIEW%2.

Tougaw, Jason. "Testimony and the Subjects of AIDS Memoirs." In *Extremities: Trauma, Testimony, and Community*, edited by Nancy K. Miller and Jason Tougaw, 166–185. Urbana: University of Illinois Press, 2002.

Twigg, Julia. *Bathing: The Body and Community Care*. London: Routledge, 2001.

Tyler, Anne. *A Spool of Blue Thread*. New York: Ballantine Books, 2015.

UK Agriculture. "Crisis in UK Agriculture and British Farming." Accessed September 13, 2015. Accessed December 10, 2016. http://archive.is/DfTp.

UK Department of Constitutional Affairs. *Mental Capacity Act 2005. Code of Practice.* London: The Stationery Office, 2007. Accessed July 22, 2016. https://www.gov.uk/government/uploads/system/uploads/attachment_data/file/497253/Mental-capacity-act-code-of-practice.pdf.

Umphrey, Don. E-mail communications, March 27, 2014.

Umphrey, Don, and Tom Robinson. "Negative Stereotypes Underlying Other-Person Perceptions of the Elderly." *Educational Gerontology* 33 (2007): 309–326.

United States Census Bureau. "College Enrollment Declines for Second Year in a Row." September 24, 2014. Accessed December 6, 2016. http://www.census.gov/newsroom/press-releases/2014/cb14-177.html.

United States Department of Agriculture (USDA). "2012 Census of Agriculture Highlights. Farms and Farmland." September 2014. Accessed December 10, 2016. http://www.agcensus.usda.gov/Publications/2012/Online_Resources/Highlights/Farms and Farmland/Highlights Farms and Farmland.pdf.

———. "USDA Census 2012, Census Highlights." May 2014. Accessed December 10, 2016. http://www.agcensus.usda.gov/Publications/2012/Online_Resources/Highlights/Farm_Demographics/no.average_age.

UPI.Com World News. "Court Orders Treatment for Ieng Thirith." December 14, 2011. Accessed December 10, 2016. http://www.upi.com/Top_News/World-News/2011/12/14/Court-orders-treatment-for-Ieng-Thirith/UPI-40721323869781/no.ixzz2FdU34Kvh.

Van Auken, Bill. "Chilean Prosecutor Charges Ex-US Officer in 1973 Murder of American Journalists." World Socialist Web Site, December 5, 2011. http://www.wsws.org/articles/2011/dec2011/chil-d05.shtml.

Van Dyk, Silke. "The Appraisal of Difference: Critical Gerontology and the Active-Ageing Paradigm." *Journal of Aging Studies* 31, no. 3 (2014): 93–103.

VEGGI Farmers Cooperative. "Ăn Quả Nhớ Kẻ Trồng Cây." October 1, 2014. Accessed November 2104. http://www.veggifarmcoop.com/2014/10/01/an-qua-nho-ke-trong-cay/.

Vitols, Maruta Z., and Caitlin Lynch. "Back in the Saddle Again: Ethics, Visibility, and Aging on Screen." *Anthropology and Aging* 36, no. 1 (2015): 11–19. Accessed December 10, 2016. http://anthro-age.pitt.edu/ojs/index.php/anthro-age/article/view/85/132.

Wall, Jeff. E-mail communications, December 12, 2012, and January 3, 2013.

Wallis, Victor. "Intersectionality's Binding Agent: The Political Primacy of Class." *New Political Science* 37, no. 4 (2015): 604–619.

Walzer, Michael. "Imaginary Jews." *New York Review of Books*, March 20, 2014, 31–33.

Waring, Marilyn. *If Women Counted: A New Feminist Economics*. San Francisco: Harper Collins, 1988.

Watts, Jonathan. "Field of Tears." *Guardian*, September 15, 2003. Accessed November 2011. www.guardian.co.uk/world/2003/sep/16/northkorea.wto.

Weems, Carrie Mae. *From Here I Saw What Happened and I Cried* (1995–1996). Accessed Decdember 10, 2016. http://carriemaeweems.net/galleries/from-here.html.

Weiner, Philip L. "Fitness Hearings in War Crimes Cases: From Nuremberg to the Hague." *Boston College International and Comparative Law Review* 30, no. 10 (2007): 185–198. Accessed December 10, 2016. http://lawdigitalcommons.bc.edu/cgi/viewcontent.cgi?article=1093&context=iclr.

Westermarck, Edward. *Wit and Wisdom of Morocco*. New York: Kessinger Publishing, 1931.

Whitehouse, Peter J., and Harry. R. Moody. "Mild Cognitive Impairment: A 'Hardening of the Categories'?" *Dementia* 5, no.1 (January 2006): 11–25.·doi: 10.1177/1471301206 059752.

Whitman, Walt. "I Sing the Body Electric." In *Leaves of Grass*, part 3. Philadelphia: David McKay, 1891–92.

Williams, Patricia J. "Cruelty, Irony, and Evasion." *The Nation*, January 11, 2016, 10–11.

Willmore, Larry. Review of Isabella Aboderin's *Intergenerational Support and Old Age in Africa*. Accessed November 19, 2015. http://larrywillmore.net/ABODERIN.pdf.

Wolff, Michael. "A Life Worth Ending." *New York Magazine*, May 20, 2012.

Womersley, Gail, Anastasia Maw, and Sally Swartz. "The Construction of Shame in Feminist Reflexive Practice and Its Manifestations in a Research Relationship." *Qualitative Inquiry* 17, no. 9 (2011): 876–886. doi: 10.1177/1077800411423205.

Wong, Ying, and Jeanne L. Tsai. "Cultural Models of Shame and Guilt." In *The Self-conscious Emotions: Theory and Research*, edited by Jessica L. Tracy, Richard W. Robins, and June Price Tangney, 209–223. New York: Guilford Press; 2007.

Woodard, Stacy, W.E. Burak, L. Kotur, P.C. Nadella, C.L. Shapiro, and J. Wilson. "Older Women with Breast Carcinoma Are Less Likely to Receive Adjuvant Chemotherapy. Evidence of Possible Age Bias?" *Cancer* 98, no. 6 (September 15, 2003): 1141–1149.

Woodward, Kathleen. "Against Wisdom: The Social Politics of Anger and Aging." *Journal of Aging Studies* 17, no.1 (February 2003): 55–67.

——. "Assisted Living: Aging, Old Age, Memory, Aesthetics." Conference Papers: *Aging, Old Age, Memory, Aesthetics, Occasion* 4 (June 15, 2012), published online on *Arcade*. Accessed December 4, 2013. http://arcade.stanford.edu/sites/default/files/article_pdfs/OCCASION_v04_Woodward_053112_0.pdf.

——. "Inventing Generational Models." In *Figuring Age: Women, Bodies, Generations*, edited by Kathleen Woodward. Bloomington: Indiana University Press, 1999.

——. "Performing Age, Performing Gender." *NWSA Journal* 18, no. 1 (Spring 2006): 162–189. Accessed October 25, 2015.

——. *Statistical Panic. Cultural Politics and the Poetics of the Emotions*. Durham, NC: Duke University Press, 2009.

——. Traumatic Shame: Toni Morrison, Televisual Culture, and the Cultural Politics of the Emotions," *Cultural Critique* 46 (October 2000): 210–240.

Wozniacka, Gosia (AP). "Woodlake Pride: Youths in Gardens, Out of Gangs." *San Francisco Chronicle*, December 11, 2011. Accessed February 25, 2016. http://www.sfgate.com/homeandgarden/article/Woodlake-Pride-Youths-in-gardens-out-ofgangs-2395289.php.

Wurtele, Sandy K., and LaRae Maruyama. "Changing Students' Stereotypes of Older Adults." *Teaching of Psychology* 40, no. 1 (January 2013): 59–61. doi: 10.1177/0098628312465867.

Yapp, Robin. "Chile Requests Extradition." *Telegraph* [UK], November 30, 2012. Accessed December 10, 2016. http://www.telegraph.co.uk/news/worldnews/southamerica/chile/8926298/Chile-requests-extradition-of-US-officer-linked-to-1973-coup-murders.html.

Yates, Pamela, director. *Granito: How to Nail a Dictator*. Film, 2011. Skylight Pictures.

Zeilig, Hannah. "Dementia as a Cultural Metaphor." *The Gerontologist* 54, no. 2 (2014): 258–267.

Zepeda, Jorge. "Second."*English Translation of Findings, Penal and Civil Judgements by Judge Zepeda* Accessed May 5, 2015. http://repositories.lib.utexas.edu/bitstream/handle/2152/19267/Horman_Sentencia_Horman_-_Teruggi_English_Full_File.pdf.

Zerwick, Chloe. *New York Times* Sunday Dialogue: "Ageism in Our Society." *New York Times*, February 7, 2015. December 10, 2016. http://www.nytimes.com/2015/02/08/opinion/ageism-in-our-society.html.

Zuckerman, Jocelyn C. "The Constant Gardeners." *OnEarth*, November 28, 2011.

Zuo, Mandy. "Pension Now Covers 143m[illion] Farmers, Just 757m to Go." *South China Morning Post*, March 9, 2011.

INDEX

ableism, xx, 32, 52, 55, 59, 183, 202; "ageist ableism" as useful term, 156; competitive, 167. *See also* cognitive impairment *entries*; disability; duty to die

activism, 16, 31, 152, 193, 204; cultural revolutions by social movements, 16, 30–31, 132, 135, 142, 175–176, 181, 190. *See also* anti-ageist activism

A.D. *See* Alzheimer's disease *entries*

adolescence, 144, 178–179

adult offspring, in relations with parents, 58–59, 122, 147, 161, 164; duty of care, 141; fear of caregiving, 141–143, 153, 156, 157; feelings when parents die, 137, 142, 158; getting support from parents, 101; helping in farm families, 89, 97, 101; hostile behaviors toward parents, 45, 172–173, 196–197; leaving farm-work for cities, 96, 98, 100, 107; in literature, 9–10, 150–152, 156; projecting own fears, 118–119, 145; published accounts begrudging treatments to parents, 72, 142–145; wanting full inheritance, 145. *See also* adults as parents in later life; family

adults as parents in later life, in relations with adult offspring, 9–11, 96–97, 101, 131, 149; afraid of them, 45; being equally adults together, 11, 59; dealing with offspring's ageism, 196–199; reconciliations, 198–200; revenge fantasies, 194–195

affects, 113; caused by age-related shaming, 6, 169–171, 174, 180, 189, 193; overcoming age-related shaming, 6–7, 32–33, 165, 174–175, 183; from silence to words and

grievances, 182–188; transmission of, 170, 171, 183

African Americans, 3, 31, 59, 66, 69, 84, 90, 137, 142; Black Panthers, 193; as farmers, 98; problems with photographic portraits of, 27, 31; shrine for an elder, 47. *See also* racism

age (category), 61–63, 67, 73; choice of, as primary identity in later life, 51; choice of, as primary identity in youth, 57, 59, 63, 202; as imposed and over-riding identity, 165–166; as one of multiple identities, 62, 189; reasons to foreground category, 16, 79; as social, historical construction, 16, 39, 83. *See also other* age, ageism, ageisms, *and* aging *entries*; intergenerational relations; midlife; old age

age anxiety, 164

age autobiography, 8, 58. *See also* author, age autobiography of

age class, xxi, 57, 76, 174; older, 16, 67, 200; youth's interests as an, 58, 74; youth's illusion of being a permanent, 57, 59, 63, 202

age critic, xi, 35, 42, 66, 120, 121, 207; as anti-ageist, 16, 25, 31, 83; author as, 6, 8, 16–17, 59, 119, 141, 148; as social constructionist, xvii, 2, 16, 19, 181

aged by culture (theory about social construction of age), xiii, 16, 212n18, 215n20; differences between "aging" and "ageism," xiii, xx, 10, 13, 15, 19, 164, 166, 171, 185, 188–189, 203; usefulness of term "middle-ageism," xviii.

aged by culture (*continued*)
  See also age studies, age theory; social
  construction of reality
age discrimination, 6; Age Discrimination in Employment Act (ADEA), xviii,
  1–2; in employment, 56, 65, 66–67, 75; in
  medical/surgical care for older adults,
  3–4, 144; starts young, xx, 2–3, 55–56,
  57, 74
age gaze, ageist, xxi, 47; appearance of
  "agedness," 4, 13, 22, 31, 172, 184, 193, 199;
  Emerson and, 15, 18; the "glimpse," 14,
  25–26, 168; harms of, xi–xii, 6, 12, 15,
  18, 24–26, 47, 168, 189; the "look," 166;
  youthful, 24, 26, 47, 168
age grading, 74
age hierarchy, 11, 32, 40, 42, 80, 149, 173,
  177; based on seniority, xviii, 20, 52, 82,
  87, 151; maturational processes, 15, 177,
  178; obstacles to respect for aging and
  older adults, 36, 41, 45, 74, 80, 101, 118,
  135, 162, 173, 181, 197, 198, 199; respect for
  aging, older adults, xvii, xviii, 18, 32, 44,
  59, 64, 87, 90, 105, 132, 175, 180, 201, 203;
  in Sages and Seekers program, 81–82
age identities, multiple (developed over
  life course), 62, 189–190; age not always
  primary among, 18, 50–51, 168; longitudinal and changing, 189–190; slogan
  identities, 51. *See also* age identity
age identity (developed over life course),
  165; and ageist identity-stripping, xviii,
  xix, 33, 74, 161, 166, 169–171; age pride,
  50–51; current or latest self (the Elder
  within), 186, 189, 190; need for continuity in identity, 91, 94, 98, 134, 168;
  in relation to age-related bodily ills,
  xix, xx; selfhood-in-relation, 164–165;
  uneven developments among identities,
  59–60, 172; Young Judge (early identity),
  57–60; youth as essentialized state, 59,
  63, 78, 81, 202. *See also* age identities,
  multiple; intersectionality
ageism, xvi, xvii, 64–65, 119; affective
  dimensions of, 6, 202, 213; becoming
  more virulent in US, 3–5, 13–14, 56, 67,
  118–119; and ethical issues, xiii–xiv, 15,
  18, 19, 132, 140, 141, 144, 154, 161, 196;
  as everyday expectable environment,
  14, 174; fear of, 190; future of, 33, 67,
  201, 192–193, 204; the Great Demotion,

xiii, xxiii, 1, 3, 59, 66, 74, 100, 171, 173,
  190, 199; as health hazard, 3–4, 14, 144,
  145; history of, 1, 77; ignorance about,
  1, 6, 11, 16, 182; implicit bias, 58, 64–65;
  like/unlike homophobia, 60, 153; like/
  unlike racism, xiii, xix, xx, 1, 3, 5, 7, 14,
  19, 61, 65, 67, 165, 180, 181, 183, 188; like/
  unlike sexism, xiii, xix, xx, 1, 7, 19, 32,
  55, 61, 148, 165, 180, 181, 183, 188; micro-
  aggressions, 8, 13, 62, 165, 194; most
  naturalized bias, xiii, 5, 173; need for a
  movement against, xi, 5, 19–20, 31, 53,
  184, 193, 203; needs study, xvi, 16–18;
  second-generation issues, 3–5, 192; starts
  young, 27, 55–56, 57, 74; violence, 10, 15,
  25, 54, 136, 140–141, 164, 170, 182, 184–
  185, 190, 195; wars against later life, xviii,
  xx, 16, 52; widespread, 15, 17. *See also*
  other ageism *and* ageisms *entries*; ageists; aging; middle-ageism
ageism (internalized), xxi, 15, 19, 32, 59;
  abjectness linked to array of ageisms,
  13, 39, 41, 138, 146, 172, 203; confusion
  about what ageism is, 6, 182–185, 188;
  de-internalization, 51, 190; expected or
  sudden assault of, 9, 100, 171, 179–180,
  182; hiding feelings about, xii–xiii, 187;
  political effect of age-shaming, 173;
  post-traumatic states, 169–171; seen as
  individual problem, 164–165, 171; sufferings from, xiii, xvi, 7, 15, 65, 137, 163–165,
  171–172, 174; wish to be young, 202;
  Young Judge, 57–59, 60, 63, 66, 81, 146,
  168, 170, 189–190. *See also* affects; emotions *entries*; shaming; trauma
"ageism" (term): indispensable, 18, 65,
  202–203; invented in 1969, 1. *See also*
  other ageism *and* ageisms *entries*
ageism consciousness, 30, 167, 190; learning new idioms of distress, 185; obstacles
  to raising, 173–174; raising, v, 31, 62, 67,
  69, 73, 162, 188, 190–191, 203. *See also*
  shaming
ageisms (in discourse), xix, 51, 57–58;
  explicit, 56, 58, 129, 143; hate speech,
  7, 52, 56, 65, 73, 79–80, 139, 141, 158,
  206; hate speech by Internet trolls, 4,
  54–55, 57, 62, 72, 76, 83, 139; in jokes,
  6, 8, 57, 62, 74, 118, 135, 163; in language
  describing people with Alzheimer's,
  113, 117–118; and laughter, 55, 61–65;

in mainstream media, xvii, 4, 70, 117, 118, 135, 137, 140–144, 147; "old hag," 12–13, 74, 194; in play scripts, 11, 148, 157, 161; representing "graying" or "aging" nation as problem, xv, xvii, xxi, 55, 88, 146; "zombie(s)," 60, 118–119. *See also* "burden"; "dementia"

ageisms (in the economy), xx, 102; being "too old" starts young, xx, 55–56, 57, 74; capitalism's role, xviii, 84, 152, 192–193; capitalism's role in academe, 66–67; capitalism's role in eroding seniority, xviii, 52, 151; capitalism's role in job discrimination at midlife, xviii, 3, 55–56; capitalism's role in pitting generations against one another, 151; middle-ageist attitudes, xviii, 56, 65, 75; neoliberalism's role, xviii, 102, 110, 196; right-wing deficit discourse, 4, 5. *See also* ageism; cult of youth; middle-ageism

ageisms (in educational systems), 68, 102; absence of older students, 66; exclusions, 102; "GOMERs" in medical education, 3, 4; job discrimination in higher education, 66–67; of students, 60–65

ageisms (in families), 10, 196–197; in attitudes of adult offspring, 44–45, 73, 141; elder abuse, 139; fear of caregiving, 141–143, 153, 156, 157; Fourth Commandment weakening, 11; psychological explanations for, 145–146. *See also* adult offspring; anti-ageism, in families; men in later life

ageisms (in farming), 89–90

ageisms (in legal systems), 5, 162, 197; leniency for uxoricides, 138–139; protection of Internet hate speech, 56; US Supreme Court decisions, xviii, xx, 2–3, 196, 206, 226n7; weakness of elder law, 102–103

ageisms (in medicine/surgery/science), 144–145; defining "aging" as disease, xix, 16, 19; malpractice, 3, 4, 144–145, 162; medical model imposed, 127, 141

ageisms (in politics): power of neoliberalism, xviii, 84, 102, 143, 196; right-wing deficit discourse, 4, 5, 144; scapegoating older adults, 5; threats to Social Security, xviii, 62, 166, 196; voting rights' exclusions, 3

ageisms (in social relations), 14, 58–59, 77, 173; avoidance of older adults, xxi, 27, 53, 57, 58, 61, 65, 127, 130, 135, 144, 161, 199; damaging younger adults too, 24, 81, 195; dehumanization, 4, 15, 25, 144; exclusions, 3, 6, 10, 13, 42, 66, 87, 136, 154, 166, 168–169; Fraboni scale of ageism, 58, 59, 61; ignoring harms, xx, 27; implicit, 58; projections (economic), 13, 118; projections (psychological) 5, 15, 25, 63–64, 147, 169, 170–171; psychological explanations for, 12, 145–146, 148, 150–151; as replacement bias, 60; silencing victims, 7, 15, 89, 141, 165, 182–184, 185–186, 188, 200; "walking while old" (assault and battery), 13–14, 58, 141. *See also* age gaze; ageist ableism; *other* ageisms *entries*; shaming; violence

"ageisms" (term), xviii; array of, xxii, 1, 15

ageisms (in visual culture), 22–25, 28, 30, 82; artists' attitudes, 22–23, 25–28, 37, 45; based in epidermalization, 7, 11–12, 14, 25–27, 43, 190; maintaining cult of youth, 52; politics of, 22–27; "posing while old," 27; social contexts of, 22–28, 50–53. *See* anti-ageism (in visual culture)

"ageist" (epithet), 12, 20; "shame-throwers," 21, 181, 203

ageist ableism, 134, 156, 158, 161; ageism and ableism, 52, 55, 59; "ageist ableism," as useful term, 156; the "calling card" against, 187–188; poverty and disability, 41; traumas of, 161

ageists, 18, 171, 176, 189, 203; ignoring harms to victims, 5, 7, 11–13, 183–184; inflicting violence, 13–14, 15, 25, 54–56, 118, 136, 141, 164, 182, 184–185, 187–188, 190, 195; lists of, xviii, 83–84, 146–147; naming and blaming, 7, 19, 182, 183, 202. *See also* violence

Age of Alzheimer's, 4, 117, 127, 135; coincides with era of the new longevity, 119

age studies, v, 60–61, 73, 90, 158, 208; and academic disciplines, 16, 61, 83; age theory, xiv, xvi, 9, 21; critical, 64, 68, 81, 84, 144; linking macro and micro, 6–7, 17, 71, 83, 98, 99; mission, 7, 16, 83–84, 200; necessity of, 16, 176; need to study ageism, 16, 81, 83; new topics, 17, 113; promotes intellectual revolution, 7, 16, 81, 83–84, 147, 209; two main principles

age studies (*continued*)
of, xiii. *See also* age critic; anti-ageist
education; gerontologists; gerontology
"aging" (term): defined as disease, xix, 16,
19; differentiated from "ageism," xiii,
xx, 10, 13, 15, 19, 89, 164, 166, 171, 185,
188–189, 203; focus on bioneurological
processes, xi, 180, 185, 189, 202; focus on
decline, xi, xiii, xvii, 173, 189; focus on
positive or "successful," xvi, xvii, 28, 43,
44, 143, 161, 194; in place, 93; redefined
as trigger for ageism, xiii–xiv, 7, 163,
166–167, 190; represented as demographic catastrophe, xx, 4, 11, 13, 23, 69,
140. *See also* aging-into-old-age; aging-
past-youth; epidermalization; narratives
of growing older
aging-into-old-age, 7, 51, 166, 172, 190;
normal coming-to-agedness, 172; shaming, as result of ageism or ableism, 24,
118, 129, 135, 160, 162, 164–166, 168–170,
172–175, 182; subjective experiences of
shame for, 163–165, 182. *See* age hierarchy; old age; shaming
aging-past-youth, xiii, xv, 16, 59–60, 151;
can lead to development, 177, 179; popular misperceptions about, xvii–xxi
agriculture (global small-scale): Agropolis
(urban farming), 103, 104; and farmers'
unions, 96, 109–110; lack of national
governments' support for small-holders,
106, 107; regenerative, 104, 110–111.
See also agro-industries; farmers; farm/
food movements; farming; farms
agro-industries (Big Farma), 88, 105, 109;
supranational market ideology, 106
Alzheimer's Defense (the "dementia"
claim in criminal courts), 112–122, 124–
125, 129, 133; and age, 114, 116, 117; mental
fitness assessment, 116–117, 121–130, 132–
133; trying accused with Alzheimer's,
125, 201. *See also* war-crimes tribunals
Alzheimer's disease (A.D.): feigning,
112–122, 124–125, 129, 133; and HIV and
AIDS, 99, 101, 135, 149, 150–151, 153;
panic about, 148, 150, 159; as plot necessity, 149–151; precursor diagnosis,
148–150; spectrum of symptoms and
abilities within, 113, 118, 120, 125, 126, 133;
synonymous with old age, 4; use of term
"dementia," as synonym for, 113–115,

118, 137, 140, 142, 144, 146, 148–149; as
women's disease, 140–141
Alzheimer's disease, persons diagnosed
with, 117, 118, 124, 141, 142, 144–145, 150;
assumed to want to die, 17, 138, 141, 158;
aversion to, 114, 118–119, 127, 158, 159, 162;
caregiving to, 130–131, 137–138, 141–143,
154, 160; dehumanized, 135, 137–140, 142,
144; determining functioning of, 127, 133,
141; human rights of, 133, 192; and incitements to suicide of, 141, 156–157, 159, 173;
and incontinence, 80, 143, 157, 162; issues
of diagnosis, 127, 148–150, 156; killing of
wives with, 136–140; literature about,
143, 150–153, 157; imagining oneself as a
future, 162; personhood care movement
for, 132, 135; relationships to, 129–133;
seen as "zombies," 17, 113, 118–119; self-
care, 135; spectrum of symptoms and
abilities among, 113, 118, 120, 125, 126,
133. *See also* cognitive impairment
entries
anti-ageism, xiv–xv, 53, 200, 202; creating
a better culture of feeling about age, 4, 6,
141–146; against decline ideology, 9, 162;
de-internalization, 51, 190; developing
moral imagination, 19, 30, 53, 76, 82, 159,
162; examining affects, 6; in families,
xiv–xv, 9, 39–42, 67, 130–133, 141–142;
imagining the life course ahead, 81–82,
177; milestones of resistance, 19, 188,
197–198, 200; needed by older adults, 32,
53; part of emotional intelligence, 8, 18,
33, 73, 76, 82, 182; preparing for ageism,
190, 199; as reason to foreground age, 16,
79; resistance to ageism by older adults,
10, 18, 173, 187, 200; social responsibilities of writers and artists, 16, 50, 53, 147,
150, 153, 157–158; therapies to combat
internalization and shame, 19, 59, 184–
185, 195, 197, 201. *See* other anti-ageism
and anti-ageist *entries*
anti-ageism (in discourse), 27, 167, 193;
"ageist" as epithet, 12, 203; blaming
ageists, 19–20, 196; documents of grievances, 1–2, 77, 108; in film and theater,
133, 159–161; pro-aging language, 28, 62;
responding to hate speech, in teaching
students, 65, 73, 76, 81; slogans, 1, 19, 20,
196, 203; value of using term "ageism,"
202–203

anti-ageism (in social relations): ageism consciousness, 31, 62, 67, 69, 162, 167, 173, 174, 188, 190; connecting younger and older adults, 81–82; learning to listen to grievance and suffering, xx, xxii, 7, 130, 132, 171, 185–186, 188, 190, 201, 204; limits of education, 200; pro-aging, 11, 28, 62, 167, 178–179; recognizing suffering and trauma, 175; risks of being ageist while young, 81, 194–195; social inclusion of older adults, xviii, 132, 134–135, 205; solidarity with, 80–82, 162; through story-telling, 200; warm emotions toward older adults, 10, 18, 24, 32–33, 50, 57, 81–82, 86–87, 90, 91, 96, 110, 135, 142, 159–161

anti-ageism (in visual culture), 17, 24, 47, 50, 53; albums, 8, 39, 41; artists' attitudes, 31, 41, 43–44; countering the age gaze, 32–36, 39–44, 45–53; documentaries about disability, 138, 142; making revolutionary anti-ageist art, 27, 31, 50, 52–53; politics of visual representation, 41–52; responsible looking, 19, 27, 51–52. See also photography

anti-ageist activism, 16, 19, 134, 141, 198; Declaration of Grievances, 204–205; lacks a movement, 5; naming grievances, 1, 77, 184, 186, 205–206; in organizations, 1–2, 7, 192–193; potential for a movement, 16, 20, 84, 173, 203–204; protecting first-generation services, 192; in public policy, 1–2, 111; for rights of older persons, 2, 77, 133, 192; second-generation issues for, 3, 4, 192; supranational support, 1–2, 108

anti-ageist education, 63, 73, 79–84; Age-Friendly University Initiative, 77; ageism consciousness, 61, 62, 65, 69, 73, 75, 81; age studies in, 67–68, 79, 82–83; the "calling card," 187–188; combatting hate speech, 65, 73, 76, 81; connecting students with older adults, 81–82; content of, 62, 64–65, 69–75, 81; through discussion, 62, 64, 69–72, 73–79; education of the emotions, 67, 73, 79, 81–84; intersectional thinking, 72, 77; methods, 62–66, 68–70, 73, 75–76; "Old Age"/Ageism barometer, 68; recognizing ageism, 75; students' learning, 60–61, 66, 68, 70, 71, 73, 79–82; writing assignments, 75–79

"anti-aging" products, services, ideology. See commerce in aging

anti-Semitism, xvii, xxi, 12

arts. See photography; writers

assisted dying, 137–138, 140, 158

author, 16, 69, 89, 97, 101, 104, 158; age autobiography of, 8–9, 58–59, 82, 85, 92, 176–177, 188, 189, 202; as age critic, 51, 119; family history of, xiv–xv, 130; father of, Martin (Marty) Morganroth, 155; granddaughter of, Vega, 57; husband of, David Gullette, 8, 41, 85, 90, 92, 104; identifying as old, xv, 9; mother of, Betty Morganroth, 129–131, 138, 155, 158, 186–188; vulnerability to ageism, 9, 169–171, 188

autism, 126, 139

Baby Boomers. See Boomers

bias. See ableism, ageism, and ageisms entries; ageist ableism; homophobia; intersectionality; racism; sexism; sexist ageism

Big Farma. See agro-industries

Big PhRMA (trade group, Pharmaceutical Research and Manufacturers of America), xix, 4, 62, 134

birthday, xx, 2, 8–9, 57, 58, 66, 163, 166

body, the old, xii, 155, 160, 175, 177, 179, 180, 185, 195; abjectness, linked to appearance of agedness, 4, 172, 184; the body-mind, 3, 33; and cult of youth, 24, 52, 181, 193; decline seen as individual problem, 6, 171; and disability, xix, 92, 99, 180; epidermalization, 7, 11–12, 14, 25–27, 43, 190; frailty, 117, 131, 144, 156, 194; given "born-into-them" labels, xix, 181; ignored in visual culture, 24, 52; represented as deficient, 25–26, 39, 44–45, 143; suffering, 138–139, 143, 150, 155; viewed by self over time, 36, 179. See also aging; disability; faces; health in later life; longevity

Boomers (US-born 1946–1964), xiv, 16, 65, 139, 145, 178; ageism turned against them, xix, 24, 71, 143, 175; misrepresented, xx, 5, 16, 24, 143

"burden," 12, 72, 141–143, 146, 206; ageism as hidden burden, 9–11, 15, 80, 128, 141, 169; discourse, vii (epigraph), 24, 62, 196; discourse heightens anticipated fear of dependency, 4, 146; discourse

"burden" (*continued*)
heightens fears of and impatience at caregiving, 4, 70, 127, 143; discourse serves as hate speech, 54, 73; history of the metaphor, 143, 181; and incitements to suicide, 71, 146, 148, 203; mainly women seen as, 12, 14, 140, 141, 143, 206; media use of term, 72, 141–144; memoir, 143; policy implications of "burden" discourse, 70, 111, 143, 144. *See also* duty to die; sexist ageism

capitalism (global, postindustrial forms of), 192–193, 203; careless of younger adults, xx; erodes seniority system, xviii, 52, 151; exploits midlife age class, xviii, 3, 56, 66; market ideology undercuts small-holders, 98, 100, 106–108, 110; outsources jobs, 6; pits generations against one another, 52, 151; tragedy of, 152. *See also* neoliberalism
caregiving, 126, 137, 143, 153; as body of knowledge, 119, 154, 156; and caregivers, 132–133, 138, 140–143, 154–156; elder abuse, 139, 141; fear of, 141–143, 153, 156, 157; focus on functionality, 127; men, killing ailing wives, 137–138, 140; personhood movement to improve, 132, 135; pressures on, 101; relief when elders die, 137, 142. *See also* "burden"
children, 3, 9–10, 14, 39–40, 42, 61, 91, 142, 145, 168, 178, 189, 195; anticipating progress in the life course, 177; being shamed in childhood, 175–177; in farm families, 96–97, 101, 160; learning ageism early, 7, 57, 67, 84, 179; learning to plant, 85–86, 91, 104. *See also* adult offspring
class (age). *See* age class
class (economic), xviii, xx, 52, 71, 91, 105, 148, 176, 178; and ageism, xvi–xvii, 14; lower income leads to poorer health and decreased longevity, xvii; middle, xviii, 92, 95, 107; poverty of older adults, 26, 41, 87, 95, 102, 106
"cognitive impairments" (term), 148; binary defiance workshops to understand, 126; and mild neurocognitive disorder, 128, 129; preferred to "dementia," 134; spectrum of loss, 120, 126, 128–129. *See also* Alzheimer's disease *entries*; mild cognitive impairment

cognitive impairments, people with, xix–xx, 15, 17, 86, 123, 127, 128, 135, 148, 194; caring attitudes toward, 129–133, 142; endangered by fear and aversion, 144–146; issues of diagnosing, 114, 119–120, 122–127, 128, 148, 150; issues of treatment for, 123, 126, 129; risks of early diagnosis, 126–127; selfhood remains, 129–131, 132–133
commerce in aging, 53; ageism in, xix, 23, 27, 52, 146, 175; "anti-aging" products, services, xix, xxi, 27; depends on cult of youth, xix, xx, 23–27, 28, 37, 41, 52, 59, 164, 181, 193; depends on decline ideology, 7; "enhancements," 146
cult of youth, xix, xx, 52, 59, 164, 181, 193, 202; in visual culture, 23–27, 28, 37, 41, 52; youth supremacy, 57–59, 81
cultural criticism, 113, 141, 146–147, 175; studies, xvii, 69, 73. *See also* age studies

death: and age, 26; anxiety about, among younger adults, 13, 55; drive, 151, 171; linked to women in later life, 13–14, 43, 139, 143; mortality salience constructed, 55; mortality salience deconstructed, 59, 142. *See also* dying
declarations, xi, xiii, 77, 177; Declaration of Grievances, 205–206; of rights for older adults, 77, 193
decline ideology, xviii, 6, 12, 16, 51, 61, 81, 173, 192
decline ideology (bioneurological view of aging), xvi, xvii, 5, 13, 26, 162, 180, 185, 202; enforced by capitalism, xx–xxi, 181; enforced by neoliberalism, 26, 28; enforced by representation, xviii, 2, 7, 143, 147, 162
decline ideology (responsible for age-shaming), 172, 173; for cult of youth, 26; for narratives of decline, 180
dehumanization, 23, 102; of older adults with cognitive impairments, 118, 135, 144; as outcome of ageism, 4, 15, 19, 76, 118, 129
"dementia" (term), 61, 65, 137, 140, 142, 144, 149, 156, 196; as defense in war-crimes trials, 113–121, 124–125, 127–128, 201; "dementia-friendly" intentions, 134, 144; issues of diagnosing, 148–150, 156; raises fear of aging into old age, 140, 146,

162; stigmatizes, 130, 135, 140, 142, 148; term to avoid, 134. *See also* Alzheimer's disease *and* cognitive impairment *entries*

depression in later life, 99, 120; due to ageism, xiii, 6, 129, 165; due to caregiving, 139–140, 154; due to impairment diagnosis, 148; due to suppressing grievance, 187, 189

dignity, 41; ageist ableist assaults on, 165; conferred on others, xviii, 42, 130, 132–133, 142; necessary to counter oppressions, 7, 77, 126, 142, 176, 187, 198

disability, older adults with, xvii, 17, 60, 138, 154, 161, 175, 179, 180; and age, 136, 145, 147, 157, 164; aversion to, 60, 137, 146, 164; cared for, 141–142, 162; disability rights movement, 16, 19, 31, 138–139, 141, 181, 202; lesser status of, 41, 129, 143, 156; mistreatment of, 4, 72, 101–102, 144–146, 172; politics of age and disability, 125, 143, 146; solidarity with, 135, 167; working, 92. *See also* ageist ableism; Alzheimer's disease *entries*; body; "burden"; killers of disabled wives

duty to die, 62, 67, 71, 146, 156, 158, 161–162, 175; implicitly about old women, 13; in relation to fear of Alzheimer's, 4, 149, 156. *See also* Alzheimer's disease *entries*; "burden"

dying, 8, 17, 73, 118, 125, 136, 142–143, 159, 194, 202; assisted, 137–138, 140, 154, 155; to avoid growing old, 144–145, 146, 159; high rate in midlife, before Affordable Care Act, 2; inequalities in rates of, xviii, 99. *See also* death; duty to die; killers of disabled wives; living with dying

elder abuse, 139, 141; disregarding autonomy of older adults, 10, 14, 197, 205
Elder within, 186, 190. *See also* age identity
elegy, 100, 149, 152–153
emotions, xiii, 21, 177, 179; created by photographic art, 18, 23, 30–31; and emotional intelligence, 19, 60, 132, 159, 182; socially manipulated, 33, 70, 141, 144, 171; study of the self-conscious, 174–175
emotions (age-related): affective outcomes of ageism, 6, 202, 213; difference between affects and feelings, 171, 183, 189; fear of aging, 140, 146, 162; fear of mortality, 55; grief, as result of ageism, 7, 15, 165, 183, 184, 194, 199; humiliation, 143, 164, 165, 172, 177; of the oppressed, xiii, 146, 186, 197–198; politics of, 175; pro-aging, xii, 18; resentment, 11, 67, 193, 200; resilience, 14, 17–18, 41, 100, 118, 135, 165, 166, 177, 178, 179, 190, 195, 210; revenge, 115, 140, 149, 173, 193–196, 200–201; shame after fifty, 178–181; sufferings silenced, 15, 89, 141, 188, 189, 200; terror of Alzheimer's, 144. *See also* affects; shaming

empathy, 19, 45, 118, 147; in literature and film, 147–148, 156, 159; may lead to moral imagination, 76, 159–161; and responsible looking, 19, 27, 51–52; social consequences of, 15, 19, 110; for victims of ageism, xiii, 171

employment. *See* middle-ageism; unemployment; workers in later life

end of life, 102, 137–139, 145, 154–155; assisted dying, 137–138, 140, 158; costs emphasized, 13, 15, 117; danger of coercion in decision making, 133, 159, 162; hospice, 137, 159, 192; long-term care insurance needed for, 155, 192. *See also* duty to die; living with dying

epidermalization, 27; ageist forms of, 7, 14, 25, 26, 27, 43; and appearance of agedness, xii, 13, 18, 172; countering ageist views, xv, 43, 45–47, 50–51, 159, 190; in other body-based biases, 7, 31, 179, 181–182; skin, 42, 61. *See also* anti-ageism (in visual culture); body

equality. *See under* human rights
essentialism, age, 57, 78; of younger adults, 59, 63, 78, 81, 202
ethics: and ageism, xiii, 144; of aging, 176, 179; and bioethicists, 11, 84, 145; issues of consent regarding older adults, 25, 45, 138, 162; of life review, 115; rights of older adults, 2, 77, 133, 141, 192
euthanasia ("mercy-killing"), 5, 153–157; issues of consent, 138, 139, 158; killing of disabled wives, 137–140
exclusions, age-related, 3, 6, 10, 42, 87, 136, 154, 166, 168–169; social inclusion of older adults, xviii, 132, 134–135, 205; solidarity with, 80–82, 162

faces: ageist attitudes toward older, 25–27, 58; developing appreciation of older faces, 32–33, 39–45, 51–52, 89; of older adults, 17, 24, 37, 50, 140, 156, 160, 179, 187; of women, 12, 14, 24, 25, 179; of younger adults, xx, 26. *See also* photography

family, 45, 53, 67, 118, 134, 149, 150, 157, 194, 198–201, 203; as caregivers, 15, 137–138, 140, 142, 149; family-identity resists ageism, xv, 9, 24, 59; human family, 53; loyalty in, xiv–xv, 118, 125; members, harming elders, 10–11, 95; older adults as integral part of, 39–41, 111, 140; photographs, 40–41, 44–48, 49–50, 89; stories, xiv, 130. *See also* adult offspring; adults as parents in later life; farms; intergenerational relations; killers of disabled wives

fantasy, 155–156; ageist, 54, 57; projective identification, 145, 147–148, 150–151, 153, 157; of revenge, 173, 193–196, 200

farmers (small-scale), in later life: and adult offspring, 96–97, 101, 107; ageism, 101–102, 107, 108, 111; ages of, 87–89, 96, 99; continuity over the life course, 91, 92, 94, 99; difficult working conditions of, 88, 93–96, 101, 105–108, 111; feed most of world's population, 88; health of, 92–93, 97, 99, 107; heterogeneity of, 89; lack of pensions, 101, 106, 111; Nicaraguan, 90, 93, 98; as professors of practice, 85–87, 90, 91, 94–97, 101; seen in US as "rednecks," 107; suicides of, 107, 110, 173; value of, 86–90, 100, 101, 103, 105, 110, 111; women's conditions as, 88, 91, 95, 99, 101–102, 106

farm/food movements, 108–111; anti-globalization activists, 8, 86, 109–110

farming (small-scale), 98, 110; African Americans' class action suit (*Pigford*), 98; and ageism, 87, 89, 102–103, 111; bank foreclosure, 3, 88, 98; crises of, 89, 95–98, 100, 105, 106; as domain of knowledge, 85–86, 90; global climate change, 15, 95, 102, 103, 107, 110, 111; governments' neglect of, 102–103, 106; losing land, 96–100, 110; market ideology, 106; no longer an inheritance, 94–97

farms, family (small-scale), 86, 99, 101, 105, 107, 109; adult children leaving for

cities, 18, 96–97; as exile for older farmers, 89; formerly a legacy career, 94–97; intergenerational connections, xiv, 86–87, 103; in nineteenth century US, 91. *See also* food crises

feminism, 1, 60, 146, 176, 180, 181, 202; effects of the women's movement, 5, 16, 19, 31; feminists and age, 11–12, 14, 43, 55, 59, 164, 175; feminist theory, xxi, 174, 175. *See also* sexism; sexist ageism

femi/senicide. *See* killers of disabled wives

fiction related to age and disability, 9–10, 39, 141, 143, 158, 196, 223n63

films about older adults with cognitive impairments, 118, 119, 133, 141, 142, 146–147, 148–149, 156–158, 159–161, 223n63

food crises, global, 89; ages of farmers, 88, 89; climate destabilization, 15, 95, 102, 103, 107, 110, 111; civil society responses to, 110–111; farm/food movements, 8, 86, 109–110, 111; few pensions for farmers, 101, 106; government neglect of old farmers, 102–103, 106; government programs, 95, 104, 108, 110, 111; loss of ecological diversity, 110; loss of farmland, 100; market ideology, 98, 100, 106–108, 110; supply issues, 103, 104, 108, 109; threats to production, 95, 100, 105–108, 110; youth out-migration, 96, 100–101; turning to Agropolis (urban farming), 103, 104; turning to food gardens, 85, 86, 90–92, 94–95, 104. *See also* agriculture; farmers; farming; farms

"Fourth Age," term critiqued, 144. *See also* body, frailty

gardeners in later life, 90, 92–93; knowledge of, 85, 94, 103; teaching younger people, 86

gardening, 104; over the life course, 91–92

gardens, 86, 94–95, 99, 103, 104, 110, 111; community, 90–92; increasingly cultivated for food, 85, 86, 90–92, 94–95, 104

gender, 36, 62, 63, 66, 73, 77, 79, 89, 174, 202; and age, 155, 175; and death, 13; studies, as one basis and model for age studies, 18, 50, 61, 70, 80, 83. *See also* sexism; sexist ageism

gerontologists, xxi, 90, 130, 144, 145, 173; ageism of, xx, 72, 146, 155, 158; and Alzheimer's, 120, 137, 146, 154, 158;

observe ageism worsening, 4; in person-hood care movement, 132; studies of ageism by, 8, 12, 35, 54, 59, 73, 137; teaching age and ageism, 60–62, 72–73, 81–83, 225n55. *See also* age critic

gerontology, 59, 61, 82, 83, 87, 130, 155, 173, 192; discovery of ageism, 1; persistence of Ciceronian narrative of aging in, xv–xvi, 15, 211n11. *See also* age studies; cultural criticism

globalization (supranational phenomena), 108–109, 200; farm/food crises, 98, 103, 105, 107, 110; market ideology, 5, 106; neoliberal austerity policies, 7, 109–110, 140, 147, 192; spread of ageism, xiii, xviii, 7, 18, 52; urbanization, 18, 96–97. *See also* capitalism

grievances, age-related, 197–198; against ageism, 77; Declaration of Grievances, 205–206; lack of audiences for, xxi, 7, 183, 184, 187, 199–200; need for documentation of suffering, xi, xiii, 10; problems of articulating, 7, 100, 171

hate speech, ageist, 7, 12, 52, 56, 65, 73, 79–80, 139, 141, 158, 206; and Internet trolls, 4, 54–55, 57, 62, 76, 83, 139. *See also* ageism (in discourse); cult of youth; essentialism; youth supremacy

health in later life, in US, 99; Affordable Care Act, 2, 183; ageism as hazard to, 3–4, 14, 144, 145; medical undertreatment a risk, 3–4, 144, 145, 162, 194; related to earlier life chances, xvii; among small-hold farmers, 92–93, 97, 99, 107; typically "good," 9, 145

homophobia, 1, 30, 60, 64, 148, 152; countering homophobia, 149–150, 175, 181; Stonewall, 193

hospice, 131, 137, 155, 157, 159, 192

human rights, 119, 124–125; civil, 56, 63, 98; equality, xxii, 2; inequality, xvii, xviii, 7, 70, 181; law of equality-in-diversity, 205; for older adults, 69, 73, 77, 103, 192, 203–204, 205

identity, 63, 91, 95, 107; born-into-them labels, xix; Elder within, 186, 190; identity politics, 50–51; relinquishing an earlier, 59–60; social identity categories, 21, 50–51, 61–63; Young Judge (early

subidentity), 57–60; youth, lived as an essentialized, 59, 63, 78, 81, 202. *See also* age class; age identity

illness in later life, 188; and alleged wish to die, 17, 138, 141, 153, 158; chronic, 15, 99, 138; and duty to die, 4, 13, 156; terminal, 138, 141, 150, 155, 158. *See also* health in later life; living with dying

intergenerational relations, 86, 100, 103, 107, 151, 158; cohort naming, xiv, 71; conflicts, 71; differences, 11, 172; Fieldwork Practicum across Generations, 81–82; responsibility, 94; rivalry for jobs, xx–xxi, 20, 52, 67, 80

international anti-ageist organizations, 1–2, 108, 111, 192

Internet, ageism on, 4, 17, 51, 54–55, 57, 62, 72, 83

intersectionality, 61–62, 76; ageism as replacement bias, 60; and compound prejudices, 60; integrating category of age, 16, 18, 64–65, 70–73, 77, 81; intersectional thinking, 72, 77. *See also* anti-ageist education

job discrimination at midlife, xviii, 3, 56

justice, 21, 30, 108, 187, 193; and age-related injustice, 119, 139, 152, 186, 196; Court of Age Appeals, 21; lack of a movement impedes, 173; for older adults, xxii, 5; for people with cognitive impairments, 126–129, 135; in war-crimes tribunals, 17, 113, 115, 121, 122, 124, 125

killers of disabled wives (uxoricides), 136–139, 141, 143; in film, 153–156; homicide-suicide in later life, 137–139; legal leniency toward, 138–139; treated as offering euthanasia, 5, 137. *See also* "burden"; duty to die; euthanasia

LGBTQ-identified people, 3, 18, 28, 181; activism among, 31, 193; ageism among, 55, 60; HIV and AIDS compared to MCI and Alzheimer's, 101, 149, 150, 153; lesbians, xviii; prepared for aging/ageism, 179. *See also* homophobia

life course, 146, 175, 176, 194; demotions of aging, xiii, xxiii, 1, 3, 59, 66, 74, 100, 171, 173, 190, 199; development, xviii, 60, 82, 180, 190, 195; longitudinal shame

life course (*continued*)
  trajectory, 177–181; maturational processes, 15, 82, 177; national responsibility
  for well-being over the, 200
life review, 41, 115, 151
literature about later life, 100, 185; burden
  memoir, 143; elegy, 100, 149, 152–153;
  and empathy, 147–148; incitements
  to suicide in, 156–157; new characters
  in, 146, 148, 157; about or by people
  with Alzheimer's, 133, 143, 148–152, 157;
  pressure to describe health status, 185;
  romantic comedy, 159–161; tragedy,
  152, 154
living with dying, people who are, 45, 138–
  139, 141; and end-of-life care, 137–143,
  145; literature about, 143, 150; need for
  long-term care insurance, 15, 137, 147,
  155, 192
longevity, xvi, 99, 134, 145, 162; era of,
  coincides with Age of Alzheimer's, 119;
  of farmers/gardeners, 92–93, 94; irony
  of increasing ageism in era of, 13, 24,
  52, 134, 140, 146, 181; life expectancy
  in US low, xvii; living longer than we
  imagined, 32; lower income leads to
  decreased, xvii; social determinants of,
  xvii, 117; of women, 13
long-term care insurance, 15, 137, 140, 147,
  155, 192

marriage, 176; in later life, xviii, 50, 159–
  161; pleasure in, 49; sex in, 159–161
MCI. *See* mild cognitive impairment
media (mainstream): ageism and middle-
  ageism in, xvii, 4, 141, 147, 161; emphasizing "burden" falling on younger
  adults, 69–70, 143; heightening fear of
  Alzheimer's, 117, 118, 135, 140; omitting
  older adults in images, 23–24; publishing begrudging accounts by adult offspring, 42, 143–145; treating killing of
  old women as euthanasia, 137–139
medical conditions in their social contexts, xvii, 145, 146, 149, 150–152, 159, 194;
  allegations of high eldercare costs, xvii,
  13, 57, 143; concept of social fates, xx, 135,
  141, 190, 199, 208; "The Conversation,"
  145; HIV and AIDS, 135, 149–151, 153;
  medical model, 127, 141, 145; new DSM-5
  label, 128–129; social construction of

reality, 6, 27, 59, 113; undertreatment
  (age-based), 3, 71–72, 144–145, 162.
  See also Alzheimer's disease *and* cognitive impairment *entries*; mild cognitive
  impairment
Medicare, 1, 2, 4, 27, 71, 142, 144, 181, 192,
  196
memory: and forgetting, 177; loss, 4, 14,
  72, 150, 157, 159, 162, 186; problems at
  midlife, 129; spectrum of loss, from mild
  to Alzheimer's, 128–129. *See also* cognitive impairment *entries*
men in later life, 197; as caregivers,
  141–142, 153–154; killing disabled wives,
  136–141, 153–154, 156; in legal system,
  5, 138–140; as victims of violence, 13.
  See also older adults
menopause, 178
"mercy-killing." *See* euthanasia
middle-ageism, xviii, 5, 56, 65, 77, 212n18;
  job discrimination, xviii, 3, 56, 65, 67, 75;
  long-term unemployment, xviii, 2, 62,
  65; and suicide, 3, 62, 173, 184
midlife, people in, 129; in cultural context, xviii, xx, 6, 9, 56, 65, 67, 80, 143,
  144, 192–193; development of, 178–179;
  failure to resist demotions, 16, 173;
  fearing later life, 72, 101, 146; the long
  midlife, 4, 23, 73; status achievements,
  178–179
mild cognitive impairment (MCI),
  129, 145, 149–151; heterogeneity of
  people with, 127–128; new DSM-5 label,
  128–129. *See also* cognitive impairment
  entries
mild neurocognitive disorder, 128, 129;
  named by DSM-5, 128–129, 134, 149
minority, old people as, xvii, 13, 16, 100,
  192; and serious consequences, xxi, 7, 24,
  136, 146, 174, 184
mortality and later life, 13, 59, 142; ageism
  raises risk of death, 3, 81; heightens fear
  of mortality, 55
movements for social liberation, xi; antiracism, 5, 19, 23, 202; disability rights,
  16, 19, 23, 31, 139, 141, 181, 202; gay and
  trans rights, 19, 23, 31, 181, 202; international anti-ageist organizations, 1–2,
  108, 192; often ignore age/ageism, 16;
  women's rights, 5, 16, 19, 31. *See* anti-
  ageist activism

narratives of growing older (life-course
imaginary), 33; aging-as-decline, xix,
5, 180; as positive or "successful" aging,
xvi, 28, 43, 44, 143, 161, 194; as progress, 2, 9, 33, 82, 94, 151; prospective, or
anticipated, 50, 83, 146; of suffering and
trauma, 65, 200; traditional Ciceronian,
seeking "truth," xv–xvi
neoliberalism, 62, 203; austerity policies,
7, 109–110, 140, 143–145, 147, 192; supranational market ideology, 106; threats
to US Social Security, xviii, 62, 166, 196;
undermines family farming, 102, 110

old age, xvi, 7, 8, 148, 188; becoming
"immutable" trait, xx; cultural diversity of, 16, 117; dying to avoid, 144–145;
fear of ageism in, 5, 72, 101, 143–144,
146, 148, 171, 190; good health in, 9,
145; imagining the future of, 84; as
minority status, xvii, xxi, 7, 16, 100,
136, 146, 174, 184, 192; negative associations with "old," xii, xix, 4, 5, 6, 10,
57, 60–61; negative associations with
"old old," 4; positive associations with
old age, 32, 36, 50; synonymous with
Alzheimer's, 4, 140; untruths about,
xvii–xviii. See also ageism entries; aging-
into-old-age; "burden"; older adults;
stereotypes
older adults, 95, 142, 143; agency of, 138,
195; always a minority, xvii, xxi, 7, 16,
100, 136, 146, 174, 184, 192; attraction
to, 29–30, 32–33, 35, 36, 39, 42, 159–160;
aversion to, 65, 118, 141–142; constructed
as abject, 146, 162, 205; heterogeneity of,
xxi, 65, 128, 172; and high gun ownership, 137; "imaginary," 25; imagining
the subjectivity of, 76–77; as majority
of farmers, 88; passing as younger, 47,
167–168, 202; poverty of, xviii–xix; psychic sufferings of, 65, 164, 169, 187–188;
represented as deficient, 4, 6, 55–56,
145, 174, 188; represented as medically
expensive, 143, 145. See also adults as
parents in later life; farmers; men in
later life; women in later life
old men. See men in later life
old women. See sexist ageism; women in
later life
1 percent, xxi, 84

pharmaceutical companies: demeaning
aging-past-youth, xix, 4, 60, 134; dysfunction and uglification industries,
xix, 175
photography (portraits) of older adults:
and age in second tier of consciousness,
42; anti-ageism in old faces shown as
old, 45; cartoonlike, 23; creating positive affects toward older sitters, 30–36,
39–44, 45–50, 81–82; family photos, 8,
39–40, 47, 89; headless, 17, 37–39; "posing while old," 27. See also visual culture
popular culture and age, 27, 52, 113, 140,
159, 166; ageism in, 141, 175, 196; need
for public comprehension of harms, 184.
See also media
poverty in old age, xviii, 7, 18, 26, 41, 87,
95, 102
public parks, 99, 103–104, 110

race, as identity category, 61
racism, xvii, 62, 68, 75, 98, 147, 148, 184;
antiracism, 5, 19, 30, 173, 181, 190, 202;
consciousness of, 1, 14, 32, 55, 59, 67, 165,
183, 190; epidermalization, 7, 27, 31, 32;
everyday, 3, 14; intersecting with ageism, xx, 64, 69, 139; against Japanese,
98; like/unlike ageism, xiii, xix, xx, 1, 14,
61, 65, 180, 188; "posing while black," 27;
systemic bias, 181, 200; value of using
term, 65, 202; "walking while black," 14.
See also African Americans
respect. See under age hierarchy
revenge, 115, 140, 149, 173, 201; role of
unexecuted fantasy in anti-ageism, 193–
196, 200. See also emotions entries
romantic comedy ("rom-com") of later
life, 159–161

Sages and Seekers program, 81–82, 83
selfhood in later life, xii, 198, 202; ageist
attacks on, xix, 7, 10, 15, 19–20; contains
earlier selves, 60; current or latest self,
189; impression management, 178, 186;
problems of representing selfhood in
later life, 25, 51, 168, 180; in representation, 25, 32, 33–34, 37, 39, 41, 45, 47–50;
supposed to be global and stable, 177
Senexa, crone goddess of age studies, v
(frontispiece), 200
seniority system, xviii, 20, 52, 82, 87, 151

sexuality in later life, 17, 36, 159–161

sexism, xiv, xvii, xx, 1, 7, 32, 55, 58, 61, 63, 67, 75, 188, 202; distinguishing ageism from, xiii, xix, 60, 64, 148, 165, 180–181, 183, 184–185

sexist ageism: associated with Alzheimer's, 140–141; associated with death, 13–14, 43, 139, 143; duty to die implicitly about, 13; lack of state protection, 5; "old hag," 12, 13, 74, 194; older people seen as "burden," 12, 14, 140, 141, 143, 206; victims of medical malpractice, 3, 144, 162; victims of uxoricide, 136–140. See also women in later life

shame, 46, 65, 142, 149, 151, 157, 163–164, 175; after age fifty, 178–181; internalized by subalterns, 182; as master emotion, 174. See also shaming

shaming, 9, 21, 60, 154; age-shaming a public crisis, 189; developing shaming-resistance, 17, 44, 165–166, 186–191; obstacle to creating a movement, 173–174; overcoming age-related shame, 6–7, 32–33, 165, 170–172, 174–175, 183, 187, 189; overcoming childhood sham-ing, 176–177; over the life course, 175, 177–178, 180–181; reasons to use "sham-ing" instead of "shame," 163, 171–172; reduction of, in historical context, 181; result of ageism or ableism, 24, 118, 129, 135, 160, 162, 164–166, 168–170, 172–175, 182; stories of suffering, 163–165, 169–170, 185–186; sufferings silenced, 15, 165, 182–183, 188, 189, 200; theory of, 9, 60, 171–175; vicarious vulnerability, 169, 171. See also affects; grievances; shame; trauma

social construction of reality, 6, 27, 59, 113; concept of social fates, xx, 135, 141, 190, 199, 208; emotion construction, 144

Social Security, US, xvii, 1, 22, 26, 77, 163, 192; average monthly income from, xviii; Cost of Living Adjustment (COLA), xviii, xix, 2, 5, 69; imagined threats to, 166; threats to, xviii, 62, 166, 196

stereotypes: compound, 60; of old age, 43, 44, 60–61, 175, 193; of older adults, 5, 32, 46, 58, 61, 73, 80, 118, 130, 145–146, 162; of older adults as demographic "catastrophe," xvii, 4, 11, 13, 20; of older adults as frail, 11, 39, 194; of older adults as homogeneous, 16, 22, 39, 58; of older adults as ready to die, 138–139, 144, 194; of older adults as unphotogenic, 24; of people with Alzheimer's, 120–121; role of decline ideology in, of older adults, xvi, xvii, 9, 16, 26, 51, 171, 173. See also "burden"

suicide, 6, 148, 150; and duty-to-die dis-course, 161; incitements to commit, of people with cognitive impairments, 149–150; international pandemic of, by farmers, 107, 173; of men who kill their wives, 137; at midlife, associated with unemployment, 3, 62, 173, 184; pre-emptive, 118, 119, 124, 135, 146, 149–153; prevention of, 155, 162; "rational," 150. See also dehumanization

systems of oppression, xiii, xiv, xvii, 179; decline ideology, xvi–xviii, 6, 7, 9, 11–14, 26, 28, 173

teaching anti-ageism. See anti-ageist education

tragedy, 152, 154

trauma, 65, 90, 95, 110, 150–151, 155; incor-porating age into theories of, xiv, 7

trauma caused by ageism or ageist able-ism, 10, 128, 141, 148, 161, 193, 194; from age-shaming, 164, 169–174, 180, 184; need for discoveries about, 7; pain of, hidden, 11, 65, 183; post-traumatic states of, 169–171, 186–187; processes of recov-ery from, 182–191, 193–198; suddenness of the event, 164; symptoms of, 163–165, 182–185, 196; vicarious vulnerability to, 73, 171. See also shaming

twenty-first century, 86, 118, 174, 175, 182

unemployment: in later life, xviii, xxi, 2, 3, 62, 65, 70, 75; and suicide, 3, 62, 173, 184; of younger people, 5, 56, 70. See also middle-ageism

United States, 89, 95, 100, 174; age of prin-cipal farm operators in, 88; and Chilean coup, 114; decreased longevity and poor health in, xvii, 2, 17; median age in, 56

urbanization, as global phenomenon for younger adults, 18, 96–97

US government, in relation to older adults, xxi, 5, 56, 95, 98, 137; Affordable Care Act, 2, 15; Congress, 4, 6; first-

generation programs for seniors, 1, 2, 95, 106–107, 192; Medicare, 4; neoliberal policies, xviii, 2, 7, 143, 147, 162; Barack Obama, 15, 77; support for agribusiness, 106; Supreme Court decisions, xviii, xx, 2–3, 5, 6, 196, 206, 226n7; threats to Social Security, xviii, 62, 166, 196
uxoricide. *See* killers of disabled wives

violence, ageist forms of, 9–10, 25, 164, 182, 184–185; causes state of alert, 14–15; hate speech as, 54–56; killing, 136–137, 139–140; physical assault or battery, 13, 141; threats of, 14, 25, 58, 162, 194; through transmitted affects, 170–171, 183, 187–188
visual culture, in relation to older adults: age politics in social contexts, 19, 22–27, 51–52; anti-ageist art, 24, 50, 53; creating a new imaginary, 30–31, 35, 44; responsible looking, 19, 27, 51–52; role of other social movements in changing, 30–31. *See also* age gaze; ageisms (in visual culture); anti-ageism (in visual culture)

"walking while old" (assault and battery), 13–14, 58. *See also* ageisms (in social relations)
war-crimes tribunals, 17, 173; accused who claim Alzheimer's, 112–122, 124–125, 129, 133; assessing fitness of the accused, 116–117, 121–130; and innocent people with cognitive impairment, 133–135; issues of diagnosis of cognition, 148–150, 156
women, work of, 89, 91, 96, 178
women in later life, 5, 35, 141, 182; as caregivers, 137, 138; goddess-matriarch, 34–36; influenced by feminism, 180; as leaders, 12–13, 109, 193; medical under-treatment of, 3, 144, 162; as nonconsensual victims of uxoricide, 153, 155, 156, 162; poverty of, xviii, 95; and right to live, 141; seen as "burdens," 12, 14, 140, 141, 143, 206; in socioeconomic context, 172, 178–181; work of, on farms, 89, 91, 101, 106. *See also* older adults; sexist ageism; shame; shaming

workers in later life, 3, 90, 96, 99, 101, 152; conditions of, xviii, xx, 2, 6, 80, 173, 181, 183, 195, 206; discrimination at midlife, xviii, xx, 3, 20, 56, 58, 65, 75, 192–193; employment of, xviii, 1–2, 22, 178; organizations of, 86, 96, 109–110, 111, 192; unemployment of, xviii, xxi, 2, 3, 62, 65, 701
writers, xii, 16, 143, 147, 154–155, 162, 175; and empathy, 159; fantasies about old people, 141, 146–147, 155, 157–159; projections onto older adults, 147–148, 150–151, 153, 157; social responsibilities of writers and artists, 16, 50, 53, 147, 150, 153, 157–158. *See also* fiction related to age and disability; literature about later life
writing classes, 68, 79; anti-ageist writing assignments, 75–79; teaching age studies in, 68–79. *See* anti-ageist education

younger adults: abandoning family farms, 18, 96–97; and ableism, 72; illusion of being a permanent age class, 57, 59, 63, 202; in-group solidarity, 168; learning ageism young, xx, 27, 57–59, 72, 183–184; misled about older adults/old age, xx; overcoming ageism, 151; risks of being ageist in youth, 81, 194–195; in Sages and Seekers program, 81–82; as students learning age studies, 60–61, 66–68, 70, 71, 73, 79–82; wanting to farm, 86–97; Young Judges, 57–60, 63, 66, 67–68, 81, 146, 168, 170, 189–190. *See also* aging-past-youth; cult of youth; younger men; younger women
younger men, 101; and ageism, xvi, 11, 62–64; as Internet trolls, 4, 54–55, 57, 62. *See also* younger adults
younger women, 96, 175; and age/ageism, 57, 80; anti-ageist, 32. *See also* younger adults
youth supremacy, 56–59, 81; and cult of youth, xix, xx, 52, 59, 164, 181; hiring preferences, 55, 56; in visual culture, 23–27, 28, 37, 41, 52. *See also* essentialism

ABOUT THE AUTHOR

Margaret Morganroth Gullette is a cultural critic and prize-winning writer of nonfiction, an internationally known age critic, an essayist, feminist, and activist. A previous book, *Agewise: Fighting the New Ageism in America*, won a 2012 Eric Hoffer Book Award and is being translated into Korean. *Aged by Culture* was chosen a Noteworthy Book of the year by the *Christian Science Monitor*. It was nominated for a Pulitzer and received an Honorable Mention from the Gustavus Myers Center for the Study of Bigotry and Human Rights. *Declining to Decline: Cultural Combat and the Politics of the Midlife* won the Emily Toth award in 1998 for the best feminist book on American popular culture. Her first book in age studies is *Safe at Last in the Middle Years: The Invention of the Midlife Progress Novel*.

Gullette's essay "The Contagion of Euphoria" won the Daniel Singer Millennial Prize 2008. Other essays, frequently cited as notable in *Best American Essays*, have appeared in many literary/ cultural quarterlies, including *Kenyon Review*, *Salmagundi*, *American Scholar*, and *Yale Review*; and in scholarly journals like *Feminist Studies*, *Representations*, *Modern Drama*, and the *Journal of the History of Sexuality*. Quotations from her writings appear in *The Quotable Woman: The First Five Thousand Years*. She has been the recipient of fellowships from the National Endowment for the Humanities, American Council of Learned Societies, and Bunting Institute. She is a member of PEN-America and a Resident Scholar at the Women's Studies Research Center, Brandeis University.

Gullette has also published in the *New York Times*, *The Nation*, *Ms.*, the *Boston Globe*, the *Miami Herald*, the *Chicago Tribune*, *American Prospect*, *Forward*, *Dissent*, and *Salon*. She blogs for *Women's ENews*, *SilverCentury*, *AlterNet*, and

Next Avenue. She has been interviewed on *The Brian Lehrer Show*, *The Callie Crossley Show*, *CultureShocks*, WBAI, and *To the Best of Our Knowledge*.

Since 1997 she has found funding for adult education programs in Newton's sister city, San Juan del Sur, Nicaragua. In 2012 she won the Marigold "Ideas for Good" Prize for the Free High School for Adults there, which she cofounded. She lives in Newton with her husband, David Gullette. They are the parents of a son, Sean Gullette, a screenwriter and director married to artist Yto Barrada, and they have two granddaughters, Vega and Tamo.